A Harmony of the Gospels
MATTHEW, MARK AND LUKE
VOLUME III
and
The Epistles of James and Jude

D1553041

CALVIN'S COMMENTARIES

CALVIN'S COMMENTARIES

A Harmony of the Gospels

MATTHEW, MARK AND LUKE

VOLUME III

and

The Epistles of James and Jude

Translator
A. W. MORRISON

Editors
DAVID W. TORRANCE
THOMAS F. TORRANCE

WILLIAM B. EERDMANS PUBLISHING COMPANY
GRAND RAPIDS, MICHIGAN

THE PATERNOSTER PRESS
CARLISLE

Translation © 1972 The Saint Andrews Press

Published jointly in the United States
by Wm. B. Eerdmans Publishing Co.
255 Jefferson Ave. S.E., Grand Rapids, Michigan 49503
and in the U.K. by The Paternoster Press
P.O. Box 300, Carlisle, Cumbria CA3 0QS

First paperback edition published 1995

Printed in the United States of America

00 99 98 97 96 95   7 6 5 4 3 2 1

Eerdmans ISBN 0-8028-0803-4

British Library Cataloguing in Publication Data
Calvin, Jean
Harmony of the Gospels — Matthew, Mark and Luke
Vol. 3 - New ed.
(Calvin's New Testament Commentaries; Vol. 3)
I. Title   II. Morrison, A.W.   III. Series
226.07

Paternoster ISBN 0-85364-682-1

A COMMENTARY ON THE HARMONY
OF THE GOSPELS

*And when he was come into Jerusalem, all the city was stirred, saying,
Who is this? And the multitudes said, This is the prophet, Jesus, from
Nazareth of Galilee. And Jesus entered into the temple of God, and
cast out all them that sold and bought in the temple, and overthrew the
tables of the money-changers, and the seats of them that sold doves: and
he saith unto them, It is written, My house shall be called a house of
prayer: but ye make it a den of robbers, And the blind and the lame came
to him in the temple: and he healed them. But when the chief priests
and the scribes saw the wonderful things that he did, and the children
that were crying in the temple and saying, Hosanna to the son of David;
they were moved with indignation, and said unto him, Hearest thou what
these are saying? And Jesus saith unto them, Yea: did ye never read,
Out of the mouths of babes and sucklings thou hast perfected praise?
And he left them, and went forth out of the city to Bethany and lodged
there. Now in the morning as he returned to the city, he hungered.
And seeing a fig tree by the way side, he came to it, and found nothing
thereon, but leaves only; and he saith unto it, Let there be no fruit from
thee henceforward for ever. And immediately the fig tree withered away.
And when the disciples saw it, they marvelled, saying, How did the fig
tree immediately wither away? And Jesus answered and said unto
them, Verily I say unto you, If ye have faith, and doubt not, ye shall not
only do what is done to the fig tree, but even if ye shall say unto this
mountain, Be thou taken up and cast into the sea, it shall be done. And
all things, whatsoever ye shall ask in prayer, believing, ye shall receive.
(Matt. 21.10-22)*

*And he entered into Jerusalem, into the temple; and when he had looked
round about upon all things, it being now eventide, he went out into
Bethany with the twelve. And on the morrow, when they were come
out from Bethany, he hungered. And seeing a fig tree afar off having
leaves, he came, if haply he might find anything thereon: and when he
came to it, he found nothing but leaves; for it was not the season of figs.
And he answered and said unto it, No man shall eat fruit from thee
henceforward for ever. And his disciples heard it. And they came to
Jerusalem: and he entered into the temple, and began to cast out them
that sold and them that bought in the temple, and overthrew the tables
of the money-changers, and the seats of them that sold the doves; and he*

would not suffer that any man should carry a vessel through the temple. And he taught, and said unto them, Is it not written, My house shall be called a house of prayer for all the nations? but ye have made it a den of robbers. And the chief priests and the scribes heard it, and sought how they might destroy him: for they feared him, for all the multitude was astonished at his teaching. And every evening he went forth out of the city. And as they passed by in the morning, they saw the fig tree withered away from the roots. And Peter calling to remembrance saith unto him, Rabbi, behold, the fig tree which thou cursedst is withered away. And Jesus answering saith unto them, Have faith in God. Verily I say unto you, Whosoever shall say unto this mountain, Be thou taken up and cast into the sea; and shall not doubt in his heart, but shall believe that what he saith cometh to pass; he shall have it. Therefore I say unto you, All things whatsoever ye pray and ask for, believe that ye have received them, and ye shall have them. (Mark 11.11-24)

And some of the Pharisees from the multitude said unto him, Master, rebuke thy disciples. And he answered and said, I tell you that, if these shall hold their peace, the stones will cry out.

And he entered into the temple, and began to cast out them that sold, saying unto them, It is written, And my house shall be a house of prayer: but ye have made it a den of robbers. And he was teaching daily in the temple. But the chief priests and the scribes and the principal men of the people sought to destroy him: and they could not find what they might do; for the people all hung upon him, listening. (Luke 19.39-40, 45-48)

In the narrative of the withered fig-tree, Matthew and Mark differ: Matthew saying that it occurred on the day following Christ's avowal of Kingship, while Mark appears to place it on the day next again. This is readily resolved. They agree that Christ spoke the word of malediction to the tree on the day after His solemn entry into the city. Mark merely notes, what Matthew had omitted, that the event was brought to the disciples' eyes on the next day. So although Mark brings out the time sequence more distinctly he makes no real difference. A wider difference does appear in his account of the traders' chastisement, as against Matthew and Luke, who state that as soon as Christ came into the city and temple He turned out those who were buying and selling: Mark is content to say then that He surveyed the scene, and puts the actual expulsion onto the following day. I reconcile these by saying that when he saw he had not spoken of the cleansing of the temple he put it in later, out of place. On the first day he tells of Christ coming into the temple, and there surveying the scene. Was there any other purpose in that close inspection than the correction of some abuse? He had been used to visit the temple frequently, and it was not the novelty of the view that struck Him. Mark ought to go on to say how those who were selling and buying in that place were turned out, but he says that Christ left the city. Afterwards he recalls the omission which deserved to be told. Perhaps some will prefer to consider that here again Mark has kept to a time sequence which the other two have lost. For although their narratives appear to run on without a break, it would not be out of the question to read as two parts what they put as one, since they do not particularly tie it to one day. All the same I prefer my previous conjecture, on the probability that Christ gave that demonstration of His power in the larger crowd of people. But no one who considers how little attention the Evangelists give to noting times will be put off by this kind of difference in narrative.

Matt. 21.10. *When he was come into Jerusalem.* Matthew tells us that the city was stirred so that we should realize that what took place was in no way concealed or surreptitious, but open to the sight of all the people and to the knowledge of the priests and scribes. The Majesty of the Spirit was revealed for all the insignificance of the outward appearance. Unless all the people had been struck with awe, how could they have endured the entry of Christ into the city in royal progress, at such risk to Himself? We must conclude that Christ made no secret of His coming; nor did His enemies stay quiet because they took no account of Him, but because they were gripped with a hidden fear. Struck by the fear of God, they dared no attempt on Him. At the same time, the lazy indifference of the populace is criticised while the enthusiasm of the pilgrims is praised. When the townsfolk hear the tumult and ask 'Who can this be?'—they at once show that they are none of Christ's company

Matt. 21.12. *Jesus entered into the temple.* Although He went up to the temple often enough, and every time this violation met His eyes, only twice did He lift his hand in correction, once at the beginning of His mission, and now a second time when He had almost come to its goal. Seeing that foul and unholy disorder held court throughout, and that the temple with all its sacrifices was given over to ruin, Christ reckoned it sufficient to give two open condemnations of its profaned state. When He revealed Himself as Teacher and Prophet sent from God, He took on Himself the duty of cleansing the temple in order to arouse the Jews to greater attention. This first incident is recorded only by John (ch. 2). So as He comes towards the end of His course, and again claims for Himself the same power, He warns the Jews of the temple's pollutions and at the same time shows that He will bring in a new order. Now there is no doubt of the fact that He is testifying to Himself as King and High Priest, who presides over the temple and

3

worship of God. This must be stressed, in case some other person should ever give himself the same licence. Admittedly the zeal which fired Christ to perform this is well suited to all worshipping people, but before anyone rushes into wild action on the pretext of imitation he must see what his calling demands and how far we should go according to the commandment of God. If foul stains have spread over the Church of God, then all God's children must burn with grief, but God has not put weapons in the hands of all. Individuals must weep, till God brings relief. I am prepared to say that they are worse than stupid who are unaffected by the pollution of God's temple, and that it is not enough for them to be distressed at heart if they do not avoid the contagion and speak out their longing for better things whenever occasion offers: but those who have no public authority must fight with the freedom of their tongues what they cannot correct by force. The question is raised, why Christ should only have set about a light, or at any rate more tolerable, abuse when He saw the temple so chock-full of superstition. The answer is that Christ had no intention of restoring all the ancient ceremonies to their former practice, and that He did not choose to give an impression of picking greater or lesser faults: His sole object was to reveal in one clear symbolic action the role He had received from God for the purification of the temple, at the same time showing how the worship of God was besmirched with sickening and palpable abuse. After all, the trading had some pretext of relieving hardship for the people, saving them going far for sacrifices and providing a convenient supply of money for the offering they might wish to make. It was not in the sanctuary that the exchange counters stood and the sacrificial beasts were offered for sale, but only in the outer court, which is sometimes called 'the temple'. Yes—but this was the intolerable profanity, that in such a place there should be set up a market for selling goods and bankers should sit for money changing; nothing more unsuitable for the greatness of the temple. And there was added bitterness in Christ's attack for the well-known fact that the practice had been introduced by the priesthood with a greedy eye on discreditable gain. We know how a man goes into a shop, well laid out with goods of various kinds, with no intention of buying anything—and yet he is caught by something attractive, and changes his mind: just so the priests spread their nets for offerings that might come their way, to cheat every single visitor of a little cash.

Matt. 21.13. *It is written*. Christ quotes two passages from two prophets: one from Isaiah 56, the other from Jeremiah 7. The passage from Isaiah certainly suited the circumstances of the time, containing a prediction of the calling of the nations. He declares that God will

4

not only restore the temple to its former glories, but also will cause all nations from all around to stream towards it, and all the world to agree in the true and sincere service of God. He spoke in a metaphor, it is certain, for the prophets use the figures of the law to sketch out the spiritual worship of God which shall be in the reign of Christ. Certainly the ascent of all nations to worship at Jerusalem was never an accomplished fact. So when he foretells that the temple should be a house of prayer for all peoples, his utterance is equivalent to a declaration that the nations are to gather into God's Church where they and the children of Abraham alike may call on the name of the true God with one voice. But since he mentions the temple, so far as it then was the visible place of worship, the Jews well deserve Christ's reproach that they had betrayed it for purposes alien to its foundation. This is the meaning, then: God intended that this temple should exist till now as a sign to draw the devotion of all His worshippers: how unworthy, how wicked that it should be turned into a common market-place! Besides, in the time of Christ the temple there was really a house of prayer so long as the Law (shade of the future) flourished. It began to be a house of prayer for all nations when the voice went out from it teaching the Gospel, to make the whole world grow into one faith. And although it was soon afterwards rased to the ground, yet to this day the force of the prophecy applies. Since the Law went out from Sion, this is the starting-place to which all who would pray aright must look. Granted there is no distinction of places, it is God's will that men should call upon Him everywhere, but as believers who profess to worship the God of Israel are said to speak the language of Canaan, so are they also to come into the temple because the true religion flowed from it, and it is also the same source of the waters which quickly and marvellously enlarged to a great flood giving life to those who drink it (as Ezekiel tells, 47.9), and which fall out in streams from the temple from the rising to the setting sun (cf. Zechariah, 14.8). When we use temples today for holding sacred meetings, the reason is different, since Christ was manifested, no outward or shadowy image is shown, as the fathers once had under the Law. It should be noted moreover that the Prophet uses the word prayer for the whole worship of God. In all the abundance and variety of ceremonies then observed, God wished to teach the Jews in brief what was the object of them all, namely, to worship Him in Spirit. This is more clearly expressed in Psalm 50, where God relates all the exercises of devotion to prayer.

Matt. 21.14. *But ye make it.* Christ means that the plaint of Jeremiah applies to their own day, in which the temple was no less corrupt. The prophet denounces the hypocrisy of men who gave themselves licence

5

to sin guaranteed by the temple. External symbols—a kind of rudimentary instruction—were instituted by God's design to lead the Jews to a true devotion, but in the regular way of hypocrites they turned truth into falsehood, making out that external rites were all-sufficient for observance, and were content to use the temple as an empty sham. So the Prophet exclaims that God is not fixed to the temple, not tied to ceremonies; it is a lie to boast in the name of the temple which they have made a den of thieves. The crimes of thieves are more audacious in their dens where they trust to go unpunished. In the same way the audacity of these hypocrites when they are covered with false piety increases almost to the point of believing that God is mocked. Seeing that the metaphor of a den takes in all forms of vice, Christ well takes this phrase of the Prophet for the present case. Mark adds that Christ forbade any man to take a vessel through the temple. Nothing is to be allowed to be on view that does not belong to the divine service. 'Vessel' in Hebrew includes any kind of goods. Altogether Christ put out anything that offended against the reverence and greatness of the temple.

Matt. 21.14. *And the blind and the lame came to him.* In case this claim to an authority beyond His usual course should be suspected of presumption, Christ supported it by miracles. He healed the lame and blind in the temple in order to make plain that the right and privilege of Messiah were His true property, for by these marks the Prophets describe Him. Here we see again, as I pointed out a little above, the danger of any single person imitating the action of Christ without considering that he reaches for the throne of the Messiah. We must believe that the lame and blind who were healed witnessed to the divine power of Christ as surely as if God from heaven approved by His own voice the outcry of the crowd.

Matt. 21.15. *But when the chief priests.* Luke narrates that the Pharisees started to complain even on the way. At that time, only the disciples were shouting, but these wanted them silenced. Christ replied that it was in vain for them to object, for God would sooner make the stones cry out than allow the suppression of His Son's Kingdom. We may well believe that, when the shouting was not reduced, but even the children joined in, the indignation of the scribes and priests rose too and their attack on Christ was renewed. It is surely by way of indirect reproach that they allege that He is grasping at children's praises. We must notice what their ill-will springs from. That it was connected with evil-thinking and virulent contempt of God is evident from the fact that they are as much pained by the miracles as by the shouts of welcome. But I am now tracing some particular thing that stung them greatly. We know how bitterly they fought for their rights, for they were utterly zealous to maintain for themselves for ever the tyrannical power they had once usurped. If the people were free to give Christ the title of King, it was no slight diminution of their supremacy. Even in trifling matters they liked their rulings to be taken as oracles from above, to which men might not say Yea or Nay except at their good pleasure. Accordingly they reckoned it ridiculous and outrageous that some man—who in their sight held no distinction—should be given the title Messiah by the mob. It would indeed have been in order for them to have taken the lead in word and action on the people's behalf, if they had lived up to their positions. Priests were created that from their lips all might seek knowledge of the Law; in short that they might be messengers and interpreters of the God of Hosts (Mal. 2.7). But their treachery extinguished the light of truth for them, and they deserve the reply Christ gives, that they gain nothing by trying to suppress the doctrine of salvation, for it will sooner break out from the stones. The point is quietly conceded. Christ does not deny that it is preposterous that the first voices to hail the advent of the Messiah should belong to the uneducated throng and to the children, but as the truth is wickedly suppressed by those who ought to be its rightful witnesses it is no wonder that God should raise up others, and to their shame make choice of children. This is a great consolation to us, for all that wicked men leave no stone unturned to hide the Kingship of Christ, we learn here that their efforts come to nothing. They hope that when some of the great crowd that advances the Kingdom of Christ are put out of the way, or are silenced by fear, their own cause will be won, but the Lord will frustrate their hopes. He will sooner make mouths and tongues out of stone than allow His Son's Kingdom to lack witnesses.

Matt. 21.16. *Did you never read.* The scribes and priests seize the opportunity to attack Christ for permitting children to call Him King. Wicked men in their pride always despise the humility of Christ's disciples. Christ meets their malice with the testimony of David, who makes even infants to be heralds of the glory of God. The text runs literally: 'Out of the mouths of babes and sucklings hast thou established strength' (Ps. 8.2). By which David means that even if all tongues were silent God needs no other spokesmen to proclaim His power than infant children, still feeding at their mothers' breasts. In themselves they are dumb, but the marvellous providence shines through them with an eloquence deep and loud. Any man who considers to himself how the child is formed in the mother's womb, is nourished there for nine months, issues at last into the light of day, and from the moment of birth finds ready food, must surely not only sense the craftsman's hand of God upon the world but will be carried

7

away altogether into admiration of Him. The sun and moon are created without power of speech, yet they are said to publish the praises of God in song clear and resounding (Ps. 19.2). Since the praises of God are heard from the tongues of infants, Christ infers that there is nothing strange in attracting children already used to speech to lend their voices.

Matt. 21.18. *In the morning as he returned.* Between the solemn entry of Christ, of which we have heard, and the Passover day, He was guest overnight at Bethany, but during the day He came to teach in the temple. Matthew and Mark relate an episode that falls into this time where Christ coming in to the city feels hungry and goes up to a fig-tree, when He finds nothing on it but leaves. He curses it, and the tree at the voice of the curse immediately withers up. First of all, I take for granted that Christ did not feign hunger, but really felt it. We know that Christ willingly faced all the infirmities of our flesh, although by nature He was free and exempt from them. But herein lies the difficulty, how He could have been deceived into looking for fruit on a bare tree, especially when the time for fruit was not ripe. Further, why was He so gravely incensed with a harmless tree? We might reasonably say that as a man He failed to recognize this kind of tree, yet it is possible that He deliberately went up to the tree knowing what to expect. Certainly it was not an outburst of bad temper that led Him to curse—this would have been not only unjust, but a ridiculous and childish revenge. Rather He overcame the bite of hunger that affected His flesh by a contrary effort to advance His Father's glory, as He says elsewhere, 'My meat is to do the will of my Father' (John 4.34). There He is contending both with fatigue and hunger. The fact that His hunger becomes an occasion for performing a miracle and teaching His disciples makes me more inclined to accept this conjecture. When hunger presses Him and there is no food at hand, He turns to find His nourishment in promoting the greater glory of God. Moreover He determined to set in this tree a sign of the end which awaits hypocrites and at the same time to expose the emptiness and frustration of their show.

Matt. 21.19. *Let there be no fruit from thee henceforward.* Let us learn from this the force of the word of cursing, namely that the tree is condemned to be barren, just as in the opposite sense God gives blessing when His voice commands fruitfulness. But it is more clear from Mark that the tree did not instantly wither, or at least it was not noticed by the disciples until they saw it the next day, stripped of its leaves. Mark also attributes to Peter alone what Matthew attributes to the disciples in general, but seeing that Christ replies in the plural we may readily infer that one put the question for the rest.

8

Matt. 21.21. *And Jesus answered.* Christ draws out His use of the miracle further by inspiring His disciples to faith and trust. In Mark, the general encouragement is put first, to have faith in God: then follows the promise that they will obtain by faith whatever they seek from God. To have faith in God means precisely the assurance and expectation from God of whatever we need. As faith, if we have any, immediately breaks into prayer and reaches for the riches of the grace of God which are revealed in the Word, that we should enjoy them, so Christ adds prayer to faith. If He had only said that whatever we wish shall be, some might have seen faith as too masterful, or too indifferent. So Christ shows that the true believers, who rely on His goodness and promises, flee to Him in supplication. This is an outstanding passage to bring out the power and nature of faith, that it is a certainty resting on the goodness of God, which does not admit of doubt. Only those who have no doubt that God is propitious to them are recognized as true believers by Christ, those who have no hesitation that He will give what they ask. We can see that Papists, who associate faith with doubt are really caught in a diabolical fiction. They actually accuse us of foolish presumption if we venture to appear before God under the conviction of His fatherly regard toward us. Yet Paul commends this benefit of Christ's with great emphasis: 'In whom we have boldness and access in confidence through our faith in him' (Eph. 3.12). This passage also teaches us that the true test of faith lies in prayer. Suppose one objects that prayers for mountains to be cast into the sea are never heard: we can easily reply that Christ does not give men a free rein in their prayers to ask whatever their own fancy suggests. He places prayers after the rule of faith, which is bound to mean that the Spirit controls all our instincts by the Word of God and keeps us well in hand. Firm and unhesitating trust in prayer is Christ's demand. And does trust of this order ever occur to human mentality unprompted by the Word of God? Therefore we see that Christ makes no promises to His disciples if they do not keep to the limits of God's good pleasure.

Luke 19.47. *And he was teaching daily in the temple.* Mark and Luke teach us first, that the class of men that constituted the Church was of the lowest order, while His opposition came from the priests and scribes and all the chief people. This is part of the foolishness of the cross, that God overlooked the excellencies of this world and chose foolishness, that is, the weak and despised. Secondly, they remind us that these fine leaders of the Church of God had to find a reason for putting Christ away, exposing their own criminal impiety thereby, for even if there had been just grounds for proceeding against Christ, they had no right whatever to pursue Him to death like a bunch of robbers, or secretly to hire assassins. Thirdly, they show how their evil conspiracy was frustrated, for Christ was appointed to die on the cross by the hidden purpose of God.

And when he was come into the temple, the chief priests and the elders of the people came unto him as he was teaching, and said, By what authority doest thou these things? and who gave thee this authority? And Jesus answered and said unto them, I also will ask you one question, which if ye tell me, I likewise will tell you by what authority I do these things. The baptism of John, whence was it? from heaven or from men? And they reasoned with themselves, saying, If we shall say, From heaven; he will say unto us, Why then did ye not believe him? But if we shall say, From men; we fear the multitude; for all hold John as a prophet. And they answered Jesus, and said, We know not. He also said unto them, Neither tell I you by what authority I do these things. Matt. 21.23-27)

And they come again to Jerusalem: and as he was walking in the temple, there come to nim the chief priests, and the scribes, and the elders; and they said unto him, By wnat authority doest thou these things? or who gave thee this authority to do these things? And Jesus said unto them, I will ask of you one question, and answer me, and I will tell you by what authority I do these things. The baptism of John, was it from heaven, or from men? answer me. And they reasoned with themselves, saying, If we shall say, From heaven; he will say, Why then did ye not believe him? But should we say, From men—they feared the people: for all verily held John to be a prophet. And they answered Jesus and say, We know not. And Jesus saith unto them, Neither tell I you by what authority I do these things. (Mark 11.27-33)

And it came to pass, on one of the days, as he was teaching the people in the temple, and preaching the gospel, there came upon him the chief priests and the scribes with the elders; and they spake, saying unto him, Tell us: By what authority doest thou these things? or who is he that gave thee this authority? And he answered and said unto them, I also will ask you a question; and tell me: The baptism of John, was it from heaven, or from men? And they reasoned with themselves, saying, If we shall say, From heaven; he will say, Why did ye not believe him? But if we shall say, From men; all the people will stone us: for they be persuaded that John was a prophet. And they answered, that they knew not whence it was. And Jesus said unto them, Neither tell I you by what authority I do these things. (Luke 20.1-8)

Matt. 21.23. *By what authority doest thou these things?* Because their other schemes and open attempts to attack Him had got nowhere, the priests and scribes now make indirect efforts to check the course of His teaching. They no longer take Him up on the truth of doctrine itself, where they had previously failed in their attacks many times, but they dispute His calling and commission. There could be some semblance to their case: no-one should push himself into the dignity of priesthood or office of prophet without waiting on God's call; far less has anyone the right to claim the title of Messiah unless it be evident that the choice is from God; not only by the voice of God but also by His oath shall a man be appointed, says the Scripture (Ps. 110.4). But when so many mighty acts had testified to the divine majesty of Christ, their dealings show perversity and evil, asking Him His origin as though they knew nothing of it all. What could be more fatuous in face of the manifest outreach of the hand of God, of the healing of lame and blind, to wonder if this might be the presumptuous gesture of some individual? In any case they already had more than ample proof of Christ's divine mission. To approve the actions of Christ was the last thing in their minds, once they had learned that God was the Author. Their insistence that He was not the legitimate minister of God comes to this—that the election had not been by their vote: as if they held complete authority. Even if they had been the rightful leaders of the Church, it would have been monstrous to set themselves against God. This explains why Christ did not directly answer their question: they were asking Him, without reason or respect, a thing that was plain to all.

Matt. 21.25. *The baptism of John, whence was it?* He questions them on the Baptism of John both to show that they had lost all right to authority in despising God's Prophet, and to convict them out of their own mouths of impudent pretence to ignorance on a subject they well understood. Remember why John was sent, the nature of his commission and his main line of action: he was sent as herald of Christ. Without the slightest defection, and without any claim for himself other than to prepare the way of the Lord, he pointed the finger to Christ, he testified that He was the only Son of God. From what source do the scribes now wish proof anew of the authority of Christ beyond the due testimony of the preaching of John? Christ was not, then, in some tricky way dodging the question put to Him, but giving a complete and consistent response. It was impossible to acknowledge that John was a servant of God without acknowledging that He Himself was Lord. He gave no backing to rash usurpation of public office by men who have no mandate other than their own audacity, any more than He intended His example to encourage the sophist's device of silencing truth: there are many with false ingenuity who plead His authority. I agree that when the wicked lay traps before us we should not always answer them in kind, but the prudent course is so to avoid their deception that we give truth its rightful place. *Baptism* here refers not only to the sign of washing but also to the whole ministry of John. Christ wished to draw out their answer in these terms: Was John God's true and accredited Prophet, or was he an impostor? This way of speaking—Was the Baptism of John from God or from men?—has a useful lesson for us: that no kind of teaching or sacred sign may be accepted in our worship unless evidently sent by God. There is no place for the inventions of human choosing. The passage refers to John, and John in another place is given outstanding commendation by the Lord and raised above all the Prophets, yet Christ declares that his Baptism ought not to be received, unless it had been sent by God. So what do we say to these fictitious sacraments which men of no account have foolishly dragged in with no bidding from God? Christ plainly declares in these words that the whole government of the Church is so dependent on the finger of God that any human innovation is proscribed.

And they reasoned with themselves. The priests show their impiety: no consideration of truth, no interrogation of their own conscience, but a disgraceful effort to shuffle off responsibility rather than admit it, in case their tyrannical power were lost to them. All wicked men pretend to be desirous to learn, but shut the door on the truth when they sense it is against their greedy interests. Christ does not let them go without an answer, but sends them away in shame and confusion. The production of John's testimony sufficiently proves that he is furnished with divine authority.

But what think ye? A man had two sons; and he came to the first, and said, Son, go work to-day in the vineyard. And he answered and said, I will not: but afterward he repented himself, and went. And he came to the second, and said likewise. And he answered and said, I go, sir: and went not. Whether of the twain did the will of his father? They say, The first. Jesus saith unto them, Verily I say unto you, that the publicans and the harlots go into the kingdom of God before you. For John came unto you in the way of righteousness, and ye believed him not; but the publicans and the harlots believed him: and ye, when ye saw it, did not even repent yourselves afterward, that ye might believe him. (Matt. 21.28-32)

The last sentence shows where the parable is aimed: Christ prefers those commonly reckoned disreputable and hateful above the scribes and priests. These latter have their masks stripped off that they may no longer trade on being ministers of God and give an empty display of religion. For although their self-seeking and pride and their cruelty and avarice were known to all they still wanted to keep up the opposite appearance. When they attacked Christ just now, they falsely claimed to be anxious for the good order of the Church, as if they were her faithful and true champions. Christ rebuffs the impudence of such a gross mockery of God and men by showing they could not be further from the position they boasted of—indeed so far from enjoying the privilege they asserted, that they ranked below tax-collectors and prostitutes. As for their profession of eminence in defence of divine worship and zeal for the Law, Christ compares it to the action of the son who makes a promise to his father with his tongue but fails to see it through. The tax-collectors and prostitutes are not excused their sins, but their unprincipled lives are compared to the action of the son, rebellious and ill-behaved, who at first rudely refuses his father's command, but in the end shows up far better, not persisting in sin to the last, but submitting with quiet compliance to the yoke they roughly refused. Now we see Christ's purpose: not only does He reproach the priests and scribes for their obstinate resistance to God and failure to heed repeated warnings, but also He strips them of the false dignity they assumed, because their unworthiness was greater than the dissipation of harlots.

Matt. 21.30. *I go, sir.* This expression comes from the Hebrew: when Hebrews wish to show obedience and testify to their readiness to serve, this is what they say, Here I am, sir. In itself an admirable virtue, to yield ready and quick obedience as soon as God gives the Word. Christ does not praise delay, for there is fault on both sides, performing a duty after a period of delay and making verbal promise without keeping to it. Christ's lesson is that the hypocrisy of the latter is less tolerable than the outburst that, after a time, submits.

Matt. 21.32. *For John came.* Seeing that John was the faithful servant of God, Christ ascribes all his teaching to the person of God Himself. He might have said more fully, God came, showing the way of righteousness by the mouth of John: but as John spoke not as a private individual but in the name of God he is rightly put in God's place. Note the considerable force here given to the preaching of the Word, for those who chose to despise the holy and religious warnings of the teacher He had sent are given the name of outright opposition and rebellion against Him. Some give the word *righteousness* a more ingenious exposition: they are entitled to their own opinion, but it

13

simply strikes me as meaning that John's teaching was pure and approved, as if to say that they had no cause to reject it. Further, when he says the tax-collectors had believed, he does not only mean that they had given verbal assent but also had taken serious resolve to embrace what they had heard. We learn that faith does not consist merely in a person giving subscription to true doctrine, but also includes something greater and deeper: the hearer is to deny himself and commit his whole life to God. When he says that even this example made no impression on them, he makes the most of their obstinate ill-will, for it was the sign of utter despair, surely, to ignore the lead of the prostitutes and tax-collectors.

Hear another parable: There was a man that was a householder, which planted a vineyard, and set a hedge about it, and digged a winepress in it, and built a tower, and let it out to husbandmen, and went into another country. And when the season of the fruits drew near, he sent his servants to the husbandmen, to receive his fruits. And the husbandmen took his servants, and beat one, and killed another, and stoned another. Again, he sent other servants more than the first: and they did unto them in like manner. But afterward he sent unto them his son, saying, They will reverence my son. But the husbandmen, when they saw the son, said among themselves, This is the heir; come, let us kill him, and take his inheritance. And they took him, and cast him forth out of the vineyard, and killed him. When therefore the lord of the vineyard shall come, what will he do unto those husbandmen? They say unto him, He will miserably destroy those miserable men, and will let out the vineyard unto other husbandmen, which shall render him the fruits in their seasons. Jesus saith unto them, Did ye never read in the scriptures,

The stone which the builders rejected,
The same was made the head of the corner:
This was from the Lord,
And it is marvellous in our eyes?

Therefore say I unto you, The kingdom of God shall be taken away from you, and shall be given to a nation bringing forth the fruits thereof. And he that falleth on this stone shall be broken to pieces: but on whomsoever it shall fall, it will scatter him as dust. And when the chief priests and the Pharisees heard his parables, they perceived that he spake of them. And when they sought to lay hold on him, they feared the multitudes, because they took him for a prophet. (Matt. 21.33-46)

And he began to speak unto them in parables. A man planted a vineyard, and set a hedge about it, and digged a pit for the winepress, and built a

14

tower, and let it out to husbandmen, and went into another country.
And at the season he sent to the husbandmen a servant, that he might
receive from the husbandmen of the fruits of the vineyard. And they
took him, and beat him, and sent him away empty. And again he sent
unto them another servant: and him they wounded in the head, and
handled shamefully. And he sent another; and him they killed: and many
others; beating some, and killing some. He had yet one, a beloved son:
he sent him last unto them, saying, They will reverence my son. But
those husbandmen said among themselves, This is the heir; come, let us
kill him, and the inheritance shall be ours. And they took him, and
killed him, and cast him forth out of the vineyard. What therefore will
the lord of the vineyard do? he will come and destroy the husbandmen,
and will give the vineyard unto others. Have ye not read even this
scripture;
> The stone which the builders rejected,
> The same was made the head of the corner:
> This was from the Lord,
> And it is marvellous in our eyes?
And they sought to lay hold on him; and they feared the multitude; for
they perceived that he spake the parable against them: and they left
him, and went away. (Mark 12.1-12)

And he began to speak unto the people this parable: A man planted a
vineyard, and let it out to husbandmen, and went into another country
for a long time. And at the season he sent unto the husbandmen a servant, that they should give him of the fruit of the vineyard: but the
husbandmen beat him, and sent him away empty. And he sent yet
another servant: and him also they beat, and handled him shamefully,
and sent him away empty. And he sent yet a third: and him also they
wounded, and cast him forth. And the lord of the vineyard said, What
shall I do? I will send my beloved son: it may be they will reverence
him. But when the husbandmen saw him, they reasoned one with
another, saying, This is the heir: let us kill him, that the inheritance
may be ours. And they cast him forth out of the vineyard, and killed
him. What therefore will the lord of the vineyard do unto them? He
will come and destroy these husbandmen, and will give the vineyard
unto others. And when they heard it, they said, God forbid. But he
looked upon them, and said, What then is this that is written,
> The stone which the builders rejected,
> The same was made the head of the corner?
Every one that falleth on that stone shall be broken to pieces; but on
whomsoever it shall fall, it will scatter him as dust.
And the scribes and the chief priests sought to lay hands on him in

that very hour; and they feared the people: for they perceived that he spake this parable against them. (Luke 20.9-19)

Matt. 21.33. *Hear another parable.* Luke puts it rather differently, in saying that Christ spoke to the crowds, whereas the utterance is directed at the scribes. The solution is easy if we grant that while Christ turned His discourse against them He revealed their depravity in the face of the whole populace. Mark says that Christ began to speak in parables, but omits the one that came first, just as in other places he selects only a part from the whole. In general the parable makes the point that there is nothing new in the priests' wild and wicked efforts to rob God of His rights. They had treated the prophets in former days with equal thievishness and were now prepared to kill the Son, yet in the end they would not go unpunished, for God will arise to defend His right. And the object is twofold, to reproach the priests for their base and criminal ingratitude, and to remove the offence which was coming in the approaching death of Christ. With their false credentials they had come to influence the simple, unsuspecting populace to accept that the Jewish religion hung on their decree and bidding. Christ forearms the weak with a lesson that as so many prophets, one after another, have been killed by the priests, no one should be distressed if He Himself were treated in the same fashion. Now let us examine it in more detail. *Planted a vineyard.* This comparison frequently occurs in Scripture. As regards the present passage Christ simply means that God in appointing pastors to His Church does not hand over His own rights into their hands but acts as a proprietor letting a vineyard or farm to a tenant to attend to the cultivation and annually to deliver the proceeds. Just as He complains in Isaiah and Jeremiah (Isa. 5.4; Jer. 2.21) that He had received no fruit from the vineyard on whose cultivation He had put out so much labour and expense, so in this passage He accuses the vine-growers themselves of seizing the produce of the vineyard like robbers with violence. Christ says that the husbandmen had taken over a vineyard in a fine state of order and upkeep from the hands of the proprietor, which considerably aggravates their fault. The more generously he had acted with them, the more hateful is their ingratitude. Paul uses the same argument when he wishes to encourage pastors to greater efforts in their duties, saying that they are stewards chosen to run God's household, which is the pillar and the ground of truth (I Tim. 3.15). Rightly so: the more splendid and honourable their rank, the greater their responsibility to God not to be idle at their task. As we have just said, the perfidy of those who laugh at the great liberality of God and the great honour which he has bestowed on them is all the more

16

hateful. God had planted a vineyard at the time when in memory of His free adoption He set them again at liberty from Egypt and made them a peculiar people to Himself, promised to be their God and Father and called them to the hope of eternal salvation. This is the planting Isaiah refers to in 60.21 and elsewhere. By *winepress* and *tower* you must understand the aids that were added to strengthen the faith of the people in the teaching of the Law, such as sacrifices and other rites. God like a provident and careful head of the house spares no effort to arm His Church with every means of defence. *Let it out to husbandmen.* God might well take care for the good order of His Church by Himself, without the work of men, but He does take men on as servants, and uses their handiwork. In former days He appointed priests, to tend His vineyard, so to speak. It is surprising that Christ should compare the prophets to those servants who are sent after the vine-harvest to demand the fruit, for we understand that they were also vine-dressers and held a common responsibility with the priests. The answer is that Christ did not need to express too closely or precisely the points of similarity and difference between the two classes. In origin it was the rule that priests were created to tend the Church thoroughly with sound doctrine: but when by idleness or ignorance they came to neglect the duties laid on them, the prophets were specially sent to strengthen their hands, in rooting out weeds from the vine, in lopping excess branches, and in other ways making up for the shortcomings of the priests. At the same time they take the people severely to task, they restore the collapse of religion, rouse fuddled minds, and bring back the worship of God and newness of life. And is not this exactly to demand for God the due produce of His vineyard? Christ applies this aptly and truly to His purpose, for the continuing and steady government of the Church was not in the prophets' hands, but was always held by the priests—just like the lazy tenant who abandons the upkeep of the farm but clings to his lease on the plea of possession.

Matt. 21.35. *And killed another.* Here Mark and Luke slightly differ from Matthew. He mentions several servants, all of whom were ill-treated and insulted, and after them a greater number still were sent. Mark and Luke speak only of one at a time, not as though they went in two and three, but one after another. They all have the same object in view, namely that the Jews will make the same attempt upon the Son as they had many times upon the prophets: Matthew is just more explicit in showing how God had struggled with the malice of the priests by sending a host of prophets. Clearly their frenzy was uncontrollable, to have resisted every measure of correction.

Matt. 21.37. *They will reverence my Son.* Properly speaking this thought does not apply to God, who had knowledge of the future and was not deceived by hopes of it turning out better, but it is usual especially in parables to transfer human emotions to Him. The addition in fact adds to the sense, for Christ wanted to give a mirror-picture of their dreadful sin, all too surely proven by the devilish fury with which they rose up against the very Son of God who had come to restore them to a right mind. They had already driven God from His inheritance as best they could in cruelly murdering His prophets. Now they would crown their wicked career by putting to death the Son, so that they might have, as it were, an empty house to reign over. Certainly it was the chief reason for the priests' fury against Christ, that they were afraid of losing their spoils—their tyrannical power. For it is Christ through whom God the Father has determined to govern, to whom He has given all authority. The Evangelists differ also a little in the conclusion. Matthew says that a confession was forced out of them, by which they condemned themselves. Mark says that Christ simply declared what penalty such miserable and wicked servants are to expect to pay. Luke at first sight differs more widely, for he says that they shrank from the penalty Christ set out. There is no contradiction if we examine the sense more closely. There is no doubt that they would have agreed with Christ over the penalty which fell to such wicked servants, but when they saw that the charge and sentence were laid against themselves, they cried 'God forbid.'

Matt. 21.42. *Did ye never read, etc.* Remember what was said a little above: seeing that the priests and scribes kept their grip on the people, it was an axiom for them to insist that they were the only true and lawful judges of the redemption that was to come: none might be received as Messiah except on their bidding and election. And so they contend that Christ's Word was impossible, that the Son and Heir of the Lord's vineyard would be killed at their hands. But Christ confirmed it with the testimony of Scripture, and stresses the question, as if to say, 'You reckon it highly absurd that the tenants of the vineyard might ever come to raise a wicked conspiracy against the Son of God, but did the Scripture (Ps. 118.22) foretell for Him a reception of glad approval and welcome, or rather that the very leaders would be His first opponents?' The passage He cites is taken from the same Psalm that contains that joyful cry, 'Save, O Lord; Blessed is he that comes in the name of the Lord.' It was an oracle of the Kingship of the Messiah, as is shown by the terms of David's appointment by God to rule—his throne should remain for ever, so long as the sun and moon gave light in the sky; and if it ever lapsed, it should be restored by God's grace to its former state. So then the Psalm contains a description of the reign of David with the addition of its continuance, which implies restor-

18

ation. If the words had applied to any temporal kingdom, Christ would not properly have applied them to Himself. Always remember what kind of kingdom God had established around the person of David, one that He would establish in the true Messiah to the end of the world. The old anointing was but the shadow. We understand that what was done in David was a prelude, a type, of Christ.

Now to return to the words of the Psalm. The scribes and priests reckoned it incredible that the Christ should be rejected by the rulers of the Church. But He proves from the Psalm that He would be placed on His throne by the wonder of the power of God and not by the will of men, and that precisely this was foreshadowed in David, whom God took up when the nobles had rejected him, to give an example and lesson of what some day He would do in His Christ. The prophet takes a metaphor from building; since the Church is God's sanctuary, Christ on whom it is founded is rightly called the corner-stone, that is, the one that supports the whole weight of the building. The comparison would not work out in every particular if you were to sift each grain of application to Christ, but it suits very well to say that the safety of the Church rests on Him, and He holds its structure together. Other prophets have followed the same form of expression, notably Isaiah and Daniel. Isaiah (28.16) makes the closest allusion to this passage when he has God use the words, 'Behold, I lay in Zion for a foundation stone, a precious and elect stone, against which both the houses of Israel shall stumble.' The same kind of expression is frequently found in the New Testament also. In sum: the Kingdom of God will be founded upon a stone which the builders themselves will throw aside as wrong and worthless. And the sense is, that the Messiah, who is the foundation of the Church's safety will not be chosen by the general election of men, but rather, when He is brought marvellously to the fore by the secret and unlooked-for power of God, He will meet the opposition and hostility of those leading men to whom the charge of the building was entrusted.

There are two things we must consider. First, in case the wicked efforts of men rising up to obstruct Christ's Kingdom should trouble our minds, God has given us warning before the event. Second, no matter what men contrive, God has at the same time testified to the victory of His power in setting up the Kingdom of Christ. We must note both with care. It appears monstrous that the Author of our salvation should be rejected, not by aliens but by those of His own house, and not by the dumb mob, but by those very chief men who held the reins of the Church. Faith needs to be fortified against the strange madness of men, or it will be taken unawares and be shaken. We now see how useful that prediction is to relieve godly minds of the terror that this sad spectacle might well strike on them. The world is upside-down when members rise against their head, tenants against their master, counsellors against their king—and builders reject the foundation-stone of the building. The second line is even more effective, where God declares that the wicked will gain nothing by rejecting Christ, for his rank remains intact. Believers who rely on that promise may in Christ scorn the perverse pride of men and cheerfully rise above it. For all their fierce contrivance Christ will hold the place the Father has given Him whatever they might wish. For all their savage insults—these honourable men, these excellent men!—Christ's rank will none-the-less remain, it will yield nothing to their vulgar spite. God's power will prevail after all; He will be the elect and precious stone which shall sustain the Church of God, His Kingdom and His Temple. The stone is said to be *the head of the corner* not in that He is only a part of the building (since it is clear from other passages that the Church is founded solidly on Him alone) but because the prophet wishes to make Him the chief support of the structure. There is some ingenious argument over the word *corner*, that Christ is placed in the corner because He brings together the two different walls, that is to say, the Gentiles and the Jews. In my opinion David meant nothing more than that the cornerstone takes the chief weight of the building.

Now the question is, how the Spirit calls men *builders* who are only intent on the ruin and destruction of God's Temple. Paul's reason for boasting of his merit as a builder was that he founded the Church on Christ alone (I Cor. 3.11). The answer is easy. Although they attend to their appointed tasks in bad faith, he gives them due credit for their calling. The name of prophet is often given to impostors; men are called pastors who ravage their flocks like wolves. But this is no title of honour, but of ignominy, to be tearing down God's Temple when they were put in charge of its construction. We do well to take warning, that a rightful calling does not prevent men from being evil and criminal enemies of Christ, instead of the servants they ought. The legal priesthood was ordained of God, the Levites received authority to govern the Church from the Lord, but did they for all that perform their duties faithfully? And did the godly have to follow them obediently even to the denial of Christ? Let the Pope now go with his mitred bishops, let them claim that they ought to be believed in all things, because they hold the pastoral office. We may allow them to have been duly called to the government of the Church—vainly can they claim any more than the title of prelates of the Church. Yet even that title of calling will not do for them, for to raise them to such tyrannical office the whole order of the Church would need to be overthrown. If they do have the right to claim jurisdiction in the ordinary sense, they are to be reckoned builders in name only if they disrupt the sacred House of God. It does not always happen that Christ is rejected by those to whom the government of the Church is entrusted. Under the Law there were many pious priests, and in the Kingdom of Christ there are pastors who labour with energy and good faith for the edification of the Church; yet because it must be fulfilled, that the builders should reject the stone, it is proper to distinguish carefully between them. The Holy Spirit has warned us in plain terms not to be deceived by an empty title or the dignity of a calling.

This was from the Lord. It is beyond the usual range of human judgment, the case of the Church's pastors repudiating their own superior, God's Son: the prophet refers us to the hidden counsel of God which we may well regard with wonder, though our intelligence cannot grasp it. Let us understand that here our lines of questioning are cut off, explicitly forbidden, for no-one may judge and measure the nature of Christ's Kingdom by human reason. Who is such a fool as to want to submit the wonderful act, which the prophet calls us to admire, to the scale of his own intelligence? Will you accept nothing of the Kingdom of Christ except what should seem in your own eyes probable? Its origin is declared by the Holy Spirit to be a mystery worthy of supreme wonder, for it is hidden from the eyes of men. Let us remember, when it is a case of the origin and restoration and state and whole well-being of the Church, that we must not depend on our senses, but give due honour to the power of God by admiring His secret work. The contrast implied between God and men is this: not only are we told to embrace the wonderful order of Church government because it is the work of God, but we are also called back from a foolish reverence for men which often obscures the glory of God: as if the prophet had said, however splendid the titles men display, it is perversity to oppose them to God. Hence the papists' diabolical impiety is refuted, that is when they do not hesitate to put the decision of their fake Church before the Word of God. According to them, what does the authority of God's Word depend on, if not on men's pleasing? God is allowed no rights but what He gets from the Church on sufferance. The Spirit's teaching in this passage is very different: once the Majesty of God comes upon the scene, let all the earth keep silence.

Matt. 21.43. *Therefore say I unto you.* Christ has directed His message so far to the chief men and rulers, albeit in the people's presence: now He urges the people themselves to the same effect: and with reason, seeing that they had been the allies and assistants of the priests and scribes in hindering the grace of God. The evil had started with the priests, but the people by their own sins had deserved to have corrupt and degraded pastors, so that in due course the whole body had become infected with much the same illness, in turning against God. This explains why the dreadful vengeance of God is proclaimed by Christ on all without distinction: as the priests were swollen with their prelacy so did the whole people pride themselves on their supposed adoption. But God is not bound to them, says Christ, but He transfers to another the honour of which they have proved unworthy. This was said once for their benefit, no doubt, but it is written for us all (Rom. 11.21) that if God chose us to be His people, let us not revel in the vain and depraved confidence of the flesh but endeavour on our part to behave as He asks His children to do. If He did not spare the natural branches what will He do with the ingrafts? The Jews thought the Kingdom of God abode with them as by hereditary right, and so continued obstinately in their vices without a care. We have suddenly come into their place, against natural order (*praeter naturam*): far less will the Kingdom cleave to us if it is not rooted in true godliness. Christ's threat to remove the Kingdom of God from those who have profaned it must strike our heart with terror: yet there is consolation for all godly men in the mark of its perpetuity. By these words Christ means that although the ungodly extinguish among themselves God's worship, they shall not succeed in abolishing the name of Christ or destroying true religion, for God (in whose hand are all the ends of the earth) will find elsewhere a dwelling-place for His Kingdom. We must learn besides from this passage that the Gospel is not preached in order that it may lie barren and idle, but that it may bear fruit.

Matt. 21.44. *And he that falleth on this stone.* Christ confirms the last sentence more fully; that is, that He suffers no loss or diminution by the rejection of wicked men: though their obstinacy be like stone or iron He will shatter them with His own hardness and will gain glory all the more from their destruction. He was amazed at the stubborn temper He saw in the Jews, and so He had to draw out their judgment in these severe terms, to stop their heedless rush. We learn two lessons: first to be content to yield ourselves to Christ's command with a mild, flexible disposition, and then to be strong in the face of the wicked when they are infatuated and madly aggressive, for a dreadful end awaits them at last. They are said to *fall* upon Christ in their rush to destroy Him not because they come down on Him from a greater height but because their madness has so deranged them that they seek, if you like, to dive on Him from the skies. All they will achieve from this, Christ teaches, is to be broken by their own assault. He foretells a very different end for their lofty ambition: the stone they dared to attack will run them into the ground.

Matt. 21.45. *They perceived that he spake of them.* The Evangelists show how little success Christ had, in case today we should be amazed that the teaching of the Gospel does not bring all men into obedience to God. We may learn that the madness of evil men cannot but be more and more inflamed by threats. The Word of God is a seal to our hearts, and is a hot iron that wounds the conscience of bad men, so that their impiety burns more strongly. Let us pray that He would lay His yoke on us freely, rather than make us more headstrong by the bare knowledge of what His vengeance is. The fact that only their fear of the people prevents them from attempting to lay hands on Christ lets us know that God had laid a restraint on them, which is indeed a sweet consolation for the faithful, when they learn that they are enabled, under the protection of God, to escape from the jaws of death.

Then went the Pharisees, and took counsel how they might ensnare him in his talk. And they send to him their disciples, with the Herodians, saying, Master, we know that thou art true, and teachest the way of God in truth, and carest not for any one: for thou regardest not the person of men. Tell us therefore, What thinkest thou? Is it lawful to give tribute unto Caesar, or not? But Jesus perceived their wickedness, and said, Why tempt ye me, ye hypocrites? Shew me the tribute money. And they brought unto him a penny. And he saith unto them, Whose is this image and superscription? They say unto him, Caesar's. Then saith he unto them, Render therefore unto Caesar the things that are Caesar's; and unto God the things that are God's. And when they heard it, they marvelled, and left him, and went their way. (Matt. 22.15-22)

And they send unto him certain of the Pharisees and of the Herodians, that they might catch him in talk. And when they were come, they say unto him, Master, we know that thou art true, and carest not for anyone: for thou regardest not the person of men, but of a truth teachest the way of God: Is it lawful to give tribute unto Caesar, or not? Shall we give, or shall we not give? But he, knowing their hypocrisy, said unto them, Why tempt ye me? bring me a penny, that I may see it. And they brought it. And he saith unto them, Whose is this image and superscription? And they said unto him, Caesar's. And Jesus said unto them, Render unto Caesar the things that are Caesar's, and unto God the things that are God's. And they marvelled greatly at him. (Mark 12.13-17)

And they watched him, and sent forth spies, which feigned themselves to be righteous, that they might take hold of his speech, so as to deliver

23

him up to the rule and to the authority of the governor. And they asked him, saying, Master, we know that thou sayest and teachest rightly, and acceptest not the person of any, but of a truth teachest the way of God: Is it lawful for us to give tribute unto Caesar, or not? But he perceived their craftiness, and said unto them, Shew me a penny. Whose image and superscription hath it? And they said, Caesar's. And he said unto them, Then render unto Caesar the things that are Caesar's, and unto God the things that are God's. And they were not able to take hold of the saying before the people: and they marvelled at his answer, and held their peace. (Luke 20.20-26)

Since the Pharisees had failed in all their attempts on Christ, they at last thought that the best means to have Him put away was to hand Him over to the governor on a charge of plotting unrest and rebellion. The tribute money (as we have seen elsewhere) was at that time a great subject for dispute among the Jews. Since the Romans had taken over the tribute-money that God in the Law of Moses had ordained to be paid to Himself, the Jews kept on complaining that it was a disgraceful and intolerable offence for profane men to seize a divine prerogative in this manner. Besides, this tribute under the Law testified to their adoption, and they felt deprived of their due privilege. Now the more meagre a man's resources, the more he can rely on his poverty to prompt him to wild action. So this device that the Pharisees think up to trap Christ is a means of catching Him out, whichever way He answers, about tribute-money: if He says it should not be paid, He will be guilty of sedition, while if He states that it ought rightly to be paid, He will be taken for an enemy to His own people and a betrayer of its freedoms. Really their chief aim is to alienate the people from Him. The Evangelists call it ensnaring, for they imagine that He is caught on every side, so that He cannot escape. Since they were His professed enemies and knew He would suspect them, they put up some of their disciples, as Matthew records, Luke calls them spies, who pretended to be god-fearing men, that is they deceitfully displayed a sincere and honest will to learn. Their pretence of righteousness is not here used in the general sense, but is applied to the present case, for they would not have been received except under the cloak of docility and genuine concern. They take Herodians along with them because they were more favourable to the Roman imperium: so the more ready to bring charges. It would repay us to note that for all their bitter dissension among themselves they hate Christ so fiercely that they conspire together to destroy Him. What kind of a sect it was, we have explained elsewhere. Herod was only half a Jew, at any rate a base, spurious professor of the Law, while those who wanted the Law observed exactly and in all parts condemned him and his tainted cult, but he had his flatterers who gave some colour to his false teaching. Hence the court religion, besides the other sects, that sprang up at that time.

Matt. 22.16. *We know that thou art true.* This is their pretended righteousness when they humbly come up to Christ, so anxious to be taught, not only covered in devotion but truly persuaded of His doctrine. If they had spoken from the heart, truly they were upright men. We may take their words as a definition of the true and faithful teacher that they pretended to see in Christ. They call Him true, one who teaches God's way, that is, a faithful Interpreter of God, a Teacher in truth, that is, without any flaw. God's way is contrasted with men's inventions and all outside doctrines, truth with ambition, greed and other low desires, which usually mar the pure course of instruction. So a true teacher must be reckoned as one who does not introduce human constructions, who does not step aside from the genuine Word of God, who hands out (so to speak) what he has taken from the mouth of God. Finally, one who has a sincere desire for edification, and suits his lesson to the use and salvation of the people, without of course any artificial colouring. For this last phrase see Paul (II Cor. 2.17), where he says he does not make merchandise of the Word of God, meaning that some persons are full of ingenuity and without openly overturning true doctrine or getting a bad name for godless opinions, still disguise and falsify the purity of doctrine, either for self-seeking or greed or from a ready ability to twist this way and that as the fancy of the flesh leads on. He compares them to dealers in that they make cheap the pure quality of the Word of God. And it is worth noting, as these hypocrites bring it in also, that Christ teaches rightly because He has no care for the person of men. Nothing pulls teachers further away from a faithful and complete rendering than going after the favour of men. It is impossible to be truly devoted to God if you are anxious to please men (Gal. 1.10). We must take notice of men, but not to the extent of winning their favour by flattery. For us to be perfect, respect of persons must have no place, for it obscures the light, and perverts a right judgment. God's Law often enough urges this upon us, and it is also the lesson of experience (Deut. 1.10 and 16.19). Christ also—John 7.24—contrasts προσω-πολημψίαν (respect of persons) and right judgment, as things directly opposed to each other.

Matt. 22.18. *Perceived their wickedness.* Since they open the conversation exactly as disciples with the best motives, how does Christ catch on to them unless His Spirit saw into their hearts? It was no human guesswork that put Him on the scent of their cunning. Because He was God, He reached into their hearts to strip them of their flattery and vain show of uprightness. Before giving His answer He gave proof of His divinity and revealed their secret wickedness. Simliar cunning is used against us daily by wicked men, but their ill-will is under the surface: we should pray Christ to guide us with the Spirit of discernment, that what was His by nature and by right may be ours by His free gift. Our need of such prudence is obvious, in that we shall constantly run God's doctrine into ill-repute if we do not avoid the traps of the wicked. Christ tells them to bring out a coin, and although it appears at first of small importance it is enough to let open the snares. In this particular, their subject status was already set out: Christ had no need to give them any new ruling. The coin was struck with Caesar's image, for the authority of the Roman imperium was approved and admitted by common use. Thus it was plain that the Jews had of their own accord legislated over tribute-money, in that they had surrendered to the force of Roman arms. They could not take up the issue of paying tribute, without raising the whole political debate.

Matt. 22.21. *Render . . . the things that are Caesar's.* Christ advises them that as their national dependence is attested by the coin they should not take up that issue; as much as to say, 'If you cannot accept paying tribute, you should not have come under the Roman imperium. The coinage (the recognized means of dealing between men) testifies to Caesar's lordship over you, while the liberty you claim has in fact perished, and been taken from you by your silent consent.' Christ's answer does not stop half-way, but provides full instruction on the question which has been raised. A clear distinction is set out here between the spiritual and civil government, that we should know ourselves to be under no external constraint from holding a clear conscience in the sight of God. The error Christ wanted to refute is the idea that a people cannot belong to God unless it is free of the yoke of human rule. Paul presses the same point home. No man should think he is giving less service to the one God when he obeys human laws, pays tax, or bows his head to accept any other burden. In short he declares that God's Law is not violated or His worship offended if the Jews in external government obey the Romans. I think he is looking askance at their hypocrisy in allowing God's worship to be violated in so many things, not to speak of their wicked conspiracy against God's authority, yet taking up with such burning zeal a trivial matter: as if he had said, You are very concerned that God's honour be not impaired by the payment of tribute-money to the Romans. You should rather take pains to give God the worship He requires of you, and at the same time render to men what is their due. Perhaps that distinction hardly seems to apply, because properly speaking when we do our duty towards men we thereby fulfil our obedience to God. But to get His message across to the man in the street Christ is content to distinguish the spiritual Kingdom of God from the political order and round of current affairs. Keep the distinction firm: the Lord wishes to be sole Lawgiver for the government of souls, with no rule of worship to be sought from any other source than His Word, and our adherence to the only pure service there enjoined, yet the power of the sword, the laws of the land and decisions of the courts, in no way prevent the perfect service of God from flourishing in our midst. The doctrine goes further. Every man has a duty as far as he is called to render to his fellow man, the child submitting freely to the parent, the servant to the master, and each to each complying obediently with the law of love, always provided that God retains supreme command, to which all human duties are (as we say) subordinate. In short the overthrow of civil order is rebellion against God, and obedience to leaders and magistrates is always linked to the worship and fear of God, but if in return the leaders usurp the rights of God they are to be denied obedience as far as possible short of offence to God.

Matt. 26.22. *They marvelled.* Here God clearly diverts the evil endeavours of His enemies to a different end, not only cheating and frustrating them of their hopes but also forcing them to go away in disgrace. It will sometimes happen that the wicked meet defeat without stopping their complaints: however unchecked their petulence, however many battles they raise against the Word of God, there are victories in God's hand equal to their number, to triumph over them, and over Satan their chief. But in this reply Christ went out of His way to display His glory, to compel them to leave in shame and confusion.

On that day there came to him Sadducees, which say that there is no resurrection: and they asked him, saying, Master, Moses said, If a man die, having no children, his brother shall marry his wife, and raise up seed unto his brother. Now there were with us seven brethren: and the first married and deceased, and having no seed left his wife unto his brother; in like manner the second also, and the third, unto the seventh. And after them all the woman died. In the resurrection therefore whose wife shall she be of the seven? for they all had her. But Jesus answered and said unto them, Ye do err, not knowing the scriptures, nor the powĕr of God. For in the resurrection they neither marry, nor are given in marriage, but are as angels in heaven. But as touching the resurrection

27

of the dead, have ye not read that which was spoken unto you by God, saying, I am the God of Abraham, and the God of Isaac, and the God of Jacob? God is not the God of the dead, but of the living. And when the multitudes heard it, they were astonished at his teaching. (Matt. 22.23-33)

And there come unto him the Sadducees, which say that there is no resurrection; and they asked him, saying, Master, Moses wrote unto us, If a man's brother die, and leave a wife behind him, and leave no child, that his brother should take his wife, and raise up seed unto his brother. There were seven brethren: and the first took a wife, and dying left no seed; and the second took her, and died, leaving no seed behind him; and the third likewise: and the seven left no seed. Last of all the woman also died. In the resurrection whose wife shall she be of them? for the seven had her to wife. Jesus said unto them, Is it not for this cause that ye err, that ye know not the scriptures, nor the power of God? For when they shall rise from the dead, they neither marry, nor are given in marriage; but are as angels in heaven. But as touching the dead, that are raised; have ye not read in the book of Moses, in the place concerning the Bush, how God spake unto him, saying, I am the God of Abraham, and the God of Isaac, and the God of Jacob? He is not the God of the dead, but of the living: ye do greatly err. (Mark 12.18-27)

And there came to him certain of the Sadducees, they which say that there is no resurrection; and they asked him, saying, Master, Moses wrote unto us, that if a man's brother die, having a wife, and he be childless, his brother should take the wife, and raise up seed unto his brother. There were therefore seven brethren: and the first took a wife, and died childless; and the second; and the third took her; and likewise the seven also left no children, and died. Afterward the woman also died. In the resurrection therefore whose wife of them shall she be? for the seven had her to wife. And Jesus said unto them, The sons of this world marry, and are given in marriage: but they that are accounted worthy to attain to that world, and the resurrection from the dead, neither marry, nor are given in marriage: for neither can they die any more: for they are equal unto the angels; and are sons of God, being sons of the resurrection. But that the dead are raised, even Moses showed in the place concerning the Bush, when he calleth the Lord the God of Abraham, and the God of Isaac, and the God of Jacob. Now he is not the God of the dead, but of the living: for all live unto him. And certain of the scribes answering said, Master, thou hast well said. For they durst not any more ask him any question. (Luke 20.27-40)

We see here how Satan bands all the wicked together, however badly they might otherwise agree among themselves, to oppose the truth of God. Between the two sects there existed bitter hostility, yet towards Christ they make common conspiracy, and the Pharisees allow their own teaching to be attacked in the person of Christ. So to this day we see how all the hosts of Satan, in other respects so much at odds with each other, rise up on all sides to harm Christ. Such a cruel hatred inflames the Papists against the Evangel that they willingly support Epicureans and Libertines and other such monstrosities if their alliance will by any means serve its destruction. In short, men came from different camps to wage war on Christ: and this was done because of the common hatred that they bore for the light of sound doctrine. The question put by the Sadducees is designed either by its absurdity to lead Him into their error, or if He rebuts it to disgrace and ridicule Him in the face of a rough and uneducated crowd. Quite possibly they may already have used the same line of mockery against the Pharisees as they now employ to trip up Christ.

Matt. 22.23. *Which say that there is no resurrection.* We have elsewhere spoken of the origin of the Sadducees. Luke (Acts 23.8) says that they denied both the final resurrection of the flesh and the immortality of souls. We would certainly agree that the correct exposition of Scripture is that the life of the soul without hope of resurrection will be a mere dream. God does not promise souls the survival of death, glory complete and immediate, and enjoyment of blessedness, but delays the fulfilment of their hope to the last day. I grant that philosophers who knew nothing of the resurrection of the flesh have discussed at length the immortal nature of the soul: but it is such foolish talk on the nature of the life to come that their opinions have no weight. · Scripture informs us that the life of the spirit depends on the hope of resurrection, and to this souls released from the body look with expectancy. Whoever destroys the resurrection is also depriving souls of immortality. Here we can see the dreadful confusion of the Jewish Church, that spokesmen for religion could take away the hope of a life to come and make men after the death of the body no different from the dumb beasts. They did not say that one must not lead a holy and upright life; they were not so profane as to make God's service superfluous (no indeed, they maintained that God was Judge of the world and human affairs were ruled by His providence), but they restricted the reward of the godly and the due punishment of the wicked to this present life. Even if it had been true that each man is treated equally according to his deserts, it was too outrageous to confine the promises of God to such narrow limits. Experience clearly shows their crass stupidity. Plainly the reward laid up for the good is kept back till a future life, and the penalties of the wicked are not paid off in

29

this life. It is a fiction beyond the wildest dreams to suppose that man created after the image of God should be extinguished in death like the beasts. And how shameful, how monstrous, when world-wide among profane and blind idolatry there still rested some thought of future life, that among the Jews (God's peculiar people) this seed of piety should be thrown aside! Not to mention that they saw the holy Patriarchs hastening towards the life of heaven, and that the covenant God made with them was spiritual and eternal, surely they must have been more than dense to be blind to such a shining light. First, this was their reward for tearing the Church of God into sects: second, this was the Lord's revenge for their wicked contempt of His doctrine.

Matt. 22.24. *Master, Moses said.* It would have done to introduce the topic bluntly—why do they go at it this way? They use Moses' name as a device to show that the marriages were lawful, contracted not at man's good-pleasure, but under the mandate and ordinance of God Himself. Now God must be consistent with Himself. Here is the subtlety of their case. If God one day gathers the faithful into His Kingdom, He shall restore to them what He had given them in the world, but what then will happen to a wife, whom God had given to seven husbands? This is the way all wicked heretics frame their lies, to distort the true teaching of religion and put to shame the servants of Christ. Papists are not ashamed openly to mock God and His Word in their efforts to steal a march on us. Paul with good reason would have a teacher well-armed against the enemies of the truth (Titus 1.9). As regards the Law, God commanded the closest blood-relations to take up the marriage of one deceased if he had died without children, the reason being that the woman who had married into a particular family should bear it offspring. If there had been children of the first marriage, a union within the degrees forbidden by Law would have been incestuous.

Matt. 22.29. *Ye do err, not knowing the scriptures.* Christ turns on the Sadducees, but it applies in general to all who invent false doctrines. In the Scriptures the light of God shines clearly upon us; to ignore them is the source and cause of all errors. The godly find extraordinary comfort in knowing they are safe from the danger of error as long as they search the Scriptures with a humble and modest will to learn what is right and true. Christ links the power of God to the Word, referring to the case in hand. For as resurrection is far beyond the grasp of human sense, we could not believe in it until our minds rise to envisage the unbounded power of God by which He is able to subject all things to Himself, as Paul teaches (Phil. 3.21). Besides, the Sadducees must have been out of their minds to make the mistake of measuring the glory of the life of heaven by present standards. We

30

are taught to find a proper and prudent sense and expression for the mysteries of the Kingdom of Heaven by joining the power of God to the Scriptures.

Matt. 22.30. *But are as angels.* He does not mean that at the resurrection the children of God will be in all respects like angels, but only so far as they shall be rid of every weakness of this present life, no longer liable to the necessities of an existence of infirmity and corruption. Luke sheds more light on the sense of the comparison when He says that they can no longer die and so will have no more need to increase their race, as on earth. He speaks only of believers, because no mention has been made of the wicked. The question arises, why He should say that being children of the resurrection they will then be children of God; for the Lord already bestows this honour upon faithful men still locked in the perishable workhouse of the flesh. How would we be heirs of eternal life after death if God did not already acknowledge us as His children? I reply, that from the time of our ingrafting by faith into the body of Christ we are adopted as sons of God and the Spirit is the witness, seal, earnest and pledge of this adoption—so that we may freely cry out with assurance, Abba, Father (Rom. 8.15; Gal. 4.6). Although we know that we are the sons of God, because it has not yet appeared what we shall be until we are transformed into His glory and shall see Him as He is, we are not yet reckoned to be His children, in actual effect. Although we are renewed by the Spirit of God, because as yet our life is hidden, it will be the manifestation of it that will truly and really distinguish us from those outside. In this sense Paul puts off our adoption to the last day (Rom. 8.21).

Luke 20.37. *But that the dead are raised.* After refuting their absurd case Christ affirms the doctrine of final resurrection by the testimony of Scripture. This is the order we must always follow with enemies of truth—repulse their lies, then let them know that they are opposed to the Word of God. Until they are convinced by the testimony of Scripture, they will always be free to grumble on. Christ quotes a passage from Moses because He was dealing with Sadducees who had little faith in the prophets, or at least held them in the same regard as we do the book Ecclesiasticus or the history of the Maccabees. Also they had cited Moses and he preferred to go back to the same authority rather than to bring up any single prophet. He did not aim anyway at a complete collection of scriptural passages; any more than we see the Apostles using the same testimonies for the same subject. The passage Christ takes up is no hasty choice, but chosen with fine judgment (even though it might appear rather obscure), for above all else Jews should have kept constantly in mind the testimony that they were redeemed by God because they were the children of Abraham. God certainly

31

declares that He comes to relieve the afflictions of His people, but He adds at once that He acknowledges the people as His own with respect to their adoption, because He had struck a covenant with Abraham. How should He mention the dead before the living unless He gives the highest rank of respect to those Patriarchs with whom He had first concluded His covenant? And how would they excel, if death had been their extinction? The account makes this plain. No one can be a father without children, nor a king without subjects. Hence God cannot properly be called Lord except of the living. Christ's argument however does not depend so much on common uses of speech as on the promise contained in these words. The Lord offers to be our God in terms of receiving us as His people, and this alone is enough to assure us of perfect blessedness. Compare what the Church says in the prophet Habakkuk (1.12), 'Thou art our God from the beginning, we shall not die'. Seeing that all to whom He affirms Himself as God are promised salvation, and that He foretells this for Abraham, Isaac and Jacob after the deaths of these men, it follows that there remains for the dead the hope of life. To the objection that their souls might survive without there being any resurrection of the flesh, I gave answer a little before that the two are connected: souls aspire to the inheritance held for them, though they do not yet reach that condition.

Luke 20.38. *For all live unto him.* These words have various meanings in the Scriptures, but Christ means here that the faithful after death in this world lead a life in heaven with God. Thus Paul says that Christ lives unto God after His reception into the heavenly glory (Romans 6.10), because He is released from the infirmities and trials of this mortal life. But Christ here deliberately warns us against judging the life of the blessed by human sense, for it is hidden in the secret keeping of God. For if during their worldly pilgrimage they are almost like dead men, much less does any semblance of life show in them after the death of the body. But God is faithful, for He will keep them alive in His presence, in a way that transcends human understanding.

Luke 20.39. *Certain of the Scribes answering.* Since they were probably all ill-disposed it was a divine prompting that forced this acknowledgment from certain ones, viz. Pharisees. Perhaps for all their desire to see Christ shamed into silent defeat, when they saw that His answer supported their case against the opposite party, they were driven by selfish enthusiasm to congratulate Him on the victory He had gained. Perhaps too the fire of jealousy prevented them wishing Christ to fall to the Sadducees. In any case it was a work of the wonderful providence of God that His worst enemies should assent to His teaching. Their insolence was checked not only by seeing how Christ was able to sustain attacks from any quarter, but also by fear of being repulsed with disgrace, as had already happened more than once. Finally they were ashamed of allowing Him to carry off the prize without a word spoken that might increase their own standing with the populace. When Matthew says *the multitude were astonished* at His teaching, we should note how deeply affected by degrading and chilling notions was the teaching of religion at the time, that it should justly have been regarded as a miracle that the hope of resurrection was proven from the Law with such skill and effect.

But the Pharisees, when they heard that he had put the Sadducees to silence, gathered themselves together. And one of them, a lawyer, asked him a question, tempting him, Master, which is the great commandment in the law? And he saith unto him. Thou shalt love the Lord thy God with all thy heart, and with all thy soul, and with all thy mind. This is the great and first commandment. And a second like unto it is this, Thou shalt love thy neighbour as thyself. On these two commandments hangeth the whole law, and the prophets. (Matt. 22.34-40)

And one of the scribes came, and heard them questioning together, and knowing that he had answered them well, asked him, What commandment is the first of all? Jesus answered, The first is, Hear, O Israel; The Lord our God, the Lord is one: and thou shalt love the Lord thy God with all thy heart, and with all thy soul, and with all thy mind, and with all thy strength. The second is this, Thou shalt love thy neighbour as thyself. There is none other commandment greater than these. And the scribe said unto him, Of a truth, Master, thou hast well said that he is one; and there is none other but he: and to love him with all the heart, and with all the understanding, and with all the strength, and to love his neighbour as himself, is much more than all whole burnt offerings and sacrifices. And when Jesus saw that he answered discreetly, he said unto him, Thou art not far from the kingdom of God. And no man after that durst ask him any question. (Mark 12.28-34)

And behold, a certain lawyer stood up and tempted him, saying, Master, what shall I do to inherit eternal life? And he said unto him. What is written in the law? how readest thou? And he answering said, Thou shalt love the Lord thy God with all thy heart, and with all thy soul, and with all thy strength, and with all thy mind; and thy neighbour as thyself. And he said unto him, Thou hast answered right: this do, and thou shalt live. But he, desiring to justify himself, said unto Jesus, And who is my neighbour? Jesus made answer and said, A certain man was going down from Jerusalem to Jericho; and he fell among robbers, which

33

both stripped him and beat him, and departed, leaving him half dead.
And by chance a certain priest was going down that way: and when he
saw him he passed by on the other side. And in like manner a Levite
also, when he came to the place, and saw him, passed by on the other side.
But a certain Samaritan, as he journeyed, came where he was: and when
he saw him, he was moved with compassion, and came to him, and bound
up his wounds, pouring on them oil and wine; and set him on his own
beast, and brought him to an inn, and took care of him. And on the
morrow he took out two pence, and gave them to the host, and said, Take
care of him; and whatsoever thou spendest more, I, when I come back
again, will repay thee. Which of these three, thinkest thou, proved
neighbour unto him that fell among the robbers? And he said, He that
shewed mercy on him. And Jesus said unto him, Go, and do thou
likewise. (Luke 10.25-37)

Luke's narrative has some resemblance apparently to Matt. 22 and
Mark 12, but is not the same. I have chosen to put them together for
the reason that this was the last question with which the Lord was put
to the test, and Luke has no mention of it. His omission seems in-
tentional, because he had related it elsewhere. I do not dispute that
it may be the same story, though Luke's version is rather different
from the rest. All agree that it was a scribe who put the testing
question to Christ, but the one described by Matthew and Mark goes
away well-disposed, for he agrees with Christ's answer, and gives the
impression of a docile and quiet character. Christ moreover replies
that he is not far himself from the Kingdom of God. Luke shows us
a man however of obdurate and inflated pride, without the slightest
mark of awakened conscience. There would be nothing exceptional
in Christ being tempted on matters of true justice and observance of
the Law and the rule of the good life more than once. It may be that
Luke told the incident out of place, or it may be that he omits the
second time of asking (considering that the first narrative covered the
doctrine well enough). It seemed to me that the lesson was so much
the same that I ought to bring the three Evangelists together.

Now what has come up to excite the scribe into putting a question
to Christ? Surely, because he as an interpreter of the Law is offended
at the Gospel teaching, which he reckons to impair the authority of
Moses. Yet it is not so much zeal for the Law that moves him, as the indignity he feels at losing his professional status. What he wants Christ
to answer is whether He would teach anything more perfect than the
Law. He does not say it in so many words, but his question is angled at
exposing Christ to the displeasure of the crowd. Matthew and Mark
do not ascribe the device to one man, but tell us it was a joint effort:

that one was chosen out of all the sect, apparently one outstanding in intellect and learning. The form of the questioning differs considerably in Matthew and Mark compared with Luke. According to Luke the scribe asks what men must do to achieve eternal life, but according to the other two, what is the greatest commandment of the Law. The object is the same, however: to attack Christ unawares, and if he can elicit any remark at variance with the Law, to raise agitation against Him on grounds of apostasy and promotion of ungodly betrayal.

Luke 10.26. *What is written in the Law?* The reply he receives from Christ is not what he had expected. Christ prescribed no other rule of pious and upright life than that handed down in the Mosaic Law, for perfect love of God and of neighbour is altogether perfect righteousness. And we must note that Christ is speaking here of gaining salvation, as He had been asked. It is not such explicit instruction as He gives elsewhere on the way men must follow to reach eternal life, but rather how they must live to be reckoned upright in the sight of God. Certainly the Law contains a way for men to order their lives to obtain salvation in God's sight. The fact that Law can only be a condemnation and is therefore called the doctrine of death, and as Paul says (Rom. 7.13) increases transgressions, arises not from any flaw in its teaching, but because it is impossible for us to fulfil its commands. Hence though no one is justified by the Law, yet the Law itself contains all righteousness, for it does not deceive its adherents in promising them salvation if any fully observe its bidding. Nor ought we to think it a strange way of teaching that God first demands justification by works, then offers it free of works; men had to be convinced of their just condemnation in order that they might take refuge in the mercy of God. So in Paul (Rom. 10.5) the two are compared to inform us that the reason for our free justification by God is the failure of our own. Christ suits His reply to the lawyer, taking account of his question. He had asked not the source of salvation, but the works by which it is to be won.

Matt. 22.37. *Thou shalt love the Lord thy God.* Mark puts in a sentence before, that the God of Israel is one Jehovah: words where God presses the authority of His Law under a twofold name. One powerful stimulus to encourage the worship of God ought to be our conviction that we worship the true Creator of heaven and earth, for doubt of course breeds apathy; again our love of Him is sweetly kindled by His free adoption of us as His people. So the Jews understand that their rule of life is ordained by the one, true God, in case they should be afraid (the usual result of uncertainty); and in case they should be held back by mistrust, God comes to them familiarly and commends to them His free Covenant. And without any doubt He sets Himself

35

apart from all idols to prevent the Jews being drawn over to another, instead of keeping to the pure worship of Him alone. It may well be that the wretched worshippers of idols have no assurance that would hold them back from the wild frenzy that draws them to their cult, but for men who have heard the Law, what excuse can remain, if they sleep through the revelation of God in person? There follows a summary of the Law, which is also found in Moses (Deut. 6.5). Though it was divided into two tables, one on the service of God, the other on neighbourliness, Moses gives a good and sensible summary that the Jews may know God's will in each commandment. By any standard it is more fitting to love God than men, yet God has good reason to make love a requirement, and not service or homage. He means by this that only the free service of our wills is acceptable to Him. Ultimately the man who comes to obey God will love Him first. Because wicked and sinful inclinations of the flesh turn us aside from the right way Moses shows that our lives will only fall duly into place when the love of God controls all our emotions. Let us therefore learn that the love of God is the beginning of religion, for God will not have the forced obedience of men, but wishes their service to be free and spontaneous. Let us learn too that under the love of God is included the reverence that is His due. Moses does not add *mind*, but only mentions *heart* and *soul* and *strength*. Although the division here into four is fuller, it does not alter the sense. While Moses wants to say in a word or two that God is to be loved fully, and that all men's powers should be devoted to this, he was content to add, to soul and heart, strength, that no part of our being should feel the lack of God's love. We know that in Hebrew the word heart often includes the mind, especially when it is linked with soul. Whatever difference there may be here and in Matthew between mind and heart I shall not elaborate, except that mind signifies for me the higher seat of reason from which all purposes and thoughts proceed. It appears from this summary that in the precepts of the Law God does not look for what men can do but what they ought to do. In this infirmity of the flesh it is not possible that the perfect love of God should reign entire: for we know how all the emotions of our soul are liable to vanity. Lastly we learn that God does not linger over the outward sign of achievement but chiefly searches the inner disposition, that from a good root good fruits may grow.

Matt. 22.39. *A second like unto it is this*. The second place is assigned to men's love for their neighbour, because the service of God ranks first. He says the command to love our neighbour is like the first since it leads from it. Every man is self-centred—love for our neighbour will never flourish unless the love of God begins to reign. Love is a mercenary thing when the children of this world are attached to each other for the advantage each wants to gain. On the other hand, the love of God cannot reign without breeding a brotherly affection among men. When Moses told us to love our neighbours as ourselves, he did not give priority to self-love; that a man should first love himself and then his neighbour (like the Sorbonne sophists' quibble, that the rule must be greater than its object). We are too much devoted to ourselves. Moses, to correct our fault, decrees that our neighbours are of equal rank, as if he were to forbid each individual from neglecting others for his own interests, for love joins all in one body. Correcting the φιλαυτίαν (self-love) that divides one from another, he brings each one into a common unity, one might say, a mutual embrace. So Paul was right to call love the bond of perfectness (Col. 3.14), and elsewhere (Rom. 13.10) the fulfilment of the Law, since all the commandments of the second table go back to it.

Luke 10.28. *This do, and thou shalt live.* I have expounded a little above how this promise agrees with the free justification of faith. God does not justify us freely because the Law fails to show us perfect justification, but because we all fail in its observance. Moreover He says that we cannot obtain life by it because of the infirmity of our flesh. The two propositions agree well. The Law teaches how men may obtain justification by works, and no-one is justified by works, for the fault lies not in the teaching of the Law but in men. Anyhow it was Christ's purpose to defend Himself from the lie which He knew was brought against Him by rough, uneducated men—that He was setting aside the Law from its place as the enduring rule of righteousness.

Luke 10.29. *He, desiring to justify himself.* The question might appear to have no relevance to man's justification. But if we remember what was said elsewhere that man's hypocrisy is most taken to task in the second table (for while men pretend fine service for God they openly break charity with their neighbours), it will readily be seen that the Pharisee has taken refuge under the false guise of holiness to avoid the light of truth. Seeing that the test of love would go against him, he tries to take shelter in the word neighbour, to avoid exposure as a law-breaker. We have already seen that the scribes falsified the Law at this point, because they reckoned none to be their neighbours but those who deserved to be. Hence their acceptance of the principle, that it is lawful to hate one's enemies. The only way out of their guilt for hypocrites is to twist all they can, to stop their lives being brought to the process of Law.

Luke 10.30. *Jesus made answer, etc.* Christ might simply have told him that the word neighbour applies indiscriminately to any man, for the whole human race is linked in a holy bond of brotherhood. Certainly the Lord uses the word in the Law for no other reason than to attract us to the delight of mutual love. It would have been a clearer commandment if it had run, Thou shalt love every man as thyself: but men are so blinded by pride and so pleased with themselves that they hardly allow any to share their place, and they avoid the duty they owe. Therefore the Lord declares all men to be neighbours, that the affinity itself may bring them closer together. For anyone to be a neighbour, then, it is enough that he be a man; it is not in our power to deny the common ties of nature. Christ wanted to elicit an answer from the Pharisee for him to condemn himself. The opinion that held sway with them was that no one can be a neighbour unless he is our friend: if Christ had asked outright he would never have come back with the straight answer that all men are included under 'neighbour'—but the parable He brings up forces him to the admission. It turns out that our neighbour is the man most foreign to us, for God has bound all men together for mutual aid. It fits in with His purpose to include some criticism of the Jews and priests in particular, for although they boasted that they were the children of the same Father and separated by the privilege of adoption from other races to be the holy heritage of God, nevertheless they held each other in savage, vile contempt, as if there were nothing of importance between them. No doubt Christ is describing their cruel neglect of love, and they knew they were guilty. But as I said the chief aim is to show that neighbourliness which obliges us to do our duty by each other is not restricted to friends and relations, but open to the whole human race.

To prove his point Christ compares a Samaritan to a Priest and a Levite. It is well known how the Jews burned with bitter hatred against the Samaritans, that for all they lived close together there was the greatest dis-unity. Christ tells of a Jew, a citizen of Jericho, who on his way to Jerusalem was wounded by thieves. He was passed by, both by the Levite and by the Priest, when they came across him lying half-dead, but the Samaritan took kind care of him. Then he asks, Which of the three was neighbour to that Jew? The ingenious Rabbi cannot avoid putting the Samaritan above the others. As in a mirror we can see the brotherhood of man which the scribes with their sophistry had tried to efface. An act of mercy, shown to a Jew by an enemy, makes plain that it is nature's leading and learning that man is made for man. Hence we see that there are mutual ties between all men.

An allegorical interpretation devised by proponents of free-will is really too futile to deserve an answer. According to them, under the figure of a wounded man is described the condition of Adam after the fall. Whence they infer that the power to act well was not quite

38

extinct, for he is only said to be half-dead. As if Christ would have intended to speak here about the corruption of human nature, and discuss whether the wound Satan struck on Adam was fatal or curable: as if He had not plainly declared, without any figurative talk, that all are dead unless He quickens them with His voice (John 5.25). I give as little respect for that other allegory which has won such regard that nearly everyone comes down in its favour like an oracle. In this, they make out the Samaritan to be Christ, because He is our protector: they say that wine mixed with oil was poured into the wound because Christ heals us with repentance and the promise of grace. And a third cunning story has been made up, that Christ does not immediately restore health but sends us to the Church, that is the inn-keeper, to be cured gradually. None of these strikes me as plausible: we should have more reverence for Scripture than to allow ourselves to transfigure its sense so freely. Anyone may see that these speculations have been cooked up by meddlers, quite divorced from the mind of Christ.

Matt. 22.40. *On these two commandments.* I now return to Matthew, where Christ says that the whole Law and the Prophets hang on these two commandments, not that He intends to restrict the whole teaching of Scripture to this, but because any instruction on the means of leading a holy and upright life should spring from these two headings. Christ is not giving a general discussion of the content of the Law and Prophets, but indicating in His answer that the requirements of the Law and Prophets are precisely that each should love God and his neighbours: as if to say that the whole foundation and structure of holy, upright living was the service of God and love for men; just as Paul says love is the perfection of the Law (Rom. 13.10). It is simply mistaken to force Christ's words into meaning that no deeper lessons are to be found in the Law and Prophets. We must keep the distinction between commandments and promises: Christ is not making any overall pronouncement on what is to be learned from the Word of God but explaining as the occasion demands to what end all the commandments are directed. The free forgiveness of sins, by which we are reconciled with God, our confidence in calling upon God which is the earnest of our inheritance to come, and all the other matters of our faith, do not hang on these two commandments though they may hold first place in the Law: for it is one thing to face a demand for debt, a different thing to be offered what we need to pay. The same thing is expressed by Mark, in other words, that no other commandment is greater than these.

Mark 12.32. *Master, thou hast well said.* Only Mark records that the scribe was appeased, and it is worth noting that one who had attacked Christ with malice and deceit not only yields to the truth without a word but openly and frankly sides with Christ. We see that he was not the kind of enemy whose obstinacy is incurable: some might be caught out a hundred times without ceasing by every means to resist the truth. We gather from the answer that Christ did not confine the rule of life to these two words alone but took the occasion to attack the false, under-cover sanctimoniousness of the scribes: they who laid all stress on outward rites took the spiritual worship of God almost for nothing—love indeed was no great subject for them. Now although the scribe was infected with this disease he had, as sometimes happens, got the grain of a right idea from the Law, which had lain choked in his heart: now it lets him be drawn without hardship away from his bad customs. It seems unreasonable that sacrifices which are part of God's service and refer to the first table of the Law, should be put after love. The answer is that although the service of God is supreme, more precious than all the duties of an upright life, its outward exercises are never so important as to require love's withdrawal. We know that love is pleasing to God for its own sake, in its simplicity, while sacrifices are neither wanted nor approved unless for what they lead to. Besides it is bare and empty sacrifice we are dealing with here: Christ sets the false show of piety over against true and sincere worth. The same teaching is found all through the prophets, warning hypocrites that sacrifices are worthless if they are not coupled with spiritual truth, and that God is not placated by offerings of beasts when love is neglected.

Mark 12.34. *And when Jesus saw.* We cannot tell whether this scribe made further progress; but because he showed himself willing to learn Christ stretches out His hand to Him and teaches us by His example that we should help any in whom the first glimmer of docility and a right mind appears. There seem to be two reasons why Christ declared this scribe to be not far from the Kingdom of God. He had an open mind to what he must do, and he had a keen eye to distinguish the outward show of service to God from the essential duties. Christ's testimony is more encouragement than praise, saying that he is near the Kingdom of God. In his person He puts heart into us all that having set out on the right way we should be all the keener to pursue it. We learn from these words that many who are still in the grip and snares of error may yet be on the way, even in blindness, being trained in this fashion when the time is full to run the Lord's race. When the Evangelists say that the mouth of His adversaries was stopped, so that they did not dare attempt any more traps for Christ, it is not right to take it in the sense that they relented from their unyielding obstinacy, for inwardly they were furious, like savage beasts shut up in dens, or like wild horses champing at the bit. But the more adamant their impenitence, the more unrestrained their opposition, the more shining the triumph Christ led over both. This victory should greatly encourage us never to break in our defence of truth, but to be sure of success. It will often happen that the enemy continue their wild assaults to the very last; but at length God has their frenzy turn back upon their own heads and, despite all, truth comes out victorious.

Now while the Pharisees were gathered together, Jesus asked them a question, saying, What think ye of the Christ? whose son is he? They say unto him, The son of David. He saith unto them, How then doth David in the Spirit call him Lord, saying,

  The Lord said unto my Lord,
  Sit thou on my right hand,
  Till I put thine enemies underneath thy feet?
If David then calleth him Lord, how is he his son? And no one was able to answer him a word, neither durst any man from that day forth ask him any more questions. (Matt. 22.41-46)

And Jesus answered and said, as he taught in the temple, How say the scribes that the Christ is the son of David? David himself said in the Holy Spirit,

  The Lord said unto my Lord,
  Sit thou on my right hand,
  Till I make thine enemies the footstool of thy feet.
David himself calleth him Lord; and whence is he his son? And the common people heard him gladly. (Mark 12.35-37)

And he said unto them, How say they that the Christ is David's son? For David himself saith in the book of Psalms,

  The Lord said unto my Lord,
  Sit thou on my right hand,
  Till I make thine enemies the footstool of thy feet.
David therefore calleth him Lord, and how is he his son? (Luke 20.41-44)

Matt. 22.42. *What think ye.* Mark and Luke explain more clearly why Christ asked this question: it was because the scribes gave support to the erroneous opinion that the promised Redeemer coming of David's line and succession would bring with Him nothing but the ordinary endowment of human nature. From the beginning Satan had tried every means to put up a counterfeit Christ, no true mediator of God and man. Since God had so often promised that the Christ

41

would spring from the seed, from the loins of David the idea was so firmly rooted in all Jewish minds that they could scarcely have allowed His human nature to be dispensed with. So Satan allowed Christ to be acknowledged true man and son of David, for it would have been useless to try to upset this leading article of faith, but (more grievously) he stripped Him of His Godhead, as if He should be any one at all of the sons of Adam. In this way the hope of eternal life to come and spiritual righteousness was done away. Ever since Christ was revealed to the world, heretics have used many devices or insinuations to subvert either His human or divine nature, either reducing His power to save us, or closing our familiar way of approach to Him. Now as the hour of His death drew near, the Lord Himself willed to attest His divinity to give all the godly sure ground of confidence in Him: if He were only human we could not glory in Him nor expect salvation from Him. We see that His purpose was not so much to assert Himself as Son of God, as to establish our faith in His heavenly power. The infirmity of the flesh in which He comes near to us gives us boldness to approach Him without fear. But if it were only this that we saw, it would fill us more with fear and despair than prompt our confidence. We must notice that the scribes are blamed, not for teaching that the Christ would be son of David, but for making Him to be no more than a man, who would come down from heaven to assume the nature and person of a man. The Lord is not explicitly speaking of Himself, but showing how wickedly the scribes are in error to expect a Redeemer merely from the world and human stock. The opinion was commonplace to them, but Matthew shows that He chose to bring it out in the presence of the people.

Matt. 22.43. *How then doth David in the Spirit.* Christ makes the point emphatically, that David spoke in the Spirit: for the prophecy of a future event is set over against a statement about the present. There is a devious argument that the Jews still take refuge in, which His words anticipate. They apply the utterance to the celebration of David's kingdom. God is acknowledged as the Author of his Kingdom that he may rise over the wild attacks of his enemies and affirm that they will gain no success against the will of God. To stop the scribes using this line of objection, Christ declared that the composition of the Psalm was not related to the person of David but under the prompting of the Spirit of prophecy was describing the Kingdom of Christ to come: this can easily be evinced from the context, that the language used does not fit David or any earthly monarch. David introduces a king clothed in a new priesthood, meaning that the old shadows of the Law must be done away. We must see how he proves Christ to have a greater excellence than mere descent from David's seed. It is because David, king and head of the people, calls Him Lord: it follows there is more than man in Him. Perhaps the argument seems weak and unappealing, as open to the objection that when David conveys the Psalm to the people he is not applying it to himself, but making someone else subject to the rule of Christ. I would take up the objection, and say that seeing he is one of the Church's members nothing could have been less appropriate for him than to exclude himself from the teaching all received. Here he calls on all the children of God as with one voice to boast of their safe keeping under the heavenly and invincible king. If he were shut off from the body of the Church, he would have no share in the promised salvation in Christ. If the words are confined to a few, the rule of Christ would not even reach David. Neither he himself nor any other can be exempted from their obedience without at the same time losing their hope of eternal salvation. The best thing for David was to be included in the Church, and he applied this Psalm as much to himself as to the rest of the people. In short, in this song of praise Christ stands as the only and supreme King, who ranks above all the faithful. No exception to the single ordering in of all can be admitted, when He is made the Church's Redeemer. There is no doubt that David also submits Himself to His rule, to be reckoned with the people of God.

Another question arises. Might not God have raised up someone of human race as Redeemer to be David's Lord and Son at the same time? For it is not God's most essential name that is used, but only *Adonai* (Lord), which in fact is often applied to men. I reply that Christ takes it for granted that He who is taken out of the number of men and elevated to the extent of headship over all in the Church is no mere man, but endowed as well with the Majesty of God. The eternal God who takes an oath to Himself and affirms that in His presence every knee shall bow swears also that He will not give His glory to another (Isa. 45.23 and 42.8). On Paul's testimony, when Christ ascended into His Kingdom there was given Him a name which is above every name, that before Him every knee should bow (Rom. 14.11; Phil. 2.9). And although Paul never said it, the fact is that Christ took rank above David and all other kings, for he also excels the angels: and this could hardly be for a mortal man unless in His flesh God were also manifest. I admit that His divine essence is not expressed exactly and in so many words, but we can readily infer that He is God, who is placed above all creation.

Matt. 22.44. *The Lord said unto my Lord.* Here the Holy Spirit leads all holy men in a song of triumph that they may sing in the teeth of Satan and all evil-doers, mocking their frenzy in working to put Christ off His throne. Let them not tremble or be afraid when they see great

43

uproar raised in the earth, for they are bidden to set the holy and inviolable decree of God against all the efforts of the wicked. It means that however mad men become, all their crafty attempts to overthrow the Kingdom of Christ will be in vain, because it does not depend on the good-pleasure of men, but on the foundation of God which shall never be moved. Whenever the Kingdom comes under heavy fire, may this celestial utterance come to our minds. This promise was put in the hands of Christ that each of the faithful might take it to his own use. God never changes nor deceives. He does not take back what has once left His lips. *Sit thou at my right hand* is taken metaphorically for the second, that is next, place occupied by God's deputy. It comes to mean holding supreme power and authority in God's name, as we know that God has given personal authority to His Son to govern His Church by His might. The expression does not mean a particular place, but includes heaven and earth in the rule of Christ. God declares that Christ will sit until His enemies are put beneath his feet, to let us understand that His reign will be invincible and all-powerful, not that He will lose His power when His enemies have been beaten; rather it will endure perpetually undiminished, as the forces of all His enemies are brought low. This explains the state of His Kingdom as we see it today, in case we are troubled at the sight of hostility on all sides.

Then spake Jesus to the multitudes and to his disciples, saying, The scribes and the Pharisees sit on Moses' seat: all things therefore whatsoever they bid you, these do and observe: but do not ye after their works; for they say, and do not. Yea, they bind heavy burdens and grievous to be borne, and lay them on men's shoulders; but they themselves will not move them with their finger. But all their works they do for to be seen of men: for they make broad their phylacteries, and enlarge the borders of their garments, and love the chief place at feasts, and the chief seats in the synagogues, and the salutations in the market-places, and to be called of men, Rabbi. But be not ye called Rabbi: for one is your teacher, and all ye are brethren. And call no man your father on the earth: for one is your Father, which is in heaven. Neither be ye called masters: for one is your master even the Christ. But he that is greatest among you shall be your servant. And whosoever shall exalt himself shall be humbled; and whosoever shall humble himself shall be exalted. (Matt. 23.1-12)

And in his teaching he said, Beware of the scribes, which desire to walk in long robes, and to have salutations in the market-places, and chief seats in the synagogues, and chief place at feasts: (Mark 12.38-39)

And one of the lawyers answering saith unto him, Master, in saying this thou reproachest us also. And he said, Woe unto you lawyers also! for ye lade men with burdens grievous to be borne, and ye yourselves touch not the burdens with one of your fingers.

Woe unto you Pharisees! for ye love the chief seats in the synagogues, and the salutations in the market-places.

And in the hearing of all the people he said unto his disciples, Beware of the scribes, which desire to walk in long robes, and love salutations in the market-places, and chief seats in the synagogues, and chief places at feasts; (Luke 11.45-46, 43 and 20.45-46)

Matt. 23.1. *Then spake Jesus to the multitudes.* With all the contention and noisy debate, with all the disturbance and confusion, with all respectable and lawful order running riot, Christ's admonition here is most timely to uphold the integrity of the authority of God. We know how quickly men turn it out of favour in their minds, especially when the life of the pastors grows more dissolute, more inconsistent with their words. The world at large takes their example as a licence to impunity, and goes astray. The same thing—and worse—happens in time of contention: the majority throw off the yoke, give free course to their passions and fling respect to the winds. At this time the scribes burned with greed and were swollen with ambition; their extortion was notorious and their cruelty terrifying; their morals so corrupt that they might seem to be set on the ruin of the Law. Besides this, their false opinions had perverted the pure, genuine sense of the Law, forcing Christ into bitter conflict with them: an astonishing fury drove them to put out the light of truth. There was a danger that many would conceive a contempt for all religion by their exposure to such corrupt influences and the tumult of debate, which Christ opportunely faces: how wrong it would be for true religion to perish, is His message, on account of the failure of men, how wrong for the Law to lose respect. Seeing that the scribes were determined enemies of the truth, for they held the Church in the grip of their tyrannical power, Christ was forced to expose their crimes, for if good and sincere men had not been released from their bondage, the door of the Gospel remained shut to them. And another reason: the common people think themselves free to do whatever their masters do, and turn their corrupt behaviour into their own standards. In case what He should say would be mis-applied, His first lesson is that whatever the life of the masters there is no justification for any of their filthy behaviour to rub off on the Word of God, nor for anyone to snatch licence to sin from their example. This caution must be noted. Many with the one objective of pouring hatred and disgrace on the heads of the

45

wicked and criminal let their zeal, without thinking, cause general upset and confusion. All discipline is flouted and respect thrown to the ground. We are left with no regard for decency, but an increasing defiance among many, crying down the sins of the priesthood in order to sin more freely themselves on the strength of it. Christ's invective against the scribes is primarily to uphold God's Law from contempt. We must take the same pains if we want our admonitions to be of use. Note at the same time, that no fear of giving offence deterred Christ from exposing the ungodly teachers as they deserved. His moderation was only motivated by fear that the wickedness of men should not bring reproach upon the teaching of God. Bringing their faults into public, Mark tells us, was not to stir up personal hatred but to check the contagion from spreading—*in his teaching he said*, etc. Meaning that the hearers were to profit by the warning to watch themselves. Although Luke appears to confine it to the disciples it is probable that the address was given to the crowd in general. It is clearer in Matthew; indeed the subject itself requires that Christ's survey should be comprehensive.

Matt. 23.2. *On Moses' seat*. It seemed satisfactory to take in here what Luke places elsewhere. It is the same teaching, in any case, and I have no doubt that Luke after narrating that the scribes received a severe and stern reproof from the Lord added the other words of reproof which Matthew retained in their proper place. We have often seen the Evangelists as occasion required collecting various sayings of Christ into one group. Matthew's narrative is the fuller, and I am basing my exposition on his account. Briefly, Christ encourages the faithful to beware of conforming their lives to the evil-living of the scribes but rather to adhere to the Law's ruling which they hear from the scribes' mouths. As I have just remarked, He reckoned it necessary to reprove them of many faults to prevent the whole people becoming infected. So in case their wickedness should ruin the message, whose ministers and heralds they were, He tells the faithful to attend to their words and not their works: in other words, the evil example of the pastors should not stop the children of God from leading an upright life. The word *scribe* suitably applies to the teachers or interpreters of the Law in Hebrew usage, and certainly they are the same whom Luke describes as lawyers. *Pharisees*, who are included with scribes, are particularly singled out by the Lord because at that time their sect's government of the Church and their interpretation of Scripture had a leading influence. We have said elsewhere that while the Sadducees and Essenes preferred literal interpretation, the Pharisees followed another way of teaching that they had taken (as it were) from the hands of their forebears, namely to look more

46

closely into the mystical sense of Scripture. This got them their name: they are called *Pherusim*, that is, interpreters. All Scripture had been spoiled by their commentaries, yet they were proud of the popularity of that sort of teaching, and their esteem flourished greatly with the people in matters of the tradition of worship and the discipline of godly living. This explains the expression, Pharisees and other Scribes, or, Scribes among whom the Pharisees held greatest esteem. When they speak to you they are good teachers of the upright life, but in the evil they do they give very bad instruction: so look to their lips rather than their hands.

The question arises, whether we should obey without discretion all that masters teach. It is agreed that in those days the Scribes had corrupted the Law by the base inventions of their evil and criminal minds. They had burdened wretched souls by unfair laws, they had polluted the worship of God with a host of superstitions, yet Christ wants their teaching respected as if it were forbidden to oppose their tryannical power. The answer is easy. It is not a simple contrast of any kind of teaching and living, but Christ's determination to separate God's holy Law from their profane deeds.

To *sit in Moses' seat* means precisely giving instruction how to live from God's Law. I am not quite sure where the expression comes from. I think it is right to refer it to the pulpit which Ezra erected for the reading of the Law (Neh. 8.4.). When the Rabbis expounded Scripture those who were about to speak stood up in order from the bench. It was perhaps a matter of usage that the Law itself should be read from a more elevated position. Whoever sits on Moses' seat, then, teaches by the Word and authority of God and not on his own account or by his own interpretation. Of course it entails a rightful calling: Christ bids men listen to the scribes because they were public teachers of the Church. Papists are satisfied for their legislators to enjoy the title and hold the office, and by so doing distort Christ's words into a sense that we must obey and hold whatever the duly appointed prelates of the Church lay down. This mistruth is more than adequately refuted in another saying of Christ's where He bids us beware of the leaven of the Pharisees. If Christ gives authority not only to reject in good conscience but actually by obligation anything that the Scribes mix in of their own to the pure teaching of the Law, then certainly we are not right to accept without a balanced judgment anything they may choose to order. If Christ intended to bind men's consciences to human precepts, He would be deceiving us in another passage when He declares it is vain to worship God by the commandments of men. Clearly Christ encourages the people to obey the Scribes just so far as they adhere to the pure and simple interpretation of the Law. Augustine was wise and well-tuned to the mind of Christ when he taught that the Scribes expounded the Law of God sitting on the seat of Moses: so ought the sheep to hear the voice of the shepherd through them, as through paid servants. And he immediately goes on to write, 'God therefore teaches through them, but if they wish to teach their own ideas, do not listen to it, do not perform it' (*Tract. in Ioan.* 46). He comes back on this opinion in *Christian Doctrine*, bk. 4: because good believers listen obediently not to any man but to God Himself, we may listen with profit to persons unprofitable in their lives. It was not the seat of the Scribes but the seat of Moses that persuaded them to teach good things, even though they did not do good things. What they did in their own lives was their own, but to teach what was their own could not be done from another's seat.

Matt. 23.4. *They bind heavy burdens.* He does not accuse the Scribes of tyrannical oppression over souls because the laws were harsh and unreasonable. Though they had brought in many trifling rites (as is clear from other passages), this is not the fault Christ refers to. He is comparing true doctrine against evil, dissolute living. The Law of God may without wonder be called a heavy burden, hard to bear, especially in view of our infirmity. Though the scribes might be asking nothing that God had not commanded, Christ's complaint is over their too rigid and heartless way of teaching it. It was common use with these proud hypocrites to demand God's due in a lordly manner from others, to be unyielding in pressing obligations, at the same time blandly letting themselves off the injunctions they laid on others, and pleasing themselves without a care. In this sense Ezekiel reproaches them for ruling with stern powers. Men who truly fear God and apply themselves honestly and firmly to train disciples to obey Him are more severe upon themselves than upon others, and therefore not such hard task-masters. Because they are conscious of their own infirmity they have a kinder eye for the weak. With these ignorant scorners of God, one can hardly imagine anything more unsuited to command or more cruel than their unconcern over difficulties which they never face themselves. No-one will show moderation in teaching another unless he has first taught himself the lesson.

Matt. 23.5. *And all their works they do.* He had already said that the scribes' living is very different from their teaching. Now he adds that if they do put on a good display it is pretence and of no consequence for they have no other concern than to win men's approval and promote themselves. Here a quiet enthusiasm for religion and a holy life is set against their façade of works which have no value but for show. A consistent worshipper of God will never lower himself to the bombast that the hypocrites puff out. It is not only self-seeking that is

48

criticised in the Scribes and Pharisees, but once the Lord has condemned every aspect of their lives for transgressing the holy Law He anticipates the shield they might put up as defence, their false sanctimoniousness, by saying that this is trifling rubbish of no worth at all that they boast of, for it has no weight but empty ostentation. He gives one example by which such self-seeking might be recognized easily, namely that by the fringes of their robes they show themselves in the sight of men as upright worshippers according to the Law. Why should their fringes be broader, why should their phylacteries be more splendid than the common fashion, unless for idle pomp? The Lord had commanded the Jews to carry certain notable and choice sentences from His Law both on the forehead and on their garments. Realizing that the flesh all too easily tends to forget the Law, the Lord wanted His people to refresh their memories. Similarly they were ordered to write such sentences on the doorposts of their houses that wherever they should turn their eyes some holy admonition should at once leap to view. But what did the scribes do? To be different from the rest of the people they carried the commandments of God printed quite richly over their garments. All this flourish betrayed their rotten pretension. We should learn from this too what ingenuity men put into concocting vain glory to hide their faults under some colour of virtue, some cloak; all the time twisting the practice of God's holy commands to suit their own hypocrisy. Nothing could be more profitable than to employ all one's faculties in contemplation of the Law, nor was it without good reason that God ordained it. But they were so far from profiting from these simple rules that they made perfect righteousness consist in adornment of robes and despised the Law in all their living. There could be no more insulting mockery of God's Law than to imagine they were observing it with fancy dress, and to call head-dress designed for the stage the Law's protection. What Mark and Luke say about long robes makes the same point. Men of the east, we know, regularly wore long garments, as is their custom today. But Zechariah (13.4) shows that prophets were distinguished from others by wearing a certain form of mantle. It is reasonable that teachers may be so dressed to be more grave and modest in their clothes than the ordinary. The scribes quite wrongly made this an occasion for luxury and display. The example has been taken up by the papal priests whose vestments are surely nothing but marks of overweening tyranny.

Matt. 23.6. *And love the chief place.* He proves by clear signs that there was no lively interest in religion among the scribes, but complete dedication to self. To seek the first places, the first seats, is the behaviour only of men who prefer proudly to advance themselves with men rather than to find favour with God. Christ chiefly condemns their desire for the title of 'Master'. Though in itself the name 'Rabbi' is a sign of excellence, the Jews had become used at that time to give it to masters and teachers of the Law. Christ maintains that this honour does not belong to any but Himself alone: it follows that it cannot be transferred to men without damaging Himself. This seems too hard, in fact ridiculous, seeing that Christ does not teach us in His own Person but ordains and appoints us masters: to keep back the title and give the office is ridiculous. When He was on earth He created Apostles to discharge the office of teaching in His Name. If it is a question of title, Paul (I Tim. 2.7) certainly had no wish to damage Christ with false, sacrilegious presumption when he asserted he was master and teacher of the nations. Christ's only intention was to gather all, from least to greatest, into line to keep His own authority entire. There is no cause for any trouble over a word. Christ is not concerned over the title assumed by those who take on the teacher's role, but confines them to their proper limits in case they lord it over their brothers' faith. We must always keep it distinct that Christ alone is to be obeyed, because for Him alone the Father's Voice was heard from heaven, 'Hear him'. Teachers are His servants, duty bound to let His voice be heard in them, and they are masters under Him so far as they represent His Person (*personam eius sustinent*). The chief point is that He must keep His own authority entire, and no mortal may claim the least part of it. Thus He is the only Pastor, yet He allows many pastors under Himself, provided He is over them all and alone, through them governs the Church. Therefore we must note the last part of the sentence. Because we are brothers He contends that no one has the right to be master over the others; it follows that He does not condemn one who exercises the role of master without violating fraternal relationships among the God-fearing. The sum of this teaching is that all should depend on the lips of Christ alone. Paul argues almost the same point when he tells us that we are rash to take one another to judgment, since all are brothers together and all must stand at the judgment seat of Christ (Rom. 14.10).

Matt. 23.9. *Call no man your father.* In almost the same sense He claims for God alone the honour of Father, as He has just claimed unique Master's rights. This name was not assumed by men for themselves but was granted to them by God. For this reason we are not only allowed to call men on earth fathers, we do wrong to deprive them of the name. The distinction some allege that men who beget children are fleshly fathers while God alone is the Father of spirits—is of no weight. I would agree that God is sometimes distinguished from men in this way (as at Hebrews 12.5), but as Paul more than once calls himself a spiritual father (I Cor. 4.15; Phil. 2.22), we must see that this fits the words of Christ. The true sense is that the honour of father is falsely given to men if it obscures the glory of God. And this happens whenever a mortal man is reckoned as father without regard to God, seeing that all degrees of relationship come down through Christ from the one God, and are so inter-connected that God is really the only Father of all. He repeats the previous sentence about Christ as Master to inform us that the true order is where God is over all and enjoys the paternal right and authority and Christ brings all to sit under His teaching and make them disciples. As is said elsewhere, Christ is the only Head of the whole Church (Eph. 1.22), because the whole body ought to be subject to Him and obey Him.

Matt. 23.11. *He that is greatest among you.* The closing sentence shows that He has not made a sophist's play over words, but rather taken care to see that no one should so far forget his rank as to claim more than his due. He declares that the highest rank in the Church is not rule but service. Whoever keeps to this standard takes nothing from God or Christ, whatever title he carries. At the same time it is vain to dress up power in the merit of service when this takes away from the master role of Christ. What good does it do the Pope, bent on the oppression of poor souls by tyrannical laws, if he calls himself 'servant of the servants' of God, unless he means to insult God to His face and play a shameful trick on men? Christ does not make much of titles, but plainly forbids His people to aspire or desire to rise any higher than promotion of brotherly concord under the heavenly Father; those who enjoy honour must be the servants of others. He adds that notable word that has been expounded elsewhere: 'he that exalts himself shall be humbled', etc.

But woe unto you, scribes and Pharisees, hypocrites! because ye shut the kingdom of heaven against men: for ye enter not in yourselves, neither suffer ye them that are entering in to enter.

Woe unto you, scribes and Pharisees, hypocrites! for ye devour widows' houses, even while for a pretence ye make long prayers: therefore ye shall receive greater condemnation.

Woe unto you, scribes and Pharisees, hypocrites! for ye compass sea and land to make one proselyte; and when he is become so, ye make him twofold more a son of hell than yourselves. (Matt. 23.13-15)

They which devour widows' houses, and for a pretence make long prayers; these shall receive greater condemnation. (Mark 12.40)

Woe unto you lawyers! for ye took away the key of knowledge: ye entered not in yourselves, and them that were entering in ye hindered.

Which devour widows' houses, and for a pretence make long prayers: these shall receive greater condemnation. (Luke 11.52, and 20.47)

His reproof becomes sharper still, not so much for their sake as to win over the plain, unaffected people from the sect. We see in Scripture how vengeance is frequently threatened on the reprobate to strip them of excuse, and how at the same time the faithful receive a profitable warning not to become enmeshed in the same crimes, but avoid a like fate falling on themselves. The scribes have overturned God's worship and corrupted holy doctrine and will brook no correction. They resist the offer of redemption in a desperate mania for their own and the people's ruin, and so must deserve the hatred and detestation of all. But their deserts were not so much in Christ's eyes, as the benefit of the simple and inexperienced. He willed at the end of His own life to leave a solemn testimony to prevent any being caught unawares or unwilling by these wicked rogues. We know what an obstacle misplaced reverence for false teachers can be for simple folk who should get loose of their errors. At that time the Jews were steeped in false teaching—indeed they had imbibed many superstitions from infancy. Difficult in itself, an uphill task to bring them back on to the path: but the greatest impediment was the strange idea they had conceived about their false teachers, that they really had to reckon them as the rightful leaders of the Church, overseers of divine worship and pillars of religion. They were so bemused that only a violent alarm could ever shake them out of it. It is not to cure the Scribes that Christ proclaims the terrible vengeance of God upon them, but to deter the rest from their folly. Just so in these days we are driven to thunder out our denunciations of the papal clergy precisely in order that those not entirely reprobate, but still ready to learn, may take thought for their salvation, and shaken by the judgment of God may break the fatal noose of superstition that holds them captive. Consider then what a cruel leniency affects those who dislike our vehemence. They dislike the tough and painful treatment dealt to wolves who continually bare their teeth to tear and devour the sheep. They can watch the wretched sheep tricked by a false cover rush of their own accord into the wolves' jaws, unless the shepherd whose heart is set on their safety drives them off with shouts. We must follow Christ's counsel, and threaten wicked deceivers with severity. At His example, we must lift our voices against them with boldness, that any who may be healed may fear for their lives and escape them. Though we make no headway against the enemies of truth, yet they must be called to God's tribunal and others must be given warning that the same curse hangs over them if they do not in time depart from their evil league.

Matt. 23.13. *Ye shut the kingdom of heaven.* Christ cries woe upon them because their fraudulent administration brought common disaster on all the people. As the government of the Church was in their hands, they ought to have been like doorkeepers of the heavenly Kingdom. What are religion and sacred instruction for, but to open the gates of heaven? All humanity, we know, is exiled from God, shut out from the inheritance of eternal salvation. The teaching of religion is like a door by which we enter into life. Thus metaphorically Scripture says that pastors are given the keys of the Kingdom of Heaven, as I have expounded at more length at ch. 16. We must keep this definition, given more plainly still in Luke's words, where Christ reproves the lawyers for having taken away the key of knowledge, for they who were guardians of the holy Law defrauded the people of their true understanding of it. Just as today the keys of the Kingdom of Heaven are entrusted to the pastors to admit the faithful to eternal life and exclude the unbelievers from any hope of it, so in former days the same responsibility was laid on the Priests and Scribes under the Law. From the word *knowledge* we appreciate the folly of the Papists' manufacture of imaginary keys like some magic power from God's Word. Christ declares that only those who serve for teaching may use those keys. If it is objected, that for all they were perverse interpreters of the Law, they still retained the keys, I reply that although the trust had been given them in respect of their office it had been suppressed by their malice and deception, and the use had expired for them. Christ says they have taken away, they have stolen, that key to knowledge with which they should have opened the door of heaven. Even so today heaven is locked in the face of the poor people under the Papacy while the very doorkeepers (at least those who are entrusted with the responsibility) use their tyrannical power to keep it shut. Unless we are utterly apathetic we shall not freely lend our assistance to those who cruelly shut the way of life against us.

Matt. 23.14. *Ye devour widows' houses.* Now He goes further, accusing them of crimes that were worthy of open hatred and detestation and blowing away the smokescreen of virtue which fooled the people. If one objects that there was no need to reprehend faults whose example could not be damaging, we must remember that the salvation of those who were tied up in the errors of the scribes could not be served except they turned right away from them. For this reason Christ is driven to show up the empty façade of virtue that continued to nourish superstition. In short, He says that even when they seem to do right they sinfully abuse the pretext of religion. Long prayers purported to be

53

a mark of unusual piety: the more a man turns to holiness the more he is given to the practice of prayer. But the Pharisees and scribes were so corrupt, says Christ, that they could not even handle the chief part of divine worship without sinfulness; because they made their constant prayers a device for filthy profiteering. They sold prayers, exactly as men hire out their day's labour for money. The lesson is not exactly that long prayers are at fault (especially as pastors of the Church should be singularly devoted to prayer) but their misuse is to be condemned as the perversion of a laudable enough practice into a bad end. The more men seek reward for hired prayers to foster (what they call) a fervid kind of devotion, the more the Name of God is profaned. This false idea had long and deep roots in popular thinking, so Christ threatens them more sharply. It is no minor offence to defile such a sacred thing. That widows were chiefly taken in is no surprise; silly women have more propensity to superstition, and rogues have always made a point of fleecing them. Paul charges the false teachers of his age with taking captive silly women laden with sins (II Tim. 3.6).

Matt. 23.15. *For ye compass sea.* The scribes had also won popular esteem for their zealous efforts to win foreigners and uncircumcised to the Jewish faith. If their tricks or other devices had thrown the wool over someone's eyes they got a marvellous reception for their so-called increase to the Church. The crowd greatly applauded their industry and achievement in leading men of other lands into God's Church. Christ on the contrary declares that their enthusiasm is so far from laudable that it increasingly calls down God's vengeance, since they pull down to greater destruction any who join their sect. Note how corrupt their condition was, how dissipated their religion. To bring disciples to God would surely have been a holy and splendid thing, yet to attract gentiles to the Jewish worship of those days (so degraded, so chock-full of wicked profanity) was nothing but leading them from Scylla into Charybdis. Besides by a sacrilegious use of God's name they provoked a heavier vengeance for themselves, seeing that their religiosity gave them wider licence to sin. An example of the same can be seen in the monks of this day: they rake in proselytes keenly from all sides, but their effect on these disordered and unclean lives is to make devils of them. In their ill-famed houses of revelry there is enough corruption to deprave even the angels of heaven. At the same time the monk's habit is a most convenient veil for covering all kinds of outrageous behaviour.

Woe unto you, ye blind guides, which say, Whosoever shall swear by the temple, it is nothing; but whosoever shall swear by the gold of the temple, he is a debtor.   Ye fools and blind: for whether is greater, the gold, or the temple that hath sanctified the gold?   And, Whosoever shall swear by the altar, it is nothing; but whosoever shall swear by the gift that is upon it, he is a debtor.   Ye blind: for whether is greater the gift, or the altar that sanctifieth the gift?   He therefore that sweareth by the altar, sweareth by it, and by all things thereon.   And he that sweareth by the temple, sweareth by it, and by him that dwelleth therein.   And he that sweareth by the heaven, sweareth by the throne of God, and by him that sitteth thereon. (Matt 23.16-22)

Matt. 23.16. *Woe unto you, ye blind guides.* Hypocrisy is almost always linked with self-seeking; popular superstition usually feeds on the avarice and greed of the pastors.   The world has its own inclination to go astray, and even deliberately draws deception and all kinds of imposture upon itself; but the final hold of perverse forms of worship is reached in the self-confirmation of the overseers themselves.   It generally happens that leading men not only blandly connive at error, because they see it to their financial advantage, but also assist in fanning their flame.   In the Papacy we see superstitions increased by countless means, when the priests gape for spoils, and are still daily thinking up more to bewilder the stupid populace.   When minds have once fallen into the obscure deception of Satan nothing is too ridiculous or even outrageous for them to take up with avidity.   So it had come about that the Jews gave more reverence to the gold of the temple and the sacred offerings than to the temple and altar.   Yet the sanctity of the offerings depended on the temple and altar: it was only a secondary interest.   We may well believe that this crazy notion started with the scribes and priests who were ready to catch on to any profit they could make.   It was a pernicious as well as a foolish error, for it led the people into a realm of crass make-believe.   Men are always more than liable to lapse from the pure worship of God: under a scheme of this kind it was easy for Satan to draw men far from the contemplation of God who were already unduly tending to foolish notions.   This is the reason why Christ castigates their error so severely.   Yet the Papists feel no shame at prostituting God's holy name to fouler mockery: for with them it rates more highly to touch the scrap of a stinking corpse than to lay hands on the Old or New Testament, or even to lift their hands to heaven.   In such ways God's worship becomes a thing of the flesh, gradually eroding His true fear.   *It is nothing.* This phrase does not mean that the temple's honour was entirely abrogated, but is intended comparatively.   When they made an extravagant fuss of the offerings, the common people were diverted to give them reverence and think less of the majesty of the temple and altar: and they had less scruple in swearing falsely by it than in swearing irreverently by the sacred offerings.

Matt. 23.18. *Whosoever shall swear by the altar.* Here our Lord does what ought to be done in the correction of error—He recalls us to the source and teaches us from the very nature of oaths that the temple is far superior to its gifts. He takes it as a principle that it is forbidden to swear by any but the one God. It follows that whatever formulas men use for oaths, God must have the honour which is due to Him alone. We also gather the reason and extent of our permission to swear by the temple, for it is the dwelling and sanctuary of God, where the glory of God shines out as in heaven. When God gives such symbols of His presence to allow men to claim His testimony and judgment, He still preserves His rights secure: it would be sinful and idolatrous to assign Deity to heaven. God gives brighter reflection of His glory in the temple than in the offerings, so that the temple's name deserves greater reverence and sanctity. Now we see in what sense Christ tells us that we swear by Him who inhabits heaven, rather than by heaven itself: He guides all forms of swearing to their rightful end and object.

Woe unto you, scribes and Pharisees, hypocrites! for ye tithe mint and anise and cummin, and have left undone the weightier matters of the law, judgment, and mercy, and faith: but these ye ought to have done, and not to have left the other undone. Ye blind guides, which strain out the gnat, and swallow the camel.

Woe unto you, scribes and Pharisees, hypocrites! for ye cleanse the outside of the cup and of the platter, but within they are full from extortion and excess. Thou blind Pharisee, cleanse first the inside of the cup and of the platter, that the outside thereof may become clean also.

Woe unto you, scribes and Pharisees, hypocrites! for ye are like unto whited sepulchres, which outwardly appear beautiful, but inwardly are full of dead men's bones, and of all uncleanness. Even so ye also outwardly appear righteous unto men, but inwardly ye are full of hypocrisy and iniquity. (Matt. 23.23-28)

But woe unto you Pharisees! for ye tithe mint and rue and every herb, and pass over judgment and the love of God: but these ought ye to have done, and not to leave the other undone.

Woe unto you! for ye are as the tombs which appear not, and the men that walk over them know it not. (Luke 11.42, 44)

Christ taxes the Scribes with the fault under which all hypocrites

labour, of being concerned and worried over small matters and neglecting the leading tenets of the Law. This disease has afflicted virtually every generation and race, that the majority of men endeavoured
to please God by observing trivial details with some attention. Since
they cannot altogether rid themselves of obedience to God they take
the second way out by redeeming glaring offences with worthless acts
of satisfaction. Look at the Papists today. They transgress the chief
commandments of God and spend all their energies on feeble ceremonies. This is the fiction Christ reproves in the scribes, who
strenuously and scrupulously pay tithes, yet take no care for the chief
articles of the Law. To bring out better their rotten ostentation He
does not speak of paying tithes in general, but on mint, dill and
(according to Luke) any kind of herb, where with the least expense
they could display their unusual regard for religion. As Christ declares the height of the Law's justice lies in mercy, judgment and faith,
we must first see what He means by these words. Also why He
omitted the precepts of the first table which really relate to the worship
of God, as if suggesting that godliness came after the duties of neighbourliness. *Judgment* is taken as equity or uprightness; it makes us
return each man what we owe him, and avoid causing fraud or injury
to others. Mercy goes further, prompting us to go to our brother's
aid at our cost, to relieve misery by counsel or funds, to protect the
unjustly oppressed, and to employ our gifted faculties in the common
cause of humanity. Faith is simply a frank integrity that tries no tricks
or malice or deceptions, but promotes the mutual sincerity among all
with which individuals like to be treated. Briefly, then, the sum of
the Law comes back to love. I know others have interpreted the word
'faith' by synecdoche to include the whole worship of God, but Christ
typically refers the real test of sanctity to brotherly love, and therefore
passes over the first table. This agrees with Luke, putting love of God
in place of faith: Christ's purpose was to show us what the Lord chiefly
asks of us in His Law. In Luke both parts are expressed, as if Christ
were saying that the chief object of the Law is that we should love God
and be fair and merciful towards our neighbours. Matthew was
content with the second part.

There is nothing wrong in the duties of love being called the leading
points of the Law, seeing that love itself is called by Paul the perfection
of the Law, for as he says in another place, the Law is fulfilled if we
love our neighbours (Rom. 13.10). Moreover when Christ was asked
previously about the Law's commandments. He only quoted those that
belonged to the second table. If it is objected that this puts men above
God, because love directed to them is rated higher than devotion, we
may easily answer that the second table is not set against the first here.

57

but rather determines, from the way the second is kept, whether we truly give God the worship of our hearts. Piety is an inward thing; God does not go about amongst us to test our love for Him. He does not need the duties we perform in fact, so that it is easy fo. hypocrites to lie and put on a false pretence of love for God. But the duties of brotherly love are a matter of general observation, plainly to be seen —so here there is better proof of their presumption. Christ had no wish to go into subtle distinctions over the parts or priorities of right-eousness, but, as far as men could grasp, to give simple teaching that the Law is only kept when men behave towards each other with justice, kindness and truth: in this way men testify that they love God and revere Him, and give a right and sufficient proof of true religion. It is not enough to do our duties to men if we do not first give God His right, but God's true worshipper must conform his life to His commands.

This is still not a complete answer to the question. The tithes that Christ puts after equity and mercy were a part of the divine worship, and in some degree were allotted to the poor, for they contained a twofold offering. The answer here is that tithes are not being compared with alms, faith and judgment, but the fictitious sanctity of the scribes is being compared with honest and consistent feelings of love. Why were they so ready and willing to pay tithes except as a way to satisfy God with the least expense and trouble? They missed the real purpose. The fluster of trivial details that they put up before God and men had no right place in the reckoning of the duties of love.

Matt. 23.23. *These ye ought to have done.* This is intended by Christ to anticipate a false objection. They might put an unfortunate inter-pretation on His words as though He made light of something God had prescribed in the Law. He declares that whatever God commands is to be observed and nothing omitted, but enthusiasm for the whole Law does not prevent us insisting on the main points. He considers it absurd for men to be busy over the tiny matters rather than start with the principal ones: tithes were a kind of extra. Christ says He has no intention of taking force out of even the least precept as long as He may advise, yes, enforce a due priority of observance. Let the whole Law remain intact, as indeed it cannot be impaired in any degree without contempt of its Author: He who forbade adultery and murder and theft equally condemned evil desires in all degrees. We under-stand that all the precepts are so interwoven that it is forbidden to pick out one from another, Wherefore it is also written, 'Cursed is everyone that does not perform all the things that are written'. In these words the righteousness of the entire Law without exception is decreed, yet such reverence does not annul the distinctions between precepts, as we have said, nor the aim of the Law to which its true devotees turn their minds, to avoid playing with it on the surface.

Matt. 23.24. *Blind guides.* This is a proverbial saying that prettily expresses the hypocrites' measly concern over trifles: they shrink from tiny faults, as if one transgression would pain them with a hundred deaths, yet the worst crimes they gracefully gloss over for themselves and their friends. They behave just like the man who strains out a little crumb of bread and swallows a whole loaf. A gnat is a tiny creature, we know, and a camel a huge beast. Could anything be more absurd than to strain one's wine or water to avoid offence to the throat by swallowing a gnat, yet to make no difficulty about gulping in a camel. But these are the things that hypocrites play with. They ignore judgment, mercy and faith, indeed dissipate the whole Law, but in minor affairs they are over austere and rigid. While they pretend to kiss the feet of God like this, they proudly spit in His face.

Matt. 23.25. *Ye cleanse the outside.* Continuing on the same line the Lord takes a figurative way of reproving the Scribes of only being worried about the shining impression they make on the world. By the outside part of the dish He means, metaphorically, outward appearances. In other words, You are only bothered about cleanliness as far as it shows on the outside: like someone vigorously cleaning the mess off the outside of a cup and leaving the inside dirty. That we are to take it in the extended sense is obvious from the second clause, where uncleanness inwardly is condemned and clearly means they are choked with intemperance and greed. He brings out their hypocrisy in trying hard to order their lives in the sight of men and gain an empty reputation for sanctity. He recalls them to a pure and sincere feeling for the good life. First cleanse the inside, He says, for it is foolish to gaze on the polish, yet drink from a cup with dregs in, or dirty in some other way.

Matt. 23.27. *Ye are like unto sepulchres.* The metaphor changes, but the object remains the same: He compares them to tombs which men of the world erect ambitiously, all beautiful and shining. As the painting or decoration of tombs catches men's attention, while inside are laid up rotting corpses, so Christ says the hypocrites give a false exterior, for they are full of deceit and wickedness. Luke's tone is different, speaking of their deception in men's eyes as tombs which are often not noticed by men who walk over them: it comes back to the same thing, that under a pretext of pretended sanctity is hidden inward decay, which they nourish in their hearts: as a marble tomb presents an appearance of beauty and pleasure to cover the decaying corpse which would offend passers-by. We learn, as I have said earlier, that Christ is thinking of the plain, inexperienced folk, caught up in the

Scribes' vain lies, when He tears their mask off. A warning well suited to the simple, that they might escape in time the jaws of the wolves. Yet the passage contains a general lesson that the sons of God should seek real purity, not a pretence.

> *Woe unto you, scribes and Pharisees, hypocrites! for ye build the sepulchres of the prophets, and garnish the tombs of the righteous, and say, If we had been in the days of our fathers, we should not have been partakers with them in the blood of the prophets. Wherefore ye witness to yourselves, that ye are sons of them that slew the prophets. Fill ye up then the measure of your fathers. Ye serpents, ye offspring of vipers, how shall ye escape the judgment of hell? Therefore, behold, I send unto you the prophets, and wise men, and scribes: some of them shall ye kill and crucify; and some of them shall ye scourge in your synagogues, and persecute from city to city: that upon you may come all the righteous blood shed on the earth, from the blood of Abel the righteous unto the blood of Zachariah the son of Barachiah, whom ye slew between the sanctuary and the altar. Verily I say unto you, All these things shall come upon this generation.*
>
> *O Jerusalem, Jerusalem, which killeth the prophets, and stoneth them that are sent unto her! how often would I have gathered thy children together, even as a hen gathereth her chickens under her wings, and ye would not! Behold, your house is left unto you desolate. For I say unto you, Ye shall not see me henceforth, till ye shall say, Blessed is he that cometh in the name of the Lord.* (Matt. 23.29-39)
>
> *Woe unto you! for ye build the tombs of the prophets, and your fathers killed them. So ye are witnesses and consent unto the works of your fathers: for they killed them, and ye build their tombs. Therefore also said the wisdom of God, I will send unto them prophets and apostles; and some of them they shall kill and persecute; that the blood of all the prophets, which was shed from the foundation of the world, may be required of this generation; from the blood of Abel unto the blood of Zachariah, who perished between the altar and the sanctuary: yea, I say unto you, it shall be required of this generation.*
>
> *O Jerusalem, Jerusalem, which killeth the prophets, and stoneth them that are sent unto her! how often would I have gathered thy children together, even as a hen gathereth her own brood under her wings, and ye would not! Behold your house is left unto you desolate: and I say unto you, Ye shall not see me, until ye shall say, Blessed is he that cometh in the name of the Lord.*
>
> *And when he was come out from thence, the scribes and Pharisees*

began to press upon him vehemently, and to provoke him to speak of many things; laying wait for him, to catch something out of his mouth. (Luke 11.47-51, 13.34-35, 11.53-54)

Matt. 23.29. *For ye build the sepulchres of the Prophets.* We do not accept the opinion of some that Christ is reproving the scribes for superstition in dressing up magnificent tombs for the Prophets in a fantastic manner, as the Papists transfer God's honour to dead saints and actually give sinful adoration to their images. They had not yet reached that degree of blindness or folly. This is not Christ's motive. The bluff that had been played on the ignorance of the populace was the reverent devotion paid to the memory of the prophets. Seeing that thus they made out that they affirmed what the prophets had taught, anyone might have believed that they were their faithful imitators and finely zealous for the service of God. Of course it was praiseworthy to erect monuments to the prophets, since in this way religion was, so to speak, brought into the daylight and set up in due honour. But they had not the least intention of restoring their teaching, which might appear to have been extinguished at the prophets' death. Although they were in themselves strangers to the prophetic teaching, indeed bitterly opposed to it, yet they honoured them after their decease with sepulchres as though making common cause with them. This is the way of hypocrites to honour God's holy ministers and true-living teachers after they have died, but in their lives to abhor them. This results partly from the human failing (observed by Horace in the words, 'Envy! You hate the worth you have: when it leaves your sight you want it'), but partly because dead men's ashes can no longer give trouble with hard and austere reproof. There is no hurt in giving an empty display of religion by some devotion for men whose living voice drove them mad. The fiction costs little—a professed enthusiasm towards those whose answer is cut off. In their day the prophets were in turn rejected with insult or harassed savagely at the hands of the Jews, often, indeed, cruelly put to death, but a later generation, though no better in character than their fathers, venerated their shadowy memory rather than embrace their teaching—the teachers of their own day were just as hateful to them. The world in general, while not daring to scorn God utterly or at least rise up against Him to His face, devises a means of worshipping God's shadow in place of God: just so it plays a game over the prophets.

The Papacy gives shining proof of this. They are not content with rightful veneration of Apostles and martyrs, but give them divine worship and think they can hardly go too far in heaping honours upon them, but their rough treatment of the faithful shows what devotion they would give the Apostles and martyrs if they were still alive to perform the duty they once performed. Is not the reason for all their fury against us, that we wish that teaching to be restored to full strength which the Apostles and martyrs sealed with their blood? These holy servants of God held their doctrine dearer than their lives. Would those who fiercely persecute the former spare the latter today? Let them adorn the images of the saints as they please with incense, candles, flowers and pomp of all sorts: if Peter were alive today they would tear him to ribbons, they would stone Paul to the ground. If Christ Himself still trod this earth, they would roast him over a slow fire. Our Lord saw that the scribes and priests of that day sought popular applause for their devout service to the prophets, and He showed up their false game. Not only do they repudiate the prophets sent them in their own day, but they actually persecute them in-humanly. This reveals the wicked fiction, the crass insolence of trying to appear devoutly respectful to the dead at the same time as they are working to silence the living.

Matt. 23.30. *If ye had been in the days.* There is reason for Christ's putting this in. He is not accusing them in the person of their parents nor particularly faulting them for being children of murderers, but He plainly reproves their stupid boast, as they were used to boast of their descent for all that they were descended from the bloody enemies of God. This is the sense of His speech: 'You reckon that the veneration you pay the dead prophets is some kind of expiation for your fathers' sin. I insist then that your boasting of sacred descent is vain, since you draw your line from sinful and criminal ancestors. Look at you: you cover your own crimes with the piety of those whose hands you admit were stained with innocent blood. But this makes your crime even greater when you imitate the unholy rage of your fathers, which you condemn at the tombs of the dead, in your slaughter of the living.' So He concludes that in this respect they are not poorer versions of their parents; in other words, 'Your generation is not the first to treat God's prophets brutally: this is the old schooling, the old habit handed down by your fathers. This way of doing is virtually bred into you.' He is not telling them to continue what they are doing, putting holy teachers to death, but in a manner of speech says that they have a hereditary right to rise up against the servants of God. They must have licence to oppose religion and so accomplish what their fathers left undone, complete the web that they began. These words do not mean that they are to despair, that they cannot come back to a healthy mind, but are a warning to the simple not to wonder if God's prophets get rough treatment from the children of murderers.

Matt. 23.33. *Offspring of vipers.* Christ has shown the scribes as criminal enemies of true teaching, perfidious corrupters of God's worship, a deadly plague, indeed, for the Church, and He comes to His conclusion with a yet more bitter outburst upon them, as though He had to shake off their conceits with violence and rush them to God's tribunal, to scare them. Christ did not regard them only, but all the people were to feel the shock of fear, that all might take care to avoid the same fate themselves. Such harsh language must have been all the more hard and intolerable to these revered teachers, for we gather that they had long been used to enjoy their rule without any daring to raise a whisper against them. No doubt many disliked Christ's permitting Himself such bitterness, and He would be held bold and intemperate for daring to speak so rudely about the order of scribes: just as today many men are too nice to bear any sharp language on the subject of the papal clergy. But Christ was dealing with hypocrites of the worst kind, men not only inflated with proud contempt for God and intoxicated with sheer self-confidence, but also men who had the common people under a spell of witchcraft. Against people of this sort He had to force His attack home. He calls them *vipers* for what they are and what they do, and promises them a punishment which they will never manage to escape if they do not quickly come to their senses.

Matt. 23.34. *Therefore behold I send.* Luke gives rather more emphasis, beginning, *therefore also said the wisdom of God.* Some interpreters explain it thus, 'I, who am the eternal Wisdom of God, declare to you.' I think it is more correct that in the normal manner of Scripture God is introduced as speaking in the person of His own Wisdom, i.e. God of old in the Spirit of prophecy announced what would befall you. I admit this sentence is not found in so many words anywhere, but as God often scolds the unchecked boldness of that people, Christ may gather it into a sentence and by a personification express more clearly what kind of judgment God held over the incurable wickedness of that race. It might have seemed a strange thing that the Lord should rashly wish to weary teachers who would make nothing by their efforts. Men do argue, that God makes a mockery of effort, when He sends His Word to the reprobate whom He already knows will remain obstinate. Indeed hypocrites reckon that it would be quite enough to have preachers of heavenly doctrine constantly in their midst, however unteachable they are in fact, and trust that God is propitious and favourable towards them as long as His outward message rings in their ears. It was a fierce boast with the Jews that they had always excelled other nations in prophets and teachers, and, as though they had deserved the great honour, took it as a certain sign of their own worth. Such futile arrogance Christ knocks down, denying them precedence over other nations on the grounds that God had given them prophets and outstanding exponents of His Scripture, contending that a favour when it is ill-placed is a more grievous reproach for them, and will bring them to a worse end. God's plan is quite different from what they imagine, for He will make them more inexcusable and raise their wicked malice to a peak or pinnacle. In other words, that a line of prophets has continually been sent you from heaven is a vain and foolish decoration for you to display, for in His secret judgment God has otherwise decided, to lay open by an uninterrupted succession of gracious invitations your stubborn wickedness, and, on your conviction, to involve parents and children alike in one ruin. As for the words, Matthew's version lacks something whose sense is supplied from Luke's text. By adding scribes and wise men to the prophets Matthew tends to make more of God's grace: their ingratitude becomes more patent in that they made no profit when God made no omission in His efforts to teach them. In place of wise men and scribes Luke has Apostles, meaning the same. The passage also teaches that God does not give salvation to men as often as He sends them His message, but is sometimes proclaimed to the reprobate whom He knows will remain obstinate, that it may be to them the savour of death unto death. The Word of God is salutary in itself and in its nature, and invites all to hope in eternal life without discrimination, but seeing all are not drawn inwardly, and that God does not penetrate all ears (because finally not all are renewed unto repentance or turned to obedience), those who reject the Word of God make it, by their incredulity, a deadly and lethal instrument. And when God knows in advance that this will happen, in order to sweep the reprobate into graver ruin, He deliberately sends them His prophets, as Isaiah brings out at greater length, 6.10. Such a way of thinking is of course very disagreeable to fleshly ways. We see how evil-minded scorners of God seize on this point to make a great howl—God, they say, is like a savage tyrant. He revels in increasing men's punishment, over whom He has no hope of success. Knowingly and willingly He adds to their blindness and their obduracy. God uses these proofs to induce humility among the faithful. Let us keep sober minds, to adore in trepidation what surpasses our vision. Those who say it is not God's fore-knowledge that prevents the unbelievers from obtaining salvation are foolishly using an idle plea to excuse God Himself. Granted the reprobate do not incur death because God foresaw it would be so; so their ruin cannot be ascribed to His fore-knowledge, but this is cavilling, which does not properly defend God's righteousness, for one may go on to object that their repentance stands in God's power, seeing that it is in His hand to give faith and repentance. A further objection: What does God mean, by fixed and deliberate purpose, in sending the light of His Word to make men blind? Why does He wish those already destined to eternal death, not content with their mere ruin, to die two or three times over? There is nothing left for us to say but ascribe glory to God's judgments and exclaim with Paul 'O profound and incomprehensible depths!' As to the question how God declares that His prophecies will lead to the destruction of the Jews while His adoption of that race was still effective and flourishing, I answer that since only a few embraced the Word with faith to their salvation, here His speech is addressed to the majority, the body as a whole. This was in accordance with the prophecy of Isaiah when he predicted the general ruin of the nation and was bidden to seal the Law of God among his disciples. We should understand that whenever Scripture assigns the Jews to eternal death, a remnant is excepted, in whom the Lord preserves some seed for the sake of His free election.

Matt. 23.35. *That upon you may come.* He not only deprives them of the basis of their false boast but shows that the gift of prophets was intended for an utterly different purpose: that no generation should be exempt from the crime of sinful rebellion. The pronoun *you* includes in general the whole race from its origin. If any object that it is not consistent with the judgment of God that a penalty for fathers' offences should be exacted from their children, there is a ready solution. Seeing that they have implicated themselves in wicked conspiracy it should not seem out of place that God in punishing all alike should throw the penalty due to the fathers into the lap of their sons. With justice then is the whole nation, in whatever centuries they have variously lived, called to account for their continuing contempt, and faced with its punishment. God, with a long measure of patience, has constantly striven with the ill-will of the whole people. The whole people is rightly held guilty of the inflexible contumacy which has persisted to the very end. Different ages had conspired to slay their own prophets, and so were fairly called to a common judgment; all the killings are laid against them, which they had perpetrated with one consent.

From the blood of Abel. Although Abel was not killed by the Jews, Christ imputes his death to them because there was an affinity of wickedness between them and Cain: otherwise there would have been no consistency in speaking of the righteous blood shed from the beginning of the world unto this generation. So Cain is made the chief and principal designer of the Jewish people because ever since they began to slay the prophets they followed in the steps of him whom they imitated. He names Zechariah not as being the latest martyr—the Jews did not even then cease murdering the prophets, but in fact their audacity and fury grew from then on, and the next generation gorged themselves in bloodshed which their fathers merely took in drops—

65

nor even because his death was more notorious, although celebrated in Scripture. There is another reason well worth noticing, although the commentators have missed it, which has resulted not only in their talking nonsense, but in their readers becoming involved in a troublesome debate. A lapse of memory might seem to have overtaken Christ that He commemorates one old murder and passes over the almost countless slaughter that came under Manasses. Not even at the time of the exile had the wicked persecution of holy men ceased among the Jews, and even in times of crisis we know how savagely they turned on Jeremiah (32.1ff.). Deliberately, the Lord does not reproach them with recent killings, but picks on this more ancient one (which indeed was the original spark of that criminal licence that afterwards exploded into unrestrained cruelty) because it was more apt for His purpose. I have just explained that the sum of all His purpose, seeing that the people did not stop their wicked ways, was to hold them guilty of all the murders which had been perpetrated over that long period. So He does not only announce the punishment for the present day atrocity but also says they must give account for the murder of Zechariah as if they had steeped their hands in his blood.

There is nothing likely about the opinion of those who refer it to the Zechariah who exhorted the people on their return from the Babylonian exile to rebuild the temple, and whose oracles are extant. Although the title of the book says he was the son of Barachiah, yet it is nowhere written that he was put to death. It is a forced exposition that he was slain between the time of building the altar and the temple. In referring to the other Zechariah son of Jehoiada the sacred narrative agrees very well with this passage. When true religion lapsed by the failures of king and people after the death of his father, he was endowed with the Spirit of God fiercely to reprehend public idolatry, and for this cause he was stoned to death in the forecourt of the temple. It is not absurd to suppose that his father Jehoiada received the same son of Barachiah as an honour, for throughout his life he affirmed true worship and deserved to be reckoned blessed of God. Whether Jehoiada held two names or (as Jerome believes) there is a textual error, there is no doubt about the matter at all that Christ refers to the impious stoning of that Zechariah which is described in II Chron. 24.22. The circumstance of place adds to the atrocity of the crime, seeing that they had clearly disregarded the sanctity of the temple. Note that *temple* here, as elsewhere, means the courtyard. Nearby stood the altar of burnt-offerings, so that the priest could offer the victims in the sight of the people. They must have been demented with anger, which neither the sight of temple nor altar could appease, when the Jews defiled the holy place with vile murder.

Matt. 23.37. *Jerusalem, Jerusalem*. In these words Christ shows plainer still His good reason for hot indignation, that the Jerusalem which God had chosen as His holy, almost His celestial dwelling-place, had not only shown itself unworthy of such an honour but (as it were, a den of thieves) had by long use taken to draining the blood of the prophets. There is pathos in Christ's voice raised up at the monstrous sight—God's holy city so sunk in mental decay that it had long tried to extinguish God's teaching by the bloodshed of the prophets. This is the relevance of the name repeated, for no ordinary word of detestation was fit for such prodigious and incredible wickedness. Christ is not reproving any particular murder, but a city so steeped in the habit that it did not cease slaying as many prophets as were sent. The participle is used as an epithet, as if Christ had said, you should have been the faithful guardian of the Word of God, teacher of heavenly wisdom, light of the world, source of true doctrine, seat of divine worship, example of faith and obedience—but you are a prophet-slayer, so that now you have caught the habit of drinking their blood. It is evident that they deserved every kind of reproach for so foully profaning the sanctuary of God. At the same time it was Christ's purpose to anticipate the impending offence. When the faithful should see Him killed at Jerusalem, they must not be shocked at any novelty in the sight. These words warn them that there is no wonder if a city used to strangle or stone prophets should cruelly slay its Redeemer. It is clear from this, how much we should attribute to locality. Although there was no city on earth which God decorated with such splendid tokens of praise or raised to such honours yet we see the depths to which it plunged by ingratitude. Let the Pope now compare his seat of brigandage with that holy city. Can he find anything to equal its honour? Its paid admirers boast to us that the faith flourished there in early days. If we allow this to be true, and yet today it is agreed to be estranged from Christ by traitorous defection, to be full of countless works of sacrilege, what is this honour of primacy that they foolishly claim? We should rather learn from this memorable example that every place that is carried to the heights by greater benefits from God, and so removed from common standards, if it should decline, is not only stripped of its decorations, but receives all the more reproach and denunciation; because it has basely defiled the glory of God by spoiling the beauty of His favours.

How often would I. There is more indignation in this than pity. For the city itself, over which recently He had wept, He still has pity: but against the scribes, the authors of its ruin, He is more hard and bitter, as they deserved. Nor does He spare the rest, who were all guilty in knowledge and approval and action: but as He puts all in the dock together,

67

He principally charges the leaders themselves, who were the cause of it all. Note the vehemence of His words. If God's grace had been rejected at Jerusalem and nothing more, it was already inexcusable ingratitude, but seeing that God's approach to the Jews had been to attract them with gentleness and friendship, and His kindness brought Him no success, the proud insult He charged them with was greatly aggravated. Besides, their obstinacy was out of control. It was not just once or twice that God had wished to gather them, but by constant, unremitting moves had sent prophet upon prophet, nearly all of whom the majority of them repulsed. We now understand why Christ compares Himself with a hen, to add to the disgrace of this sinful people who had spurned kind gestures of more than a mother's love. It is a wonderful and incomparable proof of love that He did not mind coming down to endearments to win rebels to His service. We read a fairly similar reproof in Moses, Deuteronomy 32.12 that God like an eagle gathered His people under the span of His wings. God spread out His wings to foster that people in more ways than one. Christ suits the expression to one kind in particular, namely the sending of the prophets to gather the lost and scattered into God's bosom. By this He means that whenever the Word of God is put before us He bares His breast to us with maternal kindness, and not content with that comes down to the humble affection of a hen fostering her chicks. Accordingly, our rough nature is quite monstrous, if we do not let ourselves be gathered by Him. If we consider on the one hand the dread Majesty of God, and on the other our sordid and abject condition, we must with shame come to gasp at the wonder of such great goodness.. What a thing, that God should demean Himself so far for our sake? When He puts on a mother's role, He comes a great way down from His glory: how much further when He takes the form of a hen, and deigns to treat us as His chickens! Now if this charge deserved to be brought against His ancient people who lived under the Law, it fits us far more. What I recently quoted from Moses was always true, and the complaints we read in Isaiah (Isa. 65.2) are just, that though God daily held out His hands to embrace a hard and rebellious people, and though He rose early with assiduous concern (Jer. 7.13), He gained nothing: yet to us today His invitation, through His Son, is far more familiar and kind. A dreadful vengeance awaits us as often as the teaching of His Gospel is put before us, unless we quietly hide ourselves under His wings, in which He is ready to take us up and shelter us. Christ teaches besides, that all rest in safety who gather themselves in to God in the obedience of faith, for under His wings they have an impregnable refuge.

Another part of the reproach is to be noted, that God was not immediately offended at His ancient people's perverse obstinacy, nor did He lay aside His fatherly love and motherly concern, for He did not cease to send prophet upon prophet in a continuous line. So today He has seen more than enough of the world's depravity and yet continues the course of His grace. There is a deeper significance in these words: namely that as soon as the Lord gathered the Jews together they immediately slipped away from Him. They scattered frequently because they scarcely stayed quiet a moment under God's wings. This is just like the wild behaviour we see in the world of today, as in every century. Hence it is all the more necessary for God to recall the stray and wandering to Himself. This is the culmination of desperate and ultimate depravity, for men to refuse God's goodness to the bitter end, and refuse to come under His wings. I said before that Christ is speaking in the Person of God and I mean that these words really belong to His eternal Godhead. He is not talking now of what He began to do from the time that He was revealed in the flesh, but is proclaiming how much He has been concerned for the salvation of His people from the beginning. We know that the Church was governed by God in such a way that Christ presided, insofar as He was the eternal wisdom of God. In this sense Paul says that, not God the Father was tempted in the wilderness, but Christ Himself—his first letter to the Corinthians, 10.9.

As for this passage being taken by sophists to support free will and abolish God's secret predestination, there is an easy answer. God wishes all to come together, they say: therefore all are free to come and their wish does not depend on the election of God. I answer, that the will of God as mentioned here must be judged by the result. Seeing that in His Word He calls all alike to salvation, and this is the object of preaching, that all should take refuge in His faith and protection, it is right to say that He wishes all to gather to Him. Now the nature of the Word shows us that here there is no description of the secret counsel of God (*arcanum Dei consilium*)—just His wishes. Certainly those whom He wishes effectively to gather, He draws inwardly by His Spirit, and calls them not merely by man's outward voice. If anyone objects that it is absurd to split God's will (*duplicem in Deo voluntatem fingi*), I answer that this is exactly our belief, that His will is one and undivided: but because our minds cannot plumb the profound depths of His secret election (*ad profundam arcanae electionis abyssum*) to suit our infirmity, the will of God is set before us as double (*bifariam*). I wonder at the tenacious mentalities of men who meet ἀνθρωποπάθειαν (a sense of humanity) frequently in Scripture without offence and only refuse it in this particular. I have dealt copiously with this discussion elsewhere and have no wish to take too much time over a trifle. I would briefly say that as soon as doctrine, which is the rallying-point of unity, is brought into the centre, it is God's will to gather all men together (*Deum velle omnes colligere*), so that those who do not come are without excuse. *And ye would not.* This can be said of the whole people as much as of the scribes: but I rather interpret it in connexion with the latter because they chiefly prevented the gathering-in. And Christ's whole invective in the contest is against them: after addressing Jerusalem in the singular He now reasonably enough turns to the plural. There is an emphatic contrast between God's *would* and their *would not*. It expresses the diabolical fury of men who do not hesitate to fight against God.

Matt. 23.38. *Behold your house is left unto you.* He proclaims the rasing of the temple and the ruin of the whole people. For all their impiety, crime, and all kinds of disgrace that corrupted them, they were so blinded with a perverse confidence in the outward cult and the temple that they believed they had a hold on God. They always kept this shield ready to hand, What? will God abandon this place, which He chose out of all the earth? But if He dwells in our midst, it follows that one day we will be restored. So they reckoned the temple as an invincible bastion, as if they sat in God's bosom. Christ contends that they vainly boast themselves of God's presence, for their crimes have driven Him away. By calling it *your house* He indirectly implies it is God's no longer. The temple had been erected with the view that it would cease to be God's abode and resting-place at the coming of Christ: yet it would have stood as a notable monument to the continuing grace of God had it not been ruined by the sin of the people. This was a dreadful act of God's vengeance, that a place He had so magnificently embellished He should abandon and wish utterly destroyed; yes, and to the end of the world, subject to extreme ignominy. Go on you Romanists, and despite God's will get on and build your tower of Babel!—and consider how God's temple, founded at His indication and command fell on account of the people's crimes.

Matt. 23.39. *For I say unto you.* He confirms what He had to say about the imminent vengeance of God, in that their only means of avoiding destruction will be taken from them. For this was the accepted time, this was the day of salvation, as long as He who had come as their Redeemer testified to and preached the redemption He had brought. At His departure, as at the setting of the sun, the light of life went out, and so this dread calamity which He proclaimed must fall on them. Now the question is what time He means by the phrase, *till ye shall say.* Some attach it to the final day of judgment: others reckon it a prophecy soon afterwards fulfilled, when some among the Jews begged to see Christ and worshipped Him. I do not approve either interpretation. I certainly wonder that men of learning can have tripped over such a small point as to inquire how the unbelievers shall ever say *Blessed is he that cometh*, etc. He is not talking about what they will do, but what He will do Himself. The adverb *until* has no extension beyond the time past. Joseph did not go with his wife *until* she brought forth Christ. These words of Scripture do not mean that after His birth they cohabited as man and wife but only mean that Mary before the birth of her son was a virgin untouched by man. In my opinion this is the real meaning of the present passage, that, Up to this point I have lived with you on your level of humanity, and served the office of Teacher: now the course of my calling is complete and I shall go away; nor will you enjoy my presence any longer, but you shall know me as Judge—I whom now you scorn as your Redeemer and Minister of salvation. This passage agrees with Zechariah (12.10), 'They shall look upon him whom they have pierced.' We see how Christ in a figurative way criticizes their empty hypocrisy, for as if they ardently longed for the promised salvation they sang daily from the Psalm, 'Blessed is he that cometh in the name of the Lord' (Ps. 118.26), and at the same time they mocked the Redeemer offered to them. He says that He will not come to them until they cry out in fear—too late—at the sight of His terrible Majesty, 'truly He is the Son of God'. This threat goes to all who scorn the Gospel, especially those who falsely profess His Name while they reject His teaching: one day they will admit that they cannot escape from the hands of Him whom they now cheat with a show of pretence. This is the old song the papists sing to this day who reckon nothing of Christ, until, armed with vengeance, He ascends His tribunal. We are warned as long as Christ appears to us in the Father's name, Interpreter and Mediator of salvation, He is not to be taken merely on our lips to honour, but sincerely desired as the One who shall put us and all the world under Himself.

Luke 11.53. *And when he was come out from thence.* I have already said that the previous sentences were inserted by Luke out of place. For in the course of telling how the scribes were taken to task by Christ at a dinner, he wove in the later sayings in which he dealt with their crimes shortly before His death. And so with the last reproach, which Luke puts in his thirteenth chapter, in telling another story. If any care to follow the conjecture that Christ said the same things more than once, I have no great objection. After giving the denunciations that we have just expounded, Luke draws to the conclusion that the scribes were all the more enraged at Christ, so that they did not cease to provoke by putting questions to trip Him up: this ought to be referred to the conversation held at the meal rather than this final discourse. I have not thought it of great account to be over-concerned with the time, which the Evangelist has neglected.

And he sat down over against the treasury, and beheld how the multitude cast money into the treasury: and many that were rich cast in much. And there came a poor widow, and she cast in two mites, which make a farthing. And he called unto him his disciples, and said unto them, Verily I say unto you, This poor widow cast in more than all they which are casting into the treasury: for they all did cast in of their superfluity; but she of her want did cast in all that she had, even all her living. (Mark 12.41-44)

And he looked up, and saw the rich men that were casting their gifts into the treasury. And he saw a certain poor widow casting in thither two mites. And he said, Of a truth I say unto you, This poor widow cast in more than they all: for all these did of their superfluity cast in unto the gifts: but she of her want did cast in all the living that she had. (Luke 21.1-4)

Mark 12.43. *Verily I say unto you.* This reply of Christ contains the very useful lesson that men's offerings are not to be reckoned at their outward value, but only by the motive of the heart. Piety is worth far more that gives to God whatever little it has rather than a hundred times as much out of abundance. The lesson is useful in two ways. The Lord encourages the poor, who appear to lack the means of doing well, not to doubt that they testify to their enthusiasm for Him even with a slender contribution. If they consecrate themselves, their offering which appears mean and trivial will be no less precious than if they had offered all the treasures of Croesus. On the other hand, those who have a richer supply and stand out for their large giving are told that it is not enough if their generosity far exceeds the commoners and the under-privileged, for with God it rates less for a rich man to give a moderate sum from a large mass, than for a poor man to exhaust himself in paying out something very small. The piety of this widow must have been exceptional, who preferred to deprive herself of sustenance rather than come before God's sight with nothing. Her single-mindedness is praised by the Lord, because, forgetting herself, she wished to testify that she and all she had were God's. The chief sacrifice asked of us is our denial of self. As for the sacred offerings of that time it is likely that they were not expended on rightful uses, yet as the legal cult still flourished Christ did not reject them. The abuses of men could not prevent His true worshippers from doing what was

72

holy, according to His commandment, and offering to the sacrifices and other religious expenses.

And Jesus went out from the temple, and was going on his way; and his disciples came to him to shew him the buildings of the temple. But he answered and said unto them, See ye not all these things? verily I say unto you. There shall not be left here one stone upon another, that shall not be thrown down.

And as he sat on the mount of Olives, the disciples came unto him privately, saying, Tell us, when shall these things be? and what shall be the sign of thy coming, and of the end of the world? And Jesus answered and said unto them, Take heed that no man lead you astray. For many shall come in my name, saying, I am the Christ; and shall lead many astray. And ye shall hear of wars and rumours of wars: see that ye be not troubled: for these things must needs come to pass; but the end is not yet. For nation shall rise against nation, and kingdom against kingdom: and there shall be famines and earthquakes in divers places. But all these things are the beginning of travail. (Matt. 24.1-8)

And as he went forth out of the temple, one of his disciples saith unto him, Master, behold, what manner of stones and what manner of buildings? And Jesus saith unto him, Seest thou these great buildings? there shall not be left here one stone upon another, which shall not be thrown down.

And as he sat on the mount of Olives over against the temple, Peter and James and John and Andrew asked him privately, Tell us, when shall these things be? and what shall be the sign when these things are all about to be accomplished? And Jesus began to say unto them. Take heed that no man lead you astray. Many shall come in my name, saying, I am he; and shall lead many astray. And when ye shall hear of wars and rumours of wars, be not troubled: these things must needs come to pass; but the end is not yet. For nation shall rise against nation, and kingdom against kingdom: there shall be earthquakes in divers places; there shall be famines: these things are the beginning of travail. (Mark 13.1-8)

And as some spake of the temple, how it was adorned with goodly stones and offerings, he said, As for these things which ye behold, the days will come, in which there shall not be left here one stone upon another, that shall not be thrown down. And they asked him, saying, Master, when therefore shall these things be? and what shall be the sign when these things are about to come to pass? And he said, Take heed that ye be not led astray: for many shall come in my name, saying, I am he; and, The time is at hand: go ye not after them. And when ye shall hear of wars and

73

tumults, be not terrified: for these things must needs comes to pass first;
but the end is not immediately.

Then said he unto them, Nation shall rise against nation, and kingdom
against kingdom: and there shall be great earthquakes, and in divers
places famines and pestilences; and there shall be terrors and great signs
from heaven. (Luke 21.5-11)

Matt. 24.1. *And Jesus went out.* The disciples no doubt realized that
Christ had said His last farewell, so to speak, to the temple. He was
left with the task of raising another far more splendid temple, a far more
prosperous state of the Kingdom, as had been foretold by the prophets.
He had nothing to do with that temple where everything was contrary.
It was more than the disciples could believe that the magnificent splendour of the present temple would give place to Christ. We must carefully note, considering the lavish façade of the temple was almost out of
this world, how their eyes were dazzled by the brightness of its present
aspect that they could hardly hope for the emergence of Christ's reign.
They do not put their doubts into so many words, but suggest it without
saying, when they draw Christ's eyes to the mass of stones to be overcome, indeed to be reduced to nothing, if He wished to come to power.
A similar sense of awe for the Papacy grips many people today; they
see it supported by huge wealth and vast resources and at first gasp in
amazement, so as to despise the Church whose façade is common and
poor-looking. Many take us for fools in working to bring it down, as
if a man should try and pull the sun down from the sky. It is no wonder
if such a noble sight should have held the disciples spellbound. We
may gather some idea of the building's expense from the fact that
Herod employed 10,000 workmen on it for eight years on end. No
wonder they admire the stones whose beauty was outstanding, fifteen
cubits in length, twelve in height and eight in breadth, as Josephus
records. There was such reverence for the temple even in distant parts
that one would scarcely dare to imagine that it could ever be destroyed.

Matt. 24.2. *Verily I say unto you.* Because His disciples were unable
for the size and wealth of the temple (like a veil put over their eyes) to
see their faith reach out to the coming of the true Kingdom of Christ,
He takes an oath that all things that hold their attention now will
shortly perish. This prediction of the temple's downfall made the way
smooth for the ignorant and weak. The destruction of the temple
helped the Jews not to be over-addicted to the earthly elements in their
cult of shadows: but there was the particular reason that God determined
by a terrible example to be avenged on that race that had rejected His
Son and despised the grace He offered them. So the denunciation had to
impress the disciples with the need to stand away from the company of

the rebellious people. So today the penalties which Scripture declared for the wicked should keep us off provoking God's anger by these crimes. Everything that it teaches us about the fading and passing aspect of the world should correct the vanity of our minds, which are all too eager to go after pomp and luxury and entertainment. Especially the denunciation of the terrible ruin of Antichrist and his sect ought to remove every obstacle that prevents us from following the true course of faith.

Matt. 24.3. *And as he sat.* Mark names four—Peter, James, John, and Andrew. But neither he nor Luke says as much as Matthew. They only say that they asked about the downfall of the temple and (seeing it was hard to believe) what kind of sign God would give from heaven. In Matthew they ask about the time of the coming of Christ and the consummation of the age. We must note, since they had considered from childhood that the temple would stand to the end of time and had the idea deeply rooted in their minds, that they had not thought that the temple could fall down as long as the world's created order stood. So as soon as Christ said the temple would perish, at once their minds turned to the consummation of the age. Because (one error leading to another) they were sure that immediately Christ began to reign they all would be every way blessed, their minds fly to thoughts of triumph, overlooking warfare. They link the coming of Christ and the end of the world with the overthrow of the temple as inseparable events: and they understand the end of the world to mean the restoration of all things so that nothing may be lacking to complete the happiness of the godly. We can see how they leap off to a variety of questions, because they were tied up with notions that the temple could not fall without shattering the whole world, and that the legal shadows and the whole world would have a common end. Immediately afterwards would come the brightness of the Kingdom of Christ to confirm the blessed state of the children of God, and then the visible restoration of the universe would follow, instantly bringing order out of confusion. Above all, they were under the influence of a foolishly assumed hope that in the immediate reign of Christ they would rush, out of turn, into the rest of the blessed. In Acts 1.6, when they see Christ risen from the dead, they rush headlong after the happiness laid up for us in heaven, for which we must aspire with hope and patience. Our minds run differently, for we have not been brought up under the shadows of the Law to have any superstitious infatuation about that earthly reign of Christ, yet hardly one in a hundred can be found free of the burden of a like disease. All naturally shrink from troubles, trials, any kind of cross, and our dislike of these things encourages us to wish a harvest out of season, without moderation, without a period of hope. No-one wants to be the sower, all wish to reap before time. To return to the disciples; the good seed of faith had taken root in their minds, but they did not wait for it to ripen. They were so stuffed with cheap notions as to confuse the completeness of Christ's kingdom with its beginning, and to wish to acquire on earth what should be sought in heaven.

Matt. 24.4. *And Jesus answered.* They got an answer on altogether a different understanding. They looked for the triumph that comes with warfare accomplished, but Christ urges them to long endurances as if He had said, 'You want to snatch the trophy at the starting-gates, but you must first complete the course. You drag the Kingdom of God to earth, which no-one can achieve unless he shall first have ascended there into heaven.' Seeing that this chapter contains profitable warnings for the regulation of the course of our lives, we understand that it is the work of God's wonderful purposes to turn the Apostles' error to our benefit. In short, the preaching of the Gospel is like sowing seed. We must patiently wait for the time of harvest. It is wrong to be soft and effeminate, and have our enthusiasm crushed by winter's frost, snow clouds or adverse seasons. Two things in particular Christ teaches His disciples, to beware of false doctrines and not to be upset by scandals. These words mean that His Church as long as it is a pilgrim in this world will run against these evils. This might seem inconsistent with the entirely different description of the Kingdom of Christ given by the prophets. Isaiah declares (54.13) that all men then will be taught of God. In Joel (2.18) we read, 'I will pour out my Spirit upon all flesh: and your sons and daughters will prophesy: your young men will see visions and your old men shall dream dreams.' A still more generous light of understanding is promised in Jeremiah (31.34). No man shall any more teach his neighbour, nor any man his brother saying, 'Know the Lord, for all shall know me from the least unto the greatest.' And therefore we need not wonder that the Jews hoped to be free of all clouds of error and become clear as day, 'at the rising of the Sun of righteousness', according to the prophecy of Malachi, 4.2. So the woman of Samaria said, 'When the Messiah shall come he shall teach us everything' (John 4.25). We know that there are frequent passages where peace, justice, joy and abundance of all good things are promised. So there is no wonder if at the coming of Christ they believed there would be freedom from the alarms of war, from raids, hurt of all kinds, finally from hunger and plague. Christ warns them that the godly will find false teachers no less troublesome than the false prophets were to the ancient people, and that alarms under the Gospel will be no less than in former times under the Law. Not that the prophecies which I have just cited lack effect, but that their fulfilment does not take place at once. It is enough that the faithful receive a taste of these good things

76

now, that they may cherish the hope of their full enjoyment in the future. So they were greatly deceived who wanted to have at the commencement of the Gospel an immediate and complete revelation of the things that we see being fulfilled from day to day. Besides, men's wickedness, though it cannot altogether nullify the felicity which the prophets ascribe to the Kingdom of Christ, can yet cause it delay and upset. The Lord in His struggles with men's ill-will makes a way through all obstacles for the blessings He will give. It would be strange if what was founded upon the free goodness of God should so depend on their opinion that it could be destroyed by their fault. That they may taste the fruits of their ingratitude in some measure, He drops His favours on them in very fine measure (which otherwise would have poured out in a great rich flood). Hence the maze of evil through which the faithful stray all their lives, although Christ is there to guide and to hold the torch of His Gospel before them, to assure them of the way of salvation. Hence the accumulation of trials which involve their hard campaigning, though there is no danger of defeat. Hence so many sudden alarms that worry and harass poor souls, although by leaning on Christ they may stay firm to the end. And when Christ warns His disciples to beware of impostures, let us realise that the means of defence against them will not be lacking, so long as we do not fail ourselves. Let us not doubt that whatever devices Satan contrives, we shall be safe from them if each in his own degree stands diligently on the watch.

Matt. 24.5. *For many shall come.* He does not speak of the perverse and false teachings in general, but touches on one which was like the prelude to all errors, in all the variations that Satan has attempted to use for the overthrow of the pure doctrine of the Gospel. Shortly after the resurrection of Christ impostors arose, each of them professing to be Christ. Since they had had their true Redeemer taken from their midst and put under the shame of the cross, and yet all minds were excited and inflamed with the hope of redemption and with longing, these impostors had at hand a plausible way of deceit. And there is no doubt that they had been exposed by God to this nightmare amusement for having so unworthily rejected His Son. Although the craze soon disappeared, yet God determined that they should have tumults of this kind among themselves: first to make them notorious and hated, second, to make them utterly lose confidence in salvation, and finally after so many disappointments to hasten their mad stampede to ruin. When the world turned away from God's Son whose mission was to gather us into holy concord (*in sacram unitatem nos colligere*) it was right that they should be blown this way and that, as in storms. By the same vengeance of God it came about that more were caught up with stupid credulity than were led to obedience to God with a right

77

faith. This circumstance was deliberately stated by Christ to prevent the faithful losing heart at the sight of a great crowd of madmen. We know how quickly we fall out and join the crowd, especially when we are few in number.

Matt. 24.6. *Ye shall hear of wars.* He means here the troubles in Judaea: a little later He will tell how the flame spread much further afield. As He had formerly told them to beware lest any man deceive them, so now He orders them to meet bravely the rumours of wars, and the wars themselves. There was danger that they might be overcome with calamity and fail, especially if they had promised themselves tranquility and happy repose. He says these things must take place, without giving a reason, but warning them that none of these things happens by chance or without God's providence, they must not kick in vain against the prick. Nothing is more effective in bringing us to control ourselves than to recognize that the greatest apparent confusion is restrained by the authority of God. God Himself never lacks just cause and excellent reason for allowing the world to be upset. As the faithful are best to fall in with His pleasure, so Christ is content to encourage the disciples to prepare their minds for endurance and to stand firm, for this is God's will.

But the end is not yet. He now states more openly what I have just said, that though these were serious enough, they were only the prelude to yet greater disasters, for when the fire of war caught on to Judaea it would burst out more widely. From the time of the publishing of the Gospel similar ingratitude has kindled the anger of God among other nations. Hence it transpires that they who have broken the bond of peace with God tear at each other in discords. Those who refused to obey the Kingdom of God succumb to the violence of the enemy. Those who did not bear to be reconciled with God break out in riots against each other. And those finally who disowned their claim to heavenly salvation rage against each other until they fill the earth with slaughter. Knowing how tenaciously the world would persist in evil, He goes on to add that this will be the beginning of travail, not that the faithful should consume themselves with grief (consolation ever comes to meet distress) but that they should equip themselves with patience for a long stretch. Luke adds moreover *earthquakes . . . and signs from heaven.* We have no certain record of these things. It is sufficient that they were predicted by Christ. The reader may find the rest in Josephus.

Then shall they deliver you up unto tribulation, and shall kill you: and ye shall be hated of all the nations for my name's sake. And then shall many stumble, and shall deliver up one another, and shall hate one another. And many false prophets shall arise, and shall lead many astray. And because iniquity shall be multiplied, the love of the many shall wax cold. But he that endureth to the end, the same shall be saved. And this gospel of the kingdom shall be preached in the whole world for a testimony unto all the nations; and then shall the end come. (Matt. 24.9-14)

But take ye heed to yourselves: for they shall deliver you up to councils; and in synagogues shall ye be beaten; and before governors and kings shall ye stand for my sake, for a testimony unto them. And the gospel must first be preached unto all the nations. And when they lead you to judgment, and deliver you up, be not anxious beforehand what ye shall speak: but whatsoever shall be given you in that hour, that speak ye: for it is not ye that speak, but the Holy Ghost. And brother shall deliver up brother to death, and father his child; and the children shall rise up against parents, and cause them to be put to death. And ye shall be hated of all men for my name's sake: but he that endureth to the end, the same shall be saved. (Mark 13.9-13)

But before all these things, they shall lay their hands on you, and shall persecute you, delivering you up to the synagogues and prisons, bringing you before kings and governors for my name's sake. It shall turn unto you for a testimony. Settle it therefore in your hearts, not to meditate before-hand how to answer: for I will give you a mouth and wisdom, which all your adversaries shall not be able to withstand or to gainsay. But ye shall be delivered up even by parents, and brethren, and kinsfolk, and friends; and some of you shall they cause to be put to death. And ye shall be hated of all men for my name's sake. And not a hair of your head shall perish. In your patience ye shall win your souls. (Luke 21.12-19)

Matt. 24.9. *Then shall they deliver you up unto tribulation.* Christ now foretells a different kind of trial that will come on the disciples beyond their general troubles as a trial of faith: they will be hated and despised by the whole world. It was in itself a hard and sad thing for God's children to bear, that they should be afflicted indiscriminately with the reprobate and scorners of God, suffer the same penalties which they receive for their crimes. It might seem far more unfair to bear the heavy weight of grevious troubles from which the wicked are exempt. Like grain they are first threshed along with the chaff then put to the bruising and rubbing of the mill-stone; so God gives His children a share in the afflictions of the wicked and, more than others, puts them to bear a cross, so that we might think them the most wretched of all mankind. Christ treats here in particular of the troubles which the disciples would

79

suffer for the Gospel's sake. Although it is true what Paul (Rom. 8.29) says, whom God chose He also destined to bear the cross that they might be conformed to the image of His Son. He does not, however, give all this distinctive mark of persecution sustained at the hands of the enemies of the Gospel. The type of cross of which Christ speaks now is when believers would have to endure the hatred of wicked men for the testimony of the Gospel, face their reproaches and provoke their fury. He wanted to warn the disciples that the teaching of the Gospel (whose witnesses and heralds they were to be) would never win the world's favour and applause, as He had formerly explained to them. He foretells that they will not only have to contend with a few enemies, but wherever they come whole nations will oppose them. Now this was an incredible and monstrous thing that might have shocked and shattered the stoutest minds; that the name of the Son of God could be so loaded with shame and hatred as to bring disfavour on all its adherents at all times. So Mark writes, *take heed to yourselves*. The word shows the purpose and function of the warning, that we must be ready to endure, or the trial will catch us unawares. In Mark also there is added, *before governors and kings . . . for a testimony unto them*, since Christ's disciples would be led before their tribunal. Luke in slightly different words gives the same sense, *It shall turn unto you for a testimony*. Christ means that His Gospel will get so much the greater testimony from their defence of it, at the peril of their lives. If the Apostles had only taken pains to preach the Gospel and had not constantly stood up to the angry attacks of enemies in its affirmation, they would not have given it such a shining demonstration of support. Since they did not hesitate to expose their lives nor allow any terrors of death to deflect them from their aim, men could see from their fearless perseverance how seriously they were persuaded of the rightness of their cause. It was an authentic seal of the Gospel that Apostles should go forward to the very tribunals of kings without dread, and there in plain terms confess the name of Christ. Peter calls himself a witness of the sufferings of Christ, whose marks he carried himself. Paul also in Philippians 1.17 boasts that he was set for the defence of the Gospel. It is chiefly worth noting, that those to whom God accords such honours as to make them the spokesmen of His truth should not by base evasion depart from the faith.

Mark 13.11. *Be not anxious beforehand*. This sentence and the one following we have expounded at Matt. 10. Our Lord means to relieve the disciples of the anxiety which stops us doing our duty, when we have doubts whether we can be equal to the responsibility. Not that He wants us idly to sleep with both ears shut (for nothing is better for us than to be made aware of our weakness, taught humility and be stimulated to pray), but Christ warns us to throw our worries upon our Father's knees and relying on His promised help continue eagerly upon our way. The promise is put in other words in Luke. It is not that Christ will deliver His people from death (for this must not always be expected) but that He will give them a mouth and wisdom, with which to shame their accusers. When Christ supplies them with the presence of mind and power of speech, I interpret the two terms as linked by hypallage, as if He had said He would train their tongues to make them answer prudently and suitably. He adds that his wisdom will be victorious against all enemies, for they shall not be able to contradict or resist it. Not that their impudent attack will yield to the truth, but because truth itself will triumph over their frantic audacity in vainly opposing it. Would that all who are forced to a confession of faith held to this confidence, then a different power and majesty of Spirit would arise to lay low the ministers of Satan. Sometimes indeed we are carried away by our own emotions, and rushing wild and headlong on the crest of pride we go too far, but sometimes confine ourselves within the bounds of false timidity, then sad experience shows that we lack the grace of God and the aid of the Spirit. Christ affirms in Matthew and Mark, that it is the Spirit of the Father who speaks in us, and here He declares He will give us utterance; so we may infer that it is His prerogative to fortify us with the Spirit.

Luke 21.19. *In your patience.* This means of protecting one's life, that Christ gave the disciples, is far different from what fleshly reason dictates. It is natural for a man to wish to put his life in safety. We collect on all sides the protection we think will be best, and avoid all risks. In fact we do not think we are alive to life unless we are properly protected. But Christ prescribes for our protection in life that we should walk exposed to fire and water and sword. Indeed, no man truly commits his spirit into God's hands unless he first learns to live from day to day in constant readiness to die. Briefly, Christ tells us to *possess our life* as much under the cross as under the unending fears of death.

Matt. 24.10. *And then shall many stumble.* Now He lists the temptations that shall come from bad examples. This is particularly violent and hard to overcome, for Christ Himself was a stone of stumbling to many, on whom some dash themselves and others fall back from the encounter, while others fall away. Christ seems to me in this saying to embrace many kinds of distress. Some fail who had entered upon the right path, and many turn fiercely against Christ. Some forget all reason and fair dealing and break out in mad careers. Some grow profane and cast off all sense of religion. Some take advantage of chaos for their own crimes.

Matt. 24.11. *Many false prophets shall arise.* This warning is not the same as the former when Christ predicted that many would come in his name. There He spoke only of impostors who shortly after the beginning of the Gospel made out they were Christs. Now He denounces the false teachers who will arise and corrupt true doctrine with error, as Peter teaches (I Pet. 2.8), so that the Church will be as liable to this evil under the Gospel as it was under the Law of old. Thus there is no reason why error and tricks of the devil and smears on religion should cause pious minds to weaken, for no-one is really founded upon Christ who has not learned to stand up to such aggression. This is the true test of our faith, that in all the surge of false teaching it is never overwhelmed. He says that not only will false prophets come, but they will be endowed with the art of deception to draw away sects after them. This demands no ordinary caution. The great numbers of those that go astray is like a wild whirlwind driving us off our course, unless we are thoroughly tied to God. On this matter something was said shortly before.

Matt. 24.12. *Because iniquity shall be multiplied.* How far and wide this evil extends should escape nobody, and yet very few observe it. When the wickedness of men is exposed more clearly to the light of the Gospel, the will to do good languishes and almost expires, even in upright and well ordered minds. Each man thinks to himself that the duties which one owes another are disappearing, when experience and daily practice show all men more or less ungrateful, or treacherous, or sinful. This is a serious and dangerous temptation. What could be stranger than backing a doctrine that seems actually to lessen our efforts for good and to weaken our love? When the Gospel came into the world, love whose ardour should have warmed the hearts of all men rather made them cold. Note the source of this evil, as Christ points to it: many shall faint because their weakness will succumb to the flood of ill-doing (which swells on all sides). Christ requires of His followers a courage that will stand up to the struggle. As Paul teaches us not to be weary in well-doing and humanity (II Thess. 3.13). When the love of many should fail to support the weight of iniquity Christ tells them that this barrier too must be overcome in case the faithful should break under bad example and defect. So He repeats the sentence, that no man can be saved unless he strive lawfully to persevere to the end of the course.

Matt. 24.14. *This Gospel of the kingdom shall be preached.* The Lord's speech had given no slight cause for sadness. This word of consolation is welcome either to lift up the fallen hearts or strengthen the weak, whatever Satan plots, however many various riots he works up, yet the Gospel will come through until it is spread all over the world. However hard that was to believe, the Apostles must rely on their master's Word, hope firmly against hope, and bravely strive mean-while to fulfil their tasks. When some object that the Antipodes and other remote nations so far have not even the faintest Word of Christ, the problem is readily solved. Christ is not talking of individual tracts of land or fixing any particular time but only affirming that the Gospel (which all would have thought was soon to be banished from its own home in Judaea) would be published to the furthest ends of the earth before the last day of His coming. He names this as the object of preaching, that it may be a testimony to all nations. God has never left Himself 'without witness' (ἀμάρτυρον) and particularly gave His testimony to the Jews, yet the testimony that He gave in His revelation of Himself in His Christ outshone all others. Thus Paul in his first letter to Timothy 2.6 says that he saw the light in his day because the time was ripe for calling all the world to God. Let us learn then that as often as the Gospel is preached it is just as if God Himself came in our midst and solemnly and with all authority urged us no longer to walk in vague shadows. Those who will not obey are made without excuse.

Then shall the end come. Some wrongly restrict to the destruction of the temple and the abolition of legal worship what should be understood of the end and renewal of the world. Since the disciples confused the two, as though the temple could not be put down without the ruin of the whole earth, Christ replies to the question put to Him with the caution that a long and sad epic of woes was upon them, that they must not hasten to seize the prize before they had gone through many contests and troubles. This is the answer to the last part, The end of the age will not come until I have long tested my Church with hard and wearisome temptations: this is contrasted with the false notion the Apostles had conceived among themselves. The lesson again is that no particular time is fixed, as if the last day were to follow directly upon the outcome of his predictions, for the faithful have long since experienced what we have just read, Christ did not then appear. His whole purpose was to restrain the Apostles with endurance when they were all too ready to fly right up to heavenly glory. In other words, redemption was not as close at hand as they made out, but was a path with many turnings.

When therefore ye see the abomination of desolation, which was spoken of by Daniel the prophet, standing in the holy place (let him that readeth understand), then let them that are in Judaea flee unto the mountains: let him that is on the housetop not go down to take out the things that are in his house: and let him that is in the field not return back to take his cloke. But woe unto them that are with child and to them that give suck in those days! And pray ye that your flight be not in the winter, neither on a

*sabbath: for then shall be great tribulation, such as hath not been from the
beginning of the world until now, no, nor ever shall be. And except those
days had been shortened, no flesh would have been saved: but for the
elect's sake those days shall be shortened. Then if any man shall say unto
you, Lo, here is Christ, or, Here; believe it not. For there shall arise false
Christs, and false prophets, and shall shew great signs and wonders; so as
to lead astray, if possible, even the elect. Behold, I have told you beforehand. If therefore they shall say unto you, Behold, he is in the wilderness;
go not forth: Behold he is in the inner chambers; believe it not. For as
the lightning cometh forth from the east, and is seen even unto the west; so
shall be the coming of the Son of man. Wheresoever the carcase is, there
will the eagles be gathered together.* (Matt. 24.15-28)

*But when ye see the abomination of desolation standing where he ought
not (let him that readeth understand), then let them that are in Judaea flee
unto the mountains: and let him that is on the housetop not go down, nor
enter in, to take anything out of his house: and let him that is in the field
not return to take his cloke. But woe unto them that are with child and to
them that give suck in those days! And pray ye that it be not in winter.
For those days shall be tribulation, such as there hath not been the like
from the beginning of the creation which God created until now, and
never shall be. And except the Lord had shortened the days, no flesh
would have been saved: but for the elect's sake, whom he chose, he
shortened the days. And then if any man shall say unto you, Lo, here
is the Christ; or, Lo, there; believe it not: for there shall arise false Christs
and false prophets, and shall shew signs and wonders, that they may
lead astray, if possible, the elect. But take ye heed: behold, I have told
you all things beforehand.* (Mark 13.14-23)

*But when ye see Jerusalem compassed with armies, then know that her
desolation is at hand. Then let them that are in Judaea flee unto the
mountains; and let them that are in the midst of her depart out; and let
not them that are in the country enter therein. For these are days of
vengeance, that all things which are written may be fulfilled. Woe unto
them that are with child and to them that give suck in those days! for
there shall be great distress upon the land, and wrath unto this people.
And they shall fall by the edge of the sword, and shall be led captive into
all the nations: and Jerusalem shall be trodden down of the Gentiles, until
the times of the Gentiles be fulfilled.*

*And he said unto the disciples, The days will come, when ye shall desire
to see one of the days of the Son of man, and ye shall not see it. And
they shall say to you, Lo, there! Lo, here! go not away, nor follow after*

them: for as the lightning, when it lighteneth out of the one part under the heaven, shineth unto the other part under heaven; so shall the Son of man be in his day. But first must he suffer many things and be rejected of this generation. (Luke 21.20-24; 17.22-25)

Matt. 24.15. *When therefore ye see the abomination.* Because the destruction of the temple and the city of Jerusalem and the ruin of the whole Jewish state were beyond belief (as we have just said), because it could appear particularly strange that the disciples could only be saved if they were divorced from that people to which had been entrusted the adoption and covenant of eternal salvation, Christ confirms both by the testimony of Daniel, as if saying, 'To stop you being tied down to the temple and to ceremonies of the Law God has put a certain limit upon them, and long ago testified that when the Redeemer should come sacrifices would cease: do not be troubled at being cut off from your nation.' God forewarned His people that in due time this abdication would come. The prediction had not only the effect of removing the actual cause of offence but also of strengthening the minds of the godly. In extreme disasters they might know that God looked down on them and cared for their salvation; thus they could hold on to the holy anchor and keep their moorings firm and secure in the midst of the most violent tossing of the waves.

Before going any further I must examine the passage cited by Christ. Interpreters are in my judgment mistaken in saying that this testimony comes from the ninth chapter of Daniel. We do not find there the exact words *abomination of desolation*, and it is certain that the angel does not speak of the final devastation that Christ is expounding but a dispersion of that period which came with the tyranny of Antiochus. In the twelfth chapter, however, the angel foretells (what is called) the final abrogation of legal worship which was to happen with the coming of Christ. Having encouraged the faithful to unshakable constancy he fixes absolutely the time both of ruin and restoration: 'From the time', he says, 'that the daily sacrifice shall be taken away and the abomination of desolation set up there shall be one thousand two hundred and ninety days. Blessed is he who shall wait till he come to the thousand three hundred and thirty-five days.' I know this passage through its obscurity can be distorted in various ways, but this meaning seems to me straightforward where the angel declares that, after the temple should be purged of its pollutions due to Antiochus and his idols, a time will come when it will be exposed to new profanations and lose its sanctity for ever and without any hope of restoration. Because this was a message of gloom and sorrow he again recalls the prophet to 'a year and two years and a half'. These words denote both the extent and the completion of the disaster. When evils come on without ceasing, one year seems long to go round; when the period of time is doubled the distress is all the greater. The Spirit urges the faithful to be ready not just for a year's endurance (that is, for a long time), but to realise that their afflictions must be borne for a whole stretch of many generations. Yet there is great consolation in the expression half a time, for though the afflictions will be long lasting, the Spirit shows they will not go on for ever. He had used this form of speech before; the Church's calamity will last for a time, times and half a time. Now He reckons these three years and six months in days, that the faithful in their longer extent of troubles should be the more hardened. It is the normal thing for men in adversity to count the length of time not in years or months but day to day, for one day is like a year. He calls them blessed in the end who shall persevere to the completion of that period, that is those who patiently win their way to the goal.

Christ chose only what suited His purpose: that the end of sacrifices was at hand, and that the abomination was to be placed in the temple, which would be the sign of final desolation. As the Jews were too firmly attached to their present ways to pay any attention to the prophecies where its abolition was foretold Christ tweaks their ears (so to speak) and bids them read the passage themselves with attention, to learn that there was clearly witnessed to in the prophets what they found so difficult to believe. *Abomination* comes to the same as profanation, for the word implies uncleanness, fouling and upsetting the pure worship of God. It is said to be of *desolation* because it involved the destruction of temple and state. As he had formerly said, in chapter 9, that the pollution introduced by Antiochus was like raising the flag of desolation for that time, for this is how I read the word 'wing' or 'spreading-out'. Some wrongly suppose this means the siege of Jerusalem: Luke's words do not support this error—he is not meaning to say the same thing, but something quite different. Because the city had once in years past been delivered just at the point (as it seemed) of ruin, and in case the faithful might hope for the same thing again, Christ declares that as soon as it is surrounded by its enemies it will be all over, for it is wholly deprived of help from God. The meaning is that the issue of the war will be in no doubt, for the city is doomed to destruction which it can no more escape than overturn a decree of heaven. So it is soon afterwards added, that it will be trodden underfoot of the nations. This expression denotes the ultimate ruin. As it could seem very strange that the holy city should be sold to the desires of the gentiles, the consolation is added that the gentiles are given leave for a time, until their iniquity ripens and the vengeance reserved for them breaks into the light of day.

Matt. 24.16. *Then let them that are in Judaea.* After Christ teaches by the testimony of the prophet, that with the profanation of the temple will shortly come the end of legal worship, He goes on to tell of the terrible and dread calamities that are at hand for all Judaea, so that the greatest wish will be to escape far from it. At the same time He says they will be so sudden that time will scarcely allow the most rapid flight. That is the point of the expressions, *let him that is on the house-top not go down into his house: and let him that is in the field not return:* in case they lose themselves in a desire to save their belongings. Similarly, *woe unto them that are with child and to them that give suck:* meaning of course that they will not be free and ready for flight. Also, *pray ye that your flight be not in the winter, neither on a sabbath:* here a sense of religion or the roughness of the roads or the shortness of the days might impede or delay one's haste. Christ's purpose was first to spur His followers on lest their minds should indulge too much in pictures of a blissful rest or the delights of an earthly kingdom, and second to fortify their minds against collapse in the face of common catastrophes. The caution is in strong language as was needful in view of their apathy and the awful gravity of the troubles.

Matt. 24.21. *For then shall be great tribulation.* Luke adds that there will be days of vengeance, and wrath unto this people, that all the Scripture wrote might be fulfilled. Seeing that the obstinate ill-will of the people should break God's covenant then, the earth itself and the sky must tremble under the appalling transformation. Never was any more fatal plague inflicted on the Jews than to be rejected by God through the extinction in their midst of the light of the teaching of heaven. Yet they were forced to *feel* the evil of their rejection (as the hardness of their hearts required), with sharp and severe torments. The reason for this fearful vengeance was that the desperate wickedness of the people had come to its culmination. The medicine prescribed for their disease they had not only proudly despised, but thrown out with insult. Indeed they had turned savagely on the Healer Himself, like men mad or possessed. Seeing how the Lord revenged so severely their obstinate contempt of the Gospel, along with their incorrigible frenzy, we should ever keep their punishment before our eyes, and learn that God finds nothing more intolerable than tenacious contempt for His grace. Although the same reward awaits similar despisers of the Gospel, God determined to make an exceptional impression on our memory in the case of the Jews, that the coming of Christ might shine with clearer light for the generations to come. No words can express the depths of their iniquity in putting to death the Son of God, offered to them from heaven as the author of life. So having steeped themselves in sacrilege beyond all wickedness they continued with crime after crime to bring on

87

themselves every ground for final annihilation. Christ says that there will never again be such tribulation: the rejection of Christ, whether considered in itself or in its whole nexus of sinful arrogance and ingratitude, was the most hateful of all sins of all ages, and so deserved a severity of vengeance beyond all other.

Matt. 24.22. *And except those days had been shortened.* As He amplifies the severity of the catastrophe, He brings in some words of comfort: the very name of Jew might be taken from them if God should not look to His elect and for their sake grant some alleviation. This passage agrees with that of Isaiah (1.9), 'Unless the Lord had left us a small remnant, we should have been as Sodom or as Gomorrah.' For indeed God's vengeance which had fallen in the Babylonian exile must be fulfilled again at the coming of Christ, as Paul testifies (Rom. 9.29). The greater the depth of wickedness the heavier the tide of vengeance must swell. So Christ says, 'if God had not set a limit the Jews would utterly perish, till not a single one was left: But God would take account of His free covenant, spare His elect', according to another oracle of Isaiah (10.22), 'though your people were as the sand of the sea, some remnants only shall be saved'. It is a singular proof of divine judgment when He afflicts His Church till it appears to be extinct, and yet in order to preserve some seed He marvellously snatches from destruction His elect, although few in number, so that beyond all hope they emerge from the jaws of death. So let hypocrites beware, not to rely on the title and appearance of the Church and imagine a false hope of going unpunished. God will find a way to deliver His Church when they have been handed over to their death. Wonderful comfort is given to the godly, that God will never give such free vein to His anger as to forget their safety. In punishing the Jews He blazed to a fearful extent—yet controlled His fire in an unexpected way to prevent any of His elect being lost, Here was the ground of miracle beyond belief, that seeing salvation should spring from Judaea God made rivers from a few drops of an almost dry source that would water the whole world, for (as they had drawn on themselves the hatred of all nations) they were practically brought to universal slaughter at a given sign on a single day. There is no doubt, considering how many were urging a massacre of this order, that Titus was restrained by God from giving the word to his soldiers and to others who were more than eager to see it through. As then the Roman emperor held back the final destruction of this people, the shortening of the days was to preserve some seed. Note this too, that He checked the onrush of His anger *for the elect's sake*, lest all should die. Why did He wish to keep a few survivors out of a huge number? And what reason had He for preferring these above others? Because His grace dwelt with the people whom He had adopted, and, in case His Covenant should have been in vain, certain ones by His eternal purpose were elect and destined to salvation. So Paul (Rom. 11.5) ascribes to free election the reason why a remnant had to be kept out of a very great people. So away with human merit, when we are recalled to the mere good-pleasure of God. Let there be no distinction between this one and that, but that those who are elect must be saved. To state this more clearly and fully Mark adds a pleonasm saying, *for the elect's sake whom He chose He shortened the days*. The participle alone would have done if he had not wanted to state precisely that God is not led by external causes to assign His favour to one rather than another: but because it has pleased Him to elect those whom He will save, He confirms His hidden purpose of grace in securing their salvation. It is asked how God put a limit on the troubles for the sake of the elect, so as not utterly to destroy the Jews, when many reprobate and desperate men were saved. The answer is easy, that part of the nation was delivered that God might bring forth His elect out of it, who were mixed with them, like grain from the scattered chaff. Temporal safety reaches reprobate and elect alike, but the former get no benefit; it is rightly ascribed to the latter only, since the wonderful providence of God was sent for their sake.

Matt. 24.23. *Then if any man shall say unto you.* He repeats what He had said about impostors: and with reason. There was great danger in this temptation that men in the misery of their afflictions and despairs would be deceived by a false title, go after make-believe Christs, and embrace the devil's delusions instead of God's assistance. At a time when the Jews, for their scorn for redemption, were under such duress, and needed to be dragged out of their treacherous course by vigorous means, Satan cleverly threw out to them new hopes which would lead them further astray from God. Nothing is more deadly for men who do not know which way to turn in their adversity than to be deceived, under the pretext of God's name, with lies that close the door of repentance, increase the darkness of infidelity, and in the end throw them in despair into the headlong confusion of insanity. Considering how great the danger was, the repetition was not at all superfluous, especially when Christ warns them that the false prophets will come prepared to trip them up with no trivial devices, but with signs and wonders that might stupefy the feeble minds. As God testifies to the presence of His power with miracles, making them seals on true doctrine, no wonder if impostors win favour by doing them. This mockery is a judgment of God on the ingratitude of men, that they who rejected the truth should believe a lie and fall into ever deeper mental darkness after shutting their eyes to the light that was offered. He is also giving His followers an exercise in loyalty which shines the more brightly as

89

they avoid every deception. Since the Lord declares that the false prophets and antichrists would be armed with miracles, there is no reason why the papists should be so very proud of this display or that we should be put off by their boasting. They plead miracles to support their superstitions: yes, those which the Son of God foretold would destroy the faith of many. The prudent ought not to reckon them of any importance, as if in themselves they could sufficiently prove any particular type of teaching. If they should object that this eliminates and nullifies the miracles by which Law and Gospel alike had their authority confirmed, I reply that the Spirit engraved on them a certain mark that removed doubt and fear of error from the minds of the faithful. As often as God showed His power to strengthen His people, He acted without ambiguity, to mark a true distinction resistant to every deception. Besides miracles set such a seal on doctrine that in turn it gains light and dispels the clouds which with Satan obscures simple intelligences. If we wish to guard against impostures, let us keep the link between signs and teaching intact.

Matt. 24.24. If possible, even the elect. This was added to strike a note of alarm, to have the faithful more concerned to keep carefully on guard: for where false prophets roam at will so unchecked and with such effective means of deception given them, it would be easy for the idle and incautious to be snared by their tricks. Christ urges and arouses His disciples to remain on watch. He advises them that there is no cause to be upset by the novelty of the sight, if here and there they see many fallen into error. He gives them a caution not to be caught napping by Satan; and He boosts their confidence, on which they may quietly depend, in promising that they will be safe in God's care and protection from any ruse that Satan may employ. However frail and slippery the way of the godly, yet they have firm footing on which to stand: for it could not be that men whose faithful protector is the Son of God should fall away from their salvation. They have not sufficient defences in themselves to resist the arts of Satan, but only because they are the flock of Christ, which none can pluck out of His hand (John 10.28). Note that the stability of our salvation (*salutis nostrae firmitas*) is not set in ourselves but in the hidden election of God. Our salvation is kept by faith (as Peter shows, I, 1.5), yet faith should ascend higher; we are saved because the Father gave us to His Son and the Son Himself affirms that nothing given to Him shall perish.

Matt. 24.25. Behold, I have told you beforehand. Mark expresses the Lord's intention more fully, *but take ye heed: behold I have told* you. We learn in these words that we deserve no excuse if we are amazed at the stumbling-blocks foretold by Christ: for as the Will of God ought to be our rule it is enough for us to be warned in time of His pleasure. As He declares that He is faithful and will never allow us to be tempted beyond what we can bear, we shall never lack power to resist as long as apathy does not foster weakness in us.

Matt. 24.26. *Behold, he is in the wilderness.* Luke mixes this saying in with another answer of Christ's. Being interrogated by the Pharisees about the coming of the Kingdom of God He said that it did not come with observation. Then in Luke's account, Jesus turned to the disciples and cautioned them that the days were coming when they would no longer see a day of the Son of man. These words He meant as a warning that they should walk in daylight, before they were overtaken by the shades of night. This should have been a sharp stimulus indeed to their enthusiasm to advance as long as they enjoyed the presence of Christ, when they heard the serious troubles that were impending. We cannot tell whether Christ gave His disciples the same warning twice over. I think it was probable when mention was made of the coming of the Kingdom of God that Luke inserted here sentences taken from another occasion: a thing he frequently does, as we have seen elsewhere. The passage has suffered various distortions through ignorance. To get the true sense readers must note the antitheses between the shadows and the revelation of the Kingdom of Christ in its unbounded extent. How sudden and unexpected it is, like the reach of lightning from the rising of the sun to its setting. We know the false 'Christs' (as suited the crass stupidity of that race) drew off whatever forces they could into desert recesses or caves or any hidden corners, to shake off the yoke of the Roman imperium by force of arms. The meaning is, then, that any who gather their forces into a secret locality to regain freedom by fighting are falsely putting themselves up as Christ, for the Redeemer is sent to spread His grace over every region of the world instantly, when none expect it. It is self-contradictory to shut redemption away in a corner and also spread it through the whole world. This is a warning to the disciples that the Redeemer was no longer to be sought out from Judaean fastnesses, for He will extend the borders of His Kingdom suddenly to the furthest ends of the earth. The wonderful rapidity with which the Gospel flew out to every region of the globe was a shining testimony to the divine power. It could not be the result of human industry that the light of the Gospel should flash like lightning and reach from one corner of the world to the other extreme: it is sound commendation of the heavenly glory that Christ presents. Besides by displaying the fulness of His Kingdom in this manner He wished to demonstrate that the desolate state of Judaea could not impede His reign.

Matt. 24.28. *Wheresoever the carcase is.* The meaning is: by whatever

91

methods Satan tries to scatter the children of God, this way and that, in Christ is found the holy bond of unity (*sacrum unitatis vinculum*) by which they should hold together. Real dispersion occurs when many drift away from Christ, in whom alone we have firm ground. This means is prescribed for fostering a holy union (*fovendae sanctae coniunctionis*) to prevent the separations of error tearing the Body of the Church: we must stay firm in Christ. Note carefully: it is not to the primacy of the Roman see nor to any other silliness that Christ ties us down, but the binding of His Church is of this kind alone, that all men everywhere should regard Him as their only Head. It follows that whoever adhere to Him in pure faith are beyond the danger of schism. Then let the Romanists go on to call schismatic those who refuse to be estranged from Christ and to put their own faith in a robber. When the Papists take the sense to apply to the company of those who profess one faith and explain the eagles allegorically as sharp far-sighted men, it is too absurd: plainly Christ had no other intention than to call to Himself and gather into God's care His children wherever they were dispersed. The word is not simply body, but *carcase*. Christ makes no special point about eagles other than what we might apply to crows or vultures according to the country we live in. Nor is there anything convincing in the ingenuity of other writers who say that Christ's death had a savour that attracted the elect to God. In my opinion Christ argued from the lesser to the greater. If the birds are so wise that many come together from distant regions over one corpse it would be shameful for the faithful not to be drawn to the Author of life, from whom alone they take true nourishment.

But immediately, after the tribulation of those days, the sun shall be darkened, and the moon shall not give her light, and the stars shall fall from heaven, and the powers of the heavens shall be shaken: and then shall appear the sign of the Son of man in heaven: and then shall all the tribes of the earth mourn, and they shall see the Son of man coming on the clouds of heaven with power and great glory. And he shall send forth his angels with a great sound of a trumpet, and they shall gather together his elect from the four winds, from one end of heaven to the other. (Matt. 24.29-31)

But in those days, after that tribulation, the sun shall be darkened, and the moon shall not give her light, and the stars shall be falling from heaven, and the powers that are in the heavens shall be shaken. And then shall they see the Son of man coming in clouds with great power *and glory. And then shall he send forth the angels, and shall gather together his elect from the four winds, from the uttermost part of the earth to the uttermost part of heaven.* (Mark 13.24-27)

And there shall be signs in sun and moon and stars; and upon the earth distress of nations, in perplexity for the roaring of the sea and the billows; men fainting for fear, and for expectation of the things which are coming on the world; for the powers of the heavens shall be shaken. And then shall they see the Son of man coming in a cloud with power and great glory. But when these things begin to come to pass, look up, and lift your heads; because your redemption draweth nigh. (Luke 21.25-28)

Christ comes now to the full disclosure of His Kingdom, which His disciples had originally asked Him about, and He promises that after the vexation of such great troubles will come the time of redemption. The main object of His answer was to establish His disciples in good hope, in case they should fail in courage at the ensuing chaos. For this reason He does not speak of His coming in simple terms but helps Himself to prophetic forms of speech, which the more men scrutinise, the harder they must struggle to understand the paradoxical character of events. Was it not most strange to see Christ's Kingdom held in scorn, burdened with the cross, covered in shame, overwhelmed with tribulation of every kind—in face of all the splendid utterances of the prophets in its regard? Could it not be asked what kind of majesty it was which turned sun, moon and stars to darkness, shook the world's whole system, and changed the regular order of nature? The Lord now meets tests of this kind and declares that although these oracles will not be fulfilled at once yet in the event they will be well justified. The meaning is that the predictions about a prodigious shaking of the heaven and earth should not be tied to the beginning of redemption, for the prophets had included its whole course, till it came to its finishing-point. Now that we grasp Christ's purpose, the sense of the words is easy, that the heaven will not be darkened immediately, but only after the Church has gone through its afflictions. Not that the glory and majesty of Christ's Kingdom will only appear at His final coming, but that the completion (*complementum*) is delayed till that point—the completion of those things that started at the resurrection, of which God gave His people only a taste, to lead them further along the road of hope and patience. By this way Christ keeps the minds of the faithful in suspense to the last day, in case they should think there was nothing to the testimony of the prophets on the restoration to come; for it had lain hid a long time under a dense cloud of troubles. Certain interpreters wrongly take the tribulation of those days as the ruin of Jerusalem; in fact this is a universal gathering-up

93

($\dot{\alpha}\nu\alpha\kappa\epsilon\phi\alpha\lambda\alpha\dot{\iota}\omega\sigma\iota\varsigma$) of all the evils of which Christ had already spoken. The argument encourages their enduring strength to look for a happy and joyful end, at last, to the afflictions. In other words, as long as the Church's pilgrimage in this world lasts, the skies will be dark and cloudy, but as soon as the end of distress arrives, the daylight will break to show His shining majesty. How the sun must be obscured we cannot guess today, but the event itself will reveal. As for the stars, He does not mean that they shall fall in actual fact, but according to men's way of thinking. Thus Luke predicts only that there will be signs in the sun and moon and stars. It means that there will be such a shaking of the heavenly system that the stars themselves will be thought to fall. Luke also adds that there will be a dreadful movement of the sea to make men faint for fear and alarm. Briefly, all creatures above or below will be as heralds to summon men to that terrible tribunal, which they will continue to scorn wickedly and treat outrageously to the very last day.

Matt. 24.30. *Then shall appear the sign.* In this saying Christ distinguishes more clearly between the present state of His Kingdom and the future glory. It is a kind of admission that the Majesty of Christ will not be obvious in the cloud of troubles, nor will men recognise the redemption He brings. Certainly the wild confusion of affairs we now see both obscures our minds and conceals the grace of Christ, and almost makes it vanish from our eyes, so that the salvation gained in Him is not at any rate grasped by carnal intelligence. So He declares He will appear openly at His last coming, that, endowed with heavenly power like a sign lifted high aloft, He may turn the gaze of all the world on Himself. Because He saw the majority of men would despise His teaching and oppose His Kingdom He declares that there will at once be weeping and lamentation for all peoples, for it is right that His presence should crush and bring down all rebels who scorned His rule when He was away. He says this partly to put terror into the proud and headstrong, to lead them to repentance, and partly to confirm the minds of His own amidst all the obstinacy of the world. The untroubled state of the wicked is great cause of offence when they seem to mock God with impunity. Again there is nothing to which we are more prone than to be caught in the allurements of the prosperity which they enjoy, and let go our respect for God. Lest their intoxicating pleasures make the faithful envious Christ declares it will at last turn to grief and gnashing of teeth. In my opinion He alludes to the twelfth chapter of Zechariah, v. 11, where God, giving a striking indication of judgment to come, tells them there will be mourning in every family—such as comes at the death of an only child. Let no one look for the conversion of the

94

world: too late and to no profit they will look on Him whom they have pierced. There follows an explanation of the sign that they shall see the Son of man coming above the clouds who at that time spent His days on earth in the fashion of a menial servant. He warns them that the glory of His Kingdom will be from heaven and not from earth, as His disciples had wrongly imagined.

Matt. 24.31.*And he shall send forth his angels.* He gives an instance of His authority in the sending of angels to gather His elect from the extreme corners of the earth. By the extremity of heaven is meant the furthest region. Christ speaks in hyperbole to teach the elect that even if they were swept off the ground and flung into the air yet they would be brought together to assemble under their Head unto eternal life and enjoy their hoped-for inheritance. Christ wished to comfort His disciples, that the sad dispersion of the Church should not break their spirits. We too, when we see the Church torn apart by Satan's craft, torn by the savagery of the wicked, upset by unholy doctrines, tossed by storms, we must learn to turn our eyes to this assembly. If the thing seems hard to believe, let the angelic force remind us: Christ expressly points it out to lift our minds above human means. Though the Church be now vexed by human malice, tossed between exiles and escapes of all kinds, smashed and broken even on the waves, wretchedly torn in pieces and losing all firm support on earth, we must persist in hope, for it is not by human means but by heavenly power (which will far surpass every obstacle) that the Lord will gather it in.

Luke 21.28. *But when these things begin to come to pass.* Luke gives a clearer expression to the comfort with which Christ delights the minds of His people. Though this sentence contains nothing different to Matthew's which we have just expounded it does show better the purpose of the angels' coming to gather the elect. It was necessary to contrast the general sadness and distress of the wicked with the joy of the godly, and to mark the distinction between them and the reprobate, lest they should view the coming of Christ with horror. We know that Scripture speaks, not only of the last judgment but also of all God's daily practice, in a variety of ways, according as the speech is directed to the faithful or to unbelievers. 'Wherefore would ye have the day of the Lord' (says the prophet Amos, 5.18), 'a day of smoke and darkness, not of light: of grief, not joy: of ruin, not salvation?' By contrast Zechariah (9.9) bids the daughter of Zion rejoice for the coming of her king. Rightly so: for (as Isaiah says, 35.4) the same day as brings wrath and vengeance upon the wicked brings good-will and redemption to believers. So Christ teaches that the light of gladness will arise at His coming for His disciples, that while the wicked are confused with alarms, they may leap for joy at the salvation at hand. This is the mark to which Paul (I Cor. 1.7) refers those that look for the day or coming of the Lord. Their crown and full happiness and their time of refreshment are put off till that day (II Tim. 4.8). It is therefore called here (as at Rom. 8.23) *redemption*, for we shall have then the effect, in truth and assurance, of the deliverance won for us in Christ. So let our ears be awake to the sound of the angelic trumpet, which shall not only ring out a note to strike the reprobate with the horror of doom, but will call the elect to the second life; that is, to call to the enjoyment of life those whom the Lord now revives with the voice of the Gospel. It is a sign of infidelity to panic at the presence of the Son of God for our salvation.

Now from the fig tree learn her parable: when her branch is now become tender, and putteth forth its leaves, ye know that the summer is nigh; even so ye also, when ye see all these things, know ye that he is nigh, even at the doors. Verily I say unto you, This generation shall not pass away, till all these things be accomplished. Heaven and earth shall pass away, but my words shall not pass away. But of that day and hour knoweth no one, not even the angels of heaven, neither the Son, but the Father only. (Matt. 24.32-36)

Now from the fig tree learn her parable: when her branch is now become tender, and putteth forth its leaves, ye know that the summer is nigh; even so ye also, when ye see these things coming to pass, know ye that he is nigh, even at the doors. Verily I say unto you, This generation shall not pass away, until all these things be accomplished. Heaven and earth shall pass away: but my words shall not pass away. But of that day or that hour knoweth no one, not even the angels in heaven, neither the Son, but the Father. (Mark 13.28-32)

And he spake to them a parable: Behold the fig tree, and all the trees: when they now shoot forth, ye see it and know of your own selves that the summer is now nigh. Even so ye also, when ye see these things coming to pass, know ye that the kingdom of God is nigh. Verily I say unto you, This generation shall not pass away, till all things be accomplished. Heaven and earth shall pass away: but my words shall not pass away. (Luke 21.29-33)

My understanding is not that, in those troubled times, there will be only as sure a sign of the nearness of Christ's coming as when we recognise the sure approach of summer when the trees put out their leaf. I think Christ means more than that. We see that in winter, trees draw in with the rigours of the cold and look more brave, but in the spring lose their toughness and look more tender, actually splitting and opening ways for new twigs; so with the Church, its strength is not really impaired when troubles appear to soften it to the eye of the flesh. As the inward sap diffused through the whole tree produces softness, then gathering strength breaks out to renew the dead wood, so the Lord draws from the corruption of the outward man the full restoration of His people. Briefly, they should not judge from the weak and feeble state of the Church that it is dying, but rather hope for the immortal glory for which God prepares His own by the cross and by affliction. Paul (II Cor. 4.16) affirms of individual members what should work out in the whole body: namely, if the outward man is corrupted, the inward must be renewed day by day. What Matthew and Mark had said more obscurely, *know ye that he is nigh, even at the doors*, Luke expounds more clearly, *that the kingdom of God is nigh*. And in this passage the Kingdom of God is not thought of (as so often elsewhere) at its beginning, but at its completion, and this was how those whom Christ taught used to understand it. They did not understand by it the Kingdom of God in the Gospel, which consists in the peace and joy of faith, and in spiritual righteousness, but they were looking for that blessed rest and glory which hidden under hope awaits the last day.

Matt. 24.34. *This generation shall not pass away.* Christ uses a universal term, but does not apply His words in general to all the afflictions of the Church, but simply teaches that in one generation events would establish all He had said. Within fifty years the city was wiped out, the temple rased, the whole region reduced to appalling devastation, and the world's obstinacy rose up against God. A furious passion raged to destroy the doctrine of salvation, false teachers came up to pervert the true Gospel with their impostures, religion was shocked in amazing ways, and the whole company of the godly was wretchedly harassed. Although the same evils continued without a break for many centuries to follow, Christ still spoke truly, saying the faithful would actually and openly experience before the end of one generation how true His oracle was, for the Apostles suffered the same things as we see today. It was not Christ's intention to promise His people an end to troubles within a short time (this would have contradicted His earlier caution that the end was not yet) but He encourages them to hold out by telling them exactly what to look for in that time. The meaning is that the prophecy does not refer to distant evils which a later generation would see after many centuries, but those already imminent, all massed up, so that there is no part of

97

it which the present generation will not experience. So the Lord heaps on one generation calamities of every description although He does not spare later generations, but bids His disciples be ready to bear all things with firmness.

Matt. 24.35. *Heaven and earth shall pass away.* To win faith for His words, He illuminates their certainty with a comparison which, certainly, is based more firmly and surely than the fabric of the entire world. Interpreters expound this manner of speech in various ways. Some refer the passing away of heaven and earth to the last day, on which their frail order will be no more. Others explain that, Sooner will the whole fabric of the universe perish, than the oracle we have just heard vanish. Seeing there is no doubt that Christ deliberately wished to lift the minds of His people above the destruction of the world, He seems to me to be marking the continual rising and falling that we observe in the world, as if to say that His words are not to be measured by the unstable and (as it were) stormy variations of the world, for we know how the world's affairs keep turning, and how readily our minds are distracted with them. Christ tells His disciples not to have their attention held by the world, but as from the high watch-tower of divine providence to look down on the events He had predicted. From this passage, besides, we take the useful lesson that our salvation (because it is founded on the promises of Christ) does not toss up and down in the pattern of the waves of this world but stays unshaken, as long as our faith, rising above heaven and earth, soars all the way to Christ Himself.

Matt. 24.36. *But of that day.* By this sentence Christ means to keep the minds of the faithful in suspense, in case by some false notion they might fix a time on the final redemption. We know our flights of ingenuity and how vain curiosity tickles us to know more than we should. Christ saw His disciples hurrying on to triumph, out of time. He wishes the day of His coming to be so hoped for and looked for that yet no one should dare to ask when it will come. He wants His disciples to walk in the light of faith and, without knowing times with certainty, to expect the revelation with patience. Beware then not to worry more than the Lord allows over details of time. The chief part of our wisdom consists in keeping ourselves soberly within the bounds of the Word of God. In case it should be an anxiety for men not to know that day, Christ associates angels with them: for it would really be proud and sinful to desire to have more for ourselves, living on earth, than is allowed the heavenly angels. Mark adds, *neither the Son of man.* It would be threefold, fourfold madness to grudge submission to the ignorance which not even the Son of God refused to accept, for our sake. Because many thought this unworthy of Christ they tried to alleviate its hardness with a comment of their own. Perhaps the Arian malice forced them to find a trick answer, when they attempted to prove from this that Christ was not the true and only God. Because He was unwilling to reveal it to others, they alleged that Christ did not know the last day. But since it is obvious that the same ignorance is ascribed to the angels, another more appropriate sense must be sought, and before I propose one, I must briefly dispose of the objections made by those who think it is an insult to the Son of God if any kind of ignorance is said to apply to Him. As to the first objection, that nothing is unknown to God, the answer is easy. We know that the two natures in Christ were so conformed in one Person that each retained what was proper to it: in particular the Divinity was silent (*quievit Divinitas*) and made no assertion of itself whenever it was the business of the human nature to act alone in its own terms in fulfilment of the office of Mediator. So there was nothing absurd for Christ, who knew everything, to be ignorant of something as far as man could understand. Otherwise He could not have met grief and anxiety, or have been like us. As for the objections that ignorance does not suit Christ (being a penalty for sin), this is more than stupid. It is ignorant nonsense that lack of knowledge (as is attributed to angels) flows from sin: while in another respect these critics are equally unintelligent not to recognize that Christ put on our flesh for the very reason that He might take on Himself the due penalty for our sins (*ut debitas peccatis nostris poenas in se susciperet*). As for Christ the man not knowing the last day, it detracts in no way from His divine nature, other than that He was mortal. No doubt He refers to a duty laid on Him by His Father, as I said above, when He says that it is not for Him to set this one or that on His right hand or on His left. I understand then, that as He had come down to us as Mediator, until He had fulfilled His function it was not given Him to have what He would have after His resurrection: then, at last, He plainly said that power over all things was given to Him.

And as were the days of Noah, so shall be the coming of the Son of man. For as in those days that were before the flood they were eating and drinking, marrying and giving in marriage, until the day that Noah entered into the ark, and they knew not until the flood came, and took them all away so shall be the coming of the Son of man. Then shall two men be in the field; one is taken, and one is left: two women shall be grinding at the mill; one is taken, and one is left. Watch therefore: for ye know not on what day your Lord cometh. (Matt. 24.37-42)

99

*Take ye heed, watch and pray: for ye know not when the time is.
(Mark 13.33)*

*And as it came to pass in the days of Noah, even so shall it be also in the
days of the Son of man. They ate, they drank, they married, they were
given in marriage, until the day that Noah entered into the ark, and the
flood came, and destroyed them all. Likewise even as it came to pass in
the days of Lot; they ate, they drank, they bought, they sold, they planted,
they builded; but in the day that Lot went out from Sodom it rained fire
and brimstone from heaven, and destroyed them all: after the same manner
shall it be in the day that the Son of man is revealed. In that day, he
which shall be on the housetop, and his goods in the house, let him not go
down to take them away: and let him that is in the field likewise not
return back. Remember Lot's wife. Whosoever shall seek to gain his
life shall lose it: but whosoever shall lose his life shall preserve it. I say
unto you, In that night there shall be two men on one bed; the one shall be
taken, and the other shall be left. There shall be two women grinding
together; the one shall be taken, and the other shall be left. And they
answering say unto him, Where Lord? And he said unto them,
Where the body is, thither will the eagles also be gathered together.*

*But take heed to yourselves, lest haply your hearts be overcharged with
surfeiting, and drunkenness, and cares of this life, and that day come on
you suddenly as a snare: for so shall it come upon all them that dwell
on the face of all the earth. But watch ye at every season, making
supplication, that ye may prevail to escape all these things that shall come
to pass, and to stand before the Son of man.* (Luke 17.26-37; 21.34-36)

Matt. 24.37. *And as were the days of Noah.* Christ has just put the
minds of His people in suspense, in case they should inquire over much
about the last day; but to prevent them becoming lulled into indifference
by the pleasures of the world He now encourages them to watchfulness.
He wished them to be so uncertain of His coming that from day to day,
indeed from moment to moment, they should be intently waiting. To
shake them from sleep and stir them sharply to take caution, He foretells
that the end will come suddenly upon a world sunk in dumb idleness: as
in the days of Noah all races were swallowed under unexpectedly in the
flood as they sweetly drank in their fancies; and a little later the people
of Sodom, who had no fear to abandon themselves to lust, were
burned up with fire from heaven. Since such will be the world's easy
approach to its last day there is no reason why the faithful should
settle for the example of the crowd. Now we have Christ's intention,
that the faithful should not be overwhelmed suddenly, but should
always keep watch, for the day of final judgment will come unawares.
Luke alone mentions Sodom, and that in ch. 17, where he takes occasion

to ignore the order of events and insert Christ's words. It would not have been strange if the two Evangelists had been content with one example, although two were put forward by Christ, especially since it squared in all respects: once the whole human race, as it dallied in idle pleasure, was (with few exceptions) suddenly drowned. He speaks of eating, drinking, holding marriages, and men giving their attention to other secular business at the time when God destroyed the whole world with a flood, or Sodom with thunderbolts: these words mean that they were so busy with all the comforts and delights of the present life as if no alteration were to be feared. Though He will at once go on to teach His disciples to beware of excess and earthly worries, in this passage He is not directly condemning the intemperance of those times so much as the obstinacy; this made them scorn God's threats and lie back at the prospect of their fearful death. Seeing they promised themselves a state of continuance, they did not hesitate to proceed securely in their accustomed paths. In itself it would not have been wrong or damnable to look to their necessities, if they had not set their crass folly against the judgment of God, and rushed with eyes shut to unprincipled sin as if there were no judge in heaven. Christ says now that the last age of the world will be quite witless, think of nothing but the present life, put worries a long way out of sight, and pursue the course of their lives as if the earth would always remain in the same state. These comparisons are most apt: if we consider to ourselves what happened, then we shall not be deceived by seeing the same tenor in the order of the world's affairs—and imagine it will be so for ever. Within three days of the time when each man conducted his affairs with total unconcern, the earth was submerged in a flood, and five cities were destroyed by fire.

Matt. 24.39. *They knew not until the flood came.* The source and cause of their ignorance was that incredulity had blinded their minds. As the Apostle teaches (Heb. 11.7), Noah saw from a great distance, by the eyes of faith, the vengeance of God as yet concealed, and took warning in time. Christ contrasts Noah with the rest of the world, and Lot with the Sodomites, that the faithful may learn to gather together and not wander off with the others into chaos. Note that at that time the reprobate slept in their evils because because the Lord had only granted His servants early warning for their salvation: not that the coming of the flood was altogether concealed from the inhabitants of the earth (Noah in building the ark set the baleful sight before their eyes over a hundred years) but because one man was specially warned by heavenly oracle of the future destruction of the whole earth. In these days there is a general rumour of impending judgment but only a few have been taught by God to know that Christ will come as judge, in due time. These must be aroused by the singular goodness of God and have their sense sharpened, in case they fall in with the prevailing apathy. Peter (I, 3.20; II, 2.5) for this reason compares the ark with our baptism, since a small band of men cut off from the crowd is saved amid the waters. Our minds must be directed to this small number, if we wish to get away in safety.

Matt. 24.40. *Then shall two men be in the field; one is taken.* Before writing these things Luke inserts a few sentences: the first, Matthew applies to the destruction of Jerusalem, *he which shall be on the house-top, let him not go down into the house to take his goods away.* It may be that Christ suited the same words to different events. There follows also in Luke the warning that the disciples should *remember Lot's wife*: that they should forget those things that are behind and strive for the goal of the calling from above. The reason that Lot's wife was turned into a pillar of salt was that, hesitating in case they were wrong to leave the city, she looked behind her: so denying her faith in God's oracle. She was probably drawn back by a longing for the nest where she had enjoyed peace and quiet. Since God then willed her to remain an eternal lesson, our minds must be strengthened in the constancy of faith that they may not hesitate and languish in mid course: they ought to be trained to persevere that bidding farewell to the temptations of this waning life they may aspire to heaven freely and eagerly. A third sentence is added by Luke, *whosoever shall seek to gain his life shall lose it,* that a desire for an earthly life may not prevent the faithful from hastening through the midst of death fearlessly to win the salvation laid up for them in heaven. In the same vein Christ marks the fragility of the present life in saying that souls are begotten into life (ζωογονεῖσθαι) when they are lost. In other words, men do not live in the world, He says, because ultimately the beginning of real and solid living is in renunciation of the world. Immediately Luke adds, as Matthew has also, that husband and wife will then be separated, that the mutual ties by which men are connected in the world may not hold back or delay the godly. It often happens that in looking after each other, men get nowhere. So in order that each man for himself, free and unhampered from every tie may run with haste, Christ tells us that with one couple the one partner shall be taken, the other left: not that they who are bound together necessarily have to be torn apart (their holy bond in religion will make the good woman cleave to the good man, and the children stay with the father) but Christ determined to cut away all delays and encourage each individual to hurry and not to wait in vain for the partners to which they are joined. Luke adds on the sentence, *where the body is,* etc. This should not be restricted to the last day, but as the disciples had asked, *where Lord?*—that is, how shall we stand erect in such a shaking, and remain unscathed in such serious storms? and what hiding-place will cover us all gathered together?—Christ (as in Matthew) testifies that He is the rallying-place of solid unity, where all the children of God ought to be gathered together.

Matt. 24.42. *Watch therefore.* The exhortation in Luke is more emphatic, or at least, more particular, *take heed to yourselves, lest haply your hearts be overcharged with surfeiting, and drunkenness, and cares of this life.* Anyone who lives intemperately and has his senses swamped with food and wine will never lift his mind to think of the life of heaven. As there is no desire of the flesh that does not intoxicate a man, men must attend to all these and not sink into the world, if they want to make haste to the Kingdom of Christ. In Matthew the single word 'vigilance' denotes such continuous attention as makes us walk like pilgrims on the earth with minds on the alert. In Mark the disciples are first warned to look out, that death may not overtake them unawares or drowsing: then they are told to watch, for various inducements of the flesh always creep in and drug our minds. Finally an exhortation to pray, for of course we must pray for outside help to overcome our infirmity. Luke gives the very form of prayer. First that God may grant us deliverance from so deep and difficult a maze, and then set us safe and sound in the sight of His Son. For we may never reach that point unless by wonderfully escaping innumerable deaths. As it would not do for us to pass through our course in this present life by sailing over and away from all hazards, Christ makes this the chief aim, that we may stand before His tribunal. *For ye know not on what day.* Note that the uncertainty of the time of Christ's coming (which for the most part induces idleness in men) ought to be a stimulus to our attention and watchfulness. God deliberately wished it kept hidden from us, that we should never be so carefree as to neglect our unbroken lookout. What would be the trial of faith and patience if the faithful wandered about all their lives at ease with their delights, and set themselves to meet Christ at three days' notice.

But know this, that if the master of the house had known in which watch the thief was coming, he would have watched, and would not have suffered his house to be broken through. Therefore be ye also ready: for in an hour that ye think not the Son of man cometh. Who then is the faithful and wise servant, whom his lord hath set over his household, to give them their food in due season? Blessed is that servant, whom his lord when he cometh shall find so doing. Verily I say unto you, that he will set him over all that he hath. But if that evil servant shall say in his heart, My lord tarrieth; and shall begin to beat his fellow-servants, and shall eat and drink with the drunken; the lord of that servant shall come in a day when he expecteth not, and in an hour when he knoweth not, and shall cut him asunder, and appoint his portion with the hypocrites: there shall be weeping and gnashing of teeth. (Matt. 24.43-51)

It is as when a man, sojourning in another country, having left his house, and given authority to his servants, to each one his work, commanded also the porter to watch. Watch therefore: for ye know not when the lord of the house cometh, whether at even, or at midnight, or at cockcrowing, or in the morning; lest coming suddenly he find you sleeping. And what I say unto you I say unto all, Watch. (Mark 13.34-37)

Let your loins be girded about, and your lamps burning; and be ye yourselves like unto men looking for their lord, when he shall return from the marriage feast; that, when he cometh and knocketh, they may straightway open unto him. Blessed are those servants, whom the lord when he cometh shall find watching: verily I say unto you, that he shall gird himself, and make them sit down to meat, and shall come and serve them. And if he shall come in the second watch, and if in the third, and find them so, blessed are those servants. But know this, that if the master of the house had known in what hour the thief was coming, he would have watched, and not have left his house to be broken through. Be ye also ready: for in an hour that ye think not the Son of man cometh.

 And Peter said, Lord, speakest thou this parable unto us, or even unto all? And the Lord said, Who then is the faithful and wise steward, whom his lord shall set over his household, to give them their portion of food in due season? Blessed is that servant, whom his lord when he cometh shall find so doing. Of a truth I say unto you, that he will set him over all that he hath. But if that servant shall say in his heart, My Lord delayeth his coming; and shall begin to beat the menservants and the maidservants, and to eat and drink, and to be drunken; the lord of that servant shall come in a day when he expecteth not, and in an hour when he knoweth not, and shall cut him asunder, and appoint his portion with the unfaithful. And that servant, which knew his lord's will, shall be beaten with many stripes; but he that knew not, and did things worthy of stripes, shall be beaten with few stripes. And to whomsoever much is given, of him shall much be required: and to whom they commit much, of him will they ask the more.

 I came to cast fire upon the earth; and what will I, if it is already kindled? But I have a baptism to be baptized with; and how am I straitened till it be accomplished! (Luke 12.35-50)

Matt. 24.43. *If the master of the house had known.* Luke narrates this saying of Jesus in a different place from Matthew. This is not remark-

104

able. In ch. 12 he weaves together from various discourses a summary of teaching (as we have shown elsewhere) and inserts this parable also. He gives a general preface there, that disciples should gird up their loins, carry lighted lamps in their hand, and be waiting for their Master. The parable of the wise and foolish virgins which follows shortly after in Matthew falls under the same heading. In a few well-chosen words Christ outlines how the faithful should make their pilgrim way in this world: He contrasts girt loins with idleness, and burning lights with the shades of ignorance. First Christ bids the disciples be ready and equipped for the road, that they may travel with speed through the earth and not look for any fixed and quiet resting-place anywhere but in heaven. An excellent warning: though profane men also talk about their course of life we see how they lie around the earth very content to stay as they are. God does not grant the title of sons except to those who admit they are strangers on the earth: they must not only always be ready for pilgrimage, but actually keep moving in the way to eternal life. Then as they are surrounded by darkness on every side, as long as their life is in the world, He equips them with lanterns as men who make a night journey. He gives leading emphasis to running with vigour, then, to be sure of the way, in case the faithful lose the track and tire themselves in vain, for otherwise it would be better to limp along the road than finish a journey blindly that leads nowhere. As regards girding the loins, the expression comes from the common use of Eastern nations who wear long garments.

Luke 21.26. *And be ye yourselves like.* He uses a comparison passed over by Matthew who is briefer at this point. He compares himself to a householder who is feasting gaily at a wedding or otherwise indulging his pleasure away from home, and likes His servants to behave in the house with care and sobriety, busy about their proper tasks and attentively waiting for His return. The Son of God is away from us because He has been received into the blessed quiet of heaven, yet He appoints each His duty; it would not do for us to sleep at ease. As he has promised to return to us we should at every moment stand ready to receive Him, lest He finds us alseep. If a mortal man reckons he may expect His servants to be alert for His return whatever hour He comes home, how much greater the Lord's right to order His folk always to wait for his coming, sober and watchful. To add to their alacrity, He mentions how earthly lords are so delighted at their servants' promptitude that they actually serve them, not that this was the way with all masters, but that it happened sometimes that a lord, by nature courteous and humane, allowed his servants to join him at his table as fellows. It is asked, Seeing that Scripture in various places calls us children of light, and the Lord gives us light by His word so that we walk as if in noonday (Eph. 5.8 and I Thess. 5.5), how does the Lord compare our life to the night watches? The answer to this problem is to be found in Peter (II 1.19) who says that the Word of God shines as a burning lamp, that in the dark places the path may lie clear before us. Note both aspects, then, that our way has to go through the dark shadows of the world, and that we are preserved from the danger of wandering by the light of heavenly teaching that goes ahead, especially when Christ Himself does office as our Sun.

Matt. 24.43. *But know this.* Another comparison is now used by Christ to encourage His disciples to watchfulness. If anyone hears that thieves are going about at night, his fears and suspicions do not let him sleep. We are warned that the coming of Christ will be as a thief and we are expressly foretold always to keep awake, in case He finds us sleeping and sweeps us in with the wicked. Thus we have no excuse for idleness, especially since it is not the breaking of a wall, nor the loss of our goods, that is to be feared, but a deadly wound which, unless we take heed, leads to the destruction of the soul. The object of these words is that Christ's warning may rouse us. Although judgment is delayed for a long period, yet it is imminent at any moment. It is absurd to sleep when there is suspicion in the air and danger is at hand.

Matt. 24.45. *Who then is the faithful . . . servant.* This passage is more exactly handed down by Luke who inserts Peter's question, which gave occasion for a new parable. When Christ said there was no place for idleness with the danger of His coming like a thief Peter asked whether this teaching were applied to all or to the twelve only. Always (as we have noticed elsewhere) the disciples used to reckon they were unfairly treated unless they were exempt from the common lot and given long preference over all others. Now when they are given terms that are not very attractive or pleasant, they look in all directions in their astonishment. The object of Christ's reply is that if any of the ordinary people should keep watch it is intolerable that the Apostles should be dozing. Previously, in general terms, Christ had urged the whole family to stay awake to meet Him, but now He demands exceptional diligence from His leading servants who are put in charge of the rest, that by their example they may show the way of sober attentiveness and frugal temperance. These words are a caution that they are not honoured with the distinction of doing nothing and doing what you please. Since they have a higher rank of honour granted them, a greater burden falls on them. Therefore they are particularly taught to exercise faith and prudence. Hence any may learn who are called to the responsibility of office that they are more obliged to fulfil their tasks without slackness, and, with all their care and effort, to strive to do their duty. It is enough for common servants to do their portion of their individual jobs, but the stewards must go much further, since their responsibility embraces the needs of the whole household. Otherwise Christ charges them with ingratitude, as having been chosen before others and not living up to their honour. Why should God put them over the rest unless to excel them all, in singular faith and prudence? Sober and watchful attention is laid on all without distinction, but in the pastors lethargy is more shameful and less excusable. He actually goes on to offer them reward to rouse their diligence.

Matt. 24.48. *But if that evil servant shall say, etc.* In these words Christ briefly shows the source of the carelessness that creeps on evil servants. It is because they trust in a longer delay, and thus plunge themselves further into the dark. They make out that the day of giving accounts will never come, and assure themselves of impunity, on the pretext of Christ's absence. But it is impossible that the thought of waiting for Him, as often as it comes to us, should not shake us from our sleep. Rather must it increasingly check our wild living lest we are carried off in our wickedness. So no encouragement makes a keener or more effective impression on us than to hear that grim tribunal set in our midst; which none can escape. That each of us may be watchful to discharge his duties with energy, and carefully and properly keep himself in control, let us frequently turn to think of God's final and sudden coming, which the reprobate delight to scorn. In passing, Christ warns us how easily insolence increases once we throw off restraint and chase off on a sinful career. This is not only a dissolute, worthless servant that Christ describes, but one whose boldness rises to the point of upsetting the whole house, wildly abusing his own measure of authority, dealing savagely with his fellow-servants, wastefully dissipating the lord's goods, and mocking him as he does it. The penalty is given as a deterrent is no ordinary one, for such outrageous sin deserves the greater penalty.

Luke 21.47. *And that servant.* We must weigh seriously the circumstance, recorded by Luke alone, that as a man knowingly and willingly casts contemptuous insult on the Lord, so much the greater punishment he deserves. A comparison is made between greater and lesser, to this effect. If a servant caught in imprudence does not escape a penalty, what will be done to the perverse and rebellious one who more or less deliberately tramples on his lord's authority? We must remember that those who are set over the Church's government do not sin in ignorance but cheat their Lord perversely and wickedly. A general lesson may be taken from this, that it is vain for men to take refuge in a plea of ignorance to escape their guilt. If a mortal man claims the right to choose to ask his servants to keep house without insult or upset: how much greater authority must the Son of God possess? Those who minister to Him

107

should take great pains to be instructed by his commandments and not rush about at their own discretion to business they do not understand, but remain entirely at His bidding—particularly when he has told us what we are to do, and always replies with kindness to our questions. Certainly our ignorance always goes hand in hand with idle and crass neglect. It is useless for us to seek refuge in the words, Unknown fault— Unclaimed guilt: the heavenly Judge declares against this, saying that although such lapses receive lighter punishment they will not escape it altogether. If ignorance is no excuse, what horrible vengeance hangs over those who sin deliberately, who rush madly against conscience into acts that provoke God? The more generous the instruction, the more ground for punishment, if they are not teachable and yield obedience. Evidently it is a rotten shifty device for men to reject the clear teaching of the Gospel today and try to screen their great obstinacy with their fathers' not knowing any better: as if ignorance were an adequate shield to ward off God's judgment. Granted that mistakes may be pardoned in the erring, for the same pardon to be granted to the wilful sinners is quite unfair, since they rage against God with deliberate ill-will.

Luke 21.48. *And to whomsoever much.* Christ shows another case for the more favoured disciples being beaten more severely if they despise their calling and sell themselves into general laxity. The more a man is elevated, the more he should think of the trust given him, and all the more of the account he will have to render in due course. If any of us is endued with higher gifts and fails to give the Lord a richer return, like a field cultivated at greater expense, he will pay dearly for the wasteful abuse of grace he has suppressed or profaned.

Luke 21.49. *I came to cast fire upon the earth.* We may easily infer from the final passage that this was one of Christ's last discourses and recorded by Luke out of time. The meaning is, that utmost confusion is poured on the world by Christ, like mixing earth and heaven. In a metaphor, the Gospel is compared to fire because it alters the appearance of things with violence. Since the disciples have the false idea that the Kingdom of God will come in quiet and sleep, Christ counters with a dread burning, in which the world must first be consumed. As the first marks of it were already appearing Christ urges the disciples to realise from this that the power of the Gospel is upon them. Already (he says) great movements are kindling into heat. It is not right for you to tremble at this, for it is rather ground for good confidence: for my part I rejoice to see my labours bearing fruit. All ministers of the Gospel ought to apply the same point to themselves and, in a troubled world, press on more keenly with their duties. Note that in this same fire of doctrine (which burns indiscriminately) the chaff and stubble are destroyed and the gold and silver are refined.

Luke 21.50. *I have a baptism to be baptised with.* In these words the Lord declares that only the last act awaits Him, that in His death He may consecrate the world's renewal. Since it was an awful shaking that he has spoken of, and that burning of the human race a thing full of terror, He teaches that the firstfruits must be offered in His own Person, in case the disciples later take it hard to realise their share in it. He compares death (as elsewhere) with baptism, for after submersion of the flesh, for a time, in death, the children of God shall rise soon to life again, so that death should be no more than passing through the midst of the waters. He says that He is sorely pressed until that baptism be fulfilled, in order to encourage each one of us, by His example, to bear the cross and face death. It is not natural for a man to face death, or any decline in our present state, but when we see the glory of heaven on the further shore, and the blessed and eternal peace, our longing for them shall make us face death with patience and carry us on eagerly, wherever faith and hope lead on.

Then shall the kingdom of heaven be likened unto ten virgins, which took their lamps, and went forth to meet the bridegroom. And five of them were foolish, and five were wise. For the foolish, when they took their lamps, took no oil with them: but the wise took oil in their vessels with their lamps. Now while the bridegroom tarried, they all slumbered and slept. But at midnight there is a cry, Behold, the bridegroom! Come ye forth to meet him. Then all those virgins arose, and trimmed their lamps. And the foolish said unto the wise, Give us of your oil; for our lamps are going out. But the wise answered, saying, Peradventure there will not be enough for us and for you: go ye rather to them that sell, and buy for yourselves. And while they went away to buy, the bridegroom came; and they that were ready went in with him to the marriage feast: and the door was shut. Afterward came also the other virgins, saying, Lord, Lord, open to us. Bur he answered and said, Verily I say unto you, I know you not. Watch therefore, for ye know not the day nor the hour. (Matt. 25.1-13)

This exhortation goes on similar lines to the previous one (as the last sentence shows) but is rightly added to confirm the faithful in perseverance. The Lord knew how human nature inclined to the easy ways, and that their usual course was to weary over a long period of time, take sudden dislike and give up. To cure this disease, He taught the disciples that they were not well equipped unless they had a supply of endurance over long stretches. Once the object of the parable is understood there is no reason to labour over minute details which are quite beside Christ's intention. There is great ingenuity over the lanterns, the vessels, the oil: the plain and natural answer is that keen enthusiasm for a short term is not enough unless accompanied by long unwearying effort. Christ makes the point with a most apt simile. Shortly before He had encouraged His disciples to be provided with lamps as they had to make a journey through dark and gloomy regions, but without a supply of oil the lampwick gradually dries up in the lanterns and the light fails. Christ says now that the faithful need constant replenishment of power to foster the light kindled in their hearts: otherwise their speed will give out on them halfway up the course.

Matt. 25.1. *Then shall the kingdom of heaven be likened.* This expression means the state of the Church to come, as it was to be gathered under the auspices of Messiah. A remarkable title, and used deliberately in case the faithful deceive themselves with a false picture of the blessed perfection. He took the comparison from the common customs of life. It was a childish speculation of Jerome and his like to force the passage into praising virginity. Christ only meant to relieve the weary burden that might come out of delay in His coming. He says therefore that He makes no demands but what, in ordinary use, is supplied by friends at the solemn ceremony of marriage. It was the accepted thing that virgins (for their tenderness and delicacy) should by way of respect accompany the groom to the bride-chamber. The parable turns on the fact that the duty was not satisfied by the initial girding-up and preparation unless it was continued to the end.

Matt. 25.2. *Five were wise.* At the end of the previous chapter the Lord particularly required the stewards to be wise, for it is fair that whoever bears more responsibility and puts through difficult business should behave with greater prudence. Now He asks in general some prudence of all the children of God: that they might not recklessly run and expose themselves to Satan's capture. The kind of prudence He means is the careful provision of all things needful for pursuing our course of life. Though the time is short, yet the heat of our impatience makes it appear to drag out too long. And such is our poverty that from time to time we run out of supplies.

Matt. 25.5. *While the bridegroom tarried.* This sleeping is taken in a bad sense by some, as if the faithful, along with the rest, abandoned themselves to lazy living and drowsing in the vanities of the age, but this is quite foreign to the mind of Christ and the context of the parable. It is more probably taken of death, that comes over the faithful before the coming of Christ: for we must expect our salvation not only in this time, but after this life, when we rest in Christ. I take it in the simpler sense of earthly occupations, in which the faithful are bound to be involved as long as they live in the flesh. Though forgetfulness of the

Kingdom of God should never creep over them, it is quite apt to compare the distraction of this world's business to sleep. Men cannot be so alert to meeting Christ that cares of various kinds should not distract or hinder or engage their minds. So while they watch, they are in part asleep. As regards the cry, I take it metaphorically for His sudden arrival. We know as often as anything turns out new or unexpected, men are used to making a tumult. Indeed, the Lord cries daily that He will come soon, but at that day the whole system of the world will resound, and dread Majesty will so fill heaven and earth as not only to rouse the dreamers, but actually to raise the dead from their graves.

Matt. 25.8. *And the foolish said unto the wise.* He taxes them with their late repentance, in that they do not notice their failings until the door is shut on their remedy. Folly that makes no provision for the long term is condemned, for they are pleased to live carelessly in their indigence, and allow the time for shared dealings to pass by, in despite of offered assistance. Since they did not think in time to buy oil, Christ mocks their tardy understanding, and shows how their sleepiness will be punished, when they find themselves empty and dry, with no improvement.

Matt. 25.9. *There will not be enough for us.* We know that the Lord's gifts are distributed diversely to everyone in due measure, in order that they may give mutual help to one another and devote their individual endowments to the common good, and that in this way the sacred connexion of the members of the Church is fostered. But here Christ marks the time when each will lift his own load and be called to the tribunal, that he may bring with him whatever he has achieved in his body. Rightly then is that portion of grace which each has received and laid up for himself compared to provision for a journey, which will not be enough for many. What follows directly, *go ye and buy for yourselves,* is not a warning but a reproof, meaning, 'There was a time for buying before, which you ought not to have neglected: then was there oil for sale, but now you have lost the means of obtaining it.' The papists are foolish to infer from this that the gift of perseverance can be acquired by our own powers or industry. The word buying does not indicate any price at all, as is evident from Isaiah (55.1), where it is clear that the Lord in calling us to buy demands no payment, but says that He has stocks of wine and milk which He will freely give. There is no other way of obtaining it therefore than to receive by faith what is offered to us. It follows at last that the door of the heavenly Kingdom will be shut on all who have made poor provision, for failing in mid-course. We must not here seek the details, how Christ says that the foolish virgins set out to buy, for it simply means that all must be excluded from entry to heaven who at the precise moment are not prepared.

But when the Son of man shall come in his glory, and all the angels with him, then shall he sit on the throne of his glory; and before him shall be gathered all the nations: and he shall separate them one from another, as the shepherd separateth the sheep from the goats: and he shall set the sheep on his right hand, but the goats on the left. Then shall the King say unto them on his right hand, Come, ye blessed of my Father, inherit the kingdom prepared for you from the foundation of the world: for I was an hungred, and ye gave me meat; I was thirsty, and ye gave me drink: I was a stranger, and ye took me in naked, and ye clothed me: I was sick, and ye visited me: I was in prison, and ye came unto me. Then shall the righteous answer him, saying, Lord, when saw we thee an hungred, and fed thee? or athirst, and gave thee drink? And when saw we thee a stranger, and took thee in? or naked, and clothed thee? And when saw we thee sick, or in prison, and came unto thee? And the King shall answer and say unto them, Verily I say unto you, Inasmuch as ye did it unto one of these my brethren, even these least, ye did it unto me. Then shall he say also unto them on the left hand, Depart from me, ye cursed, into the eternal fire which is prepared for the devil and his angels: for I was an hungred, and ye gave me no meat: I was thirsty, and ye gave me no drink: I was a stranger, and ye took me not in; naked and ye clothed me not; sick, and in prison, and ye visited me not. Then shall they also answer, saying, Lord, when saw we thee an hungred, or athirst, or a stranger, or naked, or sick, or in prison, and did not minister unto thee? Then shall he answer them, saying, Verily I say unto you, Inasmuch as ye did it not unto one of these least, ye did it not unto me. And these shall go away into eternal punishment: but the righteous into eternal life. (Matt. 25.31-46)

And every day he was teaching in the temple; and every night he went out, and lodged in the mount that is called the mount of Olives. And all the people came early in the morning to him in the temple, to hear him. (Luke 21.37-38)

Christ continues the same teaching, and what He had described in parables He now puts across plainly and without figure of speech. Briefly, the faithful are to encourage themselves to live in holiness and uprightness. They must look with the eyes of faith to the life of heaven, which is now concealed but will be revealed at last, at the coming of Christ. When He declares that He will sit on His throne of glory when He comes with His angels, He contrasts that last revelation with the confused and unruly agitations of earthly warfare: as if He said, that He did not appear in order to set up His Kingdom without delay, but that they needed hope and patience, lest the disciples became discouraged at the long postponement. We may gather that this was added for the sake of the disciples that they might put away their mistaken idea of present and immediate happiness, tie their thoughts to the second coming of Christ, and not give up or faint through His absence. Then, at length, He says, He will take the high title of King. Though He has inaugurated His Kingdom on earth (*regnum suum auspicatus est in terris*) and now sits at the right Hand of the Father, so as to govern heaven and earth with supreme authority, yet that throne is not yet lifted up in the sight of men from which His divine Majesty will shine out on the last day, with far greater brightness than now. Then will the glory have its full effect, which now we only taste by faith. Christ now sits on the heavenly throne as far as He needs to restrain enemies and protect the Church, but then in the open, He will ascend His tribunal to establish perfect order in heaven and earth, to lay His enemies low beneath His feet, to gather His faithful into the company of life eternal and blessed. In the end the event itself will show for what purpose the Kingdom was given Him by the Father. He says *he will come in his glory*: because as long as He lived on earth a mortal man, it lay hidden under the despised form of a servant. He calls it His own glory, though elsewhere He ascribes it to the Father, in the same sense: He means the divine glory simply which shone in the Father when it was concealed in Himself.

Matt. 25.32. *And before him shall be gathered.* He extols His Kingdom in great magnificent terms, that His disciples may learn to hope for a different kind of happiness from what they had imagined. For this alone satisfied them, namely, the liberation of their nation from the miseries that oppressed them, so that it might be manifest that God had not in vain struck a covenant with Abraham and his seed. Christ extends the fruits of the redemption brought in Him far further, for He will be judge of the whole world. To encourage the faithful to holy living, He says that it will not be the same thing for the good as for the bad, for He will bring with Him the reward which is laid up for each. Briefly He declares that the state of His Kingdom will achieve its due order when the just have obtained their crown of glory and the wicked have paid the penalty they have accrued. As for that separation of goats from sheep which is put off to that day, He means that now the wicked are mixed in with the holy and good, so that they live together in God's one flock. The comparison seems to be taken from Ezekiel (34.17, 20f), where the Lord complains of the rudeness of the goats who jostle the poor sheep with their horns, and spoil the pastures and foul the waters: and declares He will avenge it. Christ aims His words at making the condition of the faithful less bitter for them, when they are at present forced to live with the goats, to bear their hard insults and annoyances; secondly to take care for themselves, lest the contagion of faults affect them also; thirdly, that they should know their efforts to live a holy and innocent life are not mocked, when the difference is, one day, going to be made plain.

Matt. 25.34. *Come, ye blessed.* We must remember Christ's purpose: He wishes His disciples to be content with hope now, that they may look forward with patient and quiet minds to the fruition of the heavenly Kingdom. He also wishes them to strive earnestly and not weary in the right path. Referring to this second part, He promises the inheritance of the skies to none other but those who with good works aim at the prize of the heavenly calling. Before speaking directly of the reward of good works, He shows in passing how the source of salvation flows from a deeper spring. Calling them *blessed of my Father* He reminds them that their blessing started from the free favour of God. To Hebrews, to be blessed of God means to be dear or beloved with . God. Not only the faithful used this way of speaking to celebrate the grace of God among men, but also those who had fallen away from true piety still kept to this principle. 'Come in, thou blessed of the Lord', said Laban to Abraham's servant. We see how this form of praise came to them from nature, as they use it to worship God for all the good things they received. No doubt then that Christ begins from the free love of God in describing the salvation of the godly; by this, those who aspire to righteousness under the leading of the Spirit in this life, are predestinated to life eternal. What He says a little further on makes the same point, that the Kingdom is prepared for them from the beginning of the world, for they come into possession of it at the last day. Though one might easily object that a reward was laid up for their future merits, yet if anyone will examine the words without polemics he will allow that the grace of God is implicitly given the true credit. Christ does not simply invite the faithful to possess the Kingdom as if they had achieved it by their own merits, but expressly says they received it as heirs. Note another object which the Lord had in view. Though life for the godly may be nothing but a wretched, sad exile, so that the earth scarcely keeps them in existence, and though they labour under hard poverty, reproaches and all kinds of difficulties, in order that they may overcome these obstacles with a brave and keen spirit the Lord testifies that a Kingdom is made ready for them elsewhere. It is no common exhortation to be patient, when men are fully persuaded that their efforts are not in vain. In case our minds are cast down by the vaunting pride of the ungodly, in case our own miseries weaken the strength of our hope, let us always turn our thoughts to our inheritance, which awaits us in heaven: for it does not depend on any uncertain outcome, but was prepared for us from God even before we had been born. I say, for each of the elect, for here Christ turns towards the blessed of the Father. As for the words here being *the kingdom was prepared from the beginning of the world* and in another place *before the creation of heaven and earth*, there is nothing odd about this. Christ does not here fix the exact time at which the inheritance of eternal life was appointed for the children of God, but is only recalling us to God's fatherly care, in which He embraced us before we were born, and from that He confirms the certainty of our hope, for the turbulent uprisings of the world cannot hurt our life.

Matt. 25.35. *For I was an hungred.* If this were a debate on the cause of our salvation the Papists might well infer that our eternal life was merited by good works; but all that Christ was intending was to encourage His people to care for good and right conduct, and it is wrong to squeeze any meaning out of His words on the value of the merits of works. They insist on the causal particle—a weak argument: we know that it does not always signify cause, but consequence rather, when eternal life is promised to the just. There is another, plainer solution. We do not deny that a reward is promised for good works, but we say it is free, for it depends on adoption. Paul boasts (II Tim. 4.8) that a crown of righteousness is laid up for him, but where does he get his confidence unless from being a member of Christ, who is the one heir of eternal life? He says the righteous Judge will give him that crown: but where does he get that prize, except for his free adoption, and from being given that righteousness of which we are all empty? There are two things to hold on to; the faithful are called to possession of the heavenly Kingdom in respect of good works, not because they merited it through the righteousness of their works or because they were themselves the authors of the acquisition, but because God justifies those whom He first elected. Secondly, although they aspire for righteousness under the leading of the Spirit, yet they never satisfy God's Law, and no reward is due them, but what is given freely, is called their reward. Christ does not detail the whole character of the godly and holy life, but for example's sake touches on certain duties of love by which we give proof of our adherence to God. Although the service of God is higher than love for men, and so faith and supplication are of more worth than almsgiving Christ does well to bring forward instances of true righteousness which are more apparent. If a man despised God but were still warmhearted towards men, his acts of mercy would do him no good in God's pleasure, for all the time He was cheated of his due. Christ does not make righteousness add up to almsgiving, but gives the clearest signals, so to speak, of what is a holy and upright life. The faithful do not only make claims with their lips, but prove their service of God in concrete acts.

It is quite ridiculous for fanatical persons on the pretext of this passage to withdraw from the hearing of the Word and from the practice of the holy Supper and the other spiritual exercises: on the same plea they might put away faith also, and the endurance of the cross, and prayers, and chastity. Christ had no intention of binding the pattern of life contained in the two tables of the Law to part of the second table. It is foolish for monks and pinhead disputants of that sort to invent six works of mercy (as Christ mentions no more); as if even children could fail to understand that in synecdoche *all* the duties of love are being praised. To comfort the mourner, aid the unjustly oppressed, give counsel to the simple, snatch poor souls from the jaws of wolves— these are no less laudable mercies than clothing the naked and feeding the hungry. Christ in commending the works of love to us does not exclude what belongs to the service of God. He warns His disciples that it will be the authentic proof of a holy life if they give themselves to works of charity, according to the word of the Prophet, 'I wish mercy and not sacrifice' (Hos. 6.6). Even hypocrites in all their greed and cruelty and fraud and grasping and pride put up a front of pompous ceremony, to pretend to sanctity. We gather from this, that if we wish our life approved by the supreme Judge we should not wander in our own fancies but look and see what He chiefly wants from us. Those who depart from His commandments, for all their sweat and fretting over works of their own devising, will, at the last day, come to hear this (Isa. 1.12), 'Who hath required this at your hand?'

Matt. 25.37. *Then shall the righteous answer.* Christ makes the righteous doubt (yet they knew it all the time) His willingness to check the account of man's deserts. As this was not so deeply fixed in their minds as it should have been, He brings the matter right before their eyes. How can we be so slow and slack in our well-doing, unless it is that the promise is not firmly in our hearts, that all we expend on the poor will be repaid by God with interest? Christ teaches us to rise above the reactions of the flesh; whenever our poor brother asks our trust and aid, the face of a man in wretchedness should not make us hesitate to do good.

Matt. 25.40. *Verily I say unto you.* As Christ has just shown us figuratively that our minds do not yet comprehend the worth He places on duties of love, He now makes open declaration that He will reckon as done to Himself whatever we have put out upon His people. We would have to be very dull if this saying did not wring pity from our inmost being, that Christ is either neglected or given care in the person of those who need our assistance. As often as we are reluctant to help the poor let the sight of the Son of God come before our eyes, for to deny Him anything is sacrilege of the deepest order. These words show that in the end He acknowledges the good deeds that were per- formed freely with no thought of reward. When He bids us do good to the hungry and naked and strangers and captives, from whom we can expect no payment in return, we must look to Him who freely binds Himself to us; all that otherwise might have seemed lost He allows to be charged to His own account. Only the faithful are expressly commended to our pity here. Others are not to be altogether scorned, but the nearer each approaches to God the dearer He should be to us. Though there is a common tie that binds all the children of Adam, the mutual link between the children of God is more holy. Since those who belong to the household of faith are properly put above the outsiders, Christ specifically names them. His purpose was to encourage the rich and well-provided to relieve the needs of their brothers. It is also a rare consolation for the poor and down-trodden: however much reproach they bear, and are cast down in the eyes of the world, yet to the Son of God they are no less precious than the parts of His own body. To call them brothers bestows on them an incredible honour.

Matt. 25.41. *Depart from me, ye cursed.* He now comes to deal with the reprobate, who are so drunk with their own pathetic prosperity that they dream of a state of perpetual bliss. He declares He will come to be their Judge and shatter the delights in which they are now immersed, not that the coming of Christ will strike them with terror (for they think they have struck a covenant with death, and harden themselves to care nothing for it) but in showing their fearful end He warns the faithful not to envy their present fortune. As we need promises to brace and stiffen us to the effort of living well, threats too are needed to keep us in apprehension and fear. We are taught how desirable it is to be united with the Son of God, for eternal death and fire's torment await all those whom He will turn from Himself at the last day. Then He will order the ungodly to depart from Him, for there are many hypocrites now mixed in with the righteous, as if they had a close affinity with Christ. We have said elsewhere that the word *fire* metaphorically foreshadows the harshness of punishment which passes beyond our understanding. It is totally superfluous ingenuity to inquire, with the sophists, into the matter and form of this fire. By the same reckoning we would ask about the worm which Isaiah associated with the fire (Isa. 66.24 and 30.33). This author shows plainly in another passage that the expression is metaphorical. He compares the Spirit of God to a fan by which the fire is blown up, and sulphur too is added. These terms make us understand the future vengeance of God upon the wicked, more awful than all the torments of earth, which should strike us more with terror than any desire for research. Note that the fire is undying, just as the glory recently promised to the faithful. *Which is prepared for the devil.* Christ contrasts Himself with the devil who is head of all the reprobate. All the devils are rebel angels, but Scripture in many passages ascribe headship to one who gathers to destruction all the ungodly as in one body: just so the faithful gather under Christ to life, and increase in Him, until achieving perfection, they firmly cleave to God Himself. Christ says that gehenna is already prepared for the devil, to prevent the godless trusting they will escape it. They hear that they are involved in the same punishment as the devil, and he certainly, without any hope of release, was long ago sentenced and doomed to gehenna. By *devil's angels* some understand wicked men, but it is more likely that Christ speaks only of demons. There is an implicit reproach in these words that men called to the hope of salvation in the Gospel should have preferred to perish with Satan, and rejecting the Author of salvation should have cast themselves willingly into this wretched condition: not that they were any less appointed to destruction than the devil, but because in their crime we can so clearly see the reason for their ruin, in refusing the grace of their calling. Though the reprobate were appointed to death by God's secret judgment before they were born, yet as long as life is being offered to them they are not reckoned Satan's heirs and fellows; their perdition emerges from their unbelief, it is uncovered; and before it was hidden.

Matt. 25.44. *Then shall they also answer.* The same characterisation as Christ had used before is now repeated: that the reprobate may know that empty pretexts with which they now deceive themselves will do them no good at the last day. How are they so cruelly proud in face of the poor if not because they believe their malice will go unpunished? To shatter such complacency the Lord warns them that they will one day (but too late) feel what now they will not deign to consider: those who now are so plainly set at nought, are as precious to Christ as parts of His very self (*propria membra*).

And it came to pass, when Jesus had finished all these words, he said unto his disciples, Ye know that after two days the passover cometh, and the Son of man is delivered up to be crucified. Then were gathered together the chief priests, and the elders of the people, unto the court of the high priest, who was called Caiaphas; and they took counsel together that they might take Jesus by subtilty, and kill him. But they said, Not during the feast, lest a tumult arise among the people.

Now when Jesus was in Bethany, in the house of Simon the leper, there came unto him a woman having an alabaster cruse of exceeding precious ointment, and she poured it upon his head, as he sat at meat. But when the disciples saw it, they had indignation, saying, to what purpose is this waste? For this ointment might have been sold for much, and given to the poor. But Jesus perceiving it said unto them, Why trouble ye the woman? for she hath wrought a good work upon me. For ye have the poor always with you; but me ye have not always. For in that she poured this ointment upon my body, she did it to prepare me for burial. Verily I say unto you, Wheresoever this gospel shall be preached in the whole world, that also which this woman hath done shall be spoken of for a memorial of her. (Matt. 26.1-13)

Now after two days was the feast of the passover and the unleavened bread: and the chief priests and the scribes sought how they might take him with subtilty and kill him: for they said, Not during the feast, lest haply there shall be a tumult of the people.

And while he was in Bethany in the house of Simon the leper, as he sat at meat, there came a woman having an alabaster cruse of ointment of spikenard very costly; and she brake the cruse, and poured it over his head. But there were some that had indignation among themselves, saying, To what purpose hath this waste of the ointment been made? For this ointment might have been sold for above three hundred pence, and given to the poor. And they murmured against her. But Jesus said, Let her alone; why trouble ye her? she hath wrought a good work on me. For ye have the poor always with you, and whensoever ye will ye can do them good: but me ye have not always. She hath done what she could: she hath anointed my body aforehand for the burying. And verily I say unto you, Wheresoever the gospel shall be preached throughout the whole world, that also which this woman hath done shall be spoken of for a memorial of her. (Mark 14.1-9)

Now the feast of unleavened bread drew nigh, which is called the Passover. And the chief priests and the scribes sought how they might put him to death; for they feared the people. (Luke 22.1-2)

This is a further confirmation by Christ of what we have seen Him foretell His disciples on several occasions. This last telling is also the clearest, showing that He willingly offered Himself to die, and it had to be so, for only in a sacrifice of obedience could God be pleased. He further wished to prevent their being offended and discouraged by any thought that necessity dragged Him to His death. So the statement served two purposes. First, to testify, that the Son of God went to face death of His own will, to reconcile the world to the Father (since there was no other way to expiate their guilty crimes or win them righteousness). Second, to show that this was not the death forced by the violence of an oppressor, which He could not escape, but rather that He faced death of His own will. He declares that He purposely came to Jerusalem to seek to meet death there. When He was free to withdraw and pass the whole of that period in safe retreat, precisely then He knowingly and willingly came to the centre of affairs. At the time His disciples took no advantage of the warning that it was through obedience to His Father that He acted, but afterwards their faith was built up, in no ordinary sense, by this lesson. Today also it is a rare benefit for us to have set in front of us as a vivid mirror-image the spontaneous sacrifice by which all the world's transgressions were blotted out, for thus we see the Son God, eagerly and bravely advancing to death, to be Victor over death already.

Matt. 26.3. *Then were gathered together.* Matthew does not mean they were gathered during those two days but introduces the narrative to show that Christ had more than human knowledge in fixing the day of His death. How could any guesswork have led Him to it, when even His enemies were of a mind to delay it? It means that He spoke of His death in the Spirit of prophecy, at a time when no one could have suspected it was so near. John explains the reason for the holding of this meeting by scribes and priests: it was the ever increasing concourse of the people of Jesus. At that time, on Caiaphas' urging, a decree was passed that He should be put to death, since He could be got rid of in no other way, but the opportunity did not seem ripe until the festival was over and the crowd dispersed. We gather that for all that these ravenous dogs desired and longed for the death of Christ, however madly they rushed on Him, they were still restrained by God's secret hold, so that nothing should be performed by their counsel or will. As far as they can, they look to another occasion: but God, despite their wishes, hurries on the hour. It is of great importance for us to understand that Christ was not rudely hauled off to die through the passion of His enemies, but led by God. Our faith in propitiation is founded on an acceptable offering being made with the victim which He had appointed from the beginning. He wished His Son to be slaughtered on the day of Passover, that the old figure should give place to the one sacrifice of eternal redemption. Those whose only intention was Christ's overthrow thought another time more suitable: God who had appointed Him as Victim for the expiation of sin chose that very day to bring into contrast the body and the shadow. The result is a brighter revelation of the fruits of Christ's suffering.

Matt. 26.6. *Now when Jesus was in Bethany.* What the Evangelist now tells happened a little before Christ came to Jerusalem, but suitably it comes in here to let us see the sudden opportunity that pushed the priests into haste. They did not dare attack Christ with open violence, yet to secure Him by trickery was not just so easy. But now an unlooked-for plan is unexpectedly produced by Judas, and its very ease of execution changes their counsels. John's narrative is slightly different here from Matthew's and Mark's but the inconsistency, which some interpreters have wrongly inferred as grounds for making up a new account, is soon resolved. The name of the woman who anointed Christ is omitted by the two Evangelists and given by John. Yet he makes no mention of the man who invited Christ to the meal, while Matthew and Mark expressly record that they dined at the house of Simon the leper. Between John saying that the feet were anointed and our writers, the head, there is no contradiction. Unguents were not poured on the feet: but as a more generous than usual amount was poured out, John, to give fuller detail, says that even the feet were smeared with oil. Mark says, when the alabaster was broken, all the unguent spilled over the head. It agrees very well with this that it flowed right down to His feet. Let us keep certain that the same story is recorded by all.

Matt. 26.8. *But when the disciples saw.* This is also the usual practice of the Evangelists, when one has raised a matter, for several to be included, if they have all agreed. So John says that the grumbling started with Judas who betrayed Christ, and Matthew and Mark involve all the disciples together with him. None of the others of course would ever have dared to grumble if Judas' slander had not wickedly set the idea alight in their minds. There was just enough plausibility in the criticism of the needless expense to run quickly through the others like a contagion. The example teaches us of the great danger there is in malicious and poisoned tongues. Persons, by nature fair and sincere and restrained, must take prudent heed to themselves or they will be deceived by mean words and easily trapped in unjust judgments. If Christ's disciples take sides with Judas over a light and silly piece of credulity what shall become of us if we are too free to admit idle gossip—when we always make evil of good deeds? Another warning may be taken from this, not to pronounce rashly on a matter not sufficiently understood. The disciples seize on Judas' words: because there is some pretext to it, they rush to censure. They should have inquired more closely if the deed deserved blame: especially when the Master was there, on whose judgment all abides. Let us note, that opinions formed without the leading of the Word of God are of no account: none of us (as Paul shows) lives to himself or dies to himself, but all must stand at the judgment-seat of Christ to give account (Rom. 14.10 and II Cor. 5.10). Though there was a great difference between Judas and the rest—he was putting up a treacherous cover for his own theft, they were pushed into it by foolish lack of thought—we can see how they were drawn away from Christ and linked to Judas in their imprudence.

Matt. 26.10. *Why trouble ye.* It is wonderful that Christ whose whole life was a rule and example of temperance and frugality, should approve extravagant expense now, which appears very much a matter of luxury and unnecessary indulgence. Note how He defends it. He does not declare the woman to have acted rightly, in terms of something He would wish done every day, but testifies that her single act is pleasing to God, because it had to be done for a good cause. Though Christ had no desire for unguent, the anointing pleased Him because of its circumstances. We gather that some particular duties are pleasing in God's sight on occasion which should not properly be taken as an example. There is no doubt that it was by the secret prompting of the Spirit that Mary was induced to anoint Christ: as it is certain that as often as the saints are called to any extraordinary work they have been impelled by exceptional motives, attempting nothing without God's lead and guidance. There was no injunction given, that Mary should perform this anointing; there was no need for a law to be made to cover one action: as the heavenly calling is the one principle of action, she was guided by the breath of the Spirit that in sure confidence she should do this in duty to Christ. In His answer Christ not only defended one woman's action, but gave force to all who make triumph in holiness, well-satisfied that they and their works are approved by the Lord. Godly men are often criticised and indeed openly condemned unjustly, men who know themselves to be in good conscience, doing nothing other than at God's bidding: they are reckoned proud when they despise the world's judgment and are content with the approval of God alone. It is a hard temptation, and one almost impossible to resist—the crushing effect of a general, though false, consensus against us. We must learn the lesson that no men ever will be constantly encouraged to good works unless they depend on the bidding of God, and no other. So Christ here takes the issue between good and evil no further than His own assessment. In affirming the woman's good work, which the disciples had condemned, He checks by His voice the rash judgment of men who give themselves free licence to give out justice.

We should learn to rely on these words of praise and utterly disregard whatever kind of casual gossip surrounds our way in the world. Let us understand that what men condemn, God approves. See how Isaiah (50.7) calls God his sponsor when men overwhelm him with slander. See how Paul appeals to the day of the Lord (I Cor. 4.3 and 4). Our lesson is to defer no further to men's judgments than will give them a firm example of obedience to God, and when the world rises against us with a loud voice, let it be sufficient comfort for us that what is reckoned bad on earth is declared good in heaven.

Matt. 26.11. *For ye have the poor always with you.* Christ's defence of the anointing is not for our imitation but to teach us the reason for its earning favour. We should take careful note: in case we fall in with the papists and invent wrong and extravagant services for God. When they hear how Christ was willing to be anointed by Mary they reckon that He is delighted with incense, candles, splendour in vestment, and like ceremonial. Hence all their pompous ritual: they believe they would not be giving God His rightful service unless they lavish expense upon it. Christ makes a clear exception here, for what He willed to be done once would not, later on, please Him in the least. Since He says the poor will always be in the world He is distinguishing between the daily services whose practice should flourish among the faithful, and the exceptional which ceased at His ascension into heaven.

Do we want to lay out our money properly on true sacrifices? Let us expend it on the poor: for Christ says that He is not with us, to receive the service of external ceremonies. It is our sure and certain knowledge in the experience of faith (*experientia fidei*) that He is present with us in power and spiritual grace. But it is not in a visible form that He is present with us and able to accept earthly honours. They are stubborn to the point of madness, who force their ridiculous extravagance on Him, against His wish and instruction. When He says there will always be poor we gather that it is not by chance that many are in want, but they are before us by God's sure purpose, that we may exercise our love upon them. In brief, the passage says that though God calls us to dedicate ourselves and our all to Him, He asks for Himself nothing but spiritual worship, with no expense, but wishes us instead to expend upon the poor the money which foolish superstition puts out on His worship.

Matt. 26.12. *She did it to prepare me for burial.* Christ's words here confirm what we have just said, that the precious unguent was welcome, not for its scent, but in respect of burial alone. In this symbol, He wished testimony made that His grave would be of sweet savour to breathe life and salvation upon all the world. So in John, Mary is praised for the unguent being reserved unto the day of burial. Once the firm reality of the figure came to pass, with Christ leaving the tomb and pouring the life-giving odour of His dying upon, not one house only, but the whole earth—then it would be childish to repeat an action lacking in sense or benefit.

Matt. 26.13. *Wheresoever this Gospel shall be preached.* He says this action will do honour to Mary because the doctrine of the Gospel will be praised. Whence we gather that the reward of our actions does not depend on human opinion but on the testimony of the Word of God. When He says that she will be held in honoured record throughout the whole world, the comparison is an indirect reproach to His disciples, that by consent of all races in foreign and extreme regions of the globe

123

an action will be praised which the men of His own household condemned with such bitterness. Christ reproves His disciples gently for
not holding in due honour a regard for His Kingdom to come: at the
same time His words bear testimony to the calling of the nations on
which our salvation is founded. In what sense the Gospel must be
preached throughout the world, we have explained at chapter 24.

*Then one of the twelve, who was called Judas Iscariot, went unto the
chief priests, and said, What are ye willing to give me, and I will deliver
him unto you? And they weighed unto him thirty pieces of silver. And
from that time he sought opportunity to deliver him unto them.*

*Now on the first day of unleavened bread the disciples came to Jesus,
saying, Where wilt thou that we make ready for thee to eat the passover?
And he said, Go into the city to such a man, and say unto him, The
Master saith, My time is at hand; I keep the passover at thy house with
my disciples. And the disciples did as Jesus appointed them; and they
made ready the passover. Now when even was come, he was sitting at
meat with the twelve disciples.* (Matt. 26.14-20)

*And Judas Iscariot, he that was one of the twelve, went away unto the
chief priests, that he might deliver him unto them. And they, when they
heard it, were glad, and promised to give him money. And he sought
how he might conveniently deliver him unto them.*

*And on the first day of unleavened bread, when they sacrificed the
passover, his disciples say unto him, Where wilt thou that we go and
make ready that thou mayest eat the passover? And he sendeth two of
his disciples, and saith unto them, Go into the city, and there shall meet
you a man bearing a pitcher of water: follow him; and wheresoever he
shall enter in, say to the goodman of the house, The Master saith, Where
is my guest-chamber, where I shall eat the passover with my disciples?
And he will himself shew you a large upper room furnished and ready for
us. And the disciples went forth, and came into the city, and found as he
had said unto them: and they made ready the passover.*

And when it was evening he cometh with the twelve. (Mark 14.10-17)

*And Satan entered into Judas who was called Iscariot, being of the number
of the twelve. And he went away, and communed with the chief priests
and captains, how he might deliver him unto them. And they were
glad, and covenanted to give him money. And he consented, and sought
opportunity to deliver him unto them in the absence of the multitude.*

*And the day of unleavened bread came, on which the passover must be
sacrificed. And he sent Peter and John, saying, Go and make ready for us*

the passover, that we may eat. And they said unto him, Where wilt thou that we make ready? And he said unto them, Behold, when ye are entered into the city, there shall meet you a man bearing a pitcher of water; follow him into the house whereinto he goeth. And ye shall say unto the goodman of the house, The Master saith unto thee, Where is the guest-chamber, where I shall eat the passover with my disciples? And he will show you a large upper room furnished: there make ready. And they went, and found as he had said unto them: and they made ready the passover.

And when the hour was come, he sat down, and the apostles with him.
(Luke 22.3-14)

As far as influencing the heart of Judas—or turning it to better course —Christ's warning had little good effect, for he went straight and unconcerned to make his deal with the men of wickedness. How astonishingly and frightfully stupid he was to see in the pouring-out of the unguent an excuse procured for such a sin, and then, for all Christ's warning, not to realise what it was he was doing. The mere mention of burial should have softened a heart of steel, for it was readily to be inferred from that, that Christ offered Himself as a Victim for the salvation of the human race. In this mirror we can see the blindness of human desires and their effect of bewitching the mind. Judas burned with the desire to rob, and by long use had become hard in wickedness. Now since no other prey comes to hand he does not hesitate treacherously to hand over the Son of God, and Author of life, to death. Although pulled back by holy caution, he leaps ahead with violence. Luke with good reason says expressly that Satan entered into him, not that the Spirit of God had guided him before (for he could not have practised robbery and raiding had he not been Satan's slave), but Luke means that then he was altogether handed into Satan's possession and like a desperate man rushed to his own destruction. Though Satan pushes us into faults day by day and reigns over us when he hurries us into a major course of sin, yet he is finally said to enter into the reprobate when all fear of God is overthrown, the light of reason put out, shame dispelled, and he lays hold upon our intelligence. Such extreme a degree of vengeance God does not bring upon any but those who already are vowed to ruination. Let us learn to repent in good time in case, as our hardness increases, the reign of Satan becomes established in us. Once we have been tossed into his tyrannical power there will be no limit to our frenzy. Note especially that greed was the cause and origin of Judas' terrible blindness: obviously Paul was right to call it the root of all evils (I Tim. 6.10). To go on to ask whether Satan took bodily possession of Judas is frivolous speculation. It is better to consider how monstrous it is that men created in the image of God and destined to be the temple of the Spirit should be changed, not merely into foul stables or drains, but actually into the cursed abode of Satan.

Matt. 26.17. *Now on the first day of unleavened bread.* One asks why it was called the day of unleavened bread—the day preceding the slaying of the lamb. The Law did not forbid the use of leaven until they were eating the lamb. The solution of this problem is easy; the phrase refers to the following day, as is plain enough in Mark and Luke. Since the day of killing and eating the Passover is at hand, and the day began at evening, the disciples ask Christ where He wills to eat the Passover. A more difficult question arises from this, that Christ performed the rite on the day before the nation as a whole celebrated the Passover in public. John plainly declares that as Jesus was crucified the Jews were holding the Passover Eve, not Sabbath Eve. Hence they did not enter the praetorium, to avoid pollution: for on the day following they would be eating Passover. I know some try to evade this, but with very little success. No clever device can get round the fact that on the day on which they crucified Christ they did not hold the festival (on which it would have been forbidden to hold an execution) but on that day held their normal preparation, and proceeded to eat the Passover after the burial of Christ. So we must ask how Christ anticipated it. He did not allow Himself to do anything in the rite that was against the Law's directions. As for those who think the Jews put back the Passover, in their keenness to get rid of Christ, there is a wise refutation in Bucer; and in fact it falls to the ground in its own weakness. I have no doubt that the right day was kept by Christ, and that the Jews followed their long-accustomed practice. First, it is beyond controversy that Christ was killed on the eve of the Sabbath, for He was quickly buried in a near-by tomb before sun-set, because it was necessary to cease work at evening. Also no one doubts that when the Passover and other festival days fell on Friday they were put off to the following day because two days on end without work would have seemed too difficult for the people. The Jews declare that this law came down from the time of the people's return from the Babylonian exile: indeed after an oracle from heaven, in case they might appear to have made an over-bold alteration of God's commands. Now if it were a matter of custom to link the two days into one (as the Jews themselves admit and is found in their ancient records) it is quite reasonable to guess that Christ who celebrated the Passover on the eve of the Sabbath kept to the day appointed by the Law. We know the particular care He gave not to depart one jot from the letter of the Law. Seeing He wished to be bound by the Law, that He might relieve us of its yoke, He forgot not the least article of its oversight. Therefore He would have preferred to omit a usage of outward ceremonial rather than transgress an injunction sent from God and expose Himself to the slander of the wicked. The Jews themselves will not deny that the practice that, when the Passover fell next to Sabbath, the two days were treated as one rest from work, was instituted by the Rabbis. Hence it follows that when Christ departed from common use He was not trying anything contrary to the Law.

Matt. 26.18. *Go into the city to such a man.* Matthew names a particular man: the other two tell us that the disciples were sent as to an unknown man, for they were given the sign of a man carrying a water-pot. The discrepancy is easily resolved. Matthew passes over the miracle and marks him as the man who at that time was unknown to the disciples. No doubt when they came to the house they found one of their friends there. Christ gives him the order, as of right, to make ready for Him and His company, calling Himself Master; and he in return giving immediate obedience. He could have given the man his name straight out, but preferred to direct his disciples to him by a miracle, that when, soon after, they should see him at low ebb their faith should have the backing of this proof. It was no small confirmation that just a few hours before being hauled off to die He gave a clear revelation of His Godhead; testifying that men might know He was not forced by necessity but yielding freely. Perhaps at that actual moment of alarm it did them no good, yet the memory of it was something gained. It is worth our while today to overcome the scandal of the cross to know that as the very hour of death was upon Him, the glory of Godhead appeared in Christ along with the weakness of the flesh. *My time is at hand.* Though He celebrated the Passover in due accordance with the Law, He seems to add this reason deliberately to avoid any accusation of morbid haste. He says the reason for hurry which prevents Him falling in with the regular custom is that He is called to a greater sacrifice. All the same, as we have said, He makes no innovations in the ritual. As often as He drives it home, that the time of His death is at hand, He makes them realise that He hastens to perform the custom because the Father decreed it so. As for His linking true with shadowy sacrifice, He means to encourage the faithful to compare the accomplishment of the deed itself with the old images. The comparison gives no little light on the force and effect of His dying. The Passover had not been ordained for the Jews in order that they might commemorate the ancient deliverance but that they should hope for a future (and indeed a better) one at Christ's hands. This is the intention of Paul's text (I Cor. 5.7) that Christ our Passover is sacrificed for us, etc.

Matt. 26.19. *They did as Jesus appointed them.* The fact that the disciples readily obeyed, draws our attention to their holy submission. They might have hesitated when they were told to go after an unknown man whether they would get from the master of the house what they sought at their Master's command, since they knew that in many places He was not only scorned but actually hated. But they had no worried questions over the outcome, but quietly obeyed His orders. We must keep to this rule, if we wish our faith to be approved, to be satisfied by the command alone, to go at God's bidding, to expect the success He promises, and not to be over anxious.

Matt. 26.20. *Now when evening was come he was sitting.* It was not to eat the Passover that He sat, for it had to be done standing (as travellers in haste, shoes on and staff in hand in the manner of those who snatch food in haste), but after the conclusion of the solemn rite in order to take supper. That is how I interpret it. This is why the Evangelists say, *when even was come,* for they killed the lamb at the beginning of evening and ate its flesh roasted.

And as they were eating, he said, Verily I say unto you, that one of you shall betray me. And they were exceeding sorrowful, and began to say unto him every one, Is it I, Lord? And he answered and said, He that dipped his hand with me in the dish, the same shall betray me. The Son of man goeth, even as it is written of him: but woe unto that man through whom the Son of man is betrayed! good were it for that man if he had not been born. And Judas, which betrayed him, answered and said, Is it I, Rabbi? He saith unto him, Thou hast said. (Matt. 26.21-25)

And as they sat and were eating, Jesus said, Verily I say unto you, One of you shall betray me, even he that eateth with me. They began to be sorrowful, and to say unto him one by one, Is it I? And he said unto them, It is one of the twelve, he that dippeth with me in the dish. For the Son of man goeth, even as it is written of him: but woe unto that man through whom the Son of man is betrayed! good were it for that man if he had not been born. (Mark 14.18-21)

And he said unto them, With desire I have desired to eat this passover with you before I suffer: for I say unto you, I will not eat it, until it be fulfilled in the kingdom of God.

But behold, the hand of him that betrayeth me is with me on the table. For the Son of man indeed goeth, as it hath been determined: but woe unto that man through whom he is betrayed! And they began to question among themselves, which of them it was that should do this thing. (Luke 22.15-16, 21-23)

Matt. 26.21. *One of you shall betray me.* To make Judas' perfidy more detestable He brings out the shame of His sitting together with them at the holy table, all the time he was working out his treachery. If an outsider had done this it would have been more tolerable, but one of His close companions is the schemer, and after setting his wicked plot in motion, actually joins the meal in the guise of friendship; such is the incredible, monstrous deed. So Luke uses the contrast particle, *but behold the hand of him that betrayeth me.* Though Luke puts this word of Christ after the conclusion of the supper, we cannot deduce from that any exact order of time, as we know that it was often overlooked by the Evangelists. Yet I would say it is probable that Judas was present when Christ shared the tokens of His body and blood.

Matt. 26.22. *They began to say to him every one.* I do not think the disciples felt fear, as persons may be terror-struck and become anxious without cause, but seeing they shrink from the crime, they wish to be freed of any suspicion of it. It is a sign of awe that when they are indirectly blamed they do not answer their Master back in anger, but each makes Him his Judge (as we too should chiefly seek to be acquitted from His own mouth) and relying on a good conscience wish Him to testify how far removed they are from such an offence. Christ's reply does not relieve their anxiety nor point out the person of Judas, but only confirms what He had just said: that one of His friends that sat with Him at table would betray Him. It was hard on them to be left in suspense and anxiety for the moment, that they might take time to consider the atrocity of the crime, but another advantage ensued, in their appreciation that the Psalm's prophecy was fulfilled (41.9): 'he that ate pleasant meat with me hath lifted up his heel against me'. Besides, in the person of Judas the Lord wished His people in all ages to be warned not to be shattered or knocked lifeless at traitors in the household, for what He, who is the common Head of the Church, experienced, must happen to us who are His members.

Matt. 26.24. *The Son of man goeth.* Christ here encounters the offence that might otherwise shake godly minds severely. What could be more appalling than that the Son of God be foully betrayed by a disciple, exposed to the frenzy of His enemies, and taken off to a shameful death? Christ declares that all this occurred by the Will of God. The decree He proves by the testimony of Scripture, or He revealed by the mouth of His ancient prophet what had been determined. Now we see the aim of Christ's words: that the disciples should know that whatever happens is guided by God's providence and they should not reckon that chance played any part in His life, or in His death. The use of this teaching extends further still. The fruits of Christ's death have only made their lasting impression upon us when we know that He was not rudely snatched away to the cross by men, but that the sacrifice was ordained by the eternal decree of God, to expiate the sins of the world. Whence do we obtain reconciliation if it is not that Christ placated the Father by His obedience? So let us ever think of the Providence of God which Judas himself and all the ungodly (though they do not want it so, and act against it) must obey. Ever hold on to this, that Christ suffered because, by this kind of expiation, God was pleased. Christ says that Judas is not absolved from blame on the grounds that he did nothing but what was divinely ordained. Though God in His righteous judgment fixed the price of redemption for us as the death of His own Son, nonetheless Judas in betraying Christ, being full of treachery and greed, drew on himself a right condemnation. God's will for the redemption of the world in no way prevents Judas being a wicked traitor. Hence we see, though men cannot do any thing but what God has appointed, they are not for that reason absolved from guilt: their wicked desire leads them on to sin. Granted God may lead them with a rein too light to notice, to a destination unknown, yet nothing is more contrary to their purpose than to obey His decrees. No doubt to human reason these two principles appear inconsistent with each other; that God should arrange human affairs by His Providence so that nothing happens other than by His Will and bidding, and that He should destroy the reprobate by whom He achieves His ends. We see how Christ reconciles these two, placing Judas under a curse although it was divinely appointed that he should plot against God as he did, not that the treachery of Judas should properly be called a work of God, but because God bent the treachery of Judas to the fulfilment of His purpose.

I know that some interpreters try to steer clear of this rock, and say that what was written was fulfilled by Judas' action in so far as God testified by oracle what He knew beforehand. So to soften a doctrine that appears to them rather harsh they put God's prescience in place of His decree, as if God were looking down from a great height on future events but not disposing them by His will. The Spirit composes this debate quite differently: He not only gives the reason for Christ's betrayal as the fact of its being so written but equally of its being so determined. When Matthew and Mark adduce Scripture, Luke leads us direct to the heavenly decree for as he teaches us in Acts, Christ was betrayed not only with God's prescience but by His definite counsel, and, a little later, that Herod and Pilate acted along with the other wicked men in performance of what was pre-ordained by God's hand and purpose. It is a patent and foolish reversal of the facts to take refuge in prescience alone. *Good were it.* This phrase teaches us what a fearful vengeance awaits the godless, who would be more than content never to have been born. Yet this life, frail and loaded down with innumerable troubles is an incomparable benefit of God's. This makes us feel all the more what a detestable sin was theirs, that not only extinguished the precious gifts of God and turned them to ruin but makes it a better thing never to have tasted the goodness of God. This phrase too is worthy of note, *good were it for that man if he had not been born*: although Judas' state was wretched indeed, yet it was good for God that He had created him. In appointing the reprobate to the day of destruction He reveals, in this way too, His glory, as Solomon teaches. So God's secret rule is asserted against any detraction, for it presides over the counsels and works of men, as I have recently remarked.

Matt. 26.25. *And Judas answered.* We often see men with a bad conscience tremble, and yet with their fear and unseen torments there is an instinctive inertia, resulting in a bold claim of denial, but all their boldness gains for them is the discovery of their hidden crime. So with Judas, when his evil conscience tied him up he yet broke into speech: his own inward executioner stirs him up, and yet casts him down with fear and anxiety. Christ takes an indirect hit at the stupidity of his boldness and in his answer invites him to consider the crime he wanted to keep hidden. But a mind possessed by demonic rage could not grasp the sense of this. Let us learn from this example that the wicked by rash excuse merely bring judgment on themselves more quickly.

And as they were eating, Jesus took bread, and blessed, and brake it; and he gave to the disciples, and said, Take, eat; this is my body. And he took a cup, and gave thanks, and gave to them, saying, Drink ye all of it; for this is my blood of the covenant, which is shed for many unto remission of sins. But I say unto you, I will not drink henceforth of this fruit of the vine, until that day when I drink it new with you in my Father's kingdom.

And when they had sung a hymn, they went out into the mount of Olives. (Matt. 26.26–30)

And as they were eating, he took bread, and when he had blessed, he brake it, and gave to them, and said, Take ye: this is my body. And he took a cup, and when he had given thanks, he gave to them: and they all drank of it. And he said unto them, This is my blood of the covenant, which is shed for many. Verily I say unto you, I will no more drink of the fruit of the vine, until that day when I drink it new in the kingdom of God. (Mark 14.22–25)

And he received a cup, and when he had given thanks, he said, Take this, and divide it among yourselves: for I say unto you, I will not drink from henceforth of the fruit of the vine, until the kingdom of God shall come. And he took bread, and when he had given thanks, he brake it, and gave to them, saying, This is my body which is given for you: this do in remembrance of me. And the cup in like manner after supper, saying, This cup is the new covenant in my blood, even that which is poured out for you. (Luke 22.17-20)

As Luke records that the cup was twice offered, we must first ask if there is a repetition (as the Evangelists do sometimes say the same thing twice) or whether Christ, after tasting the cup, repeated the action once more: I think the latter is the likely answer. We know that the holy Fathers observed a reverent practice of tasting at the sacrifices: whence the verse of the Psalm 116.13, 'I will take the cup of salvation, and I will call upon the name of the Lord.' I do not doubt that Christ followed ancient use and tasted at the holy Supper, since it could not otherwise be duly performed, and Luke relates this carefully before proceeding to the narrative of the new mystery, whose order is different from the paschal lamb. It was also in the course of received and normal use that He is expressly said to *have given thanks* after having *taken the cup*. I have no doubt He made prayers at the beginning of the meal, since He was never used to come to table without an invocation of God. Now He wished to repeat the action, not to omit a ceremony which I have just shown to be tied to the sacred tasting.

Matt. 26.26. *And as they were eating.* I do not take these words to mean that the new and far more excellent meal was mixed in with the Passover, but rather at this point an end was put to the former feast. This is expressed more clearly in Luke, when he says *the cup in like manner after supper.* It would have been strange for one and the same mystery to be interrupted by an interval of time. I have no doubt that He proceeded directly after giving the bread to add the cup. What Luke narrates about the cup in particular I apply also to the bread. As they were eating Christ took bread, to invite them to share the new Supper. He gave thanks, which made a preparation and transition to reflect upon the mystery. So when the supper was ended they tasted the sacred bread and the wine: since Christ had aroused them from their inertia, that they should all be attentive to such a sublime mystery. Reason itself demands that this clear testimony of the life of the Spirit should be distinct from the old shadow. *Jesus took bread.* It is uncertain whether a custom today celebrated among Jews was then in use: the head of the household takes a fragment of the common bread and hides it under the cloth, then gives pieces of it to the family. As this human tradition has no foundation in God's commandment, there is no reason why we should work too curiously to seek out its origin. It is possible that it was a plan of Satan's artifice to obscure the mystery of Christ's supper. If the ceremony were then in use among Jews then Christ followed the accepted custom so as to lead the minds of His people to another one, altering the use of bread to a different purpose. This should pass without any debate: that legal figures were abolished, and a new Sacrament was here brought forward by Christ. *When he had given thanks.* Mark and Matthew use the word *blessed*, but as Luke employs in its place the word 'gave thanks' ($\epsilon\dot{v}\chi\alpha\rho\iota\sigma\tau\dot{\eta}\sigma\alpha\varsigma$) there is no ambiguity in sense. Since over the cup they use the word 'giving thanks' they are interpreting the first saying clearly enough. This makes the papists' ignorance more ridiculous, expressing the blessing with the sign of the cross as if Christ had used an exorcism. Remember what I just remarked, that the giving of thanks is linked to the spiritual mystery. Nor does Christ have regard to ordinary eating where the faithful are told to give thanks to God who sustains them in this frail life, for He was turning to the sacred action, to give thanks to God for the eternal salvation of the human race. If the food that goes into the belly should encourage and stimulate us to praise God's fatherly goodness, how much more does He stir and excite us, yes set us on fire, to this act of piety, when He feeds our souls spiritually? *Take, eat.* I do not want to be too prolix here but briefly point out the nature and content of the Lord's institution; then its objects and use, as far as we can gather from the Evangelists. It first strikes us that Christ instituted a Supper which the disciples are to share among themselves. It follows that it is a devilish invention that one man should separate himself from the rest of the company and perform the supper on his own. What could be more inconsistent, that bread should be distributed among all and be eaten separately by one? For all the papists' boast that they have the sub-stance of the Lord's supper in their Masses the nature of the thing makes evident that as often as they celebrate private Masses they erect so many trophies under the devil, to overthrow Christ's Supper. The same words show us what kind of oblation is passed down to us by Christ in the Supper. He bids the disciples to take: He Himself, there-fore, is the only one who offers. When the papists pretend that they offer Christ in the Supper they are starting from quite another source. What a wonderful case of topsy-turvy, that a mortal man bidden to receive the body of Christ should snatch to himself the role of offering it: a priest, self-appointed, sacrifices to God His own Son. At the present I am not going into all the sacrilegious froth that chokes their fictitious oblation. It is enough for me to prove that so far from having anything to do with Christ's institution, it is directly repugnant to it. *This is my body.* I find no fault with those who call these words the consecration of the bread, which make it the symbol of Christ's flesh, so long as the word is taken rightly and accurately. Christ takes and sanctifies bread, which was ordained to the body's nourishment, for another use, to begin to be our spiritual nourishment. This is the 'conversion' (*conversio*) which is mentioned among the ancient writers of the Church. But we must hold at the same time that the bread is not consecrated by whispering and blowing, but by the clear teaching of faith. It is a magical incantation when the consecration is directed to the dead element, for the bread is made the symbol of the body of Christ not to itself, but to us. Briefly, consecration is nothing but a solemn testimony by which God appoints an earthly and corruptible sign to a spiritual use, which cannot take place unless His command and promise are heard clearly for the building-up of faith. Again it is obvious that by obscure muttering and breathing the papists wickedly profane the mystery. As Christ consecrates the bread testifying to us that it is His body we must not imagine there is a change of substance (*substantiae mutatio*) but hold only to the alteration in use. If the world had not long since been bewitched by the devil's craft and, with the invasion of the monster of transubstantiation, been allowed no light of true interpretation today upon these words—it would have been superfluous to spend any longer research upon the sense. Christ declares the bread is His body: the words relate to the Sacrament. We must state that a Sacrament consists in a visible sign to which the thing signified is conjoined and this is its reality (*veritas*). This ground should be familiar enough by now: the name of a thing signified being transferred to the sign. No one with a moderate acquaintance of Scripture will deny that sacramental expression must be taken as metonymy. Figurative uses in general I pass by, for they occur often in Scripture. I only say that as often as an outward sign is called the thing it portrays, then by general consent this is taken as an instance of metonymy. If Baptism be called the washing of regeneration, if the Rock from which water flowed in the desert for the Fathers is called Christ, if the dove is called the holy Spirit, it should start no debate if the name of the things signified is transferred to the signs.

How then does it occur that men who hold reverence for the Lord's words will not allow to be applied to the Supper what is common to all Sacraments? They are delighted with the simple and literal sense. Why shall the same rule not apply to all Sacraments? Unless they allow the Rock to have been Christ in substance, the slander they throw at us is worthless. If we expound that the bread is called body because it is the symbol of the body, they make out that we are overturning the whole teaching of Scripture. But this is no recent rule of speech that we have made up, but one embraced by all, as handed down by Augustine on ancient authority, that the names of spiritual things are, improperly, ascribed to signs and that in this sense all passages of Scripture where there is mention of Sacraments must be explained. When we bring forward an axiom long accepted, what is the object of all their great uproar raised over so-called novelty and break with tradition? Let obstinate men shout as they please, among the sane and moderate this opinion will prevail, that in these words of Christ there is a sacramental mode of speech. Hence it follows that the bread which is called body is the symbol of the body of Christ.

There are two classes of men that rise against us. The papists deluded by their transubstantiation say that bread is not shown, since only the appearance remains without the reality. Paul refutes this mad notion (I Cor. 10.6), affirming that the bread which we break is the communion of the body of Christ. The very nature of Sacrament rejects their notion, for it cannot maintain its integrity unless there is a true outward symbol. How shall we learn that our souls are nourished on Christ's flesh unless a true bread is set before our eyes, not an empty shell? And what will they say about the second symbol? Christ does not say, This is my blood, but *this cup is*. According to them not only the wine but the materials of which the cup is fashioned must be transubstantiated into blood. As for Matthew's words, *I will not drink . . . of this fruit of the vine*, it is clearly shown that it was wine held out to them for them to drink. In all ways the papists' ignorance is plainly refuted. There are others who reject the figurative sense, then immediately like fanatics ask it back. The bread according to them is truly and properly the body, but they do not accep transubstantiation, as lacking all appearance of reason. But when they are asked if Christ be the bread and wine they reply that the reason for the bread being called body is that the body is received under and with it in the Supper. We may readily elicit from this reply that the name of body is improperly transferred to the bread, when it signifies body. It is amazing that those men should always be saying that Christ spoke in respect of a sacramental union and not pay attention to what they are saying. What is the sacramental union of object and sign (*sacramentalis unio rei et signi*)? Is it not that God fulfils, with the hidden power of His Spirit, the action He promises? So these other literal teachers are as laughable as the papists. So far I have expounded the simple meaning of the Lord's words: now we must add that no empty or ineffective sign is set before us, but those who by faith receive His promise are truly partakers of flesh and blood. In vain would the Lord be telling His people to eat bread affirming it to be His body unless the effect truly matched the representation. This is not a question in dispute amongst us, whether truly or merely in sign Christ offers Himself to us to enjoy in the Supper. Even though we see

135

nothing there but bread, He does not leave us with nothing or mock us when He takes our souls to feed them with His flesh. The true eating of the flesh of Christ is not only displayed in sign but demonstrated in real effect.

It is worth while observing three points here: not wrongly to confuse a spiritual act with its sign, not to seek Christ on earth or in earthly elements, and not to imagine any other eating than that which by the hidden power of the Spirit breathes the life of Christ into us—and this we only achieve by faith alone. First (as I have said) let the distinction between the sign and the thing signified remain, unless we wish to turn everything upside-down. There will be no benefit left to the Sacrament unless according to our simple capacity it leads us from the sight of the earthly element to the heavenly mystery. Whoever does not distinguish the body of Christ from the bread, and the blood from the wine, will never learn what the Supper means or what use these symbols are to the faithful. Then let there follow a right way of seeking Christ. Our minds must not settle on earth but ascend to the heavenly glory in which He dwells. The body of Christ did not put on an incorruptible life to lay aside its own nature: therefore it is still finite. He has ascended beyond the heavens (*supra coelos*) in case our gross imagination should tie us down to earthly things. Assuredly, if this is a heavenly mystery nothing could be more absurd than to draw Christ down to earth when He rather is calling us up to Himself. The last thing I believe we must notice is the manner of eating. We must not dream that the way of passing of His substance into our souls is of natural order, but we eat His flesh when by it we receive life. We must hold to the analogy or likeness (*analogia vel similitudo*) of bread and flesh; from it we learn that souls are fed with the very flesh of Christ just as bread imparts vigour to our bodies. The flesh of Christ is spiritual food, because it is life-giving to us. It is life-giving because the Holy Spirit pours into us the life that rests in it. And although it is not the same to be fed on Christ's flesh as to believe in Him, yet we must know that it is impossible to feed on Christ other than through faith, for the eating itself is an effect of faith.

Matt. 26.29. *But I say unto you.* Matthew and Mark put this sentence after the holy supper, after Christ had given the symbol of His blood in the cup. From this some infer that Luke is telling the same thing as he repeats in a short space. The knot is easily loosed for it is little to the point at issue at what moment of time Christ said this: the aim the Evangelists have in mind is that the disciples were warned both of the nearness of their Master's death and of the new and heavenly life. The nearer the hour of death came, the more they had to be encouraged not to fail. Again, as He meant in the holy Supper to set His death before their eyes as in a mirror, He deliberately testified again that He was now leaving the world. Because the message was full of gloom, comforting words are added; there is no reason to fear death when a better life ensues. In other words, 'Now indeed I hasten to my death, but from it I shall pass to blessed immortality, nor shall I live alone in separate state in the Kingdom of God but I shall have you with me to share the same life.' We can see how He leads the disciples by the hand to the cross, and thence raises them to the hope of resurrection. They had to be guided to Christ's death that they might use it as a ladder to ascend into heaven, so now, because Christ died and was received into heaven, by looking on the cross we should be led up to heaven, that His dying and life restored should hold together. As for Him promising them glory shared with Himself, this is clear from the words, *until the day when I drink it new with you.* The objection of some that food and drink have no place in the Kingdom of God is frivolous. Christ only means that as the disciples would soon be deprived of His presence He could not eat with them again until together they enjoyed the life of heaven. Moreover the company of that life is noted as having no need of the aids of food and drink, and He says there will be a new kind of drinking. The word shows that we are to understand this as allegory. In Luke he simply says, *until the kingdom of God shall come.* Briefly, Christ commends to us the fruit and effect of the redemption which His death procured. When some think these words were fulfilled on the occasion that the Lord after resurrection ate with His disciples, they depart from His meaning: for since that was an intermediate state (*medius status*) between the course of His mortal life and the goal of His heavenly life, the Kingdom of God was not yet revealed at that time. Hence He said to Mary, 'Touch me not, because I am not yet ascended to the Father.' Besides, the disciples were not yet entered upon the Kingdom of God to drink the new wine with Christ as partakers of His same glory. When we learn that Christ drank after resurrection, though He had said He would not do that, unless at the gathering of the disciples into God's Kingdom, what appears contradictory is easily resolved. He is not speaking precisely of food and drink but of the pattern of the present life. We know too that He did not then drink either to replenish His strength with food or to entertain the disciples at His feast, but only by proving His resurrection (of which they were still doubtful) to revive their spirits again. Let us be content with the natural meaning, that the Lord promises His disciples that after He has lived with them on earth as a mortal man He will afterwards have them for His companions in life blessed and immortal.

Luke 22.19. *Which is given for you.* The other two leave out this phrase and yet it is far from superfluous: the reason that the bread is

Christ's flesh for us is that in it, salvation once for all is gained for us. Just as there is no benefit in the crucified flesh itself except for those who eat it by faith, so the eating would be lifeless and of virtually no importance unless in respect of the offering of the sacrifice, once for all. Any who desire the nourishment of Christ's flesh should see it as offered on the cross, to be the price of our reconciliation with God. What Matthew and Mark pass over in silence with the symbol of bread they express over the cup: that the blood should be poured out for the remission of sins. This point should be applied to both parts. To feed as we ought on the flesh of Christ we must consider His sacrifice; it had to be given once for our salvation in order to be given to us daily.

Matt. 26.27. *Drink ye all of it.* As Christ's purpose was to bind our whole faith to Himself, so that we should seek for nothing beyond Him, He gave two symbols to assure us that our life was established in Him. This body needs both food and drink for nourishment and sustenance. Christ, to teach us that He alone is sufficient to give firm supply of all that belongs to our salvation, makes Himself our food and drink: this is a wonderful and shining goodness, that wills to assist our faith in lowering itself to the simplicity of our flesh. It makes the sinful boldness of the Pope so much more detestable, when he did not hesatiet to break this holy bond. We hear that the Son of God employed two symbols alike to testify to the fulness of life which He confers on His people. By what right may mortal man set asunder what was divinely conjoined? Besides the Lord seems deliberately to teach all, *that they may drink from the cup,* to keep the Church away from this sacrilege. Of the bread He simply said (we read) that they should take it. Why does He expressly tell them all to drink, and Mark explicitly say they all drank, unless to warn the faithful to avoid such a wicked novelty? Yet this severe ban did not deter the Pope from daring to change and violate a law fixed by God: he has prohibited all the people from the use of the cup. To prove that there is reason in his madness he makes out that one species is enough as flesh is linked with blood by concomitancy. One might as well do away with the whole Sacrament by the same pretext, since equally Christ might make us partakers without external means. Childish arguments like these help their impiety in no degree. Nothing is more odd than for the faithful freely to do without the assistance handed down by the Lord or allow themselves to be deprived and nothing is more intolerable than to tear apart the mystery in this way.

Mark 14.24. *This is my blood.* I have already warned, when the blood is said to be poured out (as in Matthew) *for the remission of sins,* how in these words we are directed to the sacrifice of Christ's death, and to neglect this thought makes any due celebration of the Supper impossible. In no other way can faithful souls be satisfied, if they

138

cannot believe that God is pleased in their regard. The word *many* does not mean a part of the world only, but the whole human race: he contrasts *many* with *one*, as if to say that he would not be the Redeemer of one man, but would meet death to deliver many of their cursed guilt. No doubt that in speaking to a few Christ wished to make His teaching available to a larger number. At the same time we must note that in Luke (saying *for you*) He addresses the disciples by name and encourages the faithful as individuals to apply the pouring-out of His blood to their benefit. So when we come to the holy table not only should the general idea come to our mind that the world is redeemed by the blood of Christ, but also each should reckon to himself that his own sins are covered. *Of the New Covenant.* Luke and Paul say differently, *New Covenant in my blood*: the sense is the same, it is only through the appointed act of a spiritual drinking of blood that the Covenant (*foedus*) may be firm and effective. One may readily gather how foolishly superstitious are papists and the like in fastening upon the words so tenaciously. For all their noise, the Holy Spirit's exposition cannot be set aside; the cup is called blood because there is a Covenant (*testamentum*) in the blood. The same way with the bread: it will follow that it is called body because there is a Covenant in the body. There is no reason now for them to contend that we should hold to the simple words of Christ and shut our ears to outside opinions. It is Christ Himself who speaks, and they can hardly deny He is a suitable interpreter of His own sayings: He shows clearly that He had no other reason for calling the bread His body than to make a lasting Covenant with us; that offering the sacrifice once for all we should now feast spiritually. There are two points worthy of note. From the word Testament or Covenant we infer that a promise is included in the holy Supper. This refutes the error of those who say that faith is not aided, fostered, supported, and increased by the Sacraments, for between God's Covenant and men's faith there is always a mutual relation. By the word 'New' He wishes to teach that the old images are at an end and give place to a stable and eternal settlement. There is an indirect contrast between this mystery and the legal foreshadowings: evidently our state is far better than the Fathers', for after the sacrifice concluded on the cross we enjoy the solid truth.

Mark 26.26. *When they had sung a hymn.* Our three Evangelists omit those divine discourses which John relates as our Lord gave them in the house and on the road. For (as we have said elsewhere) their aim was more the narrative of actual events than the doctrine contained in them. They only remark that He set out of His own accord to the place to which Judas would come, and we may know He had so arranged the times as to meet His betrayer of His own will.

Then saith Jesus unto them, All ye shall be offended in me this night: for it is written, I will smite the shepherd, and the sheep of the flock shall be scattered abroad. But after I am raised up, I will go before you into Galilee. But Peter answered and said unto him, If all shall be offended in thee, I will never be offended. Jesus said unto him, Verily I say unto thee, that this night, before the cock crow, thou shalt deny me thrice. Peter saith unto him, Even if I must die with thee, yet will I not deny thee. Likewise also said all the disciples. (Matt. 26.31-35)

And Jesus saith unto them, All ye shall be offended: for it is written, I will smite the shepherd. and the sheep shall be scattered abroad. Howbeit, after I am raised up, I will go before you into Galilee. But Peter said unto him, Although all shall be offended, yet will not I. And Jesus saith unto him, Verily I say unto thee, that thou to-day, even this night, before the cock crow twice, thou shalt deny me thrice. But he spake exceeding vehemently, If I must die with thee, I will not deny thee. And in like manner also said they all. (Mark 14.27-31)

Simon, Simon, behold, Satan asked to have you, that he might sift you as wheat: but I made supplication for thee, that thy faith fail not: and do thou, when once thou hast turned again, stablish thy brethren. And he said unto him, Lord, with thee I am ready to go both to prison and to death. And he said, I tell thee, Peter, the cock shall not crow this day, until thou shalt thrice deny that thou knowest me. (Luke 22.31-34)

Matt. 26.31. *All ye.* Matthew and Mark extend this equally to all the disciples, but Luke records it being said to Peter alone. Though the speech was intended for them all it is probable that Christ addressed them all in the person of one who needed more warning than the others, as well as needing exceptional comfort; lest after his denial of Christ, despair should completely overwhelm him.

Luke 22.31. *Behold Satan.* The other two give a shorter and simpler account of this prediction to the disciples of their falling-away. In Luke's words there is richer teaching: not only in an historical sense does Christ speak of future troubles, but He expressly says they will have a struggle with Satan, and at the same time He promises them victory. This caution is of prime importance, whenever we run into some offence, to bring to our minds the traps of Satan. As Paul teaches (Eph. 6.12) we do not have to struggle with flesh and blood, but with spiritual forces etc. The sense of the words is, then: 'When in a short time you see Me oppressed know that Satan has drawn up these forces to lay siege on you and makes the occasion suit his purpose of undermining your faith.' I have said the teaching is useful, knowing how it often happens that we are surrounded through lack of thought, disregarding temptations which we would regard as formidable if we reckoned on them being the fiery darts of such a stout and stiff opponent. Though He is speaking of that most bitter conflict where the disciples would be shattered at one blow, almost to the extinction of their faith, the teaching is of wider effect, that Satan continually goes about roaring for his prey. Since he is driven by such furious madness to destroy us, nothing is more absurd than for us to lie drowsing. Before the need to fight appears we should already be preparing, because we know our destruction is sought after by Satan, and every means of injuring us is cleverly and carefully grasped in his hands. When it comes to the encounter, let us know that all temptations, wherever they come from, are fabricated in the workshops of that foe. The simile of the *sifting* does not entirely fit in at all points: for elsewhere we have seen the Gospel compared to a fan or sieve, for the chaff to be driven from the wheat, but here it means simply to blow about or shake up with force; for the Apostles at the death of Jesus were tossed more fiercely than normal. We must hold this firm, for nothing pleases Satan less, than the purging of the faithful. It is for another purpose that he shakes them up, but it is quite right to say that they are driven and tossed in every direction, just like wheat under the winnow. We shall shortly see that a still worse fulfilment befell the Apostles. This is what the Lord meant by the words which are used in Matthew and Mark, *All ye shall be offended in me.* They mean not only an attack will come, but almost a defeat: the shameful humiliation of Christ will also crush their spirits. Whereas it was their duty to stay constantly with their Master, even to the cross, they drew back in fear. Their infirmity is shown them, so that with prayers and sighs they may take refuge in the holy protection of God.

Matt. 26.31. *For it is written.* By this word of prophecy He heartens them to overcome the offence, for God does not cease to recognise as His sheep those whom a time of scattering throws here and there. After the prophet told of the Church's restoration, for fear the imminent, extreme disasters should overwhelm pious minds with despair he declares that with the confusion, indeed the overthrow of government, there will be a sad and wretched dispersion; yet the grace of God will be victorious. Though almost all interpreters apply the passage in Zechariah (13.7) to the Person of Christ alone, I apply it more widely, as if it were said that there will be no more government on which the salvation of the people depends, because the pastors will be taken from their midst. I have no doubt that the Lord wished to include that whole period in which the Church, after the tyranny of Antiochus, was stripped of good shepherds and reduced to waste: then God gave licence in dreadful measure for the sword's career, slaying the pastors and causing the people a wretched state of distress. Yet this dispersion did not prevent the Lord stretching out His hands to gather in His sheep (so to speak). The prophet gives a general warning, that the Church must be deprived of her shepherds; yet it applies truly and properly to Christ Himself. As He was Chief of all the pastors, on Him alone hung the salvation of the Church, and in His death all hope might seem to be cut off. This was the ultimate temptation, when the Redeemer, who was the spirit and life of the people and had once begun to gather the flock of God, was suddenly snatched away by death. The grace of God was more resplendent in wonderfully bringing the remnant of the flock together again, out of waste and ruin. We see how appropriately Christ quoted this passage, so that no future scattering should frighten the disciples beyond limit; and yet they should be aware of their own weakness, and lean on their own Pastor. So it means: 'You think because you have not yet experienced your feebleness, that you are strong and unyielding: but it will soon appear that Zechariah's prophecy was true, when the shepherd is slain the flock will be scattered. Let the promise which is added re-create and sustain you; God will stretch out His hand to bring back the scattered sheep to Himself.' The passage teaches us that no unity is good for salvation unless when the sheep are kept united under the crook of Christ.

Matt. 26.32. *But after I am raised up.* He now expresses more clearly what I just now touched on, that the disciples, struck with fear, will for a short time be like scattered and lost sheep, and must yet again be recalled to the fold. Christ is not simply saying He will rise again, but declares He will be their Leader and will take them up as companions, just as if they had stayed firm together: and to increase their confidence He tells them the place where they will foregather; as if He had said, 'You, who are scattered at Jerusalem, I shall again draw in at Galilee.'

Matt. 26.33. *Peter answered.* Peter makes no pretence, but speaks with sincere emotion, yet a false confidence in his own powers led him into a foolish boast. He deserves Christ's rebuke, and soon after pays the heavy penalty for his boldness. The event shows that Peter promised more for himself than he was able to give, because he had neglected to test himself thoroughly. We see very well from this the intoxication of human self-confidence. When he receives from the Son of God a second warning of his weakness, with the added force of an oath, he is so far from yielding ground or relaxing any of his foolish assertion that he goes on to show his swelling spirit with increased efforts. It is asked, should not Peter have been free to hope for what he claimed for himself; should he not in reliance on Christ's promise have been bound to give such a promise on his own account? I answer, that when Christ promised His disciples the Spirit of unconquerable fortitude previously, He was looking to the time of renewal that followed His resurrection. Since they were not yet endowed with heavenly power, Peter in taking confidence from himself is crossing the bounds of faith. In fact he sinned in two ways. On his own rash initiative he anticipated the time and did not abide by the Lord's promise. Secondly, he shut his eyes to his own infirmity and claimed more for himself, in carelessness rather than with courage, than reason allowed. So note, that everyone should be mindful of his weakness and continually seek the aid of the Holy Spirit, and no one should assume more for himself than the Lord promises. The faithful should be so girded up for the contest that without any doubt or suspense over the victorious result they should stoutly resist fear. Trembling and panic are a sign of lack of faith. On the other hand, one must watch out for that dumb disregard which shakes off anxiety, and fills men up with pride, quenching enthusiasm for prayer. Paul finely puts his finger on the middle course (Phil. 2.12) in telling us to work out our salvation in fear and trembling, because it is God that worketh in us to will and to perform. On the one side, He humbles us and drives us to seek reinforcements elsewhere, but on the other, lest anxiety turn to apathy, He encourages us to strenuous attempts. As often as any temptation comes upon us first let us think of our weakness, and immediately in our low state learn to seek what we lack from another source: then let us think of His promised grace, which shall deliver us from doubt. Those who forget their own weakness and trust in their strength without calling on God are just like drunk soldiers who leap wildly to arms: when the liquor wears off they think of nothing but flight. It is amazing that the rest of the disciples, after Peter's rebuke, still rush into the same folly: it is obvious how little notice they took. We learn from this example to dare nothing except as far as the reach of God's Hand. Nothing falls faster or vanishes sooner than zeal which is inconsiderate. The disciples saw that there was nothing more shameful or unspeakable than deserting the Master. They are right to detest such a sin, but without the support of belief in the promise, without prayers, they mistakenly fly off into vaunting a steadiness, which they did not possess.

And he said unto them, When I sent you forth without purse, and wallet, and shoes, lacked ye anything? And they said, Nothing. And he said unto them, But now, he that hath a purse, let him take it, and likewise a wallet: and he that hath none, let him sell his cloke, and buy a sword. For I say unto you, that this which is written must be fulfilled in me, And he was reckoned with transgressors: for that which concerneth me hath fulfilment. And they said, Lord, behold, here are two swords. And he said unto them, It is enough. (Luke 22.35-38)

The whole object of Christ's saying is that He has spared the disciples thus far in not putting any burden upon them beyond their capacity. He reminds them of His earlier gentleness, so that now they can prepare themselves more eagerly for harder conflict. Why should He have kept His mere beginners out of the range of firing, in shady and quiet corners, except so as by gradual gathering of mind and strength at leisure to accustom them to battle? So in other words, 'Your conditions so far have been easy and happy, for I have wished to bring you up gently, like boys, but now the time is ripe to give you men's training.' The contrast He makes here of the two periods extends further: if they lacked nothing when they went out to their duties without supplies (in peaceful days when they might look out for themselves) but now, in days of tumult and fury, they should all the more lay aside concern for food and hasten to go where necessity calls. Christ particularly has in mind what He did with the twelve Apostles, yet He also teaches us, that while we are still novices and weak in faith He will, for the time, be gentle, until we grow up into men: so they are wrong who use His times of quiet for self-indulgence which softens the strength of faith. Let us have do doubt that Christ to-day takes due account of us, not throwing forward the novice and fledgling, but before He sends men to war He trains them in arms and capability.

Luke 22.36. *He that hath a purse.* He announces in metaphor, the vast troubles and sharpest onslaughts that were imminent, as a commander leads his troops into battle array rousing them to arms. He bids them say farewell to every other care (except their will to fight) and not even to think about food. He teaches (as is the usual thing in extreme crisis) that everything, down to wallet and purse, is to be sold for the sake of getting arms. But it is no outward battle that He calls them to. He only warns them with the simile of war how difficult are the struggles of the trials they will have to face, how heavy the assaults of spiritual encounters they must sustain. That they might more willingly throw themselves upon God's providence, He first reminded them (as I have said) how God took care to provide for them when they were empty and naked and bereft of all supplies. They who know God's support, and how it met the occasion, should have no grain of doubt, for all time to come, of the succour that would come in any kind of hardship.

Luke 22.37. *That this also which is written.* The adverb *also* is emphatic. Christ means that the whole range of His task it not complete until He has been reckoned with the evil-doers and criminals, as one of that order. In case the indignity of this action should shock their minds too much, He adduces a saying of Isaiah (53.12), which certainly can only be explained with reference to the Messiah. Since it is said there, He is to be reckoned with the transgressors, the faithful must not be alarmed at such a sight (cruel as it is), and not be put off Christ, who could not have been their Redeemer in any other sense than by taking on Himself the shame and disgrace of a criminal. There is no cure more fitted for removing offences, where we are frightened at things seeming to go wrong, than if we accept that it is God's pleasure; that what happens is not fantastic or unreasonable, since it is the effect of His decree: particularly when it was long ago foretold exactly as it came to pass. Seeing that the disciples should hope for a Redeemer as God had promised of old, and Isaiah plainly testified that to clear us of the guilt of our crimes the penalty must be transferred to Him, this should suffice to quieten the disciples' alarm, lest they made Christ of less account. So He adds, *that which concerneth me hath fulfilment*, meaning that nothing was spoken by the prophets without effect. The expression in Greek means to be accomplished, to be put into effect (τέλος ἔχει). When the prophets' words are proven by the result it should rather give confirmation to our faith than strike us with panic or anxiety. Though Christ uses this single argument to strengthen and comfort His disciples, that all prophecies must be fulfilled, this way of God's purpose has rare scope for increasing faith. Christ was put under the condemnation which we had all merited, and reckoned among the godless in order that He may present us, who are godless and burdened with wrong, to the Father as justified. Hence we are reckoned pure and free of sin in God's sight, for the Lamb pure and spotless came into our place, as we shall be saying again in the next chapter.

Luke 22.38. *Lord behold here are two swords.* It was a shameful and rough display of ignorance that the disciples, so often warned to take up the cross, should think they would have to fight with swords of steel. We cannot tell whether in saying they have two swords they believe they are well equipped against enemies or are complaining of their lack of weapons. But it is clear that they were stupid enough not to think of their spiritual enemy. As for canonists inferring from these words that mitred bishops are endowed with twofold jurisdiction, this is not only a worthless piece of allegory but an insulting mockery that attacks God's Word. Antichrist's slaves were bound to sink into this depth of madness so that they should trample in broad daylight on God's oracles by their sacrilegious contempt.

Then cometh Jesus with them unto a place called Gethsemane, and saith unto his disciples, Sit ye here, while I go yonder and pray. And he took with him Peter and the two sons of Zebedee, and began to be sorrowful and sore troubled. Then saith he unto them, My soul is exceeding sorrowful, even unto death: abide ye here, and watch with me. And he went forward a little, and fell on his face, and prayed, saying, O my Father, if it be possible, let this cup pass away from me: nevertheless, not as I will, but as thou wilt. And he cometh unto the disciples, and findeth them sleeping, and saith unto Peter, What, could ye not watch with me one hour? Watch and pray, that ye enter not into temptation: the spirit indeed is willing, but the flesh is weak. Again a second time he went away, and prayed, saying O my Father, if this cannot pass away, except I drink it, thy will be done. And he came again and found them sleeping, for their eyes were heavy. And he left them again, and went away, and prayed a third time, saying again the same words. (Matt. 26.36-44)

And they came unto a place which was named Gethsemane: and he saith unto his disciples, Sit ye here, while I pray. And he taketh with him Peter and James and John, and began to be greatly amazed, and sore troubled. And he saith unto them, My soul is exceeding sorrowful even unto death: abide ye here, and watch. And he went forward a little, and fell on the ground, and prayed that, if it were possible, the hour might pass away from him. And he said, Abba, Father, all things are possible unto thee; remove this cup from me: howbeit not what I will, but what thou wilt. And he cometh, and findeth them sleeping, and saith unto Peter, Simon, sleepest thou? couldest thou not watch one hour? Watch and pray, that ye enter not into temptation: the spirit indeed is willing, but the flesh is weak. And again he went away and prayed, using the same words. And again he came, and found them sleeping, for their eyes were very heavy; and they wist not what to answer him. (Mark 14.32-40)

And he came out, and went, as his custom was, unto the mount of Olives; and the disciples also followed him. And when he was at the place, he said unto them, Pray that ye enter not into temptation. And he was parted from them about a stone's cast; and he kneeled down and prayed, saying, Father, if thou be willing, remove this cup from me: nevertheless not my will, but thine, be done. And there appeared unto him an angel from heaven, strengthening him. And being in an agony he prayed more earnestly: and his sweat became as it were great drops of blood falling down upon the ground. And when he rose up from his prayer he came unto the disciples, and found them sleeping for sorrow, and said unto them, Why sleep ye? rise and pray, that ye enter not into temptation. (Luke 22.39-46)

Matt. 26.36. *Then cometh Jesus.* Luke only says the mount of Olives, but Mark and Matthew give more detailed reference to the place. Yet Luke says what is more to the purpose, that Christ came there, as He was used to do. We gather He did not seek a corner to hide in out of the way, but offered Himself to death, almost by arrangement. John says the place was known to His betrayer because Jesus used to come there often. So in this passage we gain another indication of his obedience, for He could not have pleased the Father but by a voluntary death. *Sit ye here.* By leaving the disciples at a distance He is sparing their weakness: like a man in combat, settling his wife and children in a peaceful place when he arrives at the moment of his supreme test. Though He wished them all to stay out of the firing area, He took three companions closer with Him, as if they were the chosen flower, in whom was more strength. He did not take them in a belief that they would be equal to bear the assault, but to give a proof of the general failure of them all.

Matt. 26.37. *Began to be sorrowful.* We have already seen the Lord wrestle with the fear of death, but now as He comes hand to hand with temptation, the ordeal is called a beginning of grief and sorrow. We gather that the true test of power only comes in the moment itself: then the weakness of the flesh betrays itself, which before was hidden, and the inner emotions pour out. Though God had trained His Son in some preliminary bouts, now at the closer aspect of death He deals a heavier blow and strikes Him with unaccustomed terror. As this seems to be below the dignity of Christ's divine glory that He was affected with panic and sorrow, many interpreters are vehemently concerned to find a way out. Their efforts were thoughtless and fruitless: if we are ashamed of His fear and sorrow, our redemption will trickle away and be lost. Ambrose was right, I think, when he said, 'there is no need of excuse. Indeed, I find nothing more wonderful than His piety and majesty. He would have done less for me, if He had not borne my affliction. He grieved for me, who on His own account had nothing to grieve over; He laid aside the delights of His eternal Godhead, to feel the weariness of my infirmity. I boldly speak of this sorrow, because I preach His cross. He did not assume an appearance of incarnation, but a reality. He had to bear grief in order to conquer sadness, and not shut it out: they do not have the praise of fortitude who are drugged by wounds, and not hurt.' Thus far Ambrose.

Those who pretend the Son of God was immune from huamn passions do not truly and seriously acknowledge Him as a man. When the divine power of Christ is said to have reposed as it were in concealment for a time (*quasi abscondita ad tempus quievisse*) to allow Him to fulfil the Redeemer's role of suffering, this is so far from being an absurdity,

147

that the mystery of our salvation could not have been fulfilled other-wise. Cyril is correct. 'That the suffering of the cross was in a certain respect not voluntary for Christ, but voluntary through the will of the Father, and for our salvation, you may learn easily from His prayer, "Father, if it is possible, let this cup pass from me." For the same reason, in that the Word of God is God, and is Life in its very nature, no one thinks that He feared death in any respect. But being made flesh He allows the flesh to suffer its own, and so, as truly man, He is frightened in the very presence of death, and says, "If it is possible, Father, let this cup pass from me: but since it is not possible, not my will, but thine be done." You see how human nature even in Christ Himself has its own suffering and fear, but through its union with the Word is drawn back into the fortitude suited to God.' At length he concludes: 'You see that death was not voluntary for Christ as far as the flesh was concerned, but it was voluntary, because by it, according to the will of the Father, salvation and life were given to all men.' Thus far Cyril.

Yet the weakness of the flesh which Christ took on Himself must be separated from ours, for it was very different. None of our feelings are free of sin, for they all exceed the limit and proper moderation. Though Christ was troubled by sadness and fear, yet He did not rebel against God, but remained composed in the true rule of restraint. There is no wonder, since He was innocent and pure of all stain, that the emotion was displayed in Him, although it witnessed to human infir-mity, was pure and unsullied. From the corrupt nature of men nothing flows out but trouble and rottenness. So let us keep the distinction; Christ in His fear and grief was weak, but without any spot of sin, while all our emotions, bubbling out to excess, are sinful. The kind of emotion with which Christ was tried is worth notice. Matthew says He was affected by grief and sorrow (or trouble of mind), Luke that he was was seized with anguish, Mark added that He was dismayed. Where did that grief and trouble and fright come from, if He did not see in death something more sad and more fearful than the separation of soul and body? Certainly He endured death not only to move from earth to heaven, but rather to take on the curse that we had fallen under and relieve us of it. It was not simple horror of death, the passing away from the world, but the sight of the dread tribunal of God that came to Him, the Judge Himself armed with vengeance beyond under-standing. Our sins, whose burden was laid on Him, weighed on Him with their vast mass. No wonder if death's fearful abyss tormented Him grievously, with fear and anguish.

Matt. 26.38. *My soul is exceedingly sorrowful.* He shares His sorrow with them to awaken their sympathy. He was well aware of their failings but wanted them afterwards to feel the more shame for their apathy. His words express the deadly wound of grief, as if He had said He was faint with grief, or almost dead. As Jonah replied to the Lord (4.1), 'I am angry even unto death.' I make the remark because there is some foolish philosophising in the old writers dealing with this passage too ingeniously, that Christ's soul was not sad in actual death but only to the point of death. Here again we should bear in mind the cause of all the grief: death in itself would not have so agonised the Spirit of God's Son unless He realised that He had to deal with the judgment of God.

Matt. 26.39. *He went forward a little.* We have seen elsewhere that to excite Himself to a greater intensity of prayer the Lord prayed without witnesses. Led away from the sight of men, we gather our thoughts better, to be more intent on what we are doing. It is not necessary to withdraw into distant corners whenever we wish to pray (indeed it is not always suitable), but when some greater necessity presses upon us, since prayer's fervour flows more freely in solitude, it is useful for us to pray alone. If the Son of God did not neglect this assistance it would be more than mad pride not to apply it to our own use. Besides, where God is the sole Judge and there is no fear of self-seeking, there the faithful soul uncovers itself more intimately and in greater simplicity, unburdens its desires, sighs, anxieties, fears, hopes, and joys into the lap of God. God allows His people many foibles when they pray in private, which would be reckoned forward in the sight of men. By the very gesture of falling on the ground He testifies to the real intensity of His prayer. Even bowing the knee as a symbol of honour and reverence is regularly practised in prayer; Christ lies full on the earth as a Suppliant and places Himself in the lowest attitude for the greatness of His grief. *O my Father if it be possible.* It is vain effort for those who would make out that this is not so much the description of a prayer but only a complaint. I admit it is abrupt, yet I have no doubt that Christ's call was a prayer. It is no objection that He asks a thing impossible of being granted Him, for believers' prayers do not always flow on a straight course to their ending. They do not always keep an even moderation, and are not always composed in strict order, but rather are involved and confused and even in conflict with themselves, or stopping in midstream, just as a ship tossed by storms makes for any harbour, and cannot hold to its right and regular course as in a quiet sea. We must remember what I just said, that Christ's emotions were not turbulent in the way that ours shake pure moderation from our minds. But within the capacity of a sane and unspoiled human nature, He was struck with fright and seized with anguish, and so compelled to shift (as it were) between the violent waves of trial from one prayer to another. This is the reason why He prays to be spared death, then holds Himself

149

in check, submits Himself to the Father's command, and corrects and revokes the wish that had suddenly escaped Him. It is asked how He begged for the Father's eternal decree of which He was not ignorant to be rescinded. Even accepting the condition, *if it is possible*, it seems absurd to make God's plan liable to alteration. It is right to be utterly firm that God cannot withdraw His plan. In Mark, in fact, Christ seems to contrast God's power with His decree, *all things*, He says, *are possible unto thee*. But God's power does not rightly extend so far as to weaken His truth by making it variable or changeable. I would answer that there is nothing odd if Christ, following the way of the faithful, did not turn His eyes to the divine plan but rested His desire that burned within Him upon His Father's knees. Faithful men in pouring out their prayers do not always rise to speculate upon the secret things of God or take time to consider what may be possible, but are sometimes carried off in haste by the fervour of their prayer. Moses prays that he may be blotted out of the book of life. Paul prayed that he might be anathema (Exod. 32.22; Rom. 9.3). This was no rehearsed prayer of Christ's, but the force and onset of grief wrung a cry from Him on the instant, which He at once went on to correct. The same vehemence took from Him any present thoughts of the decree of heaven, so that for a moment He did not think how He was sent to be the Redeemer of the human race. Often heavy anxiety clouds the eyes from seeing everything at once. Briefly, there is nothing strange if in His prayers He did not maintain an immediate attention to everything and keep them in due proportion. As for Christ's words in Mark, that to God all things are possible, He does not intend to bring His power into conflict with His immutable truth and constancy, but because hope had gone (as is the case in desperate straits) He cast Himself on the essential power of God. By the word beaker or *cup* there is elsewhere signified God's providence, which assigns to each a measure of the cross and affliction, even as the master of the house gives an allowance to each of his servants, and distributes portions to his children. *Nevertheless not as I.* We see how Christ from the very start checks His feelings and in good time brings Himself back into line. Here the first question is, how was His will free of all fault, when it did not agree with the will of God. If God's Will is the one rule of what is good and fair, it follows that all desires that dissent from it are faulty. I answer, although it is true rectitude to conform all our desires to God's pleasure, yet there is a certain kind of indirect dissent which is blameless and not reckoned as a sin, just as a man might wish the state of the Church to be peaceful and prosperous, and might desire the children of God to be freed from their pains and all superstitions to be removed from their midst and the licence of the wicked repressed, that they might no longer be hurt. Though these things are all right in themselves and may properly be sought by the faithful, yet God's pleasure is otherwise. He will have His Son reign in the presence of His enemies, have His people trained under the cross, and the victory of faith and the Gospel made glorious over against the hostile devices of Satan. We see how prayers may be holy which appear to differ from the will of God, for He does not wish us to ask always with exactness and scruple what He has decreed, but allows us to beg from Him what our intelligence can grasp as desirable. But this does not dispose of the question altogether. Since it was just said that all Christ's desires were properly controlled, how does He now correct Himself? The way He brings His emotions into obedience to God suggests that He had transgressed the limit. Certainly in His first cry there does not appear to be the quiet moderation of which I spoke: He declines and refuses to perform, as far as He may, the office of Mediator. I answer, it was no fault, when the terror of death fell on Him and the darkness covered Him, that He forgot all else and let forth that cry. There is no need for ingenious debate whether it could be possible for Him to become forgetful of our salvation: the one thing should suffice us, that when he broke out in deprecation of death He was not thinking of other things that might have shut the door upon His prayer. If it is objected that the first movement (which had to be checked before it ran away any further) was not controlled as it should have been, I reply, that in our corrupt nature one cannot find emotional heat linked with restraint, as it was in Christ. We should give God's Son all honour, and not reckon Him by our standards. In us, all the emotions of the flesh seethe and leap up boldly—or at least drag up some dirt with them. Yet Christ's passion of grief and fear was such that He held Himself in limits. As various musical sounds, different from each other, make no discord but compose a tuneful and sweet harmony, so in Christ there exists a remarkable example of balance between the wills of God and of man; they differ from each other without conflict or contradiction. This passage clearly shows how unintelligent were the old heretics called 'Monothelites', who made Christ to be endowed with only one simple will, holding that as far as He was God, He only willed the Father's Will. It follows then that His human soul had different desires from the hidden purpose of God. Now if Christ had so to keep His will captive as to subject it to God's command, although it was rightly trained, how carefully must we restrain the licence of our desires, which are always running wild and headlong and are full of contumacy? If the Spirit of God so guides us that we wish nothing that is not agreeable to reason, God must have our obedience, in that we bear it patiently if our prayers are not granted. This is faith's due limit, to allow God to decide differently from what we desire. Particularly, we must hold to the rule that, where we have no certain and special promise, we must not ask anything except on condition that God may fulfil His decree, which cannot be done unless we yield our wishes to His instruction.

It is then asked, What advantage prayer was to Christ? The Apostle to the Hebrews (5.7) says that He was heard for His fear (for this is how the passage should be expounded, and not as is commonly read, for His reverence). Now this would not meet the case, if Christ had simply feared death, for He was not delivered from it. It follows that through fear of a greater evil He was led to ask off death. When He saw the wrath of God put before Him, as He set Himself before His tribunal, burdened with the sins of the whole world, He was bound to be terrified at the profound abyss of death. Though He met death, yet its pangs were loosed (as Peter tells, Acts 2.24), and He came out of the battle victorious. Thus the Apostle rightly says that He was heard for His fear. Ignorant men rise up at this point and clamour that the action is unworthy, for Christ to have feared to be swallowed up in death. I should like them to answer me, What kind of fear do they think it was that drew out from Christ drops of blood? Such deadly sweat could only have flowed from a dire and unusual horror. If anyone today were to sweat blood, and in such quantity that it fell to the ground in drops, it would be a portent beyond belief, and if this should come from a fear of death we would ascribe it to a feeble, womanly spirit. Those therefore who say that Christ did not pray the Father to snatch Him out of the gulf of death attribute a softness to Him that would disgrace even the man in the street. If anyone object that the fear I speak of comes from lack of faith, there is a ready answer. When Christ was struck with the horror of the divine curse His fleshly sense was affected while His faith remained undamaged and unshaken. He had an integrity of nature which could take the effect of temptations without hurt, while we are pierced with their stings. Besides, people who exempt Him from feeling temptations make Him Victor without a fight. And it is quite forbidden to suppose that He made a pretence, when He complained of mortal sadness in His soul. The Evangelists did not lie when they recorded that He was overcome with sorrow and in great fear.

Matt. 26.40. *And he cometh unto the disciples.* Although He was not without fear or free of anxiety, He laid aside His struggle in prayer and took a space of relief. The faithful do not need such persistent prayer as never to stop addressing God. By Christ's example let them go on praying as long as their weakness allows, then stop for a short time, take breath, and then anew betake themselves to God. It would have been no small relief to His sorrow to have had the disciples as companions and partners: on the other hand, it was a bitter addition to His distress to be abandoned by them also. Even if He needed no-one's aid,

152

yet as He had taken our infirmities upon Himself willingly, and supremely wished in this struggle to give a proof of that emptying of Himself of which Paul speaks (Phil. 2.7), it is no wonder that it added a heavy and painful weight to His grief, for those whom He had made His companions to fall asleep. He takes them to task without pretence. With genuine feeling, He testifies to the pain He has received in being let down. It was a fair reproach for their laziness, that in His extreme anguish they could not bear to watch even one hour.

Matt. 26.41. *Watch and pray*. Because the disciples slept at their Master's hour of danger they are brought to themselves, to waken up to a sense of their own evil. Christ declares that unless they watch and pray they may be suddenly caught by temptation. In other words, 'When you take no thought for me, at least do not neglect yourselves; because what happens here is your affair, and unless you beware, temptation will suddenly swamp you. To enter into temptation is to succumb to it.' Let us note the means of resistance here prescribed, not relying on our own power and efforts to gather our spirits, but rather being conscious of our weakness and seeking arms and strength from the Lord. Our watchfulness will do no good without prayers. *The spirit indeed is willing*. Lest fear make the disciples lose heart, He corrects their idleness gently with a measure of consolation and with ground for good hope. First He warns them, however keenly they rush in pursuit of right action, they must still struggle with the weakness of the flesh, and so prayers are never superfluous. We see He allows praise for their readiness, in case their infirmity should drive them to despair: yet they are urged to prayer, because they are not yet sufficiently possessed of the power of the Spirit. This caution properly applies to the faithful who in the regeneration of the Spirit of God desire to do right, yet still labour under the weakness of the flesh. Though the grace of the Spirit flourishes in them, according to the flesh they are weak. Though their weakness is shown to the disciples alone, what Christ says to them applies to all in turn; we ought to draw from this a general rule, to keep careful watch, with prayer: for there is not in us any such outstanding strength of the Spirit as may prevent our frequent collapse under the weakness of the flesh unless God by His assistance strengthens and sustains us. But we should not be frightened to excess: a sure remedy is set before us, which is not far to seek, nor sought in vain. Christ promises that men earnest in prayer, who carefully put away the idleness of their flesh, will be victorious.

Matt. 26.42. *Again a second time he went away*. It seems from these words of Matthew as if Christ, with fear subdued, entrusted Himself to the Father more freely and with a clearer mind. No longer does He ask or the cup to be taken from Him, but passing over that appeal He

153

insists rather on this, that He may obey the purpose of God. In Mark, such a progression is not to be found; even when Christ went back a second time He is said to have repeated the same prayers. I have no doubt that as often as He prayed He felt driven by fear and terror to beg release from death. Yet it is probable that on the second occasion He strove more to fulfil His obedience to the Father, and was encouraged by His first encounter with temptation to approach death with greater confidence. Luke does not exactly record that He prayed on different occasions, but only says that as anxiety pressed upon Him He did so at more length and with more intensity, as if the course of His prayer had been unbroken. But we know that the Evangelists sometimes omit details and sketch out a summary account. As for his saying towards the end that Christ came to His disciples, this is hysteron-proteron: as in another part, where he says an angel appeared from heaven, before speaking of Christ's agony. To reverse the order is not strange: that we should know the angel was not sent to no purpose, the need is then explained. The account that follows supplies the reason, so to speak. Though it is the Spirit of God alone who supplies courage, there is no objection to God using His angels as servants. We may infer the enormity of suffering that Christ endured, when God had to give Him aid in a visible form.

Matt. 26.43. *And found them sleeping again.* This was not the drowsiness of hang-over, nor of crass stupidity, nor after-effect of fleshly exhilaration, but rather, as Luke tells us, it came from excessive grief. So we see better how prone our flesh is to torpor, in which even peril itself leads us to forget God. On every side the occasion is suited to Satan and ready for the traps he sets for us. If we fear no enemy, he drowns us in a drunken sleep: and in fear and grief by which we should be prompted to prayer, he overwhelms our minds and stops them rising to God: so in all ways men fall aside and lose their place with God, until He gathers them in. Note this circumstance; the disciples, for all their sharp reproof, fall back to sleep almost in the same instant. This is not spoken of the whole band, but of those three whom Christ had chosen as His chief companions. How will it be with the flock, when the flower behave like this? Repeating His words again was not vain repetition (as Christ had condemned in the hypocrites above, who hoped they would gain something by futile chatter, but never seek it honestly and from the heart), but Christ showed by His example that our minds must not be broken or wearied with prayer if we do not immediately receive what we ask. It is no superfluous repetition of words when the experience of rejection does not damp the ardour of our prayer, but makes us ask a third and fourth time, to achieve what God appears to have denied.

Then cometh he to the disciples, and saith unto them, Sleep on now, and take your rest: behold, the hour is at hand, and the Son of man is betrayed into the hands of sinners.   Arise, let us be going: behold, he is at hand that betrayeth me.

And while he yet spake, lo, Judas, one of the twelve, came, and with him a great multitude with swords and staves, from the chief priests and elders of the people.   Now he that betrayed him gave them a sign, saying, Whomsoever I shall kiss, that is he: take him.   And straightway he came to Jesus, and said, Rabbi; and kissed him.   And Jesus said unto him, Friend, do that for which thou art come.   Then they came and laid hands on Jesus and took him. (Matt. 26.45-50)

And he cometh the third time, and saith unto them, Sleep on now, and take your rest: it is enough; the hour is come; behold, the Son of man is betrayed into the hands of sinners.   Arise, let us be going: behold, he that betrayeth me is at hand.
And straightway, while he yet spake, cometh Judas, one of the twelve, and with him a multitude with swords and staves, from the chief priests and the scribes and the elders.   Now he that betrayeth him had given them a token, saying, Whomsoever I shall kiss, that is he; take him, and lead him away safely.   And when he was come, straightway he came to him, and saith, Rabbi; and kissed him.   And they laid hands on him, and took him. (Mark 14.41-46)

While he yet spake, behold a multitude, and he that was called Judas. one of the twelve, went before them; and he drew near unto Jesus to kiss him. But Jesus said unto him, Judas, betrayest thou the Son of man with a kiss? (Luke 22.47-48)

Matt. 26.45. *Sleep on now, and take your rest.* We may agree that Christ speaks here in irony: but we must grasp the point of the irony. As Christ had no success in warning His disciples, He not only makes an indirect criticism of their indifference, but also declares that however idle they want to be, there will not be much longer to spend.   So it means: 'So far I have wasted my words on you, I shall now cease urging you.   But however much I may let you sleep, the enemy will not allow it you, but will force you to watch against your will.'   So in Mark there is added, *it is enough*: as if He had said, There is no longer time to sleep.   In this way the Lord often corrects men for their inertia, making men who are deaf to words awake to the compulsion of disaster. Let us learn to attend to the Lord's words in good time, in case what He wishes to elicit from us freely may latterly be wrenched out by necessity.

Matt. 26.46. *Arise, let us be going.*   These words reveal that since His prayer, He has found new reserves of arms.   Before He had been willing

155

enough for death, but at the sudden crisis He had a serious struggle with the weakness of the flesh, till He might have been glad to withdraw from death, if the good consent of the Father had been allowed Him. With prayers and tears He gained new strength from heaven: not that lack of strength had ever made Him waver, but in the weakness of the flesh, which He had freely assumed, He wished to wrestle in anguish, in painful and hard combat, that in His own person He might win the victory for us. Now His fears are allayed and His nerves are mastered, now again to offer a willing sacrifice to the Father—He tries no escape—He advances of His own accord, to meet death.

Matt. 26.47. *And while he yet spake.* The Evangelists take pains to express that whatever happened was foreseen by the Lord: whence it may certainly be gathered that outside violence only dragged Him to die in so far as evil men worked out God's secret design. Though the spectacle brought to the disciples' eyes was gloomy and terrifying, yet it gave grounds for confidence; they might take courage when the event showed that nothing occurred by chance. Christ's prediction directed them to look to the glory of the Godhead itself. As for the armed band being sent by the priests, a tribune and cohort being obtained on request from Pilate, it is plain that they were so shocked and disturbed in their evil conscience as to do everything in alarm. Whatever was the need of such a great force to arrest Christ, who they knew to have no armed bodyguard? It was the divine power of Christ, which they had been made to feel with many proofs, that tormented them inwardly—hence all this panic preparation. On the other hand, it shows their monstrous frenzy, that they do not hesitate to rise up against God relying on armed force.

Matt. 26.48. *Now he that betrayed him.* I am sure that either awe for the Lord or shame for his crime prevented Judas from openly daring to side with the enemy: the caution he gave the soldiers in Mark, *and lead him safely away*, I guess arose from his remembering all the many proofs Christ had given of His divine power at other times. Yet it was astonishing madness to hide under a cheap pretence, when he came before the sight of the Son of God, or to oppose His unbounded might with human effort.

Matt. 26.49. *Hail, Rabbi.* I have no doubt that he was putting a show of sympathy and anxious concern for the danger his Master was in when he spoke like this: this is why Mark has the pathetic repetition, *Rabbi, Rabbi*. Though Christ's Majesty impressed him, yet the devil had such a fascination on his mind that he trusted that he could well conceal his treachery under a kiss and gentle words. This greeting and salutation, then, was a pretext of compassion. I think the same of the kiss, though it was a common enough habit among the Jews to greet their friends with a kiss. Judas who had only left Christ a little before seems now to have become suddenly alarmed and offers the Master a parting kiss. He outdoes them all in his false show of respect, appearing to be terribly hurt at separation from the Master, but how little he gains by his falsehood is evident from Christ's reply.

Matt. 26.50. [1]*Friend, why are you here?* Luke is more exact, *Judas, betrayest thou the son of man with a kiss?*—except that there is greater intensity in this reproof; that he abuses the Master's good-will and the high honour placed on himself by going wickedly to the supreme betrayal. It is not an ironical greeting, when Christ calls him friend, but a challenge to his ingratitude, that from an intimate friend, who sat with Him at table, he has become the betrayer, as had been predicted in the Psalm (41.9), 'If an outsider had done this, it would have been bearable: but a close and familiar friend, who did eat bread pleasantly with me, who went with me into the temple of the Lord, has prepared snares against me.' Here we see clearly what I noted before, with what artifice hypocrites conceal themselves, what screens they put up when thy come before the presence of the Lord, and their crimes are brought into the midst. It goes the more heavily against them in judgment that they who were taken to Christ's bosom should rise up treacherously against Him. The name of *friend* (as we have said) has a bitter sting to it. The Church will ever be liable to this evil, just as Christ bore it in His person, and will foster traitors in her midst. So it was said a little before, 'The traitor approached, who was one of the twelve.' Lest we should be disturbed overmuch at these examples the Lord wishes to test our faith two ways. From outside, Satan attacks us and the Church in open warfare, and from within, he works our secret ruin through hypocrites. We are taught, we who are of His disciples, to serve God with sincerity. The defections we see today should quicken us to trembling and to zeal for true religion, as Paul says, 'Let everyone that calleth on the name of the Lord depart from iniquity.' We are all bidden to kiss the Son of God: so we must see that none do this as the traitor, else it will be a dear price we pay to be elevated to such degree.

And behold, one of them that were with Jesus stretched out his hand, and drew his sword, and smote the servant of the high priest, and struck off his ear. Then saith Jesus unto him, Put up again thy sword into its place; for all they that take the sword shall perish with the sword. Or thinkest

[1] R.V. renders differently.

thou that I cannot beseech my Father, and he shall even now send me
more than twelve legions of angels? How then should the scriptures be
fulfilled that thus it must be? In that hour said Jesus to the multitudes,
Are ye come out as against a robber with swords and staves to seize me?
I sat daily in the temple teaching, and ye took me not. But all this is come
to pass, that the scriptures of the prophets might be fulfilled. Then all the
disciples left him, and fled. (Matt. 26.51-56)

But a certain one of them that stood by drew his sword, and smote the
servant of the high priest, and struck off his ear. And Jesus answered
and said unto them, Are ye come out, as against a robber, with swords
and staves to seize me? I was daily with you in the temple teaching,
and ye took me not: but this is done that the scriptures might be fulfilled.
And they all left him, and fled.

And a certain young man followed with him, having a linen cloth cast
about him, over his naked body: and they lay hold on him; but he left the
linen cloth, and fled naked. (Mark 14.47-52)

And when they that were about him saw what would follow, they said,
Lord, shall we smite with the sword? And a certain one of them smote the
servant of the high priest, and struck off his right ear. But Jesus answered
and said, Suffer ye thus far. And he touched his ear, and healed him.
And Jesus said unto the chief priests, and captains of the temple, and elders,
which were come against him, Are ye come out, as against a robber,
with swords and staves? When I was with you daily in the temple,
ye stretched not forth your hands against me: but this is your hour, and
the power of darkness. (Luke 22.49-53)

Matt. 26.51. *And behold one of them that were with Jesus.* Luke says
that the disciples made common cause to fight for their Master. Again
it is evident how much more spirited and ready we are for fighting,
than for bearing the cross. We should always prudently reckon what
the Lord bids, us, what He requires from each of us, in case the exuber-
ance of our zeal boils over without reason or restraint. As for the
disciples being said to have asked Christ, they did not do it with any
intention of obeying His orders, but testified by these words that they
were braced and ready to hold off the enemy's force. Peter did not
wait for command or permission to be given him to strike out, but
leapt rashly into wrong use of force. At first sight such energy seems
praiseworthy, in that the disciples had forgotten their weakness,
though they were not equal to the opposition, and offered their bodies
in their Master's service and did not hesitate to face certain death: they
prefer to perish with their Master than have Him put under while they
live to see it. But because they attempt out of turn to do more than

God's calling allows or permits, they are duly condemned for their rashness. So we learn, for our services to be pleasing to the Lord, to depend on His bidding. Let no-one lift a finger unless as far as he shall have been commanded. A particular reason for carefully and properly holding ourselves in check is that instead of well-ordered zeal it is mostly wild imbalance that rules in us. Peter's name is not mentioned here by the Evangelists. John testifies that it was he, and from the context a little later it will be obvious that it was Peter whose name is not mentioned here. Yet we may readily infer from Luke that the others also joined in the same disorder: Christ is not addressing one only, but saying to them all in general, *suffer ye thus far.*

Matt. 26.52. *Put up again thy sword.* In these words Christ confirms the Law's precept that private individuals were forbidden to take up the sword. We should specially notice the sanction which follows: this Penalty was not fixed by men's choosing to avenge their own blood, but God Himself in severely banning murder testified how dear to Him is the human race. First then He refuses the defence of Himself by force of arms, because God forbade violence in the Law. This is the general reason: he goes on to add a special one. The question arises, however, if we are never allowed to use force against unjust force seeing that Peter was dealing with godless and wicked villains, and yet is censured for snatching up a sword. If there is no exception for moderate defence in this affair, it seems that Christ ties our hands completely. Although we dealt with this question at greater length in the fifth chapter, yet I must repeat my judgment now in a few words. First we should make a distinction between the civil court and the court of conscience. If anyone resists a robber, because the laws arm him against a common enemy of the human race, he will not be liable to punishment in public courts. As often as defence is opposed to unjust aggression, the penalty which God commanded earthly judges to exact is annulled. Yet the goodness of the cause in itself does not absolve the conscience of guilt, unless there is also pure motive. For a man to defend himself duly and freely he must first strip himself of hot anger or hatred, of any desire for vengeance, of all wild bursts of temper, that his action of defence may have nothing in it unruly. Since this is rare, indeed scarcely ever occurs, it is right for Christ to recall us to the general rule, to keep off the sword altogether. The injunction has been foolishly misapplied by some fanatics, so as to take the sword from the hands of the judges. They claim it is forbidden to strike with the sword. I grant it is true that no man may take the sword at his own pleasure to commit murder. But I deny that magistrates (who are God's servants, through whom He works out His judgments) are to be counted on the same basis. In fact these words of Christ's explicitly confirm their authority. When He declares that murderers must be removed from their midst, it follows that the sword is put into the hand of judges to punish wrongful killings. It happens sometimes that man-slaughter is punished in other ways, but this is the ordinary practice by which God willed the cruel violence of wicked men to be checked, lest their career go unpunished. Certain canonists have dared to go to such a pitch of impudence as to teach that the sword was not taken away from Peter, but that he was ordered to keep it out of sight until the chance came to draw it. We can see from this how crassly and boldly these dogs have made a game of God's Word.

Matt. 26.53. *Or thinkest thou that I cannot.* Now follows the special reason I mentioned a little above. Christ lets them know that He would have a far better and more legitimate form of defence at hand if it were not that He must obey His Father's decree. Briefly, since He was by the eternal purpose of God destined for sacrifice, and this was witnessed to in Scripture oracles, He must not fight against it. So Peter's rashness is censured on other grounds, not only for attempting to undermine heaven's decree but also blocking the path of mankind's redemption. The Lord, to prove their foolishness more plainly, makes this comparison. If he had to find a guard to protect His life, He could lay hand on not eleven angels but a large and invincible army. Since He does not call on the angels to bring Him aid, far less does He resort to inconsidered means, from which He can hope for no benefit. The disturbance the disciples created was of no more use than the croaking of a few frogs. Certain interpreters waste their efforts over this, how Christ could have secured angels at His Father's hands when His decree was that He should meet death. They find inconsistent that He should have exposed His Son to death, bare and unarmed, because it had to be so, and had once for all been decreed, and yet might have been in-fluenced by prayers to send Him assistance. But Christ's words are conditional: that He had a far better way to protect His life, except that the Father's will was against it. This removes all inconsistency, Christ held off asking His Father, precisely because He was sure it would conflict with His decree. We gain a useful lesson from this, that injury is done to God by those who take refuge in forbidden means under the pretext of emergency. If anyone is deprived of legitimate means and support, he is swept headlong into evil counsels and vicious methods: for few attend to God's secret protection, which alone should be enough to give us peace. Danger may be imminent upon us. Since in the flesh no way out is obvious, we turn our minds this way and that, as if there were no angels in heaven which Scripture says so often are set as guardians of our salvation. Thereby we lose their aid. Those who are forced by restlessness or excessive worry to put out their hands to forbidden measures against trouble are certainly renouncing the providence of God.

Matt. 26.54. *How then should the scripture be fulfilled?* Christ means by this word that He must make no attempt to escape death, to which He knew He was called by the Father. He did not Himself need the Scriptures to teach Him that He was divinely appointed to die then, but since mortals cannot grasp what God has determined in Himself until the Word reveals it, Christ thinks of His disciples and rightly brings before them the testimony God had given of His will. We know that whatever troubles fall on us are inflicted by God Himself, but since we do not know the result, we do not rebel against His authority in seeking the remedies He allows. When His will has been discovered there is nothing left but to accept it. Though the lesson Christ gives here is simply that He must patiently endure His death, because on Scripture's testimony it had to be so, the application of this teaching goes further, that Scripture is the right restraint for the arrogance of the flesh. God shows us what pleases Him in order that He may keep us in obedience to His will. Paul gives Scripture this role of training us to be patient and supplying our need in adversity, as far as we may need comfort. In Luke Christ tells off the disciples more curtly, *suffer ye thus far*. It is a sharp reproof of their boldness, for going as far as to commit capital offence; at the same time it gives hope of pardon if they go no further in their sinful fury.

Luke 22.51. *And he touched his ear.* Peter's foolish zeal had left a serious mark of disgrace on his Master and His teaching. No doubt Satan would have used this means of trying to load the Gospel with lasting reproach, that Christ had raised insurrection with the help of cut-throats and rioters. I think this is the reason why Christ healed the wound He inflicted. A dreadful, monstrous stupor must have held His enemies, from not being moved by the sight of such a wonder. Less wonderful perhaps that they failed to see Christ's power on another person: for though His own voice had laid them low, they still did not cease their rage. It is a spirit of vertigo with which Satan maddens the reprobate when they leave the Lord and tumble into blindness. Particularly in that servant who has healed, we see a prime example of ingratitude: the power of Christ did not convince him, he did not regret his hardness of heart, he was not won over by kindness to become disciple instead of foe. It is a foolish comment of the monks that he was also healed in mind so as not to damage Christ's work, as if daily God's goodness were not poured out on undeserving men.

Matt. 26.55. *As against a robber.* In these words Christ expostulates with His enemies for heaping infamy on Him by coming out with a large show of force: for it means, 'Why did you need to put on such armour, as if there were some robber to be overcome? I have always lived among you unarmed and quiet. When I taught in the temple it would have been easy to arrest me without detailing troops.' Though he complains of their evil intention in rushing a violent attack on Him like a revolutionary, He is again pricking their bad conscience; led by a traitor, they can only approach him with trembling and many signs of diffidence.

Matt. 26.56. *But all this is come to pass.* A rather different account in the other two. What Matthew says in his own person, Mark seems to attribute to Christ. Luke uses different words, namely *this is your hour and the power of darkness.* The mind of the Holy Spirit is certain however; whatever the plots of the wicked, nothing was done at all except by the bidding and providence of God. For (as was said before) God gave no testimony through His prophets but what He had determined with Himself. Here we are taught first that however Satan and all the godless break the leash and exult themselves, God's hand is still master pulling them as He wills despite their wishes. Secondly we learn, although the wicked fulfil what is predicted in the Scriptures yet since God does not use them as His rightful servants but secretly pushes them into a course they have no mind for—they are not excusable, God tightly uses their evil minds, but the blame sticks to them. Note besides, that Christ said this to obviate offence which might have greatly worried weak minds, seeing Him so rudely harassed. He not only had regard for the disciples, but wished also to rebuff the enemies' pride, in case they should triumph over a victory won. So He says in Luke, *this is your hour*, meaning for a short time the Lord allowed them this freedom. *The power of darkness* is taken as the devil's, a term that also had the full effect of undoing their glory. However they exalt themselves Christ shows that they are nothing but the devil's retinue. When all is chaos and confusion and the devil spreads darkness and seems to uproot the whole structure of the universe, we should know the light of God's providence shining high in heaven. At length He will order what is upset. Let us learn to lift up the eyes of faith to His serenity. When it is said that *all the disciples fled* we may again gather that they were much more ready for rash action than for following their Master.

Mark 14.51. *And a certain young man.* How it has happened that some have imagined this to be John, I do not know, nor should we greatly care: it is more to the point to grasp the reason for Mark telling the story. I reckon that this was his intention, that we should know that in disorder, shameless and unrestrained (as is the way with ruined causes) the wicked proceeded to arrest a young man, unknown and suspected of no crime, who only just slipped from their clutches, without his clothes. It is likely that the young man mentioned, being a follower of

Christ's, heard the riot in the night; put on no clothes but a linen wrap, and hoped either to reveal the plot or at least to perform some duty of devotion. It is certainly evident, as I have just remarked, that those wicked men acted with savage violence when they did not spare a young man who had leapt from his bed half-dressed at the uproar.

And they that had taken Jesus led him away to the house of Caiaphas the high priest, where the scribes and the elders were gathered together. But Peter followed him afar off, unto the court of the high priest, and entered in, and sat with the officers, to see the end. Now the chief priests and the whole council sought false witness against Jesus, that they might put him to death; and they found it not, though many false witnesses came. But afterward came two, and said, This man said, I am able to destroy the temple of God, and to build it in three days. (Matt. 26.57-61)

And they led Jesus away to the high priest: and there come together with him all the chief priests and the elders and the scribes. And Peter had followed him afar off, even within, into the court of the high priest; and he was sitting with the officers, and warming himself in the light of the fire. Now the chief priests and the whole council sought witness against Jesus to put him to death; and found it not. For many bare false witness against him, and their witness agreed not together. And there stood up certain, and bare false witness against him, saying, We heard him say, I will destroy this temple that is made with hands, and in three days I will build another made without hands. And not even so did their witness agree together. (Mark 14.53-59)

And they seized him, and led him away, and brought him into the high priest's house. But Peter followed afar off. (Luke 22.54)

Luke follows a different order of events from Matthew and Mark. We shall endeavour to reconcile these differences in their own place. Now we should glance briefly at what is worth noting in the account of Matthew and Mark. First, to remove the scandal of the cross, look at the benefit Christ gives us in His self-emptying: thus will the incomparable goodness of God and the efficacy of grace dispel by their own light whatever is ugly and shameful in the scene. For the Son of God to be arrested, bound, and put under the restraints of the flesh, was degrading. But as we realise that by His bonds we are loosed from the tyrannical power of the devil and from the guilt which in God's sight kept us prisoner, not only is that stumbling-block removed upon which our faith might have struck, but there follows in its place a great wonder at the immense grace of God, who reckoned our deliverance so precious that He handed over His only-begotten Son to be bound by the wicked. This will also be a singular pledge of Christ's love towards us: He did not spare Himself, but willingly put the shackles on His wrists, that He might relieve our souls of far worse chains.

Matt. 26.57. *They led him away to Caiaphas.* Although major jurisdiction, as they say, had been taken from the Jews, there was something left of the judicial power which the Law confers on the high priest (Deut. 17.8) so that in losing absolute authority they had still a secondary court of discipline. This is why Christ is taken for examination to the high priest, not for final judgment to be given at the tribunal, but so that the priests could later bring him before the Governor with its judgment already round His neck. Caiaphas the Pontiff was also named Joseph. The historian Josephus (*Hist.* bk. 18) says he was raised to the rank of high priest by Valerius Gratus, Governor of Judaea, when Simon, son of Camithus, was removed from office. The Evangelists only give the surname, perhaps because he was more generally and more popularly called by it. Matthew says the priests assembled at Caiaphas' house, not that they were meeting at midnight before Christ was brought in, but because the place had been arranged. They were to come quickly together as soon as news came in the early hours, though we have just seen that some of priestly rank were out in the night with the troops on Christ's arrest. We have often seen elsewhere that the Evangelists were not too exact about the time sequence. In this present passage they had nothing else in mind than to show how the Son of God was overtaken by the wicked conspiracy of the whole council. This is the fearful and appalling sight set before our eyes: at that time in all the world there was no other temple of God or rightful worship or face of the Church beyond that at Jerusalem. The supreme Pontiff was the image of the one Mediator between God and men. Those who came to that council represented the entire Church of God, yet they all conspired together to extinguish the one hope of salvation. As was declared in the oracle of David (Ps. 118.22), 'the stone rejected by the builders would become the head-stone of the corner'. Similarly in Isaiah (8.14) it had been predicted, the God of hosts would be 'a stone of offence' to the whole people of Israel, on which they would strike. It was duly foreseen by the Lord, that such impiety of men should not trouble faithful souls.

Matt. 26.59. *Sought false witness.* The Evangelists remark in these words that the priests had no intention to inquire into the case, so as to come to a right decision after examining the facts. They had already settled on Christ's death: they were only looking for a way of putting Him down. Equitable dealing was now quite out of the question, for there was no preliminary examination of the case. In seeking false witnesses their cruel treachery is revealed. And when their hopes are disappointed and they still persist, we see all the better the blindness of their obstinacy. In the dark clouds of their fury the innocence of the Son of God shone out, so that the very devils knew He died an innocent man. Besides we should note, they are called *false witnesses*, not because they are men who produce a lie made out of nothing but because they slanderously pervert right words and distort them in a criminal sense, as in the instance here detailed of the fall of the temple and its restoration. Christ had said, when the temple of His body was destroyed, He would raise it up in three days. These false witnesses do not think up a new utterance, but debase His words, as if He had boasted to perform some sorcery over building the temple. As the slander was trifling and worthless, we may readily gather how blinded the priests and scribes were in their madness when they put Christ to death, without any pretext.

And the high priest stood up, and said unto him, Answeres thou nothing? what is it which these witness against thee? But Jesus held his peace. And the high priest said unto him, I adjure thee by the living God, that thou tell us whether thou be the Christ, the Son of God. Jesus saith unto him, Thou hast said: nevertheless I say unto you, Henceforth ye shall see the Son of man sitting at the right hand of power, and coming on the clouds of heaven. Then the high priest rent his garments, saying, He hath spoken blasphemy: what further need have we of witnesses? Behold, now ye have heard the blasphemy: what think ye? They answered and said, He is worthy of death. Then did they spit in his face and buffet him: and some smote him with the palms of their hands, saying, Prophesy unto us, thou Christ: who is he that struck thee? (Matt. 26.62-68)

And the high priest stood up in the midst, and asked Jesus, saying, Answerest thou nothing? what is it which these witness against thee? But he held his peace, and answered nothing. Again the high priest asked him, and saith unto him, Art thou the Christ, the Son of the Blessed? And Jesus said, I am: and ye shall see the Son of man sitting at the right hand of power, and coming with the clouds of heaven. And the high priest rent his clothes, and saith, What further need have we of witnesses? Ye have heard the blasphemy: what think ye? And they all condemned him to be worthy of death. And some began to spit in him, and to cover his face, and to buffet him, and to say unto him, Prophesy: and the officers received him with blows of their hands. (Mark 14.60-65)

And the men that held Jesus mocked him, and beat him. And they blind-

folded him, and asked him, saying, Prophesy: who is he that struck thee?
And many other things spake they against him, reviling him.

And as soon as it was day, the assembly of the elders of the people was
gathered together, both chief priests and scribes; and they led him away to
their council, saying, If thou art the Christ, tell us. But he said unto them,
If I tell you, ye will not believe: and if I ask you, ye will not answer.
But from henceforth shall the Son of man be seated at the right hand of the
power of God. And they all said, Art thou then the Son of God? And
he said unto them, Ye say that I am. And they said, What further need
have we of witness? for we ourselves have heard from his own mouth.
(Luke 22.63-71)

Matt. 26.62. *And the high priest stood up.* We may be sure that Christ
kept silence under the attacks of the false witnesses both because they
deserved to have no answer and because He had no desire to be acquitted,
knowing His hour had come. Yet Caiaphas triumphed at His silence as
though He were dumb with defeat—as is usual with men who have a
bad conscience. It was the height of wickedness to pretend that Christ
was blameworthy on the basis of the witnesses' charges. His question,
what is it which these witness against thee? is as much as to say, 'What other
reason could these men have for their attack unless the compulsion of
their beliefs? They would not have come out against you without good
cause.' As though He did not know that they were suborned by
corrupt means, but this is the headstrong behaviour of people who
throw off all shame in their wickedness, as long as they are superior in
authority and force. Again Christ kept silent, not only because the
objection was worthless but because as a man appointed for sacrifice He
had put away all care for defending Himself.

Matt. 26.63. *I adjure thee by the living God.* The Pontiff reckoned this
crime sufficient for Christ's condemnation, if He had professed Himself
to be Christ, but since they all claimed to look for redemption from the
Christ, he should first have asked if He were in fact the man. To say
that there would not be a Christ, by whose hand the people would find
deliverance, was more than they would dare. Jesus comes into their
midst with the title of Christ. Why did they fail to take note of the
facts themselves? Why not examine the signs on which a right judgment
could have been based? Their decision to destroy Christ had been
taken finally, and they were satisfied with this pretext of sacrilege,
namely His assumption of the glory of Godhead. Yet Caiaphas ex-
amines the matter on oath as though he were prepared to look into the
matter properly and give way, while all the time his mind is full of a
perverse hatred and contempt for Christ, and is so blinded by pride and
self-seeking that he takes it as a settled case, on the mere admission of fact,

without any inquiry over the rights, that he has powers for a fair con-viction. We may gather from Caiaphas' words that the title of Messiah was much used among the Jews at that time as a name for the Son of God: it would only have been from regular usage that this line of interrogation started. From Scripture too, they had learned that He was no less Son of God than son of David. It seems Caiaphas used the appellation perhaps to terrify Christ, perhaps to increase the ill-feeling against Him, as if he had said, 'See where you are going. You cannot say you are Christ without also taking on the name of Son of God, as Scripture assigns it to Him.' It is the same object as in Mark's version, using *Blessed* in place of God. With this pretence of reverence he makes the charge weigh heavier on Christ, as if He had profaned God's holy Name.

Matt. 26.64. *Thou hast said.* In Luke there is inserted another reply in which Christ criticises the malice of the priests for not asking out of a desire for knowledge. He says, *If I tell you ye will not believe*: meaning by these words that even if He proved Himself to be Christ a hundred times over, He would make no effect on stubborn minds. They had not only heard, they had seen miracles with their eyes. And these, without Christ's speaking, asserted Christ's heavenly and divine power, nay shouted out, 'He is the Redeemer promised of old.' He then makes a declaration, which although given at greater length in Matthew is in the same sense. Jesus confesses that He is the Christ, not for the sake of avoiding death, but rather to inflame His enemies' anger more against Himself. Although he was then an object of scorn in His poor state, and almost at collapse, He declares that in His day He will come with royal Majesty, so that they may tremble before the judgment, of Him whom now they refuse to acknowledge as the Author of their salvation. The meaning is that they are greatly deceived if they reckon who He is, on the basis of present appearances, for He must be brought low, and al-most to nothing, before He appears in the garments of His Kingship, with nobility and magnificent splendour. The word *henceforth* dis-tinguishes His second coming from His first.

From this may be drawn a useful lesson with wider application: How do the wicked come to be so unconcerned? How do they reach such a pitch of mad rebellion, except that the crucified Christ is not for them a great reward? They must be recalled to that dread judgment which, in their folly, they cannot flee. For all that they pull silly faces, as hearing a fairy tale, when they are told of the future coming of Christ, the Judge will not fail in His purpose when He calls them to His tribunal, and bids them be cited at the Gospel call, to render them more in-excusable. The declaration is of greatest benefit to believers now, for with eyes of hope they may see Christ seated at the right hand of the

Father and wait with patience, and likewise be certain that the wicked's rage against Him while He is absent will not be without consequence: for they in turn will be forced to look on Him coming down from heaven, whom now they both despise and trample proudly beneath their feet. The metaphor contained in the word *right hand* must be well enough known, for it occurs frequently in Scripture. Christ is said to sit at the right hand of the Father, because, appointed supreme King (to rule the world in His name), He holds the seat second from Him in honour and power. Christ sits at the Father's right hand, because He is His deputy: and this is called the right hand of power because now God only exercises His authority through the hand of His Son, and on the last day will execute judgment.

Matt. 26.65. *Then the high priest.* We see from this how little the godless had benefited from those miracles by which Christ had witnessed to His Divinity. But it is no wonder that they despised the Son of God under the humble form of a servant, for they were touched with no concern for the promised salvation. If they had not utterly cast off all sense of religion, they should in their lamentable state have looked urgently for their Redeemer. Now when He is presented to them, and they, without any inquiry, reject Him, are they not, as far as they may, extinguishing all the promises of God? First the high priest declares Christ a blasphemer: then the rest concur. The tearing of garments shows clearly how boldly and spitefully these profane scorners of God put up a false pretence of zeal. It was proper for the high priest, should he hear God's name shamefully violated, both to burn and feel pain inwardly and to give an outward gesture of aversion, but in making no inquiry, he makes himself absurd, and invents blasphemy. Yet this treacherous hypocrite puts on a false mask and teaches the servants of God how seriously blasphemies are to be treated. He gives an example, to condemn those whose disgraceful weakness of character is undisturbed by insult to religion, but who make no more of it than the hearing of silly jokes from a cheap comic.

Matt. 26.67. *Then did they spit in his face.* Either Luke has inverted the order of the narrative or the Lord suffered the same great insult twice: the latter seems likely to me. I have no doubt that the servants had the nerve to spit on Christ and hit him rudely, from seeing him condemned to death by the Council at their first judgment. The object of all their mockery was to show how absurd it was for a man to be leader of the prophets if he could not, when blindfolded, look out for the slaps they aimed. God's providence however changed their rudeness to a very different course, for the Face of Christ marred with spittle and blows has restored to us that image which sin had corrupted, indeed destroyed.

168

Now Peter was sitting without in the court: and a maid came to him, say-
ing, Thou also wast with Jesus the Galilaean. But he denied before them
all, saying, I know not what thou sayest. And when he was gone into
the porch, another maid saw him, and saith unto them that were there,
This man also was with Jesus the Nazarene. And again he denied with an
oath, I know not the man. And after a little while they that stood by
came and said to Peter, Of a truth thou also art one of them; for thy
speech betrayeth thee. Then began he to curse and to swear, I know not
the man. And straightway the cock crew. And Peter remembered the
word which Jesus had said, Before the cock crow, thou shalt deny me thrice,
and he went out, and wept bitterly. (Matt. 26.69-75)

And as Peter was beneath in the court, there cometh one of the maids of
the high priest; and seeing Peter warming himself, she looked upon him,
and saith, Thou also wast with the Nazarene, even Jesus. But he
denied, saying, I neither know, nor understand what thou sayest: and he
went out into the porch; and the cock crew. And the maid saw him, and
began again to say to them that stood by, This is one of them. But he
again denied it. And after a little while again they that stood by said of
Peter, Of a truth thou art one of them; for thou art a Galilaean. But he
began to curse, and to swear, I know not this man of whom ye speak. And
straightway the second time the cock crew. And Peter called to mind
the word, how that Jesus said unto him, Before the cock crow twice, thou
shalt deny me thrice. And when he thought thereon, he wept. (Mark
14.16-72)

And when they had kindled a fire in the midst of the court, and had sat
down together, Peter sat in the midst of them. And a certain maid seeing
him as he sat in the light of the fire, and looking stedfastly upon him, said,
This man also was with him. But he denied, saying, Woman, I know
him not. And after a little while another saw him, and said, Thou also
art one of them. But Peter said, Man I am not. And after the space
of about one hour another confidently affirmed, saying, Of a truth this
man also was with him: for he is a Galilaean. But Peter said, Man, I
know not what thou sayest. And immediately, while he yet spake, the
cock crew. And the Lord turned, and looked upon Peter. And Peter
remembered the word of the Lord, how that he had said unto him,
Before the cock crow this day, thou shalt deny me thrice. And he went
out, and wept bitterly. (Luke 22.55-62)

Peter's fall, here described, brilliantly mirrors our own infirmity.
His repentance in turn is a memorable demonstration for us of God's
goodness and mercy. The story told of one man contains teaching of
general, and indeed prime, benefit for the whole Church; it teaches

those who stand to take care and caution; it encourages the fallen to trust in pardon. First, we must note that Peter acted without thought in entering the court of the high priest. It was the disciple's duty to follow his Master. But as he was warned of the lapse he would make, he should rather have hid in some corner and not run into an occasion of sinning. It often happens that the faithful throw themselves into temptations under the appearance of virtue. We must ask the Lord that the Spirit may hold us on firm rein, in case we go beyond the mark and at once pay the penalty. We must ask, as often as we undertake any thing, that He may not allow us to fall in the midst of our efforts or at the outset of the task, but may supply from heaven strength to the end. A sense of our weakness should not be a reason for doing nothing, for not going wherever God calls us, but it should check our rashness, in case we attempt more than our calling. It should prompt us to pray, that God who gave a right beginning, may add the grace of persever-ance.

Matt. 26.69. *A maid came unto him.* Here we see that it does not take a heavy fight to break a man, nor many forces and devices. Whoever is not dependent on God's hand will soon fall, at a breath of wind or the noise of a falling leaf. Peter certainly was no less brave than any of us, and had already given no ordinary proof of his high courage (though his boldness was excessive). Yet he does not wait to be brought to the tribunal of the Pontiff, or until the enemy threatens his violent death, but, at the voice of a young woman, he is scared, and straight out denies his Master. A moment ago he had seemed to himself a soldier, even unto death. Let us remember that our powers are so unequal to bearing large-scale attack that they fail even at the mere shadow of a fight. So God gives us a due reward for our treachery, in disarming us and stripping us of all virtue, till we tremble at nothing at all, once we have cast off our fear for Him. If a lively fear of God had dwelt in Peter's heart, it would have been an insuperable rampart. But now, stripped and defenceless, he panics when danger is still far off.

Matt. 26.70. *He denied before them all.* This is a circumstance that aggravates the offence; Peter, in denying his Master, did not take note of the crowd of witnesses in his fear. The Spirit precisely wishes to impress on us that the sight of men should embolden us to hold firm to our faith. If we deny Christ in the sight of the weak, they may be shocked and cast down by our example, and thereby we destroy all the souls we can. If, in the presence of wicked scorners of God and enemies of the Gospel, we cheat Christ of His due testimony, we expose His sacred name to the ridicule of all. As a bold and free confession builds up pious minds and puts the unbeliever to shame, so defection involves a public collapse of faith for the Church and a shaming of sound doctrine. The higher a man stands the more he should take care to himself, for he cannot fall from his rank without doing greater damage. The form of denial set down here shows sufficiently that wretched sophists gain nothing by their ingenuity, when with ambiguous and smart-spoken tricks they make evasions, if they are called to give an account of their faith. Peter does not explicitly deny the whole teaching of the Gospel. He only denies he knew the man, but because under Christ's person he buries indirectly the light of the offered redemption, he is condemned as a foul and base betrayer. He had just heard from the Lord's mouth that a confession of faith was a pleasing sacrifice in God's sight, so his denial is quite beyond excuse, robbing God of His due service and Christ of His honour. Take this point; as soon as one departs from a simple and sincere profession of Christ, one robs Him of His rightful witness.

Matt. 26.71. *Another maid saw him.* We tend to guess, from Mark's account, that it is the same maid: he certainly does not say she is a different one. There is nothing contradictory, in fact it is likely, that one girl's remark went round them all, the first pointing him out to many over and over again, the others going up to find out for sure and spreading the discovery further still. John says that the second questioning came not from the maid, but from a crowd of men. Obviously the report that started with the girl was picked up by the bystanders, who turned it against Peter. There is another difference between Mark and the other three. He mentions the cock crowing twice, the others say that it only crowed when Peter had denied the Lord for the third time. This problem too has an easy solution, since Mark says nothing to contradict the report of the others. What they pass over in silence, he relates explicitly. I have no doubt when Christ said to Peter, 'Before the cock crows', He meant the cock-crowing in its various repetitions. Cocks do not only crow once but repeat their calls several times, yet all the cock-crows of one night are called the cock-crowing. So Matthew, Luke and John say that Peter denied the Lord thrice before the end of cock-crowing. Mark gives the greater detail, that Peter came in quite a short space of time to his third denial, and did not repent at the first cock-crow. We do not say profane historians are in disagreement if one of them tells a thing the others leave unmentioned. Although Mark's narrative is different it is not at odds with the others. It is to be noted that once Peter found he could not slip out of it with a simple denial, he doubles his crime by putting in an oath. A little later when he is pressed more strongly he goes as far as cursing.

We see how once a sinner has fallen he is rapidly taken into worse plight. Those who begin with minor faults rush from them headlong into the foulest crimes, which at first they would have abhorred. This

171

is God's just punishment, once we deprive ourselves of the assistance of the Holy Spirit, that He allows Satan to work his power on us with violence, tossing us this way and that in our utter addiction and slavery. This is particularly the case with denial of the faith. When a man, for fear of the cross, turns aside from the pure profession of the Gospel he goes further if he sees he has not satisfied his enemies. And what he had not dared to make a simple confession of, he must now adjure outright without the chance of concealment. Then this also must be observed, that virtually in one moment of time Peter defected three times over: whence it appears how slippery and steep is the slope on which we fall, whenever Satan drives us. There will certainly be no limit to our fall unless the Lord reach out His hand to hold us. When the vigour of the Spirit of grace died in Peter, as often as he was asked about Christ, whoever approached, he was ready to deny with a hundred, yes a thousand denials. Disgraceful as it was for him to fall three times, yet the Lord spared him, and checked the mouths of the enemies, in case they made more attacks. So the Lord must daily bridle Satan, or he would overwhelm us with temptations beyond number. Though he does not cease to come against us with all kinds of trickery, unless the Lord had regard for our weakness and held off the brunt of his rage, we should have to encounter a vast onslaught of temptation. In this respect we must glory in the Lord's mercy, that He allows no more than the bare hundredth part of our enemy's evil purpose to make way against us.

Matt. 26.74. *Then began he to curse.* At the third denial Peter's faithlessness towards his Master reached its highest peak. Not content with an oath, he passed to cursing, calling damnation on his body and soul. He wills himself cursed of God, if ever he knew Christ. This has the force of saying, 'May I perish, if I have any part in the salvation of God.' Christ's goodness is the more wonderful, that He healed the disciple brought forth from such a pit. This passage teaches that it is not direct blasphemy against the Spirit for a man fallen through weakness of the flesh to deny the truth he knows. Peter had certainly heard from the Lord's mouth what a detestable treachery it was to deny Him before men, and what a terrible vengeance awaits them, at the hands of God and the angels, who desert their confession of faith in cowardly fear of the cross: not for nothing, a little before, had he preferred death and torment to denial of Christ. Now in full knowledge and after due warning, he comes to grief, yet wins pardon afterwards. It follows that he sinned from weakness, and not from incurable malice. He would willingly have offered to Christ the due devotion that he owed, but fear had extinguished his sparks of right desire.

Matt. 26.75. *And Peter remembered.* Besides the cock-crow Luke tells us there was the sight of Christ: for he had first ignored the cock's crow, as we have learned from Mark. So he had to meet Christ's eyes to come to himself. This is the experience of each one of us. Which of us does not neglect with deaf ear and unconcern—not the many and various songs of birds (and yet they prompt us to glorify God)—but the actual voice of God, which in Law and Gospel clearly and distinctly resounds for our learning? And it is not for one day only that our minds are seized with this dumb stupidity, but on and on, until He grants us a sight of Himself. This alone converts the hearts of men. It is well worth noting, that it was no ordinary look (since He had already looked on Judas, who became none the better of it), but with the turning of His eyes on Peter, there went the secret power of the Spirit piercing his heart with the radiance of His grace. Whence we learn, that as often as a man has lapsed, repentance for him only starts from the look the Lord gives. *Wept bitterly*. It is likely that Peter went out through fear, not daring to weep where witnesses could see: again he displayed his weakness. We gather that he did not win pardon by any satisfaction, but from the kind fatherly affection of God. The example teaches us that however lame our repentance, yet we may have good hope. As long as it is sincere, God scorns not even feeble repentance. Peter's secret tears testified in the Face of God and of the angels that his sorrow was true. Hidden from the eyes of men he puts before him God and the angels: from the inmost feelings of his heart flow those tears. We should note this, since we see many in floods of tears, as long as there is someone to watch, eyes are dry as soon as they are by themselves. No doubt tears that are not forced from us by God's judgments, spring from self-seeking and hypocrisy. It is asked whether true penitence requires weeping. I answer that the faithful often sigh unto God with dry eyes, and confess their fault, to obtain pardon: but in the graver sins it is too stupid and unfeeling not to be wounded with grief and sorrow to the point of shedding tears. Scripture, after convicting men of their crimes, urges them to sackcloth and ashes.

Now when morning was come, all the chief priests and the elders of the people took counsel against Jesus to put him to death: and they bound him, and led him away, and delivered him up to Pilate the governor.

Then Judas, which betrayed him, when he saw that he was condemned, repented himself, and brought back the thirty pieces of silver to the chief priests and elders, saying, I have sinned in that I betrayed innocent blood. But they said, What is that to us? see thou to it. And he cast down the pieces of silver into the sanctuary, and departed; and he went away and hanged himself. And the chief priests took the pieces of silver, and said, It is not lawful to put them into the treasury, since it is the price of blood.

173

And they took counsel, and bought with them the potter's field, to bury strangers in. Wherefore that field was called, The field of blood, unto this day. Then was fulfilled that which was spoken by Jeremiah the prophet, saying, And they took the thirty pieces of silver, the price of him that was priced, whom certain of the children of Israel did price; and they gave them for the potter's field, as the Lord appointed me. (Matt. 27.1-10)

And straightway in the morning the chief priests with the elders and scribes, and the whole council, held a consultation, and bound Jesus, and carried him away, and delivered him up to Pilate. (Mark 15.1)

And the whole company of them rose up, and brought him before Pilate. (Luke 23.1)

Matt. 27.1. *Now when morning was come (they) took counsel.* After the supreme Pontiff and his council, at an unsuitable hour of night, put through an inquiry over Jesus, they decide at daybreak to send him before Pilate. In this they preserve a form of justice, in case their haste be suspect, and they should rush (as is the way of riots) to Pilate too early. It is likely that when Christ was taken out of their meeting they continued to debate with themselves, and determined without longer delay what they intended to do. It has already been said that by the time that Christ left them, and met Peter, it was after cock-crowing, and break of day. The Evangelists do not mean that they went away from that place, but simply relate that at the first light of dawn Christ was appointed by them to die, and they did not waste a minute in the energetic execution of their crime. What Luke said before, that *as soon as it was day the assembly was gathered*, should not be explained as referring to the very beginning, but to the last act, which is here appended, as if to say, once day broke, since the Lord had confessed He was Son of God, they confirmed their decree that He should die. If they had been allowed to decide on life and death over a man, they would all have struggled with each other in their rage to savage Him with their hands: but as Pilate presided over capital offences, they are forced to defer to his tribunal. Their previous trial sets up the trap. The stoning of Stephen was an act of sedition (as comes in troubled times). The Son of God had to be condemned in proper form by an earthly judge, so that He might clear our guilt in heaven.

Matt. 27.3. *Then Judas . . . when he saw.* The adverb does not indicate a particular moment of time in Matthew. He will shortly add, that when Judas saw the payment for his treachery spurned by the priests, he threw it back in the temple. Now they came straight from Caiaphas' house to the Praetorium, and stayed there till Christ was condemned. They would hardly have been found in the temple on that day, but as he is dealing with the tragic madness of the Sanhedrin, he also inserted the death of Judas (in which their blind obstinacy and almost iron hardness of heart appears). He says that Judas was touched with repentance, not that he repented, but that he was displeased with the crime he had committed. God often opens the eyes of the reprobate to begin to feel and to shudder for their wrongs. Those who really grieve to the point of repentance are said not only μεταμελεῖν but also μετανοεῖν: hence the word μετάνοια for the real conversion of man to God. Judas conceived a weariness and horror, not leading him back to God but plunging him into despair, that he might be an example of a man banned from the grace of God. Paul rightly speaks of sorrow as salutary which leads to repentance (II Cor. 7.10), but if a man stumbles just at the doorstep, confused and vague grief will do him no good. Rather this is the just punishment God brings on the wicked who have boldly scorned His justice; he hands them over to Satan for torment without hope of relief. True penitence is a dislike for sin, conceived from fear and respect for God which at the same time creates from itself a love and desire for justice. The wicked are far from this state of mind, for they would really wish to put no end to their sinning, and as far as possible to attempt to mock God and themselves, but in spite of digging in their heels, their conscience racks them with a blind horror, so that without hating their sin yet they feel it heavy and painful, with grief and trouble. Hence their grief is no benefit to them: they do not freely turn themselves to God, nor aspire to anything better, but are attached to their wicked desires and rot in the torment that they cannot escape. In this way, as I have just said, God avenges their stubbornness. Although He draws His elect to Himself reluctantly, with correction, in due time He heals the wounds He has inflicted, that they may come to Him of their own desire, acknowledging Him as the hand that struck them, the wrath that put them to right. The former have no hatred of sin, but flee from it in dread: they are wounded with an incurable stroke and perish in their griefs. If Judas had heeded Christ's warning, there was still room for repentance, but since he had scorned such a generous call to salvation he is handed over to Satan's rule, which tosses him head-first into despair. If the papists were right in what they teach about penitence in their schools, one could find nothing lacking in Judas, as all their definition of it would apply to him. We can pick out the contrition of heart, the confession by the mouth, the satisfaction in deed, which they speak of. Whence we gather that they only grasp the outer shell, and omit the chief part which is the conversion of man to God, when broken with shame and fear, the sinner renounces himself, in order to give himself over to follow righteousness.

Matt. 27.4. *What is that to us?* This is the record of the priests' folly and madness, not warned by the grim example of Judas to take thought to themselves. I know how hypocrites are used to indulge their own fancy, and readily concoct a supposed distinction between their case and that of Judas. They thought they were not companions in crime, for all that they had taken advantage of the betrayer's perfidy. Yet Judas not only confesses his sin, but declares Christ's innocence: it follows that they have engineered the destruction of an upright man and are thereby guilty of a cruel murder. No doubt God wished to sear their consciences, to disclose the concealed corruption. Let us learn, when we see the wicked put to fright, and they have something in common with us, that these are incitements to repentance which it is doubly culpable for the stubborn to neglect. We must understand that people cannot be absolved from a man's crime if they have in any way involved themselves in it. Far less can the instigators of a crime gain any advantage from severing the tie with their agents to avoid bearing the same penalty.

Matt. 27.5. *And hanged himself.* This is the price for the pleasant path along which Satan charms the wicked; he turns them to frenzy, so that they cut themselves right off from the hope of salvation and find no comfort other than in death. Judas throws down the thirty silver pieces for which he had sold his own salvation as well as Christ—though others would have allowed him to use them, he deprives himself of their benefit, and with the sacrilegious reward for Christ's death throws away his life also. Without God moving His hand, the wicked are robbed of their desires; they gain their object yet disown the enjoyment of it and actually make a noose for themselves. They are their own executioners, forcing the penalty upon themselves, yet do they in no way lighten or abate the fierceness of God's anger. *It is not lawful to put them.* It is very obvious that the hypocrites, by pursuing the outward form, are making a gross mockery of God. As long as they do not profane their Corban they pretend to be pure in everything else and have no concern for the atrocious deal which fastened the vengeance of God as much on them as on Judas. If blood money may not be deposited in the sacred treasury, how could they draw it in the first place, for their only wealth came from the temple offerings and what they are now hesitant to put back in as polluted could have been taken from no other source? Is not the pollution from their own hands? The more the wicked try to conceal their crimes the more the Lord watches to make them public. They thought that the crime would be buried in a show of decency, if they were to purchase a bare field for burying strangers. But God's wonderful providence turned this quite into reverse, making the field a lasting memorial to their treachery, from its previous obscurity. They did not give it the name under which it was later known; public concensus called it the field of blood, as if God had commanded their shame to be published in every tongue. To care for strangers' burial was a plausible idea if any happened to die at Jerusalem who had come up there to sacrifice from distant lands. As part of them would be from Gentile stock I quite agree with ancient writers who see in this symbol a sign of hope given to the Gentiles, by being included on the price of Christ's death. I take it no further—the comment is subtle rather than solid. The word 'Corban' is Aramaic, deriving from the Hebrew קרבן of which mention has been made elsewhere.

Matt. 27.9. *Then was fulfilled that, etc.* How the name of Jeremiah crept in I cannot confess to know nor do I make much of it: obviously Jeremiah's name is put in error for Zechariah (13.7). Nothing of this sort is said of Jeremiah, or anything like it. The other passage, if not applied carefully, might seem ill-forced into a false sense, but if we adhere to the rule that the Apostles followed in citing Scripture it will be easily understood that what we find there fits Christ well. The Lord lamented that all the time He had performed the duties of shepherd, ruling over the people, He had wasted His work, and has been forced by the burden and pain to give it up altogether: He breaks His staff and says He will no longer be Pastor. He adds that when He asked His pay, He was given thirty pieces of silver. By these words He means that He was treated as cheaply as a common, low, working man. The ceremonies and empty displays that the Jews reckoned as His benefits, He compares to thirty silver pieces, as the price of a mean, no-account cowherd or labourer: so he tells them to throw it to a potter in the temple, as if to say, 'This fine present which would be as shameful for me to accept as for them to offer, is an insult; they can spend it on repairing tiles or bricks for stuffing the temple's cracks.' To make it more sure that Christ, against whom the people had from the start been malicious and ungrateful, was the God of armies, it was necessary, when He was revealed in the flesh, for Him to fulfil in His own Person now in actual fact and visible form what had previously been said of Him in a figurative sense. When their malice compelled Him to bid them farewell, to withdraw His work from them for their ingratitude, they valued Him at thirty silver pieces. This scorn for the Son of God was the peak of their impiety. *The price of him that was priced.* Matthew does not quote Zachariah's words, he only alludes to the metaphor, under which the Lord there complains of the people's ingratitude. The point is the same, when the Jews owed themselves, each one, and all that they had, to the Lord, it was indeed an insult to dismiss Him with a slave's wage, as if He had deserved no more for ruling them all those centuries than some cowherd for his one year's work. He complains that He is rated at such a mean price, when He is beyond all reckoning. When he says at the end, *whom certain of the children of Israel did price,* the language is vague. Judas made a bargain with the priests who acted in the name and person of the whole people. Hence Christ had been, as it were, put up for auction by the Jews through the voice of the crier. The price made was fit to be given to a potter.

Matt. 27.10. *As the Lord appointed.* In this phrase Matthew confirms that nothing was done apart from the providence of God. Although they aim differently, they unwittingly fulfil the old oracle. How could it ever have occurred to them to purchase a field from a potter unless the Lord had bent their error to the furtherance of His decree?

Now Jesus stood before the governor: and the governor asked him, saying, Art thou the King of the Jews? And Jesus said unto him, Thou sayest. And when he was accused by the chief prie.ts and elders, he answered nothing. Then saith Pilate unto him, Hearest thou not how many things they witness against thee? And he gave him no answer, not even to one word: insomuch that the governor marvelled greatly. (Matt. 27.11-14)

And Pilate asked him, Art thou the King of the Jews? And he answering saith unto him, Thou sayest. And the chief priests accused him of many things. And Pilate again asked him saying, Answerest thou nothing? behold how many things they accuse thee of. But Jesus no more answered anything; insomuch that Pilate marvelled. (Mark 15.2-5)

And they began to accuse him, saying, We found this man perverting our nation, and forbidding to give tribute to Caesar, and saying that he himself is Christ a king. And Pilate asked him, Art thou the King of the Jews? And he answered him and said, Thou sayest. And Pilate said unto the chief priests and the multitudes, I find no fault in this man. But they were the more urgent, saying, He stirreth up the people, teaching throughout all Judaea, and beginning from Galilee even unto this place. But when Pilate heard it, he asked whether the man were a Galilaean. And when he knew that he was of Herod's jurisdiction, he sent Him to Herod, who himself also was at Jerusalem in these days.

Now when Herod saw Jesus, he was exceeding glad: for he was of a long time desirous to see him, because he had heard concerning him; and he hoped to see some miracle done by him. And he questioned him in many words; but he answered him nothing. And the chief priests and the scribes stood, vehemently accusing him. And Herod with his soldiers set him at nought, and mocked him, and arraying him in gorgeous apparel sent him back to Pilate. And Herod and Pilate became friends with each other that very day: for before they were at enmity between themselves. (Luke 23.2-12)

Matt. 27.11. *Now Jesus stood.* Though it was an ugly sight, and far removed from the dignity of the Son of God, that He should be taken to the tribunal of a profane man to defend a capital charge in chains, like a wrongdoer: yet we must remember that upon the teaching of the cross (foolishness to the Greeks, a stumbling-block to the Jews) our salvation depends. The Son of God wished to stand bound before an earthly judge and there submit to the death sentence, that we might not doubt that we are freed of guilt and free to approach to the heavenly throne of God. If we consider what benefit we have in Christ's standing trial before Pilate, the stain of such base submission will immediately be removed. These are the only men offended by the condemnation of Christ—proud hypocrites, stupid and crass scorners of God, unashamed of their own righteousness. God's Son stood trial before a mortal man and suffered accusation and condemnation, that we might stand without fear in the presence of God. His enemies have tried to fasten undying shame upon Him, but we should rather look to the end to which God's providence directs us. If it should come to our minds how terrible is that tribunal of God, and that we could not have been absolved there unless Christ had in turn stood trial on earth, it will never shame us to boast of His chains. As often as we hear how Christ stood, in sad and cheap array, before Pilate, we shall take grounds for confidence from it; that relying on His intercessions we may come before, happy and eager. The same point is found in the silence next mentioned. Christ said nothing when the priests pressed Him from every side, in order to open our mouths by His silence. Hence the glorious freedom which Paul acclaims (Rom. 8.15) that we can call out with full voice, 'Abba, Father' (to which I shall refer again directly).

Art Thou the King of the Jews? Though there were many and various charges on which they hoped to destroy Christ it is likely that the name of King was maliciously picked on by them to draw the highest ill-favour upon Him in Pilate's eyes. The same is expressed in Luke, that they represented him as *perverting our nation and forbidding to give tribute to Caesar and saying*, etc. Nothing was more hateful to Pilate than this charge, as his greatest concern was to keep the state of the empire in peace. We see from John that the case was raised on various counts, but it is clear from the whole context that this was the chief head of accusation. Just so today, Satan endeavours to make the Gospel hated and suspect on this pretext, that Christ in raising up His Kingdom

179

undermines all the kingdoms of the world, wrecking the rights of kings and magistrates. The pride of kings is often so blind that they reckon Christ cannot rule without risk to their own authority. Thus they always give credence to a case that once was laid against Christ without cause, and so Pilate lays the other matters aside and presses Him mainly on the charge of sedition, for if he had found that Christ caused any disturbance in public order, he would eagerly have condemned Him without delay. This is the reason why he interrogated him on king-ship. Though in our three Evangelists Christ's reply is ambiguous, it is easily inferred from John that Christ plainly admitted the charge, but He made it no crime, since He denied He was an earthly King. He had no intention of clearing Himself carefully, as accused men do, which is the ambivalent answer of the Evangelists. In other words, while He did not deny that he was a King, He remarked indirectly on the un-deserved slander which His enemies laid against Him.

Matt. 27.12. *He answered nothing.* The reason for the Evangelists saying that Christ kept quiet, when we have just heard His reply come from their lips, is that He voluntarily kept from using the defence He had prepared. His earlier answer about the Kingdom was not to win release, but only to assert that He was the Redeemer, long-promised, before whose Face every knee should bow. Pilate wondered at His patience, that Christ by silence should let His innocence suffer when He might have been ready to refute the heartless and empty slanders. Christ's integrity was such that the judge saw it clearly without an advocate. Pilate wanted Christ not to let Himself down, as He might be acquitted without great ill-will. So far, Pilate's fair dealing is praise-worthy, having a favourable regard for Christ's innocence and urging Him to a defence. In case we should wonder at Christ's silence, thinking what He did strange, we should hold on to the purpose of God who was willing for His Son (whom He had appointed to be victim, for the expiation of our sins), though pure in Himself, to be found guilty on our behalf. Christ kept silence, to be our spokesman now, and by His pleading to free us of our guilt. He kept silence, that we might be able to boast that we are justified by His grace. In this way the prophecy of Isaiah was fulfilled (53.7), that like a sheep led to the slaughter, etc. Meanwhile that good confession shone forth, as Paul says (I Tim. 6.12), not of words but of deeds. By this He did not suit His own advantage, but won acquittal for the whole human race.

Luke 23.4. *And Pilate said.* As Christ was to bear the penalty for our offences, it was necessary that He should first be acquitted by His judge's lips, that afterwards it might be plain that He was condemned for another's sake than His own. As Pilate did not dare, for the shout-ing of the crowd, to absolve Him completely, he freely accepted the chance that was offered him of passing Him to the judgment of Herod. This Herod was surnamed Antipas, and had been left the tetrarchy of Galilee, when Judaea was attached to the province of Syria, and Archelaus exiled to Vienne. Though Luke will shortly tell that this gesture of prestige pleased Herod, who had previously been on bad terms with Pilate, yet he did it not so much to gain his favour as by a decent excuse to clear himself of the ill-will, and to escape the need to condemn Christ.

Luke 23.8. *Now when Herod saw Jesus he was exceeding glad.* It is manifest how far pride intoxicates the wicked, then at once deranges them. Though Herod did not acknowledge Christ as the Son of God, he at least gave Him the status of prophet. Which made it all the more unjust to be delighted at His poor state and disgrace. He reckoned he had received a hurt, as long as he had not met Christ face to face. Now he sees Him put at his free mercy, and triumphs—as over a conquest. We see what kind of love wicked and profane men have for the prophets, in whom the power of God shines. Herod had long desired to see Christ. Why then did he not wish to hear Him and benefit from His teaching? He chose to be a mere spectator of divine power, rather than to reverence it as he ought, with piety and humility. This is the genius of the flesh, so to seek God in His works as not to submit to His command, so to seek the sight of His servants as not to wait to hear Him speaking through them. Herod, hoping to have some miracle from Christ, actually preferred to throw Him like a criminal at his feet, than to admit Him as a Teacher. It is no wonder if God hides His glory from the wicked, who ask for sport from Him, like the performance of some actor.

Luke 23.11. *Herod set him at naught.* It could not be otherwise that a proud man enjoying his luxuries of royal honour and wealth, should scorn Christ, whose whole presence then was contemptible. Yet Herod's high manner is not excusable, for it shut out the grace of God, and there is no doubt that God, to punish him for his former indifference, deliberately hardened his heart at such a sight. He was not worthy to see one spark of the heavenly glory in Christ, as he had been so long blinded to the full spendour, which had made his heritage famous on all sides. Luke tells that Christ was despised not by Herod only but by all his little cluster, that we should know that God rarely receives true honour in the halls of kings. Since practically all men of court are addicted to ceremonial, such a vanity seizes their minds that they carelessly despise the spiritual graces of God, and go past them with their eyes shut. By this contempt for Christ, we win new dignity, to be esteemed with God and with angels.

Luke 23.12. *Became friends.* From the fact that Christ was the token of friendship restored between two wicked men, let us learn how much the children of God are despised in the world, and religion itself. It is likely, since each of the two was forced by self-seeking, that they came into discord over government, but whatever was the origin of their quarrel, as far as earthly business, neither would have yielded one particle of his rights to the other. Yet because Christ is set at naught, Pilate can easily send Him down to Herod and in turn Herod send Him off to Pilate. We see the same today. Judges disagree over thieves and other criminals, but toss around the children of God with contempt. Hatred of piety often makes wicked men friends together. Though they had nothing in common before, they will plot together for the ruin of God's Name. When the children of God are handed over, even to death, by wicked men on opposite sides, they make up their mutual friendship at no great price, on the cheapest terms they know; they make no difficulties, any more than a man throwing a crust of bread to a dog. Among us, however, it is a different kind of peace that Christ should bring about. Having been first reconciled to God (*Deo primum reconciliati*) let us help one another in holy and sacred agreement, to promote righteousness, and exert ourselves in acts of brotherly duty and mutual humanity.

Now at the feast the governor was wont to release unto the multitude one prisoner, whom they would. And they had then a notable prisoner, called Barabbas. When therefore they were gathered together, Pilate said unto them, Whom will ye that I release unto you? Barabbas, or Jesus which is called Christ? For he knew that for envy they had delivered him up. And while he was sitting on the judgement-seat, his wife sent unto him, saying, Have thou nothing to do with that righteous man: for I have suffered many things this day in a dream because of him. Now the chief priests and the elders persuaded the multitudes that they should ask for Barabbas, and destroy Jesus. But the governor answered and said unto them, Whether of the twain will ye that I release unto you? And they said, Barabbas. Pilate saith unto them, Why, what evil hath he done? But they cried out exceedingly, saying, Let him be crucified. (Matt. 27.15-23)

Now at the feast he used to release unto them one prisoner, whom they asked of him. And there was one called Barabbas, lying bound with them that had made insurrection, men who in the insurrection had committed murder. And the multitude went up and began to ask him to do as he was wont to do unto them. And Pilate answered them, saying, Will ye that I release unto you the King of the Jews? For he perceived that for envy the chief priests had delivered him up. But the chief priests stirred up the multitude, that he should rather release Barabbas unto them. And Pilate again answered and said unto them, What then shall I do unto him whom ye call the King of the Jews? And they cried out again, Crucify him. And Pilate said unto them, Why, what evil hath he done? But they cried out exceedingly, Crucify him. (Mark 15.6-14)

And Pilate called together the chief priests and the rulers of the people, and said unto them, Ye brought unto me this man, as one that perverteth the people: and behold, I, having examined him before you, found no fault in this man touching those things whereof ye accuse him: no, nor yet Herod: for he sent him back unto us; and behold, nothing worthy of death hath been done by him. I will therefore chastise him, and release him. But they cried out all together, saying, Away with this man, and release unto us Barabbas: one who for a certain insurrection made in the city, and for murder, was cast into prison. And Pilate spake unto them again, desiring to release Jesus; but they shouted, saying, Crucify, crucify him. And he said unto them the third time, Why, what evil hath this man done? I have found no cause of death in him: I will therefore chastise him and release him. But they were instant with loud voices, asking that he might be crucified. And their voices prevailed. (Luke 23.13-23)

Matt. 27.15. *Now at the feast the governor was wont.* We have here a description of both the implacable cruelty of the priests and of the furious obstinacy of the people. Both must have been seized with an amazing kind of frenzy not satisfied with plotting the death of an innocent man unless, in their hatred for him, they also released a robber. So Satan whips on the wicked; once they have begun their career they shrink from no crime however horrible, and blindly, crazily, heap sin upon sin. No doubt Pilate tried to influence them by shame and so chose the most criminal character by contrast with whom Christ might be released. The very atrocity of the crime of which Barabbas was guilty deserved to make him an object of popular hatred, that at least by comparison Christ might be released. But no sense of propriety deters priests or people as a whole from demanding a rebel and murderer being given to them. Meanwhile we must consider God's purpose, by which Christ came to be crucified as the basest of men. Indeed the Jews rage against Him with blinded fury, but since God had ordained Him to be the κάθαρμα (sacrificial outcast) for the expiation of the world's sins, He suffered Him to be placed lower than a robber and a murderer. That God's Son was brought down to that level is a fact no one will really consider without the utmost horror and displeasure with himself and detestation for his own sins. Yet here also emerges great ground for confidence, that Christ plunged into the depths of disgrace precisely to win, by His abasement, an ascent for us into the heavenly glory. Thus He was reckoned worse than a thief, to bring us into the company of angels. If this achievement is rightly valued, it will be enough and more to abolish the scandal of the cross. That it was the Governor's practice on the festival to set free one of the prisoners to please the crowd was an example brought in without sense or reason, involving God's worship in considerable corruption: nothing was less suitable than to mark festival days with a show of impunity for crime. God armed magistrates with the sword to punish severely the crimes that cannot be tolerated without public disaster. Clearly He does not want the worship of upset laws and penalties. This is what comes of men devising for themselves rash ways of worshipping God (since nothing should be tried without his express Word), that they bring insult upon Him under the pretext of honour. We must keep a clear head and not offer God anything but what He demands. He is not pleased with profane gifts, for they rather provoke His anger.

Matt. 27.19. *And while he was sitting.* Although it is possible that some daytime thoughts caused this sleeplessness, there is very little doubt that Pilate's wife was affected not with a natural sensation (as happens to us daily), but was distressed by God's particular intervention. A popular idea is that the devil, to delay the redemption of the human race, put the notion into the woman. This is not right, since it was his influence that so greatly inflamed the priests and scribes to ruin Christ. We should rather hold that Christ's innocence was given many proofs by God the Father to make it clear that for another's (that is, our own) sake He met His death. He wished Pilate often to speak His acquittal before condemning Him, so that in His undeserved condemnation the satisfaction won for our sins should blaze out. Matthew puts this in explicitly, that no one should be surprised at Pilate's anxious concern to argue over a despised man, in face of all the tumult of the mob. By the terrors his wife felt in the night, God made him protect the innocence of His Son, not to snatch Him from death, but only to testify that He was given the punishment of another, which He had not deserved. We have spoken elsewhere of dreams, how they are a kind of visions.

Matt. 27.20. *Now the chief priests.* The Evangelist points to the chief instigators of the evil, not that foolish credulity excuses the crowd (being under outside influence); but to let us know that its anger against Christ was not spontaneous. They pay obedience to the priests and forget all fair dealing and restraint, also their own salvation. This teaches us how fatal is the authority of godless men, who may easily sway the mob, this way and that, to any crime—nothing is more unsteady. We must hold to the Evangelist's purpose: the people's voice called so bitterly for Christ's death, not because He was universally hated, but because the majority, for their own interests, so much wanted to follow the lead of their superiors that they threw away respect for equity, and engaged their tongues, hired them out, to the wicked conspiracy of a few.

Matt. 27.22. *What then shall I do unto Jesus.* As Pilate saw that they were so blind in madness that with all shame they were ready to rescue a robber from death he tried another device to push them back into their sound mind: the death of Christ would brand them with disgrace, because it was commonly said of Jesus that he was King and Christ. As if he had said, 'If you have no pity for the man, at least consider your honour. Strangers will commonly think that you have all been punished in His death.' Yet not even so was the ardour of their rage assuaged, but they go on to cause hurt to their own public interest more than to Christ individually. In Mark, Pilate, to put yet keener pressure upon them, says that they themselves call Jesus King, meaning that the title was so regularly used that it had become His habitual surname. But with all shame cast aside they insistently urge for Him to be slain—the act that brought dishonour on the whole human race. In John an answer is expressed, which our three leave unsaid: that they have no King but Caesar. So they prefer to be robbed of their hope of the promised redemption, and bound to perpetual servitude, than accept the Redeemer offered them from God.

Luke 23.16. *I will therefore chastise him and release him.* If a lesser offence had been committed, apart from a capital charge, the Roman governors were used to have the offenders beaten with rods: this form of punishment was called *coercitio*. There was no justice in Pilate acquitting Christ of all guilt, yet wanting to punish Him as if convicted of a lesser offence. He not only declares that he has found nothing in Him worthy of death, but actually asserts His innocence without qualification. Why then have Him flogged? This is how men on earth behave, whom the Spirit of God does not set firm on the steady course of right. Though they desire to serve equity, they allow themselves to be turned aside to acts of moderate injustice. They try to make a fair excuse that they have not sinned grievously, and actually claim some praise for their clemency, in sparing the innocent to some degree. They do not consider that though extreme cruelty may be avoided justice is as much violated with rods as with the axe—and it is of more worth than the life of a man. As regards the Son of God, if He had been dismissed in this manner He would have borne the shame of the beating without helping our salvation. It was on the cross, as in a splendid chariot, that He made triumph over His enemies and ours. Would that the world were not today full of so many Pilates! We see the same thing accomplished in the members as began with the head. With the same savagery as the Jewish priests shouted for Christ to be dragged off to die, the popish clergy chase after His servants. Many of the judges offer themselves as executioners, willingly pursuing their fury, but when they shrink from bloodshed, to snatch innocent men from death, they flog Christ Himself, (the sole righteousness of God). To force God's worshippers to save their lives by denial of the Gospel— what else is this than subjecting Christ's Name to the indignity of rods? The violence of the enemy is the excuse they pretend, a cloak to cover their treacherous fear, which if in Pilate was inexcusable, in them deserves the utmost detestation. Though our three Evangelists omit this, yet it is clear from John, that Christ was beaten with rods, while Pilate was still struggling to save His life, that the ugly spectacle might appease the rabid mob. John adds also, that it was not to be placated, until the Author of life was done away.

So when Pilate saw that he prevailed nothing, but rather that a tumult was arising, he took water, and washed his hands before the multitude, saying, I am inncoent of the blood of this righteous man: see ye to it. And all the people answered and said, His blood be on us, and on our children. Then released he unto them Barabbas: but Jesus he scourged and delivered to be crucified.

Then the soldiers of the governor took Jesus into the palace, and gathered unto him the whole band. And they stripped him, and put on him a scarlet robe. And they plaited a crown of thorns and put it upon his head, and a reed in his right hand; and they kneeled down before him, and mocked him, saying, Hail, King of the Jews! And they spat upon him, and took the reed and smote him on the head. And when they had mocked him, they took off from him the robe, and put on him his garments, and led him away to crucify him.

And as they came out, they found a man of Cyrene, Simon by name: him they compelled to go with them, that he might bear his cross. (Matt. 27.24-32)

And Pilate, wishing to content the multitude, released unto them Barabbas, and delivered Jesus, when he had scourged him, to be crucified.

And the soldiers led him away within the court, which is the Praetorium; and they call together the whole band. And they clothe him with purple, and plaiting a crown of thorns, they put it on him: and they began to salute him, Hail, King of the Jews! And they smote his head with a reed, and did spit upon him, and bowing their knees worshipped

186

him. And when they had mocked him, they took off from him the purple, and put on him his garments. And they led him out to crucify him.

And they compel one passing by, Simon of Cyrene, coming from the country, the father of Alexander and Rufus, to go with them, that he might bear his cross. (Mark 15.15-21)

And Pilate gave sentence that what they asked for should be done. And he released him that for insurrection and murder had been cast into prison, whom they asked for; but Jesus he delivered up to their will.

And when they led him away, they laid hold upon one Simon of Cyrene, coming from the country, and laid on him the cross, to bear it after Jesus.

And there followed him a great multitude of the people, and of women who bewailed and lamented him. But Jesus turning unto them said, Daughters of Jerusalem, weep not for me, but weep for yourselves, and for your children. For behold, the days are coming, in which they shall say, Blessed are the barren, and the wombs that never bare, and the breasts that never gave suck. Then shall they begin to say to the mountains, Fall on us; and to the hills, Cover us. For if they do these things in the green tree, what shall be done in the dry?

And there were also two others, malefactors, led with him to be put to death. (Luke 23.24-32)

Matt. 27.24. *So when Pilate saw.* As sailors who have run into too violent a storm give way in the end and let themselves be drawn onto an opposite course, so Pilate, when he finds himself unequal to resisting the tide of popular feeling puts down his judicial power and follows their mad uproar. Though he had tried to hold out for a long time, he cannot plead necessity as excuse; for he ought to have endured anything rather than be swung off his course. The childish performance he goes through is no lessening of his guilt. How can he scrub off the stain of his crime with a few drops of water, when no expiation could have cleared it? Though he did not chiefly aim to purge his stains in God's sight, he set a sign of disapproval before the crowd, perhaps to urge some repentance for their anger, as though he had said to them, 'Look, you are forcing me to an unjust killing, and I fall in only in fear and abhorrence. What shall become of you, what grave penalty awaits you from God, you who are the chief instigators?' Whatever might be Pilate's purpose, God wished His Son's innocence attested in this way, that it might be more clear that our sins were condemned in Him. The supreme and only Judge of the universe stands before the tribunal of an earthly judge. He is condemned to the cross as a criminal; indeed He is placed between thieves as if He were their leader. The ugliness of this scene might at first sight greatly agitate men's minds unless the thought came to us that the penalty that was due to us was

187

laid on Christ; now with the guilt removed, let us not hesitate to advance into the sight of the heavenly Judge. The water, which was no use to Pilate for cleansing dirt, should today have a different and very good use, to clear our eyes of all that hinders us from seeing lucidly, in the midst of condemnation, the righteousness of Christ.

Matt. 27.25. *His blood be on us.* There is no doubt that the Jews called down this curse on themselves without a thought, as if they had a firm and right relationship with God. Their unconsidered zeal drove them to the point that they plot an inexpiable crime and with a solemn oath cut themselves off from any hope of pardon. Whence we gather how carefully we are to avoid wild rashness in all judgments. When men dare, without inquiry, to tear off here and there as they think best, they are bound at length by their blind impulse to plunge into madness. This is God's just punishment, which He brings on the pride of those who do not deign to make choice between right and wrong. The Jews thought that in killing Christ they would do welcome and obedient service to God, but whence came their contemptible error, if not from their wicked contumacy and scorn of God himself? So they deserve to be cast into such madness as to secure their own final ruin. We should learn, when it is a matter of the service of God and His holy mysteries to keep our eyes open, and reverently and soberly to consider the case, lest hypocrisy and pride affect our reason. As God would never have allowed this voice of cursing to have left the people's lips unless their impiety were already desperate, so justly in after time did He avenge it, with fearful and unparalleled means: yet, in a wonder beyond belief, He left Himself some remnant, lest His covenant should be extinguished by the ruin of the whole race. He had adopted the seed of Abraham to be His chosen race, a priestly kingdom and inheritance. Now the Jews, as with one voice, make plans to refuse such an act of grace: who would deny that the whole race had been torn up, by the roots, from the kingdom of God? But God in their very treachery (*perfidia*) displays the constancy of His faith (*fidei suae constantiam*), and to show that His Covenant was not struck with Abraham to no effect He rescues those He freely elected from the general destruction. Thus His truth ever arises superior to all the obstacles of human incredulity.

Matt. 27.26. *Then released he unto them Barabbas.* Our three Evangelists do not say exactly what we find in John, that Pilate ascended the tribunal to deliver his sentence from there. They only record that he was so overcome by the passion of the crowd and the wild uproar as to hand Christ over, shamefully, to death. We must note both points, that his assent was forced from him against his will, yet he represented judicial form in his person when he condemns this man, whom he declares innocent. Unless God's Son had been pure of every offence He could not by His death have been the source of expiation, and unless He had gone bail for us and undergone the penalty we deserved we should still be involved in the guilt of our crimes. God wished His Son condemned in due form, that for His sake He might absolve us. The cruelty of the punishment is also a powerful confirmation of our faith, impressing us with a fear of God's wrath, making us humble at our sense of wrong. If we wish to profit as we ought from thinking on the death of Christ we should start at this point: according to the severity of the penalty He bore, so should we abhor our sins. So may we be disgusted and ashamed of ourselves, and also affected with a genuine grief, for which we should seek relief with ardour, at the same time as we tremble for fear. We must have hearts harder than stone if we are not wounded to the core with the wounds God's Son endured, if we do not hate and detest our sins which God's Son bore such punishment to expiate. As God's dread punishment here comes to view, step by step richer ground for confidence is set before us: we must not fear that our sins will any more come into God's judgment; God's Son has released us from them, at this great price. It was no ordinary manner of death He endured to win us life. With the cross He took cursing on Himself, that no more uncleanness might be found in us.

Matt. 27.27. *Then the soldiers of the governor*. This additional insult has a real place in the narrative. That God exposed His only-begotten Son to mockery of every kind, we know was no mere comic interlude. We should first consider our deserts, then the satisfaction offered by Christ should raise us to good. Our foul condition is such as God might abominate, and all the angels spit upon, but Christ, to make us stand in the sight of the Father pure and unstained, was willing to be spat upon Himself and befouled with all insult. So the ugliness He once endured on earth now wins us grace in heaven, and also restores the image of God, which had not only been polluted with the filth of sin, but almost effaced. So also God's inestimable mercy upon us shines out, in lowering His only-begotten Son to these depths, for our sake. By this proof Christ witnessed to His amazing love for us, in refusing no insult at all for our salvation. These are things that ask for secret meditation, not fancy words. We learn that Christ's Kingdom is not to be reckoned by fleshly sense but by the judgment of faith and the Spirit. As long as our minds are stuck to the earth it will seem contemptible to us, yes, even full of shameful disgrace, but once by faith they have risen up to heaven not only will they meet the spiritual Majesty of Christ obliterating all the shame of the cross, but also the spitting and blows, the cuffs and other mockery will lead us to the vision of his glory. As Paul says, He was given a name and highest rule, that in His presence every knee should bow, because He willingly emptied Himself even to the death of the cross (Phil. 2.8 and 10). So even if today the world rudely laughs at Christ, we should learn to overcome these scandals with loftiness of mind, not stop over those things the wicked wrongly fastened upon Christ, but on the marks of honour the heavenly Father has endowed Him with, the sceptre and the crown He accorded Him that He might have eminence not only far over men but even above the angels. Mark mentions purple instead of scarlet, changing the colours, but we need not sweat over this. It is not likely that Christ was dressed in a precious robe: we may gather it was not real purple but something that had a resemblance to it, as a painter imitates the real thing in his pictures.

Matt. 27.32. *They found a man of Cyrene.* This circumstance expresses the height of the cruelty both of the Jewish race and of the soldiers. There is no doubt that it was usual for malefactors to carry their crosses to the place of execution, but as only stout robbers were crucified they were equal to bearing such a burden. The case was different with Christ, so that the very weakness of His body made plain that it was the sacrifice of a lamb. It may well be that, terribly hurt by the scourge and seriously pulled down by many injuries, He stumbled under the weight of the cross. The Evangelists say that a country man of no account was forced by the soldiers to carry the cross, for as the punishment was detested the very contact with it was thought by all to carry pollution. The man who was hauled from the dregs of the crowd to this sordid and ignoble task is ennobled by God through His heralds. It is by no means superfluous that the Evangelists give his name carefully and record his home and family. There is no doubt that this preliminary scene is a warning to us from God that we are of no status or worth in ourselves; all our dignity and renown spring from His Son's cross.

Luke 23.27. *And there followed him.* Though in public the whole people had joined in one shout of condemnation for Christ, yet we see that some had not forgotten His teaching or His miracles. Thus in all the wretched falling-away, God had kept Himself some little remnant. Though these women's faith was weak, yet we may believe it was the hidden seed of devotion which later in its own time produced fruit. At the time, their weeping served to condemn the wicked and outrageous cruelty of the men, who with the scribes and priests had plotted the death of Christ. Luke's intention however was different. That we should know that when restraint is thrown aside and men's wickedness exults in all confusion, God does not idly view their behaviour, but sits as Judge in heaven, and shall soon exact the penalty for this unrighteous savagery. His vengeance must not be scorned for being deferred to its proper time, but even before it appears, it is to be feared.

Luke 23.28. *Weep not.* Some have thought that the women are reproached for pouring out useless tears in foolishness and senseless emotion. Yet Christ is not merely correcting them for weeping out of place and out of reason, but He tells them of the far greater cause for weeping that comes from the impending, dread judgment of God as if saying, His death is not the end for Jerusalem and the race as a whole, but the beginning of their woes. He means that He was not abandoned to the passion of the wicked without remaining in God's concern. It is obvious from the punishment that followed after, that Christ's life was precious to God the Father, at the very time that all thought Him utterly deserted and cast off. These words testify to the high courage of Christ's spirit, for He could not have spoken so unless His path to death were unflinching and unafraid, but the chief object is that even in His hideous and wretched state He was under God's regard. The wicked who now triumph as victors in their pride will not enjoy their mad pleasure for long, for a reverse beyond belief will shortly follow. This teaching is of benefit to us today, as we understand that Christ was no less dear to His Father when for the moment He was deprived of His help; our salvation counted so much to Him, that He did not spare even His only-begotten Son. He gave remarkable proof of this when He utterly destroyed the holy city, where He had chosen His one Sanctuary to be, and rased it along with its inhabitants. Let us learn from this to proceed to consider the cause of Christ's death: seeing that God avenged it so severely, He would never have let His Son face it, unless it were an expiation for the sins of the world.

Luke 23.29. *For behold the days are coming.* He declares an imminent disaster, out of the ordinary, dire and never before heard of, the open revelation of divine retribution: as if He had said, 'That race will be caught up in no one or simple kind of ruin, but will be crushed beneath a heap of all sorts of enormous troubles, so that it would be far better to be engulfed in the fall of mountains, or swallowed up in earthquake, rather than pine away in the fierce pains of a lingering death.' These were no idle threats, for the event with its atrocities followed the thunder of the words, as we may see in Josephus. Moreover, since the desire to be crushed by the mountains and the cursing of their off-spring were expressions of the deepest despair, Christ taught by these words that the Jews will at last realize that their warfare has been not with mortal man but with God. So God's enemies pay the right reward for their sacrilegious frenzy, when in vain they would heave up the earth as a shield against His vengeance—they who before dared to attack heaven itself.

Luke 23.31. *If . . . in the green tree.* Christ confirms in this sentence that His death will not be unavenged and that the Jews whose iniquity is already ripe, indeed half rotten, will not wait long. He takes an everyday simile to show that they cannot avoid the divine fire lighting on them and at once devouring them in its flame. We know how dry wood is usually thrown first on the fire, but if the wet and green wood is already alight, there will be far less delay for the dry. The words *if they do* may be expounded in the indefinite sense, meaning, if green wood is thrown onto the fire before time, what do you think will happen to the old and dry? Or one may prefer it as a comparison of men and God: in other words, Christ said the wicked who are like the dry wood have brought unfair destruction upon the just, and in their turn will find God ready for them. How could they who are doomed to destruction ever escape the hand of the heavenly Judge, who only allows them to do as they please against the good and innocent for limited periods of time? Whichever way one prefers to take it, it comes to this, that the women's tears are out of place, unless they look also in fear to the dread judgment of God that overhangs the evil-doers. As often as the bitterness of the cross afflicts us, beyond measure, we should relieve it with this consolation, that God who now allows His people to be oppressed unjustly will not in the end suffer that the evil-doers should come off unscathed. Unless this hope is our support we must sink under our afflictions, just as they did. Though it is natural and more usual to start a fire with dry rather than wet wood, God follows the other order. He gives peace and rest to the wicked, and works His people with various troubles; the more wretched their condition then, if one reckons by present appearances. Here is the remedy to hand: let them patiently look for whole course of divine judgment. It will turn out that the wicked make little profit from their short remission. When God has humbled His faithful with the paternal rod, He will draw His sword and attack those whose crimes, for the moment, He seemed not to be watching.

And when they were come unto a place called Golgotha, that is to say, the place of a skull, they gave him wine to drink mingled with gall: and when he had tasted it, he would not drink. And when they had crucified him, they parted his garments among them, casting lots:[1] *and they sat and watched him there. And they set up over his head the accusation written, THIS IS JESUS THE KING OF THE JEWS. Then are there crucified with him two robbers, one on the right hand, and one on the left.* (Matt. 27.33-38)

And they bring him unto the place Golgotha, which is, being interpreted,

[1] A.V. adds: *that it might be fulfilled which was spoken by the prophet, They parted my garments among them, and upon my vestments did they cast lots.*

The place of a skull. And they offered him wine mingled with myrrh:
but he received it not. And they crucify him, and part his garments
among them, casting lots upon them, which each should take. And it was
the third hour, and they crucified him. And the superscription of his
accusation was written over, THE KING OF THE JEWS. And
with him they crucify two robbers; one on his right hand, and one on his
left. And the scripture was fulfilled, which saith, And he was reckoned
with the transgressors. (Mark 15.21-28)

And when they came unto the place which is called The Skull, there
they crucified him, and the malefactors, one on the right hand and the other
on the left. And Jesus said, Father, forgive them; for they know not
what they do. And parting his garments among them, they cast lots.
    And there was also a superscription over him,[1] *THIS IS THE KING*
OF THE JEWS. (Luke 23.33-34 and 38)

Matt. 27.33. *And when they were come unto a place,* Jesus was led to
the place where malefactors were usually executed to make His death
the more shameful. Though it was a matter of custom, we should
weigh God's purpose more closely. He wished His Son thrown out of
the city, as unfit to share men's society, in order to take us into the
heavenly Kingdom along with the angels. So the Apostle in the
Epistle to the Hebrews (13.12) relates this to the old type of the Law.
As God ordered the bodies of animals to be burned outside the camp
when their blood was taken into the Sanctuary for the expiation, so, he
says, Christ went out of the gates of the city, that bearing the curse that
weighed on us He should be like the one rejected, and in this way
expiate our sins. The more insult and shame He bore in the face of the
world, the more acceptable and noble the spectacle He gave in His
death to God and the angels. The foulness of the place was no hindrance
to His erecting there the glorious trophy of His victory. Nor did the
stench of corpses that lay there prevent the sweet savour of His sacrifice
breathing over all the world and reaching up to heaven.

Matt. 27.34. *They gave him wine.* Though the Evangelists do not
carefully go through every single thing in its order, that one can certainly mark the details of time, yet I think it is a reasonable guess that,
before the Lord was lifted on the cross, out of custom there was offered
Him, from a cup, drugged wine with myrrh or some kind of mixture,
clearly composed of gall and vinegar. There is sufficient agreement
among practically all interpreters that this was a different drink from
the one recorded by John, of which we shall shortly be speaking. I
only add that it seems to me the cup was offered to the Lord when He

---

[1] A.V. adds: *in letters of Greek, and Latin, and Hebrew.*

was about to be crucified: only when the cross was lifted up on high was the sponge dipped in. When He began to ask for drink, I am not concerned to argue, but if we take everything into account it is not absurd to suppose that after He had refused the bitter mixture, it was from time to time pushed in His face as a piece of mockery. Matthew will go on to say that while the soldiers were giving Him drink they taunted Him, that He could not get Himself away from death. Whence we gather that in offering a remedy, they mocked Christ's impotence, for He had complained that He was forsaken by God. As regards John's account, one point is enough to hold on to, that Christ asked for ordinary drink to be given Him to quench His thirst, but that vinegar mixed with myrrh and gall was pushed up to Him to hurry on His death. He bore his torment so patiently that the dragging pain made Him seek no hurrying on of death. This was part of His sacrifice and obedience also, to endure all the extremities of slow weariness. I think they are wrong who count the vinegar as being among the remaining torments cruelly inflicted on God's Son. The more probable conjecture is to think that this kind of potion was suited for making the blood flow out, and so was usually given to the criminals that their death might be hastened. Hence Mark calls it wine mixed with myrrh. Christ (as I have just noted) did not refuse the wine or vinegar because He was put off by its bitterness, but to show that He was quietly advancing towards death as His Father had laid down, and was not rushing headlong in an impatience of pain. John's words were not contradictory, saying that the Scripture was fulfilled, *in my thirst they gave me vinegar to drink* (Ps. 69.11). The two accounts agree perfectly: a remedy was given Him to finish the agony of His slow death, yet Christ was afflicted grievously by all means, so that the very alleviation was a part, an addition to His pain.

Matt. 27.35. *They parted his garments.* Certainly this action of the soldiers was also customary, to divide among themselves the spoils of the condemned man: perhaps one feature was exceptional, drawing lots over the tunic woven in one piece. Though nothing happened to Christ in this regard that was not suffered by all the condemned, yet this narrative deserves the utmost attention. The Evangelists portray the Son of God as stripped of His clothes that we may know the wealth gained for us by this nakedness, for it shall dress us in God's sight. God willed His Son to be stripped that we should appear freely, with the angels, in the garments of his righteousness and fulness of all good things, whereas formerly, foul disgrace, in torn clothes, kept us away from the approach to the heavens. Christ Himself allows His raiment to be torn apart like booty to make us rich with the riches of His victory. As Matthew says, thus was fulfilled the prophecy of David (Ps. 22.19) *they part my garments among them*, etc. It is right to take it that literally (as the expression is) and in actual fact there was set forth in Christ what David metaphorically and figuratively complains of in himself. David means by the word 'garments' his fortunes and honours, as if saying, that in his lifetime and sight he was made a prey for his enemies, who had raided his house, and, far from sparing the rest of his goods, had made off with his wife too. The metaphor amplifies the cruelty of this, when it indicates how his vestments were divided up by lot. Seeing he was a shadow and image of Christ he foretold, in the Spirit of prophecy, what Christ would suffer. In Christ's Person, it is worth noting how the soldiers looted His garments, for we see in this dividing-out the signs and marks by which He used to be distinguished. At the same time, the offence that fleshly sense sometimes takes at His nakedness is here done away, for He suffered nothing but what truly and properly the Spirit's oracle declared to belong to the Person of the Redeemer.

Mark 15.25. *And it was the third hour.* This seems to contradict John's testimony, when he says, that Christ was condemned about the sixth hour. But if we put together other passages and reckon that the day was divided into four parts, and that each part was named from the first hour it started from, the solution will not be difficult. The whole period that ran from sunrise to the second part was called the 'first hour'. The second part up to mid-day was the 'third hour' to them. The 'sixth hour' starting at mid-day went on to three or four in the afternoon. When the Jews saw that Pilate was wearing out the time and mid-day was approaching, John says they made a great uproar, so that the whole day should not be wasted. This did not prevent the Lord being put on the cross around the end of the third hour. It is clear enough that after His riotous condemnation He was immediately hailed off: the Jews had such a burning desire to be rid of Him. Mark means therefore not the beginning but the end of the third hour. It is more likely that Christ did not hang more than three hour on the cross.

Luke 23.34. *And Jesus said.* By this word Christ showed He was the quiet and tame lamb that must be led to the slaughter, as Isaiah the prophet had testified (53.7). He not only remits their punishment, but He commends to God His Father, the salvation of the men by whom He was more than cruelly harassed. It would have been great enough not to think of retaliation: as Peter (I, 2.20-23) when he urges us to patience by the example of Christ, says: He did not repay cursing for cursing, nor avenged His hurts, but was content with this alone, that God was His vindication. Yet this is a far superior virtue, far more outstanding— to pray God to forgive His enemies. If anyone thinks this sentence does not really match the one I have just cited from Peter, there is a ready answer. That Christ was led by feelings of pity to ask God for pardon for his persecutors did not prevent His accepting God's righteous judgment which He knew was decreed for the reprobate and stubborn. When Christ saw both the Jewish populace and the soldiers rage on Him in blind aggression, though their ignorance was not excusable, yet He felt pity, and intervened to beg them off. Yet as He knew God would be an avenger, He allowed Him to give judgment against the desperate. In like manner, ought the faithful to check their feelings in putting up with evil, and desire their persecutors to be saved, without doubting that their lives are under God's protection. Relying on this consolation, that in the end the wicked's licence will not go off unpunished, they should not faint under the weight of the cross. Moderation of this kind is the example Luke here gives in the Person of our Leader and Master, for when He might have called down a curse on His persecutors, to their ruin, He not only checked Himself from cursing but actually prayed for their good. We must note, if ever the whole world rises against us and all strive to overwhelm us, that this is the best means of overcoming temptation, to think of the blindness of those who attack God in us. The result will be that the conspiracy of many turned on us, alone and helpless, will not unnerve us out of measure. Just as in reverse, daily experience shows us the power of the device for shaking weak minds, if they see that they are attacked by a vast multitude. If we learn to raise ourselves to God, it will come easily to us to look down on the ignorance of the faithless as from a high position, for all their force of arms and great supply, they yet do not know what they do. It is likely that Christ did not pray for all without distinction, but only for the wretched populace who were carried along by thoughtless zeal, not deliberate wickedness. As there was no hope remaining for the scribes and priests, prayer for them would have had no effect. There is no doubt that the prayer was heard by the heavenly Father, whence it resulted that many of the people who had spilled His blood came afterwards to drink it.

Matt. 27.37. *And they set up over his head.* What is briefly noted by Matthew and Mark is given in more detail by Luke; the title was written in three languages. John goes into it still more fully. Let readers seek there what I here omit for brevity's sake. Let me only say that it was done by God's providence, that Christ's death was published in three tongues, for even if Pilate had no other purpose than to draw shame on the Jewish race, God saw further than he. By this presage He gave wide testimony that His Son's death would be famous, that all peoples everywhere would acknowledge Him as the Jews' promised King. This was not a true preaching of the Gospel, for Pilate was unworthy that God should make him a witness to His Son, but what His true ministers were afterwards to declare was foreshadowed in

196

Pilate. We may take him to be a herald of Christ, as Caiaphas was a prophet.

Matt. 27.38. *Then are there crucified.* This came as the culmination of His shame, that Christ was hung in the middle of two thieves: they gave Him first place as though He were the thieves' leader. If He had been taken to the cross alone, His case might have seemed to be separate from other malefactors, but now He is both mixed with them, and lifted high as the most hated of all. So Mark applies the oracle of Isaiah (53.12), *he was reckoned among the transgressors.* The prophet expressly says of Christ, that He will not deliver His people from death in splendid array, but will undergo the penalty due to their sins. So to rescue us from guilt this means of expiation was necessary, that He should bring Himself down to our condition. Here we see how fearful was the severity of God's wrath against sins, when Christ, the eternal righteousness, had to be put in line with thieves to placate it. We can see Christ's incomparable love for us, that to bring us into the company of the holy angels He endured to be counted one with the wicked.

And they that passed by railed on him, wagging their heads, and saying, Thou that destroyest the temple, and buildest it in three days, save thyself: if thou art the son of God, come down from the cross. In like manner also the chief priests mocking him, with the scribes and elders, said, He saved others; himself he cannot save. He is the King of Israel; let him now come down from the cross, and we will believe on him. He trusteth on God; let him deliver him now, if he desireth him; for he said, I am the Son of God. And the robbers also that were crucified with him cast upon him the same reproach. (Matt. 27.39-44)

And they that passed by railed on him, wagging their heads, and saying, Ha! thou that destroyeth the temple, and buildest it in three days, save thyself, and come down from the cross. In like manner also the chief priests mocking him among themselves with the scribes said, He saved others; himself he cannot save. Let the Christ, the King of Israel, now come down from the cross, that we may see and believe. And they that were crucified with him reproached him. (Mark 15.29-32)

And the people stood beholding. And the rulers also scoffed at him, saying, He saved others; let him save himself, if this is the Christ of God, his chosen. And the soldiers also mocked him, coming to him, offering him vinegar, and saying, If thou art the King of the Jews, save thyself.
And one of the malefactors which were hanged railed on him, saying, Art thou not the Christ? save thyself and us. But the other answered,

and rebuking him said, Dost thou not even fear God, seeing thou art in the same condemnation? And we indeed justly; for we receive the due reward of our deeds: but this man hath done nothing amiss. And he said unto him, Verily I say unto thee, To-day shalt thou be with me in Paradise. (Luke 23.35-37 and 39-43)

Matt. 27.39. *And they that passed by.* These circumstances carry great weight: there is set before our eyes the final self-emptying of the Son of God, to show better the price He put upon our salvation: at the same time we may reckon ourselves liable to all the punishments He endured and be urged all the more to repentance. The scene reveals how wretched a state we were in if we had had no Redeemer. All that Christ took upon Himself should be taken as relief to us. This was the hardest trial of all His pains, that all should have treated Him as a man cast off and forsaken of God, with vexation, spite and insult. So David in the Psalm (22.7) bearing Christ's character laments this above all His woes. There is no more cruel wound for pious minds than for the wicked to undermine their faith with the reproach that they are fallen from God's protection and grace. This is the harsh persecution which Paul says Isaac suffered from Ishmael (Gal. 4.29), not that he attacked him with sword and armed force, but that he tried to wreck his faith by laughing at God's grace. David first endured these trials, then Christ Himself, that they should not over-alarm us today by their novelty. There will never be lack of wicked men to seize upon our troubles. This is Satan's regular device, whenever God does not appear at our behest, but rather conceals His aid for a little time—to allege that our hope was in vain, as though His promise were empty.

Matt. 27.40. *Thou that destroyest the temple.* They make out that Christ's teaching was worthless because the power that He claimed for Himself now that He needs it is not actually displayed. If their reckless ill-speaking had not robbed them of sense and judgment they would very soon after have seen the truth of His saying. Christ had said, 'Destroy this temple and in three days I will raise it up.' Now they set off a triumphal march at the beginning of the destruction and fail to wait for the three days to elapse. Such is the rudeness of the wicked against all the sons of God, that under pretext of the cross they try to cut them off from the hope of everlasting life. Where (they say) is that immortal glory, of which credulous men foolishly boast? Seeing that they mostly lie in disgrace and abandon, some drag out a thin existence, some are driven to flight and exile, some rot in gaol, some are burnt to ashes at the stake. They are so blinded by the present corruption of the outward man that they make the hope of the renewal of the life to come vain and ridiculous. We must wait, however, for the full time of the building's completion, as promised, and not take it hard if we are crucified with Christ, in order afterwards to be companions of His resurrection. *If thou art the Son of God.* The proof which the wicked demand of Christ is such that by showing Himself to be Son of God He must cease to be Son of God. The terms on which He took on mortal flesh and descended to earth were to secure, by the sacrifice of His death, the reconciliation of men with God the Father. To show Himself Son of God He had to hang on the cross. Now these reprobates say that the Redeemer will not, for them, have the place of God's Son unless He comes down from the cross, refuses the Father's command, says farewell to the expiation of sins, and renounces the character assigned to Him by God. Our lesson here is to confirm our faith, in that the Son of God for the sake of our salvation willed to stay fixed to the cross till He had gone through the cruellest torments of the flesh, fearful agony of spirit, and death itself. In case we should be inclined to tempt God in a way like them let us allow God, as often as He thinks fit, to hide His power that He may exercise it again at the right moment, by His own judgment. The same deep fault appears in the second reproach, as follows, *if he is the King of Israel let him now come down from the cross and we will believe on him.* They had no right to embrace any King except according to what was written in the prophets. Isaiah and Zechariah expressly show Christ in poor shape and affliction, condemned and accursed, faint and poor and despised, before He ascends the royal throne. The Jews are all wrong to seek for someone different to acknowledge as King: thus they declare that they have no good-will for the King whom the Lord had promised to give them. But we on the other hand (that our faith may rest firmly upon Christ) must seek our point of strength at His cross, nor reckon it possible for any to be rightful King of Israel unless He has fulfilled the role of Redemption. We gather how fatal it is to wander aside from God's Word after our own speculations, and fall away. Since the Jews pictured themselves a King at the dictation of their own minds, they spurned Christ crucified, as they reckoned it absurd to believe in Him. For us, this is the best and highest reason for belief, that freely for our sake He endured the shame of the cross.

Matt. 27.42. *He saved others.* Here was the least excusable instance of ingratitude, to count all the miracles that He had formerly performed before their eyes for nothing because they were offended at his present humiliation. They allow He saved others. By what power, or by what means? Cannot they here, at least, see God's work and have reverence for it? Yet as they maliciously obscure and, as far as they can, try to extinguish the light of God that shone in the miracles, they are unworthy of making a right judgment on the weakness of the cross. As

Christ did not at once tear Himself away from death, they reproach Him with impotence. This is too much the way of the wicked at all times, to measure God's power by present appearances, thinking what He does not do He cannot do; to start a false account of His inability whenever He does not come up to their false desire. Let us hold, that Christ, though He well might, did not straightway deliver Himself from death, because He did not wish to do so. Why did He overlook His own safety for the time, unless it was that our safety altogether was a greater concern to Him? Why did He not wish to free Himself, except in order to save us all? We see how the ill-will of the Jews forced to the defence of their incredulity all the things that really strengthen our belief.

Matt. 27.43. *He trusteth on God.* As I have just said, the sharpest dart of temptation that Satan holds is to pretend that God has forgotten us, because He does not soon or instantly rush to our aid. As God watches over His people's safety, and not only brings help in due time, but often before the crisis (as Scripture teaches in many places), it seems that He does not love those whom He does not help. This line of argument leads to despair, that we trust vainly in God's love, when His aid does not plainly appear. As Satan suggests this kind of fallacy to our minds, he uses his agents to argue that our salvation is betrayed and lost by God, since He delays His assistance. So we must reject the falsity of this argument. That God does not love those whom He seems to desert for a time. There is nothing more absurd than to restrict His love to particular moments of time. God promised He would be our Deliverer, but if at times He is blind to our troubles we should bear the delay with patience. It is contrary to the nature of faith to insist on the adverb *now*, as He trains us by His cross and adversity to be obedient, and urges us to prayers and the invocation of His name, for these are the true testimonies of His fatherly love, as the Apostle says in the Epistle to the Hebrews. The particular thing in Christ was that though He was the beloved Son, He was not taken from death until He had settled the penalty we owed: that was the price at which our salvation was redeemed. The priests again act perversely, when they infer that He is not the Son of God because He performs the role laid on Him by the Father.

Matt. 27.44. *And the robbers also . . . the same reproach.* Matthew and Mark ascribe to the robbers, by synecdoche, what Luke plainly shows was correct for one of them only. We should not take this way of expression hardly: the two Evangelists had no other intention than to teach how Christ was assaulted with insults from all sides, till not even the thieves, already half-dead, spared Him. So David in Psalm 22.7 laments His woes and underlines their indignity with the fact that He was the scorn of all kinds of men, the butt of the crowd. Though they omit the memorable incident that Luke gives the second thief, there is nothing odd in this, that they say Christ was mocked by them all, even down to the thieves, since the saying is not applied to individuals, but the class in general. So now we turn to Luke.

Luke 23.39. *And one of the malefactors.* This insult which God's Son suffered from the thief won us the extreme honour of being recognized among the angels as their brothers. At the time an example of mad self-will is described for us in this ruined man, who even in the midst of agonies does not cease the wild frenzy of his blaspheming. Obstinacy is the usual revenge of desperate men, when they cannot escape their pains. Though he rebukes Christ for not being able to save Himself or others, his complaint is turned against God Himself. Just so the wicked, when they fail of their desires, would willingly drag God down from heaven. They would do better to accept their blows and be quiet. It is obvious how iron-hard is the evil of their hearts, which no punishment can bend.

Luke 23.40. *But the other answered.* In this wretched man there is held out to us a singular picture of the unexpected and unbelievable grace of God, first that he was suddenly changed in the hour of death into a new man, from the gate of hell raised to heaven, then that he won pardon in a moment for all the crimes in which his whole life had been sunk, so as to be received into heaven before the Apostles and the first-fruits of the new Church. First a shining instance of God's grace is seen in the conversion of this man. It was not by the native instinct of the flesh that he changed his cruel brutality and proud contempt for God to an instant repentance, but by the leading of the hand of God. As all Scripture teaches, penitence is His work. The grace is all the more excellent in coming contrary to anyone's expectation. Who would ever have thought that a thief in his last breath would have become both a devout servant of God and a leading teacher of faith and devotion to the whole world, so that we too may seek from his lips the rule of true and proper confession? The first-fruits he gave of repentance was the sharp reproof he gave to check the sinful rudeness of his fellow; then he gave a second, in humbling himself by sincere confession of his own crimes and giving Christ due glory for His righteousness. Finally he gave a wonderful testimony of faith, casting himself and his whole salvation on the protection of Christ, whom he then saw hanging on the cross and near to death. Dost thou not even fear God? Though interpreters twist these words variously, their sense seems simple to me, 'What does this mean, that not even this condemnation impels you to the fear of God?' The thief emphasises the hardness of his fellow, that at the last resort he still does not begin to fear God. To remove all ambiguity, readers should know that a headstrong and wicked reviler who thought he might mock with impunity is summoned to God's tribunal, for even if he had been dense all his life he should then have begun to tremble, when he felt God's Hand armed against him, and the account of all his crimes soon to be made up. It was a sign of abandoned, diabolical obstinacy that when God had him in the grip of the last judgment he did not then return to a sound mind. If there had been any drop of goodness in the man's heart he would have been forced at least to take refuge in the fear of God. To sum up these words, they are desperate men and deprived of all fear of God, who are not amended by their punishments. Ἐν τῷ αὐτῷ κρίματι I interpret, not as in the same condemnation, but in this present condemnation: as if he had said, 'Seeing that you are now in the jaws of death, you should wake up and admit that God is your Judge.' We take a useful lesson from this, that it is outright opposition to God not to be taught humility by punishment. Those who have any experience of the fear of God must be taken aback and silenced by shame.

Luke 23.41. *And we indeed justly.* Taking the condemnation as reproof might seem to apply equally to Christ, so the thief distinguishes Him from the plight of himself and his fellow. He allows that the penalty, common to them all, was inflicted justly on himself and his fellow, but not on Christ, who had been seized for execution not through His own offence, but through His enemies' cruelty. Remember what I just said; the thief gave a proof of repentance such as God demands of us all, in admitting that he received the reward due to his deeds. Note this particularly, that the brutality of the punishment did not prevent him bearing its harsh pains with patience. If we are truly sorry for our sins, we must learn to admit them freely and without pretence as need arises, and not hide from the disgrace we have deserved. The only means of burying our sins before God and the angels is not to attempt to hide them in the sight of men with useless deceptions. Among all the tricks that hypocrisy plays, the most regular is involving others with oneself, to excuse oneself on their account. The thief however is as eager to proclaim Christ's innocence as simply and freely to condemn himself and his companion.

Luke 23.42. *Lord remember me.* I do not know if there was ever, from the foundation of the world, a more rare or memorable example of faith: so much the more admiration is due to the grace of the Holy Spirit that gave here such a shining illustration of itself. The thief, not only untrained in the school of Christ, but rather a man who in a career of sinful killing had tried to extinguish all sense of right, suddenly penetrates more deeply than all the Apostles and the other disciples, upon whom the Lord Himself had spent so much effort, to teach them; not only so, but he adores Christ as King on the gallows tree, celebrates His

reign in the fearful and unspeakable loss, and proclaims Him Author of
life in the hour of dying. Even if he had been imbued with a right faith,
and had heard much of Christ's calling already, and had been confirmed
in this by the miracles, this knowledge could have dissolved at the over-
clouding of such a shameful death. For a rough, newfound man, quite
corrupt in mind, to understand salvation and the glory of heaven from
the very rudiments on the cross itself—this was more than marvellous.
What marks, what tokens adorned Christ as he saw Him, that should
raise his mind to kingship? Indeed it was to step from the depths of
hell to the heights of heaven. To the flesh it was moonshine and farce
for a rejected and condemned man (whom the world could not bear)
to receive an earthly kingdom more noble than all the empires of earth.
We see how keen was the sight of his understanding, that could discern
life in death, exaltation in ruin, glory in disgrace, victory in destruction, kingship in slavery. If the thief raised Christ, by faith, as He hung
on the cross, almost overcome with evil words, to the heavenly throne,
woe to our idle minds, if we do not lift our gaze to Him who sits
on God's Right Hand, if we do not plant our hope of life upon His
resurrection, if we do not reach out to the heaven that He has entered.
From another aspect if we consider in what state he begged Christ's
mercy, our admiration of his faith increases. Life-blood draining from
his torn body, he awaits only the executioners' last stroke, and yet he
finds his peace in the grace of Christ alone. First, whence could that
confidence in pardon have sprung, if he did not sense in Christ's death
(which to all others seemed so hateful) a sacrifice of sweet odour, able to
expiate the sins of the world? And when he bravely disregards his
agonies, completely forgets himself, seized by a longing for the unseen
life, he goes beyond all human sense. The mortification of the flesh and
patience and burning devotion are lessons we shall not be ashamed to
learn from this teacher, whom God sets before us to reduce the pride of
the flesh. The more eagerly each follows him, the closer he will come
to Christ.

Luke 23.43. *Verily I say unto thee.* Though Christ has not yet
triumphed over death openly He demonstrates in His very exhaustion
the effect and fruits of it. By this means He declares that He was never
robbed of His power of Kingship. The divine King has no more lofty
or spendid office than restoring life to the dead. Even if under God's
mighty Hand He might give the appearance of a man almost beyond
relief, yet as He did not cease to be the world's Preserver, He ever kept
reserves of heavenly power to fulfil His task. Note first, His amazing
ease in taking the thief to Himself with no delay, with such kindness,
promising that He would share with him the blessed life. There is no
doubt that He is prepared to admit all into His Kingdom without

exception, who take refuge in Him. We may state for sure that if He remember us, we shall be saved. And it cannot be that He will forget those who entrust their salvation to Him. If the thief had such an easy passage into heaven that he could repose on Christ's grace in the final desperation of all things, much more today will Christ the Victor over death reach out His hand to us from the throne, to gather us into the company of life. For it would be absurd, since He had nailed to the cross the handwriting that was against us, and made havoc of death and Satan, and in His resurrection triumphed over the prince of this world, not to be so easy and ready as He was with the thief, to grant us passage from death to life. Whoever then with true faith gives the guardianship of his soul, in death, to Christ will not be long detained or languish in suspense, but at his prayer Christ will come to him with the same kindness as He bore toward the thief. So no more of that repulsive commentary of the sophists on penalties retained when guilt is remitted, for we see how Christ immediately frees a man from the penalty when He clears him of his guilt. That the thief still goes through to the last the punishment he had been awarded, is no objection; for there is no compensation to be imagined in that, and no expiation to placate God's judgment (as the sophists rave on): it indicates simply that the Lord trains His elect by bodily punishment to have displeasure and hatred for their sin. Christ takes the thief, who has been led by fatherly chastening to deny himself, into His bosom; He does not send him off to the fire of purgatory. Besides, we should note the keys that open the door of the Kingdom of the skies to the thief: there is no papal confession here, satisfactions are not accounted. Christ is content with penitence and faith to welcome him willingly when he comes.

This confirms what I have just touched on, if any man resents going in the path of the thief and following his lead, he deserves eternal ruin for his own wicked pride keeps him away from the road to heaven. In the person of the thief, Christ gave us all an equal pledge of obtaining pardon, and so again He adds to the honour of that poor man, in order that we should strip off all our own glory and boast in the mercy of God alone. If each of us would examine this in truth and seriousness, the vast score of our offences would rightly put us to shame and we should not be annoyed that a ruined man, who won salvation by pure grace, should be the leader and standard bearer. And as at that time the death of Christ bore fruit, so we gather that souls, when they leave the body, have survival: otherwise Christ's promise would be illusory, for all that He confirms it on oath. We should not debate in detail and with cleverness about the place of paradise. Let it be enough for us that whoever by faith are set in the body of Christ are partakers of His life, and so after death enjoy peace, blessing and happiness, until the total revelation, at the coming of Christ, of the perfect glory of the life of heaven. One thing still remains, that the promise to the thief was not relief for his present distress, nor reduction in any degree of the penalty for the body. We are here warned not to reckon God's grace with fleshly sense: it will often happen that God will allow great affliction to fall on those to whom He has favour. So if in the body we are in wretched agony, we must take care that that sharpness of pain does not dispel the favour of divine goodness for us. Rather all our troubles should be eased and abated by this one consolation, that once God has taken us to His favour, whatever troubles we endure is an instrument for our salvation. Not only shall our faith emerge victor over all kinds of tribulation, but shall take quietness and sweetness from the midst of the ordeal of punishment.

Now from the sixth hour there was darkness over all the land until the ninth hour. And about the ninth hour Jesus cried with a loud voice, saying, Eli, Eli, lama sabachthani? that is, My God, My God, why hast thou forsaken me? And some of them that stood there, when they heard it, said, This man calleth Elijah. And straightway one of them ran, and took a sponge, and filled it with vinegar, and put it on a reed, and gave him to drink. And the rest said, Let be; let us see whether Elijah cometh to save him. And Jesus cried again with a loud voice, and yielded up his spirit. And behold, the veil of the temple was rent in twain from the top to the bottom; and the earth did quake; and the rocks were rent; and the tombs were opened; and many bodies of the saints that had fallen asleep were raised; and coming forth out of the tombs after his resurrection they entered into the holy city and appeared unto many. Now the centurion, and they that were with him watching Jesus, when they saw the earthquake, and the things that were done, feared exceedingly, saying, Truly this was the Son of God. And many women were there beholding from afar, which had followed Jesus from Galilee, ministering unto him; among whom was Mary Magdalene, and Mary the mother of James and Joses, and the mother of the sons of Zebedee. (Matt. 27.45-56)

And when the sixth hour was come, there was darkness over the whole land until the ninth hour. And at the ninth hour Jesus cried with a loud voice, Eloi, Eloi, lama sabachthani? which is, being interpreted, My God, my God, why hast thou forsaken me? And some of them that stood by, when they heard it, said, Behold, he calleth Elijah. And one ran, and filling a sponge full of vinegar, put it on a reed, and gave him to drink, saying, Let be: let us see whether Elijah cometh to take him down. And

*Jesús uttered a loud voice, and gave up the ghost. And the veil of the
temple was rent in twain from the top to the bottom. And when the
centurion, which stood by over against him, saw that he so gave up the
ghost, he said, Truly this man was the Son of God. And there were also
women beholding from afar: among them were both Mary Magdalene,
and Mary the mother of James the less and of Joses, and Salome; who,
when he was in Galilee, followed him, and ministered unto him; and
many other women which came up with him unto Jerusalem.* (Mark
15.33-41)

*And it was now about the sixth hour, and a darkness came over the whole
land until the ninth hour, the sun's light failing: and the veil of the
temple was rent in the midst. And when Jesus had cried with a loud
voice, he said, Father, into thy hands I commend my spirit: and having
said this, he gave up the ghost. And when the centurion saw what was
done, he glorified God, saying, Certainly this was a righteous man. And
all the multitudes that came together to this sight, when they beheld the
things that were done, returned smiting their breasts. And all his acquaintance, and the women that followed with him from Galilee stood afar off,
seeing these things.* (Luke 23.44-49)

Matt. 27.45. *Now from the sixth hour.* Though in Christ's death the
weakness of the flesh obscured for a short time the glory of the Godhead and God's Son lay in the disgrace of shame and contempt, and
(as Paul says) was emptied out, yet the heavenly Father did not fail to
mark it with some distinction. In His final rejection He raised some
portents of the glory to come, to support devout minds against the
scandal of the cross. To the Majesty of Christ, came the superb testimony of the sun's eclipse, the earthquake, the cloven rock, the tearing
of the veil, just as if heaven and earth gave their due service to their
Maker and Designer. It is first asked, for what reason was the sun's
eclipse. The ancient poets in their tragedies describe the sun's light
being withdrawn from the earth when any foul crime is committed,
and so aim to show a portent of divine wrath: this was a fiction that
drew from the common feelings of nature. Some interpreters think
that darkness was sent from God at Christ's death as a sign of His
abhorrence, as if God by blackening out the sun should be hiding His
own Face from the most loathsome of all crimes. Others take the
extinction of the sun's light as a token of the fall of the Sun of righteousness. Others prefer to attach it to the blindness of the people, that
shortly afterwards ensued. When the Jews rejected Christ and He was
taken from their midst they were deprived of the light of heavenly
teaching, and had nothing left to them but the shadows of despair.
I am inclined to think that as the people in their folly had shut out the

light, God aroused them with darkness to consider His amazing purpose, in the death of Christ. The unusual reversal of the order of nature would have made a serious impression on their senses, if they had not been utterly hardened, and made them look for the future renewal of the world.

Further, they were shown a sight full of terror, to make them tremble at God's judgment. It was certainly an incomparable proof of God's anger that He did not spare His only-begotten Son and was only placated by this price of expiation. That the scribes and priests and a great part of the people carelessly overlooked this darkening of the sun, and passed through it with eyes closed, should strike us with horror, for their formidable degree of stupidity. They must have been more foolish than dumb beasts to have continued their mockery with such a portent of the force of heavenly judgment, and with open warning. This is that spirit of folly and giddiness by which God makes the reprobate reel, after He has long striven against their malice. A lesson meanwhile; once they were under the spell of Satan's craft, the glory of God, however conspicuous it might be, was hidden from them. At least their minds were so darkened that seeing, they do not see. As the warning was general, it should be useful for our understanding today, that the sacrifice by which we were redeemed was of no less importance than if the sun fell out of heaven, or the whole structure of the world collapsed. So we shall abhor our sins the more. When some extend this eclipse of the sun to every corner of the globe, I doubt if they are correct. Even if it has been recorded by one or two writers, the history of those times was too widespread for such a remarkable miracle to have been overlooked by so many others, who have given accurate accounts of things far less worth remembering. Besides, if the eclipse had been common to the whole world, men would more easily have missed its significance. While the sun shone elsewhere, Judaea was plunged into shadow; this made the prodigy more notable.

Matt. 27.46. *And about the ninth hour Jesus cried.* There appeared to be more than human vigour in Christ's cry, but it is certain that intensity of grief forced it from Him. This was His chief conflict, harder than any other agony, that in His anguish He was not given relief by His Father's aid or favour, but made to feel somehow estranged. He did not only offer His body as the price of our reconciliation with God, but also in His soul He bore our due pains: He was truly made the Man of sorrows, as Isaiah says (53.3). They are very unenlightened who make stress of the torment of the flesh outwardly, and hold back this part of redemption: for Christ to make satisfaction for us He had to stand trial at God's tribunal. There is nothing more dreadful than to feel God as Judge, whose wrath is worse than all deaths. When the

207

trial came on Christ in this form, that He was now against God and doomed to ruin, He was overcome with dread (which would have been enough to swallow up all mankind a hundred times over) but He came out Victor, by the marvellous power of the Spirit. It is no fiction or play-acting that prompts His complaint, that He is forsaken by the Father. When some say that He followed popular mood in speaking so, their sneer is pathetic. It is an inner sadness of soul, with violent fire, that drives Him to break out in a cry. The redemption He worked out was not for the spectator (as I have just said), but, that He might go surety for us, He truly wished to undergo God's judgment in our place. Does it seem strange that a voice of despair fell from Christ's lips? The solution is easy. Although the physical senses feared death, faith was firm set in his heart; for by it He saw God present, while He complained of His absence. We have said in another place how the Godhead yielded to the infirmity of the flesh, in the interests of our salvation, that Christ might fulfil the whole role of Redeemer. We have noted a difference between natural sense and the intelligence of faith: so nothing prevents Christ, as far as ordinary sense dictated, taking thought of His estrangement from God, and at the same time, by faith, realizing that God was on His side. This is quite clear from the two parts of the complaint. Before uttering the temptation, He first says He takes refuge in God as His God, and so with the shield of faith bravely re-pulses the sort of dereliction that shot at Him from the other side. In this fearful torment His faith was unscathed. Though He laments that He is forsaken, He takes confidence in the close assistance of God. The words are chiefly worthy of note, clearly, from the fact that the Spirit, to engrave them better in men's minds, chose to record them in the Syriac language. This is precisely to make Christ speak the actual words that then fell from His mouth. More shame on the indifference of those who pass over with mild amusement such sorrow in Christ, such dreadful trembling. Those who reckon that Christ took on the office of Mediator on condition of bearing our guilt in soul as in body will not wonder at the struggle He had with the pangs of death; as though under the wrath of God, He were cast into the labyrinth of evil.

Matt. 27.47. *This man calleth Elijah.* In my opinion they are wrong who apply this to the soldiers, as uneducated and ignorant of the Syriac language, unaccustomed to Jewish religion: they suggest that they made a mistake over the likeness of sounds. I do not think it at all likely that they slipped through ignorance, for they were rather making deliberate mockery of Christ and were determined to slander His words on pur-pose. Satan has no device more suited for hurting the salvation of the godly than to put them off calling on God's Name. He urges his servants to this as best he can, to shake the desire to pray out of us. So he impelled the wicked enemies of Christ rudely to turn His prayer into mockery, wishing by this stratagem to make Him lose His chief armour. This is a very grave temptation, when we seem to be so far from success that God more exposes His name to insult than shows Himself propitious to our prayers. The irony—the barking of dogs, if you prefer—comes to this; they were denying that Christ had any dealings with God, for He was calling on Elijah, so seeking help at other hands. We see that He was harassed on all sides, that He might be overcome with despair and cease calling upon God, which was to renounce salvation. If today the hired rabble of Antichrist, and the rogues within our doors, debase with their low slanders what we have said rightly, let us not be amazed that the same falls on us, as fell upon our Head. Though they transfigure God into Elijah, when they have had their hearts content of laughter over us, God will, in the end, hear our groans and will show that He vindicates His glory, and brings retribution on their dirty lies.

Matt. 27.48. *And straightway one of them ran.* The likely conjecture may be inferred that as Christ had once rejected the drink it was repeatedly offered Him as an annoyance. At the same time it is likely that vinegar was offered him in a cup at the beginning, before He was lifted up high, and afterwards a sponge was placed to his lips when He was hanging on the cross.

Mark 15.36. *Saying, let be.* Mark records these words as being spoken by the soldier reaching out the vinegar, *Let be, let us see*, etc. Matthew attributes the words to the others: there is no contradiction. It is likely that the joke, started by one, was taken up eagerly by the others and caused an upcry among them all. The word to *let be* is not a prohibition but mockery. The first to mock Christ urged his companions in irony, Let's wait, he says, and see if Elijah will come. At once the others follow, passing the jingle along the line, as often happens when men think alike. There is no reason to insist on the plural or singular number: *let be* means the same in either form. The word is used as an interjection, as if one said '*hist!*'

Matt. 27.50. *And Jesus cried again.* Luke, who does not relate the first cry of anguish, records the words of the second call, which Matthew and Mark omit. He says that He cried, *Father into thy hands I commend my spirit*, testifying that although He was sore shocked with many violent trials yet His faith was unshaken, and stood its ground undefeated. There could be no clearer declaration of triumph than for Christ to boast without fear that God is the faithful Guardian of His soul (which all were thinking lost). And as He would be speaking to deaf ears He took His words direct to God and entrusted His testimony of confidence into His very bosom. He wished His words to be heard by men, but even if it did no good in men's sight, He was content if God were His only witness. Faith has no more real or solid approbation than when a godly man, seeing himself attacked on all sides, and unable to find comfort in men, despises the world's madness and unburdens on God's lap his griefs and cares, and rests quietly in the hope of His promises. Though the form of prayer seems to be taken from Psalm 31.9, I have no doubt that He adapted it for His present use according to the emergency of the moment, as if He had said, 'I see Father, that I am by every voice appointed to destruction, and my soul is somehow carried this way and that. Although according to the flesh, I feel no help from You, yet that will not prevent My resting My spirit in Your hands and, without anxiety, taking support from the hidden protection of Your goodness.' Yet we must note that David in that passage I have cited did not only ask that his soul's taken into the hand of God, should stay safe and sound after his death; but commended his life to God, that surrounded by His defence in life and in death, he should have good fortune. He saw himself continually beset with many deaths. There was no other course but to commit himself to the invincible protection of God. And when he set God the Guardian over his soul, he boasts that it is safe from every danger. Likewise he prepares himself readily to face death, when God so pleases, for the Lord Himself also holds the souls of His people in death. Now as Christ has lost the first alternative, to commit His soul to the protection of the Father in the frail course of this earthly life, He advances eagerly upon death, seeking to be preserved beyond this world. For the chief reason that God takes our souls into His trust is that our hope should transcend this shadowy existence.

Now let us remember that it was not for His personal interest that Christ commended His soul to the Father, but He gathered up, as it were, all the souls of his faithful in one bundle, to keep them safe with His own. By this prayer He won the right to keep all souls, so that the heavenly Father, for His sake, not only deigns to take them into His keeping, but resigning His role entrusts them to Him for preservation. So Stephen in dying entrusts his soul into His hands: 'Lord Jesus', he says, 'receive my spirit' (Acts 7.59). Following his example, whoever shall believe in Christ will not, in death, breathe out his soul into the air, but will resort to a sure Custodian, who will keep safely whatever is entrusted to Him by the Father. The cry again shows the vehemence of His feelings. There is no doubt that Christ, in the anguish of the temptations that beset Him, let out this cry at last with deep and burning effort. Yet for our sakes He wished to testify with a loud and ringing call that His soul would be safe from death and unhurt, that we might bear the same confidence and march out with eager step from the crumbling hovel of the flesh.

Matt. 27.51. *And behold the veil.* When Luke combines the rending of the veil with the eclipse of the sun, as if it occurred before the death of Christ, he turns the order round. The Evangelists (as we have seen often enough) do not always observe an exact time sequence. It was not appropriate for the veil to be rent, except at the completion of the sacrifice of expiation. At that time, Christ the true and eternal Priest, abolishing legal fore-types with His own blood, opened for us the way to the celestial Sanctuary, that we should no longer stand away in the courtyard, but freely advance into the sight of God. As long as the cultic representations (*umbratilis cultus*) survived a veil was set over the earthly Sanctuary, to keep off from there not only the feet but even the eyes of the people. Christ, blotting out the handwriting that was against us (Col. 2.14), tore away every obstacle, that we might be all one royal priesthood dependent on Him as sole Mediator. The rending of the veil not only abrogated the ceremonies that flourished under the Law but also opened heaven, that God might now intimately welcome the members of His Son to Himself. Besides, the Jews were warned that an end was set upon their external sacrifices, and that after this there would be no use for the old priesthood. Even if the building of the temple were to stand, there could no longer be service of God there, under the accustomed rite, for now, as the substance of the shadows and the reality was fulfilled, all legal figures were transformed into spirit. Though Christ offered a visible sacrifice, it is spiritually (as the Apostle in the Epistle to the Hebrews teaches, 9.14) that we must reckon it in order to take hold of its reward and fruits. These wretches gained no benefit from having the outward Sanctuary laid bare by the rending of the veil, for inwardly the veil of their faithlessness robbed them of a view of the light of salvation. What Matthew adds regarding the earthquake and cleaving of rocks, I think it likely, occurred at the same moment. And in this way, not only the earth gave testimony to its Maker, but witness is summoned against the hardness of that ruined race. It is revealed how prodigious was their obstinacy, when it was unmoved by the shattering of the earth and the cleavage of stones.

Matt. 27.52. *And the tombs were opened.* This was a particular portent in which God testified that His Son had entered death's prison, not to stay there shut up, but to lead all free who were there held captive. At the time when in Christ's Person was seen a contemptible weakness of the flesh, the splendid and divine power of His death had reached down even to the underworld. That is the reason why He, who was soon to be shut in a tomb, opened the tombs elsewhere. Yet we may doubt whether this opening of the tombs happened before the resurrection, for the resurrection of the saints which is shortly after added followed in my opinion the actual resurrection of Christ. It is absurd for some interpreters to imagine that they spent three days alive and breathing, hidden in tombs. It seems likely to me that at Christ's death the tombs at once opened: at His resurrection some of the godly men received breath and came out and were seen in the city. Christ is called the Firstborn from the dead and the First-fruits of those who rise (I Cor. 15.20; Col. 1.18), because by His death He began the new life, and by His resurrection completed it, not that the dead at His dying immediately revived, but because His death was the source and start of their life. This reasoning agrees very well, seeing that the breaking of the tombs was the presage of new life, and the fruit itself, the effect, appeared three days later, as Christ rising again led other companions from the graves with Himself. And in this sign it was shown that neither His dying not His resurrection were private to Himself, but breathe the odour of life into all the faithful.

Yet here begins a question as to why God wished some to rise again, when all the faithful are within the scope of the resurrection company of Christ. I reply that the time was not yet ripe for the whole body of the Church to be gathered in to its Head, but an instance of the new life was published in a few to show what all could hope for. We know that the terms on which Christ was received into heaven were that the life of His members should remain hidden, until it was revealed at His coming. In order that the minds of the godly might be raised more keenly to hope, it was good that a few should sample the resurrection which all would in time enjoy. A second question is more difficult. What afterwards became of these saints? It seems absurd if after once being admitted to the fellowship of new life with Christ they again returned to dust. As there is no easy or ready solution so there is no point in labouring wearily over a matter we need not understand. It is not likely they passed long in the company of men: they only had to be seen for a short time, that as in a mirror or picture they should manifest the power of Christ. Since God wished in their person to confirm among the living the hope of life in heaven, there would be nothing strange if once they had performed this task they again rested in their tombs. Yet there is more likelihood that the life they were given was not taken from them, for if it had been mortal it could not have been a proof of real resurrection. And although the whole world will rise again, and Christ will rouse no less the wicked into judgment than the righteous to salvation, yet as He truly rose again for the sake of the Church He rightly only accorded to saints the honour of sharing His resurrection.

As for Matthew calling Jerusalem with the distinction of *holy city*, he gives no credit to the merits of its citizens thereby (we know it was crammed with every mark of criminality, and more like a bandit's cave). But because of its divine election, no conception on the part of men could efface its holiness, which was grounded in God's adoption, until its reprobation was made public. To put it more briefly, on men's part it was profane, but on God's part holy, until the destruction or desecration of the temple, which took place not long after the crucifixion of Christ.

Matt. 27.54. *Now the centurion.* Seeing that Luke mentions the mourning of the people, it was not only the centurion, with his soldiers, who recognized Christ as Son of God, but the Evangelists speak of Him explicitly to fill out the narrative, for it is amazing that a profane man uneducated in the Law and with no experience of true piety should have made such a judgment from the signs he saw. The comparison has a strong effect on the condemnation of the folly of the city, for apart from the feeble crowd, none of the Jews was moved by the shock and tremor of the world's structure; a fearful sign of their derangement. In such crass blindness, God did not allow the testimonies He gave on His Son's account to go without notice. Not only then did true religion open the eyes of sincere worshippers of God to a sense of the light of the glory of Christ published in heaven, but the very natural senses compelled outsiders, even soldiers, to confess what they had learnt neither from the Law nor from teachers. Mark says, the centurion spoke thus because Christ in dying had given out a great shout. Some interpreters think that it is the extraordinary strength that is noted, coming from a man who had kept His faculties even to the point of death. And certainly as Christ's body was virtually exhausted it was humanly impossible for chest and lungs to have force enough for a loud shout. I rather think it was Christ's persistent endurance in calling on God's Name that the centurion praised. It was not only Christ's shouting that led him to treat Him with honour, for his confession was drawn from him as he saw His remarkable power matched by miracles in heaven. It says he feared God, but it should not be explained as meaning a full repentance. It was only a sudden and passing impulse as often happens to empty men, set on this world, struck with fear for God when He exerts His dread power, but as there is no living root beneath, indifference grows on quickly and obliterates the impression. The centurion was not so changed as to dedicate the remaining time of his life to God, but was only a momentary herald of the Deity of Christ. As for his saying in Luke merely, *Certainly this was a righteous man,* this has the same force as if he had said plainly, 'He was Son of God', as the other two Evangelists say. The report had gone everywhere that Christ was executed for behaving as if He were God's Son. Now if the centurion credits Him with being righteous and acquits Him of the charge, he is at the same time declaring that He is Son of God, not that he understood exactly in what way Christ was begotten of God the Father, but that he did not doubt there was something divine in Him; that he was convinced on evidence that He was no common man, but was sure He was of divine origin.

As regards the crowds, they beat their breasts in sign of warding off the price of their guilt, for they felt a public expiation was involved, for the unjust and wicked killing. As they went no further, their lamentation was to no use for them, unless perhaps for some it was the beginning, or the preparation, of a better repentance. The only lamentation recorded for us is that which God drew from them for His Son's glory. Let the example teach us, that it counts little or nothing for a man to feel horror at the presence of the power of God until his fright abates and the fear of God abides calmly in his heart.

Matt. 27.55. *And many women were there.* I interpret this addition as telling us that while the disciples had fled this way and that, and scattered, there were certain of that company whom the Lord retained as witnesses. Though John the Apostle did not leave the cross, there is no mention of him here. Only the women are praised, who kept Christ company up to His death, for with men fleeing in terror, their singular devotion to their master shone out the more clearly. They must have had a rare enthusiasm and fire in them. Though they could serve no purpose, they did not cease in His utmost shame to give Him reverent attendance. Not all the men had fled, as we gather from Luke: he says *and all his acquaintance . . . stood afar off.* Not without reason however do the Evangelists give first place to the women, as worthy to be put before the men. In my judgment the tacit contrast is serious criticism of the Apostles. I am speaking of the body as such: because one alone remained, the three Evangelists keep quiet about him (as I have just said). For the chosen witnesses it was a great disgrace, to withdraw from that scene, on which depended the salvation of the world. In their later publication of the Gospel they must have borrowed from the women the chief part of the story. If God's providence had not been equal to the disaster in a wonderful way, we too would have been deprived of the knowledge of redemption. Though we might not think there is so much authority in women, if we weigh the matter up, how the power of the Spirit supported them in that trial, there will be no reason for our faith to waver, since it rests on God, the true Author of their testimony.

Meanwhile notice the way of God's incredible goodness, that there should flow, even to us, the Gospel of expiation by which God is reconciled to us. In the general falling away of those who should have led others, God stirred some of the flock to pull themselves together, in their terror, to be the witnesses of that story—without which faith we could not be saved. Of the women themselves we shall shortly be saying something further. Meanwhile, it is enough to note that in their zeal for learning they were led from their home country, to hang continuously on Christ's words, not sparing effort, nor means as long as they enjoyed His teaching of salvation.

And when even was come, there came a rich man from Arimathaea, named Joseph, who also himself was Jesus' disciple: this man went to Pilate, and asked for the body of Jesus. Then Pilate commanded it to be given up. And Joseph took the body, and wrapped it in a clean linen cloth, and laid it in his own new tomb, which he had hewn out in the rock: and he rolled a great stone to the door of the tomb, and departed. And Mary Magdalene was there, and the other Mary, sitting over against the sepulchre. (Matt. 27.57-61)

And when even was now come, because it was the Preparation, that is, the day before the sabbath, there came Joseph of Arimathaea, a councillor of honourable estate, who also himself was looking for the kingdom of God; and he boldly went in unto Pilate, and asked for the body of Jesus. And Pilate marvelled if he were already dead: and calling unto him the centurion, he asked him whether he had been any while dead. And when he learned it of the centurion, he granted the corpse to Joseph. And he bought a linen cloth, and taking him down, wound him in the linen cloth, and laid him in a tomb which had been hewn out of a rock; and he rolled a stone against the door of the tomb. And Mary Magdalene and Mary the mother of Joses beheld where he was laid. (Mark 15.42-4)

And behold, a man named Joseph, who was a councillor, a good man and a righteous (he had not consented to their counsel and deed), a man of Arimathaea, a city of the Jews, who was looking for the kingdom of God: this man went to Pilate, and asked for the body of Jesus. And he took it down, and wrapped it in a linen cloth, and laid him in a tomb that was hewn in stone, where never man had yet lain. And it was the day of the Preparation, and the sabbath drew on. And the women, which had come with him out of Galilee, followed after, and beheld the tomb, and how his body was laid. And they returned, and prepared spices and ointments. And on the sabbath they rested according to the commandment. (Luke 23.50-56)

Now follows the burial of Christ, a transitional passage from the ignominy of the cross to the glory of the resurrection. One reason for God wishing His Son to be buried was to give better testimony that He had died a real death, on our account. But the chief object that we must regard was, that by this means the curse which He had for a while undergone began to be lifted. His corpse was not thrown into a pit in the common way, but buried with respect in a hewn sepulchre. It was still the weakness of the flesh that occupied their eyes. There was no clear vision of the divine power of the Spirit before the resurrection. God meant this as a kind of foreshadowing of what He would shortly bring to pass, that He would raise His Son in splendour and victory, above the heavens.

Matt. 27.57. *And when even was come.* Understand that Joseph came not in the dark but before sunset in order to offer this service of devotion to his Master without violating the sabbath, for the sabbath started from that evening. It was necessary for Christ to be laid in the tomb before night fell. From the death of Christ to the observance of sabbath there were three clear hours. John does not only name Jospeh but also Nicodemus his companion, but he was the first to start the arrangements, and Nicodemus only followed his lead and instigation. Thus in the short account of the three Evangelists it was enough to record what was done by him alone. Even if we should reckon Joseph's efforts as deserving high praise, our first consideration should be God's providence, that He chose a man of noble rank among his own people, of highest worth, to begin to cover the shame of the cross with honourable burial. Seeing that he exposed himself to the spite and hatred of the whole race, and to very great risk, there is no doubt that he drew his great confidence from the hidden prompting of the Spirit. Granted he had been already one of Christ's disciples, he had never dared so openly and freely to confess his faith. Now at Christ's death a sight full of despair comes to view, that might shatter even strong minds, where did he get this sudden generous courage to fear nothing, in the worst peril, and advance with less hesitation than he had in quieter times? Let us be sure that God's Son was buried under divine persuasion by the hand of Joseph. This should be the focal point of the circumstances here recorded.

Joseph is praised for his devotion and integrity of life, that we may learn to recognize God's work in God's servant. The Evangelists call him rich to teach us that it was by a wonderful, sublime courage that he overcame every obstacle that might otherwise have held him back. For as the rich are proud, they find nothing more difficult than freely to face the scorn of the crowd. We may know what an unpleasant, degrading business it was to take the corpse of a crucified man from the executioner's hand. Besides, as his fortune was the more splendid, he might have been the more cautious and timid (men who are tied up in their money usually keep clear of any crisis point), except that his boldness had been sent him from heaven. He is given his degree of rank, namely councillor or senator, that God's power might be displayed in this respect also. It was no man out of the mob that had been put up to bury Christ's corpse, in haste and secrecy, but as equal to the responsibility a man of high standing was brought forward. The less credible it seems that such service of devotion should have been prepared for Christ, the more clearly it appears that it was all guided by God's counsel and hand.

The example teaches us, that the rich are so far from being excused if they cheat Christ of His honour, as to be doubly guilty if they make the opportunities, that should stir them on, into obstacles. I agree that it is all too regular and common an occurrence for these men to withdraw from the yoke (men who appear to be above other people, effeminate and soft, too occupied, too nervous), but we must start an altogether different way of thinking; unless wealth and honours are aids to the service of God, we are making a false use of them. The events of this moment show how easily God may correct the base fears that stop us doing our duties. Joseph earlier did not dare, in doubtful circumstances, to profess himself frankly as Christ's disciple, but now, in face of the enemies' fiercest fury and savage attacks, he takes courage and does not hesitate to throw himself into open conflict. We see then how, in a moment, God shapes our hearts to new passions, raises with the spirit of boldness those who before were in collapse. If Joseph summoned up his confidence when Christ hung dead on the cross, in his holy desire to do Him honour, and we today, after His resurrection from the dead, have not at least the same flourishing zeal for His glory in our hearts—then woe to our idle ways!

Mark 15.43 and Luke 23.51. *Who also himself was looking for the kingdom of God.* This is the highest commendation given Joseph, that he was looking for the Kingdom of God. He also praises too his uprightness, but this expectation of the Kingdom of God is the root and source of righteousness. By the *kingdom of God* understand the promised restoration in Christ. The complete ordering, that the prophets always promised would appear at the coming of Christ, cannot exist until God gathers under His rule the folk who had scattered. So this is a praiseworthy mark of Joseph's piety; in the ruined condition of affairs, he fostered the hope of redemption, which had been promised by God. This is the beginning of the fear of God and a concern for holy and right living. Nor can any man ever attach himself to God unless he hopes in Him as his Deliverer. Let us note, that though salvation was promised to all the Jews without distinction in Christ, His promise was common

217

to all; yet it is only of a very few that the Holy Spirit testifies what here we read of Joseph. It is obvious that the incomparable grace of God was then almost completely buried in oblivion, by that whole people. Practically everyone had something boastful to say about the coming presence of Christ, but in few minds was God's Covenant set firm, that they might rise by faith to a spiritual renewal. Certainly their folly was astounding. We need not wonder that the purity of religion decayed when faith in salvation was extinct. Would to God there were no similar corruption in this unhappy generation! Christ once appeared to the Jews and to the whole world as Redeemer, as had been testified by the oracles of the prophets. Ordering affairs out of wild confusion into a right and proper state, He set up the Kingdom of God, and prescribed us a time of combat to train our patience, until He should again come down from heaven as the Perfecter of that Kingdom which He had inaugurated. How many in fact aspire to this hope, even in a moderate degree? Are men not almost all tied to earth, as if there were no promise of resurrection? While the greater part of men, forgetting their aim, drift this way and that—let us remember that it is the true virtue of the faithful to seek what is above: and especially since the time that the grace of God shone down on us through the Gospel, 'to teach us that denying ungodliness and worldly lusts we should live soberly and righteously and godly in this present world, looking for the blessed hope and appearing of the glory of our great God' (Titus 2.11-13).

Matt. 27.59. *And Joseph took the body*. The three Evangelists treat the burial rather briefly: they say nothing of the aromatic unguents that only John speaks of. They narrate simply that a clean linen cloth was purchased by Joseph. So we gather, He was decently buried. No doubt a rich man, in giving up his sepulchre to the Lord, would have provided suitable finery and ornament in other respects. It came about more by the secret purpose of God than by men's planned intention, that the Lord obtained a new and still unsullied tomb, He who was First-born from the dead, the First-fruits of them that rise. God by this symbol distinguishes His Son from the whole company of the human race, and in His very tomb set out the newness of life.

Matt. 27.61. *And Mary Magdalene was there*. Mark and Matthew merely state that the women watched what was done, and noted the place where the body was laid. Luke, at the same time, expresses their intention to return to the city and prepare spices and unguents, and two days later to attend to His burial in due order. So we recognize that their minds were filled with a better odour, which the Lord breathed into His dying, that He might lead them to His sepulchre and raise them higher.

Now on the morrow, which is the day after the Preparation, the chief priests and the Pharisees were gathered together unto Pilate, saying, Sir, we remember that that deceiver said, while he was yet alive, After three days I rise again. Command therefore that the sepulchre be made sure until the third day, lest haply his disciples come and steal him away, and say unto the people, He is risen from the dead: and the last error will be worse than the first. Pilate said unto them, Ye have a guard: go your way, make it as sure as ye can. So they went, and made the sepulchre sure, sealing the stone, the guard being with them. (Matt. 27.62-66)

Matt. 27.62. *Now on the morrow.* In this narrative it was not so much Matthew's purpose to show the obstinate fury with which the scribes and priests pursued Christ as to give us, in mirror image, a view of the incredible providence of God, in proving the resurrection of His Son. Clever men plot together, well trained in fraud and perfidy, they devise a plan to blot out the memory of the man that had died. They see they have gained nothing unless they suppress faith in a resurrection. Yet, as they try to achieve this, they seem almost deliberately to bring it out into the light of knowledge. Christ's resurrection would have been more obscure, or, at any rate, their ability to deny it would have been all the greater, if they had not taken care to place witnesses over the tomb. We see God frustrating the purposes of astute men, catching them up in their own devices as in snares, drawing and forcing them into His service. Christ's enemies did not deserve to receive the revelation of His resurrection, but it was right that their insolence should be exposed and their pretext for maligning Him removed, indeed, for their own consciences to be convicted, that they might not have the excuse of ignorance. Note this: God, as it were hiring them for pay, used their work to publish the glory of Christ, for when they found the sepulchre empty, they were left no chance of lying in denial of it. Not that they departed from their lunatic wrongdoing, but for all sound people, enjoying right and sane judgment, it was a proof that Christ, whose body had been shut in a tomb, had risen, that after soldiers had been appointed to keep it sealed on all sides, He was not found.

Matt. 27.63. *We remember that that deceiver.* This thought was suggested to them by divine prompting, not only that the Lord might take His just revenge for their sin (He regularly troubles bad consciences with secret pains) but chiefly to restrain their unholy tongues. Again we see what folly seized them once Satan had bewitched them. They actually name him *a deceiver* whose divine power and glory had so recently been displayed, with so many miracles. It was not the clouds they resisted now, but mocking the sun's eclipse they were (so to speak) spitting in the face of God. These examples teach us to attend to the glory of God in good time, and with reverent, sincere attention, in case our hardness leads to a grim and fearsome blindness of heart. At first sight it seems harsh and unreasonable that the wicked should so rudely do Christ spite in His death. That their wildness may not disturb us, we should always consider wisely the end to which God turns it. The wicked think they will subvert the whole teaching of Christ and His miracles by this single blasphemy which they spew out in their pride, but God actually uses them to vindicate His Son from all mark of imposture. As often as the wicked prepare the ruin of all things, with their slanders, and burst out in a flurry of malicious words, let us wait with level and calm minds, till God brings His light out of the darkness.

Matt. 27.65. *Ye have a guard.* Pilate means by these words that he falls in with their wish to set soldiers on guard duty. The permission stopped them even more getting away with any evasions. Although without compunction they still dared to cry out against Christ after His resurrection, in fact Pilate's signet ring blocked their mouths as effectively as the sepulchre.

Now late on the sabbath day, as it began to dawn toward the first day of the week, came Mary Magdalene and the other Mary to see the sepulchre. And behold, there was a great earthquake; for an angel of the Lord descended from heaven, and came and rolled away the stone, and sat upon it. His appearance was as lightning, and his raiment white as snow: and for fear of him the watchers did quake, and became as dead men. And the angel answered and said unto the women, Fear not ye: for I know that ye seek Jesus, which hath been crucified. He is not here; for he is risen, even as he said. Come, see the place where the Lord lay. And go quickly, and tell his disciples, He is risen from the dead; and lo, he goeth before you into Galilee; there shall ye see him; lo, I have told you. (Matt. 28.1-7)

And when the sabbath was past, Mary Magdalene, and Mary the mother of James, and Salome, bought spices, that they might come and anoint him. And very early on the first day of the week, they come to the tomb when the sun was risen. And they were saying among themselves, Who shall roll us away the stone from the door of the tomb? and looking up, they see that the stone is rolled back: for it was exceeding great. And entering into the tomb, they saw a young man sitting on the right side, arrayed in a white robe; and they were amazed. And he saith unto them, Be not amazed: ye seek Jesus, the Nazarene, which hath been crucified: he is risen; he is not here: behold, the place where they laid him! But go, tell his disciples and Peter, He goeth before you into Galilee: there shall ye see him, as he said unto you. (Mark 16.1-7)

*But on the first day of the week, at early dawn, they came unto the tomb,
bringing the spices which they had prepared.   And they found the stone
rolled away from the tomb.   And they entered in, and found not the body of
the Lord Jesus.   And it came to pass, while they were perplexed there-
about, behold, two men stood by them in dazzling apparel: and as they
were affrighted, and bowed down their faces to the earth, they said unto
them, Why seek ye the living among the dead?   He is not here, but is
risen: remember how he spake unto you when he was yet in Galilee, saying
that the Son of man must be delivered up into the hands of sinful men, and
be crucified, and the third day rise again.   And they remembered his
words.   (Luke 24.1-8)*

Now we come to the closing passage of our redemption. This is the
source of our lively confidence in our reconciliation with God, that
Christ came forth from hell as Victor over death, and showed that the
power of the new life was in His hands. As Paul rightly says (I Cor.
15.14), there would be no Gospel and the hope of salvation would be
vain and trifling, unless we held that Christ is risen from the dead. Thus
our righteousness came to be won, and our access to heaven laid open.
Then was our adoption assured; Christ in resurrection exerted the
power of his Spirit and proved Himself Son of God. Though He
displayed His resurrection otherwise than our fleshly sense would have
looked for, yet the means that pleased Him should also seem best to us.
He came out of the tomb without witnesses, so that the empty place
might be the first sign, then willed that angels should announce to the
women that He was alive. A little later, He appeared to them, then to
the Apostles, and so on several occasions. Gradually He brought them
along, according to their own capacity, into fuller understanding. He
made a start with the women, and not only let them see Him but gave
them the message of the Gospel for the Apostles, making them their
teachers: this in the first place was a rebuke to the inaction of the
Apostles, who were lying all but dead for fright while the women
were anxiously hurrying to the tomb—and duly gained no mean
reward. Though the intention to anoint Christ was not free of censure
(they were reckoning Him still to be dead), He pardons their weakness
and honours them with exceptional distinction, taking the apostolic
office away from the men for the moment and committing it to them.
Besides, this is an instance of what Paul remarks (I Cor. 1.27), that God
chooses the things that are foolish and weak in the world, to bring
down the loftiness of the flesh. We shall never be properly prepared to
learn this item of our faith, unless we lay aside all pride, and submit to
the testimony of the women, not that our faith should remain confined
in such narrow limits, but that the Lord, to prove our obedience,

wished us to become foolish before He admits us to the fuller under-standing of His mysteries.

As regards the narrative, Matthew only says the *two Marys came to see the sepulchre*: Mark adds a third, Salome, and says *bought spices that they might . . . anoint him*. We gather from Luke that not two or three, but several, came. We know this is the usual way of the sacred writers, to mention particularly a few out of a greater number. The likely con-jecture is that Mary Magdalene with another companion (perhaps sent ahead, perhaps running on of her own wish) came before the others to the sepulchre. This seems implied by Matthew's words, that the two *came to see*: without seeing, they could not go on with anointing Christ. The task they had in mind to perform he does not mention, for his one chief object was to witness to the resurrection. It is asked how the women's efforts, being mixed with superstition, were agreeable to God. I do not doubt that they would refer the custom of anointing the dead as it was handed down from the Fathers to its proper end, which was, to seek comfort in the mourning of death from the hope of life to come. I grant they sinned, in that their minds did not rise at once to the preach-ing they had heard from their Master's mouth, but as they keep to the general principle of a final resurrection, their lapse is pardoned, when it might have rightly spoiled the whole show—as the saying is. God often accepts the works of saints with fatherly kindness, though often without His indulgence they would be unpleasing indeed, rightly rejected, with shame and punishment. Christ's wonderful goodness shines out in presenting Himself alive to the women with grace and courtesy, when they wrongly sought him among the dead. And if He did not let them come to his sepulchre in vain, we may agree that if anyone now aspires to Him with faith he will not be frustrated, for distance of place makes no obstacle for the faithful to enjoy Him who fills heaven and earth by the power of His Spirit.

Mark 16.1. *And when the sabbath was past*. This has the same effect as Matthew, *Late on the sabbath day as it began to dawn*: similarly in Luke, *On the first day of the week (prima die sabbatorum)*. As we know that the Jews began their days from the first shadows of evening, all may under-stand that the women planned among themselves to visit the sepulchre at the end of the sabbath, so as to arrive there before dawn. Two Evangelists say 'the first day of the sabbaths', namely the first day in order between two sabbaths. Some have translated *one* and have caused many to err, through ignorance of the Hebrew language. Although אחד sometimes means *one*, and sometimes *first*, the Evangel-ists (as in many other places) following the Hebrew phrase have said μίαν. I have stated their meaning more clearly in case the ambiguity should deceive us. In the purchasing of spices, Luke's narrative differs considerably from Mark's. The former says that they returned to the city and made ready spices: then, according to the precept of the Law, they rested a day before continuing their journey. Mark, referring two different things to one context, distinguishes the occasions less accurately than Luke: he confuses the first actions with their setting out. In the actual events, they agree very well, that after the holy rest they left home, still in the darkness of the night, to reach the sepulchre at the very break of day. Again we must bear in mind what I have previously remarked, that the rite of anointing the dead, though shared by many godless races, was only in legitimate use among the Jews. Their fathers had handed it down to them to foster them in the faith of a resurrection. To embalm a body which has lost its feeling, without this in view, would have been a cold and empty consolation; think of the Egyptians, who took scrupulous pains in this respect, and gained nothing by it. In this sacred sybolism God showed the Jews an image of life in death, that out of the decay and the dust they might hope to receive new vigour. The resurrection of Christ has reached into all tombs with its lifegiving perfume, to breathe life upon the dead. Hence these outward ceremonies are now abolished. He Himself had no need of these ministrations, but it was the women's simplicity and ignorance, for they did not truly understand that He was immune from corruption.

Mark 16.3. *They were saying among themselves.* Only Mark expresses this doubt, but as the others tell of the stone removed by the angel we may easily gather that they were in complete perplexity, and unsure of their plans, until God's Hand revealed the way in. We learn from this that in their fit of zeal, they had come without taking advice. They had seen the stone set over the tomb, to prevent anyone from entering. Why did it not come to their minds in the leisure of their homes, unless fear or wonder struck them, and their sense and memory failed? As it is a holy excitement that blinds them, God does not hold the fault against them.

Matt. 28.2. *And behold, there was a great earthquake.* The Lord showed the glory of His presence by many signs, that He might better move the hearts of the holy women to reverence. As it was not a thing of light moment to know that victory over death had been obtained by God's Son (on which all our salvation depends), all doubts must be removed, that the divine Majesty may present itself to their eyes openly, and not in obscurity. Matthew says there *was an earthquake,* by which the power of heaven that I have spoken of might be felt. By this portent, the women should be roused to expect nothing now of human or earthly sort, and should lift up their minds to a new and unexpected work of God. The splendour of the Godhead shone out also in the

223

dress and form of the angel, radiant in light: that they should sense it was no mortal man that stood near, bearing the features of man. Even though no brilliance of light or whiteness of snow can be matched to the immense Glory of God, and, if we will know Him truly, we must not think in terms of colour, yet He warns us of His approach with outward signs and invites us to Himself, as far as our weakness can grasp. But we must know that the visible marks of His presence are offered to us that our minds may apprehend Him as invisible. Under bodily forms, a taste is offered us of His spiritual essence, that we should seek Him in Spirit. There is no doubt that to the outward symbols there was tied a certain inward effectiveness, to engrave a sense of the Deity upon the women's hearts. Though at the first, they are amazed, it will appear from the context that they gradually came to their senses and began to learn, that they might feel it was the present Hand of God. The three Evangelists, to put the matter briefly, pass over what is narrated more fully in John, ch. 20, down to v. 12, which we know is nothing unusual for them. One difference is, that Matthew and Mark mention one angel only, while John and Luke have two. This kind of contradiction is easily resolved, as we know that instances of synecdoche are frequently to be found in Scripture. Two angels were seen, first by Mary, then by the others with her. As one took the role of speech, and took the lead in converting their minds, it was enough for Matthew and Mark to relate his message. Besides, when Matthew says *an angel sat upon the stone* he makes in these words a hysteron-proteron, or at least, he neglects the order of events, since the angel did not appear at once, but while the women were held in suspense and worry at the strangeness and wonder of the event.

Matt. 28.4. *For fear of him the watchers did quake.* The Lord caused the guards terror as if He held a cautery to their consciences, forcing them to feel His divine Power, though they had no wish to. At least the terror had the effect of preventing them from laughing off the rumour of resurrection that was soon to spread abroad. Though they were not ashamed of prostituting their tongues, yet inwardly they were compelled, willy-nilly, to admit what before men they wickedly denied. Nor should we doubt that when they had the chance to speak more freely they would have confessed to their friends the things they were paid not to dare to say out in public. Note the distinction between two kinds of terror which Matthew contrasts. Soldiers, accustomed to tumult, were terrified and so struck with panic that they fell down half-dead: no power raised them from the ground; but in the like alarm of the women, a comfort soon came to restore their spirits—which had nearly deserted them, so that they might at least begin to hope for something better. It is certainly right that God's Majesty should strike horror and fear alike on holy and on reprobate, that at His face all flesh should keep silence. But when the Lord Himself has humbled and subdued His elect, He soon relieves their fears, lest they be overcome and fall away: not that only, but He heals the wound inflicted, with the sweetness of His grace: the reprobate, however, He panics (as they say) to exhaustion, or allows them to languish under slow torments. As regards these soldiers, they were like dead men, but with no serious effect. They are scared almost out of their minds, for a moment, but at once forget their fear, not that the memory of their fear was wholly obliterated, but because that lively and effective apprehension of the divine power to which they had been forced to yield soon flowed out of them. The chief thing to hold is this, that their fright was as great as the women's, but they received no healing to relieve it. Only to the women did the angel say, *fear not*, holding out to them the ground of joy and relief in the resurrection of Christ. In Luke is added the reproach, that *they sought the living among the dead*, just as if the angel tweaked their ear, to stop them drifting further into despair.

Matt. 28.7. *And go quickly, and tell his disciples.* Here God gives the women extraordinary honour through the angel, trusting them with proclaiming to the Apostles themselves the chief part of our salvation (*praecipium salutis nostrae caput*). In Mark they are expressly told to take the message to Peter, not because he then excelled in rank, but because his shameful lapse had need of special comfort, that he should know he was not disowned by Christ, however disgracefully and wickedly he had fallen. He had already entered into the sepulchre and had seen the traces of Christ's resurrection, but God denied him the honour, which soon after He gave to the women, of hearing from the voice of the angel, that Christ was risen. This certainly shows us the confusion in which he still laboured, that he took refuge again in his hiding-place for fear, as if he had seen nothing, while Mary sat by the sepulchre weeping. There is no doubt that she and her companions received in the sight of the angel the reward for their patience. That the angel sends the disciples to Galilee was done, I believe, for Christ to show Himself to more people. We know that he had spent longer time in Galilee. He wanted to give more generous time to His own, that they might gradually collect their spirits for His departure. Also the acquaintance with the places helped them to recognize their Master more certainly. It had to be confirmed in all points for nothing to be lacking in their faith's assurance. *Lo, I have told you.* In this form of speech the angel declared that what he said was true. But it does not come from himself as if he were the first author, but he underlines Christ's promise. So in Mark's account he simply recalls Christ's words to their minds. Luke takes the speech further, that the disciples had been warned by Christ that He must be crucified, etc.—yet the sense is the same, for He had predicted His death along with His resurrection. Then it is added, *And they remembered his words*, teaching us that although they had not gained much in Christ's teaching yet it was not lost, but rather overclouded, until in good time it should bear its fruit.

And they departed quickly from the tomb with fear and great joy, and ran to bring his disciples word. And behold, Jesus met them, saying, All hail. And they came and took hold of his feet, and worshipped him. Then saith Jesus unto them, Fear not: go tell my brethren that they depart into Galilee, and there shall they see me. (Matt. 28.8-10)

And they went out, and fled from the tomb; for trembling and astonishment had come upon them: and they said nothing to any one, for they were afraid.
   Now when he was risen early on the first day of the week, he appeared first to Mary Magdalene, from whom he had cast out seven devils. She went and told them that had been with him, as they mourned and wept. All they, when they heard that he was alive, and had been seen of her, disbelieved. (Mark 16.8-11)

and returned from the tomb, and told all these things to the eleven, and to all the rest. Now they were Mary Magdalene, and Joanna, and Mary the mother of James: and the other women with them told these things unto the apostles. And these words appeared in their sight as idle talk; and they disbelieved them. But Peter arose, and ran unto the tomb; and stooping and looking in, he seeth the linen clothes by themselves; and he departed to his home, wondering at that which was come to pass. (Luke 24.9-12)

Matt. 28.8. *And they departed quickly.* The three Evangelists pass over what John says of Mary Magdalene, that before she saw the angels, she returned to the city and complained with tears that Christ's body had been removed. Only the second return to the city is treated here, in which she and her companions announced to the disciples that Christ had risen, as they had learnt from the voice and testimony of the angels, and from the sight of Christ Himself. Before Christ showed Himself they were already running off to the disciples, as they had been bidden by the angel. On the way, they had the further assurance that they might with greater certainty assert that the Lord had risen. Matthew says *they departed with fear and great joy*, meaning by these words that they were delighted by the message of the angel and yet at the same time struck with fear, till they were in a fever of happiness and alarm. Sometimes opposite emotions lay hold on the hearts of the godly and swing them to and fro, until at last the peace of the Spirit creates a balanced mind. If faith had been a solid part of their being, it would have subdued their fear and quite calmed them for their mixture of fear and joy shows that they have not yet properly taken the angel's words to heart. Here Christ demonstrated a singular mark of kindness, in meeting them in their doubt and trepidation, to remove such hesitation as was left. Mark's account differs not a little, that *they fled* and *trembling and astonishment had come upon them*, that they were dismayed for fear. The solution is not so difficult, for though they had a mind to obey the angel, their ability was not equal to it until the Lord Himself loosed their tongues. What follows appears more contradictory still. Mark does not say that Christ met them all, but only *appeared first to Mary Magdalene* at break of day: Luke completely omits this vision. The omission, as it is not very unusual in the Evangelists, does not seem too strange to us. As regards the difference between Matthew and Mark, it is possible that the Magdalene may have had a great favour before the others, or perhaps that Matthew applies to them all, by synecdoche, what befell one in particular. Yet it is more likely that she alone was named by Mark because she had a first sight of Christ, in a special way before the others, apart from Christ's appearance to her companions in due course: Matthew attributes it to them all in common. It was a remarkable act of kindness for Christ to reveal His heavenly glory to a wretched woman who had been possessed by seven devils. In being willing to offer the light of eternal and new life, He began at a point where in men's eyes nothing but scorn and shame existed. In this way Christ has given documentary evidence of the fact that when once He extends His grace toward us He continues to do so with the utmost liberality, while at the same time putting down all the pride of the flesh.

Matt. 28.9. *Took hold of his feet.* This does not appear to agree with John's words, where he testifies that Mary was forbidden to touch Christ, but it is easily reconciled. The Lord, in seeing how Mary clung too much to His feet, embracing and kissing, told her to go back. He had to correct superstitious affection and show the purpose of His resurrection which Mary lost, partly by her earthly, gushing emotion, partly by foolish enthusiasm. At first, the Lord allowed her to touch His feet, that she should lack no assurance. Straight after, Matthew adds that *they worshipped him*: a proof that their recognition was certain.

Matt. 28.10. *Then saith Jesus unto them.* We gather that the fear from which Christ delivered them was not a proper one: though it arose from wonder, it was opposed to tranquil confidence. That they may rise up to Christ, the Victor over death, they are bidden to be of good cheer. The same words teach us that the Lord's resurrection is only truly acknowledged by us now if we take courage, and dare to boast, that we are made partakers of that same life. Our faith should go at least so far, that fear loses its domination. Moreover, in telling them to give the news to the disciples, by their mission Christ reunited the scattered Church (*dissipatam ecclesiam de integro collegit*) and restored its collapse. As the resurrection faith chiefly revives us today, so then the disciples had to regain the life from which they had fallen. Note also Christ's unbelievable humanity in deigning to address as *brothers* the renegades who had shamefully deserted Him. There is no doubt that He freely wished to relieve with a kind word the sadness with which He knew them to be distressed. But since it was not only Apostles that He included under *brothers*, let us be assured that by Christ's command, this message is extended to reach down the years to us. We cannot hear the story of the resurrection without emotion, when Christ courteously invites us, from His own lips, by the right of brotherly compulsion to accept His benefits. That some interpreters understand Christ's relatives by the word *brethren* is refuted by the context, which more than adequately shows their error: John says explicitly that Mary came to *the disciples*, while Luke adds that the women came *to the Apostles*. Mark also agrees, writing that *Mary went . . . and told these things to the disciples as they mourned and wept.*

Mark 16.11. *And they when they heard.* Mark records the testimony of Mary alone, yet I am sure that Christ's orders were jointly related by them all. This passage confirms better what I have just said, that there is no discord between the Evangelists in one attributing to Mary Magdalene in particular what, according to the rest, was shared by them all (admittedly not in equal degree). The disciples were in the grip of a shameful apathy not to realize that what they had often heard their Master speak of was accomplished. If the women had told something quite unheard of, they might have had some reason for disbelieving the incredible message given them, but they must have been excessively dense to treat as a fable or dream this deed, so often promised and asserted by God's Son, when its fulfilment is told them by eye-witnesses. Their incredulity had robbed them of right understanding, and they both reject the light of truth, and even spurn it as an hallucination, as Luke tells. This shows us they had so far succumbed to temptation that the whole savour of Christ's words had almost departed from their minds.

Luke 24.12. *But Peter arose.* I have no doubt that Luke has reversed the order of the narrative, as we may readily gather from John's account. In my judgment, the word *ran* might well be taken in the plu-perfect tense. Those with a moderate knowledge of Scripture know that it was regular for Hebrews to relate afterwards events they omitted at the right point. Luke uses the circumstance to underline the Apostles' hardness in scorning the women's words, when Peter had already seen the empty tomb, and had been forced to wonder at the clear sign of resurrection.

Now while they were going, behold, some of the guard came into the city, and told unto the chief priests all the things that were come to pass. And when they were assembled with the elders, and had taken counsel, they gave large money unto the soldiers, saying, Say ye, His disciples came by night, and stole him away while we slept. And if this come to the governor's ears, we will persuade him, and rid you of care. So they took the money, and did as they were taught: and this saying was spread abroad among the Jews, and continueth unto this day. (Matt. 28.11-15)

Matt. 28.11. *Now while they were going.* It is not only credible, but the event itself shows, that the soldiers who were set to guard the tomb were bribed with money so that they were ready to lie, at the priests' will. They knew well that the priests feared nothing worse than that a report should gain ground to the effect that Christ had risen again after three days, for they knew they had been sent there precisely to look after the corpse and suppress the report. Men who are devoted to gain and looking for profit on every side, once they lose the fruits of their diligence, find new methods of squeezing out the cash. According to Matthew *some of the guard came;* it is not certain whether a few smart ones took plans apart from the rest, or whether they were sent in the name of all. Conjecture rather inclines to this second part, for Matthew says later that, not to one or two, but to the soldiers in general was a reward paid out for perjury. It is certain anyway, whether they plotted together or only a part of them, that they made profit from the cruel and implacable hatred of the priests against Christ: reckoning them involved in crime, they put pressure on their bad conscience to extort money for themselves. The priests (as happens with most criminals) having an evil conscience, in order to hide their misdeeds were forced to bribe the soldiers with a large sum. It is obvious from this that the reprobate, once they have rushed headlong into sin, are always caught up in new wickedness, as they seek to protect themselves from shame in men's eyes and take no thought for their offences against God. These wretched men are not only buying off the soldiers with a heavy donation but, if their crime were brought to justice, are exposing their

229

name and life to peril. What else forces them to put themselves to such hazard, on top of the expense incurred, except their obstinate rage which will not let them withdraw until they heap sin upon sin?

Matt. 28.15. *This saying was spread abroad.* It was the final culmination of God's vengeance in blinding the Jews, that by the soldiers' perjury Christ's resurrection was buried and such an empty lie accepted. Clearly they were deceived by an error of their own choice to think that Christ was not risen; just so, is the world a willing victim of the mockery Satan's impostures afford. If a man had but opened his eyes, it would not have needed a long enquiry. Armed soldiers allege that Christ's body was stolen from them by civilians, frightened and few in number, an unarmed company of folk. How could you believe it? They say that they were asleep when it was done. Then how do they know He was stolen? If there were any suspicion of the disciples, why did they not get onto their tracks? Why did they not start an outcry? It was a childish excuse, that would not have got them off for nothing if they had been dealing with an upright judicious Governor. Yet it was done with Pilate's connivance, to leave no trace of the crime. We see it happening every day. Profane judges take little pains when the truth is attacked by fraud and malice; rather, if they have no fear of unpleasant consequences, they seem to go into collusion with treacherous rogues. Though it might seem hard that God should endure a false rumour to go around, to the extinction of His Son's glory, we should give due honour to His just recompense. The race deserved to have its light obscured by clouds, for we see the greedy way in which they snatched at an empty and trifling lie. As almost all had stumbled on the stone of offence, their eyes had to be darkened, that they might not see the cup of giddiness poured out for them: in short they were cast into all kinds of madness, as was predicted in Isaiah's oracle (6.8). God would never have allowed them to be deceived by such a foolish piece of credulity, except to deprive of the hope of salvation men who had despised their own Redeemer. The same kind of penalty today falls on the world's ingratitude, loosing the reins on the wicked, that they may come out all the worse. Though this lie had some success with the Jews, it did not prevent the truth of the Gospel flying abroad to the furthest ends of the earth, for it always rises victorious over the world's obstacles.

And after these things he was manifested in another form to two of them, as they walked, on their way into the country. And they went away and told it unto the rest: neither believed they them. (Mark 16.12)

And behold, two of them were going that very day to a village named Emmaus, which was threescore furlongs from Jerusalem. And they communed with each other of all these things which had happened. And it came to pass, while they communed and questioned together, that Jesus himself drew near, and went with them. But their eyes were holden that they should not know him. And he said unto them, What communications are these that ye have one with another, as ye walk? And they stood still, looking sad. And one of them, named Cleopas, answering said unto him, Dost thou alone sojourn in Jerusalem and not know the things which are come to pass there in these days? And he said unto them, What things? And they said unto him, The things concerning Jesus of Nazareth, which was a prophet mighty in deed and word before God and all the people: and how the chief priests and our rulers delivered him up to be condemned to death, and crucified him. But we hoped that it was he which would redeem Israel. Yea and beside all this, it is now the third day since these things came to pass. Moreover certain women of our company amazed us, having been early at the tomb; and when they found not his body, they came, saying, that they had also seen a vision of angels, which said that he was alive. And certain of them that were with us went to the tomb, and found it even as the women had said: but him they saw not. And he said unto them, O foolish men, and slow of heart to believe in all the prophets have spoken! Behoved it not the Christ to suffer these things, and to enter into his glory? And beginning from Moses and from all the prophets, he interpreted to them in all the scriptures the things concerning himself. And they drew nigh unto the village, whither they were going: and he made as though he would go further. And they constrained him, saying, Abide with us: for it is toward evening, and the day is now far spent. And he went in to abide with them. And it came to pass, when he had sat down with them to meat, he took the bread, and blessed it, and brake, and gave to them. (Luke 24.13-30)

Luke 24.13. *And behold two.* While Mark only touches on this story lightly, Matthew and John omit it completely. As it was of great benefit for our understanding and worth remembering, Luke is serving a good purpose in narrating it so carefully. I have often noted how the Spirit of God shared out the parts appropriately to each Evangelist, so that what did not strike one or another may be learned from the rest. There are numerous appearances of which mention is made in John, but of which the three say no word. Before coming down to details, it would be worth saying this briefly in preface, that these two witnesses were chosen, not for the Lord to persuade the Apostles through them that He had risen, but to reprove their slowness. At first they made no headway, but eventually, with other assistance, their testimony held great weight with them. Who exactly they were is doubtful, except that from one's name (whom Luke later calls Cleopas) we may infer that this was not one of the eleven. *Emmaus* was an old town, of some account, which afterwards the Romans called Nicopolis. It was not far away from Jerusalem, as sixty furlongs came to seven thousand four hundred paces. The location is not named for its fame but to make the story accurate.

Luke 24.14. *And they communed with each other.* It was a sign of devotion that they kept trying to foster their faith in Christ, though it was weak and slight. Their conversation had no other object than to put reverence for their Master as a shield against the scandal of the cross. Though their discussion and debate revealed an ignorance worthy of blame, seeing that after previous warning of the coming resurrection of Christ, they were astounded when they heard of it, yet their willingness to learn showed Christ a means of approach, to remove their error. Many deliberately raise questions, because they intend to reject the truth with contumacy, but those who have a mind to embrace the truth with tranquillity, even if they waver over small objections, and stick on light scruples, find favour in God's eyes by their holy desire to obey; with outreached hand He leads them to the ground of certainty, that they may cease from their tossing. We must hold on to the fact that when we inquire of Christ, if it comes from a patient desire to learn, a door is open for Him to help us; indeed we invite Him to teach us Himself, while profane men, with their evil words, put Him at a distance.

Luke 24.16. *Their eyes were holden.* The Evangelist particularly mentions this in case anyone should think Christ's bodily form was altered. Though Christ stayed like Himself, He was not recognized, as the eyes of the beholders were checked. This removed any suspicion of a spectre or false piece of imagination. We are taught to admit the weakness of all our senses, that neither eyes nor ears perform their function, except as far as the facility is continually afforded them by heaven. Our members are endowed by nature with their gifts, but to teach us that they are ours at His command, God keeps the use of them in His Hand, and whatever our eyes see or ears hear from day to day must be reckoned among His gracious gifts. If He did not animate our senses from moment to moment, their whole force would soon disappear. I admit that our senses are not often withheld as on this instance, that they should make such a mistake over an object put before us, yet by one example God shows that it is in His power to guide such faculties as He has conferred on man, that we should know our nature to be under His direction. If the eyes of the body, which are most apt for our looking, are checked as often as God pleases, and fail to see the forms presented to them, our minds would have no greater strength of discernment even though they were still intact. In this wretched state of corruption, once their light is taken from them, they run into deceptions of all sorts, and are so affected with utter dullness that they can do nothing but err, as happens all the time. True discrimination between right and wrong does not then depend on the acuteness of our intelligence but on the wisdom of the Spirit. It is chiefly in contemplation of heavenly things that our dullness is proven, as we not only imagine false appearances to be true, but turn clear light into darkness.

Luke 24.17. *What communications are these that ye have one with another?* What we then see Christ doing openly we daily feel happening secretly —He freely comes up to us and teaches us. It is obvious from Cleopas' reply how anxious, as I have just said, and worried they were over Christ's resurrection, yet they felt reverence for His teaching and were not on the point of giving up. They do not expect Christ to anticipate them and make Himself known to them, or that this traveller, whoever he may be, will speak of Him with respect: rather, Cleopas throws out a few sparks from the little, obscure light he had, to illuminate his mind a little—if he were lacking in knowledge or information. Christ's name all over at that time was so much hated and disgraced that it was not safe to speak of Him with respect, but despising the ill-will, he names him as God's Prophet and professes to be one of His disciples. Though the distinction of being called Prophet was a long way below the divine Majesty of Christ, even the moderate commendation he gives deserves praise, as Cleopas had no other intention than to win for Christ disciples, who would submit to His Gospel. We cannot tell whether it was through ignorance that Cleopas spoke of Christ with less distinction than He merited or whether he wanted to begin from the better known rudiments and to go up by slow degrees, Certainly a little later he does not simply rank Christ in the common order of prophets, but says that he and others believed He would be Redeemer.

Luke 24.19. *Mighty in deed and word.* Almost the same form of words is used by Luke in Acts 7.22 in the person of Stephen, when he speaks of Moses, and says he was powerful in words and deeds. It is not certain here whether Christ is called powerful in deed on account of His miracles (as if to say, He was endowed with divine virtues which showed Him to be sent from heaven) or whether it was a wider application to the effect that He excelled in facility of teaching, in holiness of life, in outstanding accomplishments. The latter sense is the one I favour. Adding *before God and all the people* is far from superfluous. He means that Christ's excellence was so well testified by men and known by clear

233

evidence, that it had no need of pretence or inane display. One may gather from this a short definition of the true prophet, one who adds the power of deeds to his speaking, and takes care to excell in the sight of men and sincerely to conduct himself as under the eyes of God.

Luke 24.21. *But we hoped.* It will be clear from the context that the hope they had formed of Christ was not broken off, though that is our first impression from their words. An account that started with the condemnation of Christ might put off a man who had felt no leaning towards the Gospel—seeing He was condemned by the leaders of the Church. Hence Cleopas puts before the scandal the hope of redemption. Though afterwards he shows how he clings to this hope despite fears and almost total collapse, he carefully draws in all the aid he can to support it. The third day is probably mentioned by him, simply because the Lord had promised He would rise again on the third day. When he recounts that the body could not be found by the women, that they had seen a vision of angels, and that what the women reported about the empty tomb was confirmed by the men's testimony also, everything adds up to the fact that Christ had risen. Thus, this godly man, caught between faith and fear, nourished his faith and struggles, as a man, to overcome his fear.

Luke 24.25. *And he said unto them.* The reproof seems to be rather sharp and stern considering the man's weakness, but weighing up all the circumstances one may easily understand that there was reason in the Lord's rebuking him roughly, as one of those on whom He had spent long efforts with virtually no return. Note, that what He says is not restricted to these two, but in reproof of a common fault. He wished it heard directly from their mouths by the rest of their companions. Christ had ever so often forewarned them of His death, spoken of the new and spiritual life, and confirmed His teaching with the oracles of the prophets, but He might have spoken to deaf ears or rather to trees and stones, for shattered by His death they did not know which way to turn. Such unsteadiness He rightly attributes to foolishness. He blames their inattention, that they were not more inclined to believe. He does not so much reprove them for being dull and slow at learning— though He was the finest Master they could have, but for not having attended to the words of the prophets—as if to say, they had no excuse for their stupidity, because it was due to themselves alone for the prophets' teaching was lucid in itself and well explained to them. So today the greater part of men bear the same blame for their ignorance, being hard to teach and headstrong. Let us note, when Christ sees His disciples over apathetic He arouses them by starting with reproof. This is how we must subdue those whom we have found to be hard or sullen.

Luke 24.26. *Behoved it not the Christ to suffer these things.* There is no doubt that the Lord went through the Messiah's character as it is described by the prophets lest the death of the cross cause offence, and in a journey of three or four hours there was enough time for a generous explanation. Not in three words did He state that Christ had to suffer, but He related at length that He had been sent to expiate the sins of the world by the sacrifice of death, to be the κάθαρμα that removed the curse, and to clear the pollution of others by guilt imputed to Himself. Luke put down the sentence as a question, for the sake of greater emphasis, from which we gather that the necessity of His death was revealed with reasons (*rationibus ostensam fuisse mortis necessitatem*). Briefly, the disciples were wrong to be alarmed at the death of their Master (without it Christ could not fulfil His role, for His sacrifice was the chief part of the redemption) and by so doing they erected a door against His entry into His Kingdom. Note this carefully. As Christ loses His honour unless He is rated Victim for sin, His only entrance into His glory is His self-emptying (Phil. 2.7) from which He emerges as Redeemer. To turn this upside down, is as we see today, a sin committed amongst us, for among the multitude of those who splendidly declaim on Christ the King and extol Him with divine titles of praise, scarcely one in ten thinks of the grace brought to us by His death.

Luke 24.27. *And beginning from Moses.* This passage shows us how Christ is revealed to us through the Gospel, for understanding of Him comes from the light of the Law and the Prophets. No-one was ever a more gifted or suitable Teacher of the Gospel than the Lord Himself, and we see that He borrows from the Law and the Prophets the proof of His teaching. If one objects that starting from the rudiments He brings the disciples gradually to bid farewell to the prophets and pass over to the perfect Gospel, it is here easily refuted: it will be stated later that all the apostles had their minds opened, not to knowledge divorced from the aid of the Law, but to understand the Scriptures. That Christ may be seen by us today through the Gospel, Moses and the Prophets must take their place as forerunners. Readers must be warned not to lend their ear to fanatics who, by suppressing the Law and the Prophets, wickedly mutilate the Gospel. As if God would wish anything to be useless that He had ever found in testimony to His Son. In what way passages are to be applied to Christ that are frequently written in the Scriptures, is not the task of the present book to explicate. It would be sufficient to hold, in brief, that not for nothing was Christ called the end of the Law. Moses foreshadows Him, darkly and afar off, without giving detail; yet it is clear beyond any debate, that except there be one Head, in the stock of Abraham, above the rest, in whom the people may draw into one body, the Covenant that God struck with the sainted

Fathers will be wasted and brought to no effect. As God ordered the tabernacle and rites to be arranged to match the heavenly type, it follows that sacrifices and all temple ceremonies, unless their truth rested upon a further source, would be vain and fruitless mockery. This line of proof is unravelled fully by the Apostle in the Epistle to the Hebrews (9.1). Assuming the principle that the visible rites of the Law are shadows of spiritual things, he shows that Christ must be sought in all the legal priesthood, in sacrifices, in the order of the sanctuary.

Bucer puts out a wise conjecture somewhere, that in this obscure material the Jews were used to a certain method of interpreting Scripture which the Fathers had handed down to them. Without going on to uncertain ground I am satisfied with the simple and sincere approach we frequently find throughout the prophets, who were extremely apt interpreters of the Law. Christ is rightly inferred from the Law, if we think how the Covenant which God struck with the Fathers depended on a Mediator. The Sanctuary by which God testified to the presence of His grace was consecrated with blood, the Law itself with its promises was sealed with the sprinkling of blood, while one priesthood was chosen out of all the people to stand in God's sight in the name of all, not as any mortal man but in the garments of holiness, and no hope was given men of their reconciliation there with God unless a victim were offered. Add the outstandingly notable oracle, concerning the continuance of the kingship in the tribe of Judah. The prophets themselves (as we have mentioned) made the greatest effect with their description of the Mediator, yet they drew their first understanding of this from Moses. The precise duty laid on them was to renew the remembrance of the covenant, reveal the spiritual service of God more distinctly, establish the confidence of salvation upon the Mediator, and demonstrate more clearly the means of reconciliation. Since it had pleased God to delay the full revelation to the coming of His Son, their interpretations were not unneeded.

Luke 24.28. *And they drew nigh unto the village.* There is no reason for some interpreters to suppose that this is another place than Emmaus: the journey was not so long that they had to rest at an earlier lodging. We know that seven thousand paces (even if a man take his pleasure and walk slowly) take altogether about four hours. I have no doubt that Christ went as far as Emmaus. When it is asked whether pretence is appropriate for Him who is the eternal Truth of God, I answer that God's Son was under no obligation to bring all His purposes into the open. Yet as pretence is a kind of falsehood, the problem is not quite resolved, especially as many use this as an example for liberty to tell lies. I answer, that Christ made pretence without a lie, in what is told here, just as He made Himself out to be a traveller: it is the same case with each. Augustine's solution is rather more sophisticated (*Contra Mendacium ad Consentium*, bk. 1, ch. 13; and *Quaestiones super Evangelia*, ch. 51). He wants this fiction treated along with tropes and figures of speech, and then among parables and fables. One point is enough for me. As Christ veiled their eyes for a time when He spoke with them, so that assuming apparently a different character they took Him for a common stranger: so He presented, at that moment, a plan of going on further, not to invent something He would not actually do, but really to conceal the mode of His departure. No one will deny that He was going further, for He was then set apart from the ordinary concourse of men. He did not deceive His disciples by this fiction, but held them for a little in suspense, till the time for His revelation was ripe. It is just too absurd to adduce Him as patron of falsehood. We may no more make up things after His example than we may equal His divine Power in closing the eyes of them that see. Nothing then is safer than observing the rule laid on us, of speaking the truth in sincerity. Not that the Lord Himself ever departed from the Father's Law, but, because He kept the real intention of the Law, without literal rules, the weakness of our intelligence needs further restraint.

Luke 24.30. *He took the bread.* Augustine and many others with him have felt that the bread was not offered by Christ for eating, but as the symbol of His sacred body. It is plausible to say that the Lord was recognized at last in the spiritual mirror of the Supper, for the disciples, seeing Him with the eyes of the body, had not known Him. But as this conjecture rests upon no likely indication, I would take Luke's words more simply to say that Christ took bread in His hands and gave thanks, as He was used. Clearly He was accustomed to a particular form of prayer, to which He knew the disciples had become used intimately. He used this sign to remind and arouse their thoughts. We learn from the Master's example, as often as we eat bread, to offer a thanksgiving to the Author of life, that we may be known amongst profane men.

And they went away and told it unto the rest: neither believed they them.
*   And afterward he was manifested unto the eleven themselves as they sat at meat; and he upbraided them with their unbelief and hardness of heart, because they believed not them which had seen him after he was risen.* (Mark 16.13-14)

And their eyes were opened, and they knew him: and he vanished out of their sight.   And they said one to another, Was not our heart burning within us in the way, while he opened to us the scriptures?   And they rose up that very hour, and returned to Jerusalem, and found the eleven gathered together, and them that were with them, saying, The Lord is risen indeed, and hath appeared to Simon. And they rehearsed the things that happened in the way, and how he was known of them in the breaking of the bread.

And as they spake these things, he himself stood in the midst of them, and saith unto them, Peace be unto you. But they were terrified and affrighted, and supposed that they beheld a spirit. And he said unto them, Why are ye troubled? and wherefore do reasonings arise in your heart? See my hands and my feet, that it is I myself: handle me, and see; for a spirit hath not flesh and bones, as ye behold me having. And when he had said this, he shewed them his hands and his feet. (Luke 24.31-40)

Luke 24.31. *And their eyes were opened.* These words teach us that there was no metamorphosis in Christ to trick men's eyes with a change of forms (like Proteus of the poets' imagination) but rather, the eyes of the beholders mistook Him, being under a veil themselves. So shortly after He did not vanish from their sight by His body becoming invisible in itself, but because their clear vision was obscured by God withdrawing His powers from them. It is no wonder that as soon as Christ was recognized He suddenly disappeared. It was no use for them to go on seeing him, in case (their minds being in any event far too earthbound) they should want to draw Him back to the life of earth again. As far as was necessary for their witness to the resurrection, He let them see Him. His sudden departure taught them, that He was to be sought out of this world, for His ascent to heaven was the complement of the new life.

Luke 24.32. *Was not our heart.* Recognizing Christ made the disciples achieve a lively insight into the secret and hidden grace of the Spirit which He had formerly gifted them. God sometimes so works on His people that for a time they are unaware of the activity of the Spirit (yet they have a part in it) or at least do not recognize it distinctly but only feel it by an unseen instinct. The disciples had begun to burn already (as is now recalled) but had not noticed. Only now that Christ is known to them do they begin to think how they had previously taken in His grace, without savouring it, and realize how dull they were. They accuse themselves of their slowness, as if saying, 'How did it happen that we did not recognize Him as he spoke? Seeing that He reached into our hearts, we should have known who He was.' They did not infer that it was Christ from the bare sign of His speech setting their hearts on fire; but, because they gave Him His due honour—'when He spoke with His mouth, our hearts glowed with the inward fire of His Spirit'. Paul boasts that the ministration of the Spirit was given him (II Cor. 3.8), and Scripture often gives marks of approval to ministers of the Word, as that they convert hearts, illuminate the minds, and renew men to make them pure and sacred victims: and this is not to put forward a display of their own power, but rather what the Lord does through them. Christ alone enjoys both properties, of speaking a word outwardly, and effectively shaping the heart, to obedience of faith. There is no doubt that He then engraved a singular impression on the hearts of the two men, that they might at last realise that in speaking He had breathed a divine warmth into them. Though the Word of the Lord is always fire (Lk. 3.16), a peculiar and unusual kind of fiery vigour produced itself then in Christ's speech, as a shining witness of His divine power. He alone baptizes in the holy Spirit and with fire. Let us remember that it is the true fruit of heavenly teaching, whoever may be its minister, to light the fire of the Spirit in men's hearts, to refine and purify, yes, to consume, and to whip up a true fever of love for God, and snatch all men to heaven in its flames.

Luke 24.33. *And they rose up that very hour.* The circumstances of the time, the distance between places, shows the enthusiasm that burned in these two to share the news with their fellow-disciples. It was evening when they reached the inn, and not before nightfall that the Lord revealed Himself to them. To make a journey of three hours at that untimely hour of night was far from agreeable, yet they rose up in the very instant, and hurried to Jerusalem, with speed. Indeed if they had waited for the morrow, their delay might have raised doubts. As they dearly preferred to lose their night's peace rather than fail to make the Apostles sharers of their joy, their haste adds to the narrative. When Luke says they *rose up at that very hour*, we reckon they reached the disciples about midnight. By Luke's testimony again, they were still gathered together. This shows their anxiety and burning concern in watching almost all night, questioning all the time, for fuller information and more testimonies to the resurrection of Christ.

Luke 24.34. *Saying, The Lord is risen.* These words mean that those who brought glad news to confirm the hearts of the Apostles received in turn an account of another vision. There is no doubt that this reward of mutual confirmation came to them from God for their devoted energy. And from reckoning the time, one may gather that after Peter had returned from the sepulchre, he had been in a ferment of agitation until Christ showed Himself to him, and on the very day that he visited the sepulchre, he obtained the answer to his prayer. Hence the rejoicing among the eleven that there was now no doubt, for the Lord had appeared to Simon. This does not seem to agree with Mark's words, when he says neither were these two given belief by the eleven—*neither believed they them.* How could it be that rejecting the new witnesses they tossed around in hesitation, after being already certain? In saying *he is risen indeed*, they agree that the matter is beyond debate. I say first, that the general statement includes a synecdoche, for there were some more resistant, less ready, and Thomas more stubborn than them all. Then, we may easily infer that their persuasion was of the kind that comes on astonished men who afterwards were liable to be plunged into various doubts. However it may be, it is certain from Luke that the greater part of them in that condition of ecstatic excitement not only freely embraced what had occurred but fought against their own hesitancy. The word *indeed* cuts off any ground for doubt. Yet we shall see in a while, that a second and third time, they tumbled back into a state of alarm through amazement.

Luke 24.36. *Jesus himself stood in the midst of them.* Though John tells the same story at length, he differs in some circumstances. Mark in his brief account is also rather different, but as regards John, he only assembles what Luke omitted. The two may easily be reconciled. All in all there is no contradiction, unless perhaps one wishes to argue over times. It is said there that Jesus arrived in the evening, while it is clear from Luke's context that He appeared late at night, that is to say, after the disciples had returned from Emmaus. I do not think we should press too exactly the time of evening. What is said here could aptly and well be extended till late at night, seeing that the Apostles had shut the doors at eventide and kept themselves hidden at home; and then Jesus came to them. John does not describe the start of the evening but simply means that day was over and the sun set, and so it was in the dark of night that Jesus came, beyond their hopes, to the disciples. Another question arises, as Mark and Luke record that the eleven were gathered when Christ appeared to them. John says Thomas was then absent. There is nothing strange that eleven is put as the number of the Apostles even if one of the company were missing. We have just said, and the event itself shows it, that John goes into details more carefully, as it was his purpose to relate the things omitted by the others. There is no doubt at all that the same story is told by the three, since John explicitly testifies that only twice was Christ seen by the disciples at Jerusalem before they went to Galilee. He says, for the third time *he appeared to them at the sea of Tiberias.* He had previously noted two visions, one which took place on the day after the resurrection, and the other that followed eight days later: though if one should prefer to expound this on the basis of the second being that which is recorded in Mark, I have no great objection.

Now I return to Luke's words. He does not state that Christ opened for Himself, by His divine power, doors that were closed, but his use of the word *stood* hints at something like that. For how could the Lord suddenly stand in their midst at night unless He came in miraculously.

The same form of salutation is given by both, *Peace be unto you*: by which Hebrews mean that they wish a person joy and prosperity.

Luke 24.37. *But they were terrified.* John does not speak of this terror, but as he says also that Christ showed His hands and side to His disciples we may imagine a part omitted by Him. It is not unusual for the Evangelists, in trying to be brief, only to give some part. We learn from Luke that, terrified by the strangeness of the scene, they dared not believe their eyes. A little before, they were sure that the Lord was risen and had spoken forcefully as of a matter well understood. Now when their eyes see it, wonder stuns their minds, and they imagine it to be a spirit. Their error is not without fault, as it derives from weakness, yet they were not so self-forgetful as to be frightened of magic. They do not think it is a trick but rather tend to hold that in spirit, through a vision, an image of the resurrection is set before them, rather than that Christ Himself were there alive, who had recently died on the cross. They did not reckon the vision suspect as being an empty spectre to deceive them, but seized with fear, they thought that what was really presented to their eyes was only displayed in spirit.

Luke 24.38. *Why are ye troubled?* These words warn them to pull their minds together out of their fear and with restored strength of mind to judge for themselves upon the matter with full recognition. As long as men are gripped with alarm, they stay blind in the clear daylight. That the disciples may get sure understanding, they are told to consider the matter with minds settled and composed. In the second part Christ corrects another fault; by shifting between different notions they are hindering each other. He says *reasonings arise,* meaning the knowledge of the truth is so choked up by them that seeing they do not see, since they do not check their wrong imaginations, but rather allow them free rein, they let them rise higher. We know this is too true by experience: as clouds, when the morning has been clear, rise up and cover over the bright sunlight, so when we allow our minds to rise too freely against God's Word, we lose sight of what was previously quite clear to us. Granted, when something occurs that looks strange, we may use our imaginations to look into it from all sides. It cannot be otherwise when our minds are moved this way and that by confused matters, but we must keep a limit and clear head, not to let the flesh rise higher than it should, and send its fancies soaring into heaven.

Luke 24.39. *See my hands.* He calls on their bodily sense as witnesses, in case they think a shadow is put before them and not a body. First He distinguishes between a bodily man and a spirit, as if saying, 'Sight and touch will prove me to be a true man, as I lived with you before, for I am clothed with the flesh which was crucified and still bears its marks.' And as Christ declares His body to be palpable and compact with solid

241

bones and by these marks distinguishes it from spirit, this is the wise and right passage for our men to cite in refuting the crass error of the transubstantiation of the bread into body, the local presence of the body, which men preposterously create over the Supper. They wish Christ's body to be there, where it has no sign of body. It will follow on these lines that it has changed its nature, and has ceased to be what it was, ceased to exist in the way Christ proves it to be a real body. If it be objected, that then His side was pierced and his feet were holed with the wounds of the nails, as well as His hands, yet now Christ is unwounded and entire in heaven, this cavilling is easily refuted, for it is not a matter of what condition Christ appeared in, but what He testified about the true nature of His flesh. This is the real property He attributes to it, that it may be touched, and so is different from spirit. So today that distinction of flesh and spirit must remain, as we may take it to be settled by Christ's words for ever. We should think of the wounds, that by this sign it was testified to all that Christ was risen for us, rather than for Himself. For being Victor over death and endowed with blessed and heavenly immortality, He continued for a time to bear the leftovers of the cross for the sake of His people. This was wonderful kindness towards His disciples, that He preferred to lack something Himself of the perfect glory of the resurrection than deprive them of such assistance to their faith. It has been foolish, old women's nonsense to imagine that He is still marked with His scars when He comes to judge the world.

Mark 16.14. *The eleven themselves as they sat.* The participle ἀνακειμένοις I think is put to mean not, sitting at table (as some have rendered it), but simply, sitting: reasonably so, if it be agreed that this is the first vision here being described—a meal would hardly have been appropriate towards midnight. Besides, if the table had been laid, it would hardly fit what Luke says a little later that Christ asked if they had anything to eat. It is a Hebrew word, *sitting* meaning to rest in any place. The rebuke that follows applies more to the first vision than the second, for as (on John's witness) the disciples were glad when they had seen the Lord on the day after Passover, that was when they were rebuked for incredulity. Several apply these words of Mark to Thomas alone, but it seems forced. I prefer to explain simply that Christ, when He first appeared to the disciples, rebuked them for not believing the eyewitness to His resurrection. Yet their hardness of heart is not only condemned on the ground of their failure to believe men, but that after being convinced by the event itself they did not, even then, embrace the Lord's testimony. As then Peter and Mary and Cleopas and his companion were not the first witnesses of the resurrection, but only underline Christ's words, it follows that the rest of the Apostles did injury to the Lord in disallowing belief in His words, even though they were proven by the outcome. So their hardness of heart is deservedly reproved as base obstinacy, and is joined to their lethargy, as if they had deliberately wished to suppress what was clearly true: not that they intended to smother their Master's glory or make it out to be nothing, but because their folly stood in their way and made them unreceptive. It is not willing obstinacy that is condemned (as was formerly said) but blind indifference, that sometimes hardens men although they are not wicked or rebellious.

And while they still disbelieved for joy, and wondered, he said unto them, Have ye here anything to eat? And they gave him a piece of a broiled fish. And he took it, and did eat before them.

And he said unto them, These are my words which I spake unto you, while I was yet with you, how that all things must needs be fulfilled, which are written in the Law of Moses, and the prophets, and the psalms, concerning me. Then opened he their mind, that they might understand the scriptures; and he said unto them, Thus is it written, that the Christ should suffer, and rise again from the dead the third day; and that repentance and remission of sins should be preached in his name unto all the nations, beginning from Jerusalem. Ye are witnesses of these things. And behold, I send forth the promise of my Father upon you: but tarry ye in the city, until ye be clothed with power from on high. (Luke 24.41-49)

Luke 24.41. *And while they still disbelieved.* This passage too shows they were not wilfully incredulous, like men who resolve not to believe, but while their will led them to believe avidly, they were held back by the force of their emotion and could not accept it. Certainly the joy that Luke mentions only arose from faith, yet it was an obstacle that stopped their faith emerging victorious. Let us note, then, how much we should suspect the intensity of our emotions, which although they spring from good principles pull us right across the correct road. We are warned how carefully we must fight against the hindrances of faith, when the joy that came from the presence of Christ was a cause of incredulity for the disciples. We see in turn how kindly and courteously Christ indulges their weakness, not refusing to give new assistance and support in their shakiness. As He had won newness of life in heaven, He had no more need than the angels of food and drink, but He freely condescends to join in mortals' common usage. In all the course of His life He had subjected Himself to the necessity of eating and drinking: now when he is free of it, he takes food to persuade the disciples of His resurrection. So we see that He lays aside thought for Himself and wishes always to be ours. This is the real and godly thought from the story, on which the faithful may well ponder, and say farewell to curious questions—whether this corruptible food were digested, what kind of nourishment Christ's immortal body might take from it, and what became of the excrement. As if it had not been in the power of Him who created all things from nothing to reduce a morsel of food to nothing when it was His will. Christ truly tasted the fish and honey to show Himself a man, and there is no doubt that by His divine virtue He consumed what did not need to pass over as nourishment. I have no doubt the angels at Abraham's table, being endowed with real bodies truly ate and drank in this way. I do not admit from this that they were filled with food and drink for any infirmity of the flesh, since they had put on human form for the sake of Abraham, and the Lord granted to his servant that these heavenly guests should eat in front of his tent. If we admit that the bodies that they temporarily assumed were reduced to nothing after they had fulfilled their mission, who will deny the same took place with what they had eaten?

Luke 24.44. *These are my words.* Though it will later appear from Matthew and Mark that a similar discourse was held in Galilee, it is yet likely that the one now narrated by Luke occurred on the day following the resurrection. John records that on that day *he breathed on them*, to confer the Holy Spirit, and this agrees with the words of Luke that follow, *Then opened he their mind that they might understand the scriptures.* And in these words Christ indirectly rebukes their dull and careless forgetfulness, that after particular instruction on the coming resurrection they were as astounded as if they had never heard of it. The effect of His words is as if to say, 'Why do you hesitate, as if this were a new or unlooked for event, when it was declared by me often enough. Why should you not rather recollect my words? For if you have reckoned on me as true up to this point, you should already have learned this from my teaching, before it came to pass.' Christ's tacit complaint is, in brief, that as His doctrine had not lasted He had wasted effort on the Apostles. He rebukes them more sharply for their lethargy, saying that He did not bring them anything new, but only recalls to their minds the testimony of the Law and the Prophets, with which they should have been imbued from childhood. Even if they had been entirely ignorant of religious doctrine, it was utterly absurd for them not to accept straightway what they certainly knew had been sent them from God. It was an agreed principle for the whole people, that there was no religion except that which is contained in the Law and the Prophets. The division of Scripture given here is wider than in other places. Besides the Law and the Prophets, the Psalms are added in third place, for though they may well be included with the Prophets they have actually a distinct quality of their own. The two-part division that we see elsewhere still includes all Scripture.

Luke 24.45. *Then opened he their mind.* As the Lord had before acted the role of Teacher and made no headway with His disciples, He now begins to teach them inwardly, by His Spirit. Words float into thin air to no effect, until minds are illuminated with the gift of understanding. It is true that the Word of God is like a lantern, but it shines in darkness and among the blind, until the inner light is shed upon their eyes by the Lord (Ps. 146.8), whose own office it is to enlighten the blind. It is obvious how great is the corruption of our nature, when the light of life offered to us in heavenly oracles does us no good. If we do not see with our understanding what is right, how will our wills be adequate to show obedience? We must admit that we fail in all points. The heavenly teaching is of no use or effect to us unless as far as the Spirit shapes our minds to understand it, and our hearts to accept its yoke. To be adequate disciples of Him, we must put away all confidence in our own intellect and seek light from heaven, abandoning the foolish notion of free will, we must yield ourselves to God's direction. Paul is right to bid men become fools, to be wise unto God (I Cor. 3.18), for there is no worse screen to block out the light of the Spirit than confidence in our own intelligence. Let readers note also, that the disciples did not have their minds opened to see God's mysteries without assistance, but to see them as they are found in the Scriptures. Thus is fulfilled what is written at Psalm 119.18, 'Open thou mine eyes that I may behold wondrous things out of thy Law.' God does not bestow His Spirit on His people to abolish the use of His Word, but rather to make it bear fruit. Fanatical men do wrong to use the pretext of revelations to allow themselves freedom to despise Scripture. What we here read of the Apostles is effected by Christ on us all today. He guides them to understand the Scripture by His Spirit, He does not rush them off into vague ἐνθουσιασμούς. It is asked, why Christ preferred to lose a whole three years' effort on teaching them, rather than open their minds at once. I answer, first, that although there was no rapid fruit of His efforts yet it was not without benefit, for when the new light was given, they had the benefit of the earlier time. I interpret *Their minds were opened* not only to mean they were ready to be taught for the future, but that they remembered the teaching they had previously taken for nothing—it took good effect. Secondly, we should know that the ignorance of those three years taught them that they won their new wisdom, only from the light of heaven. Besides, Christ in this instance gives a sure proof of His Godhead, since He was not only Minister of the outward voice, sounding in the ears, but reached into minds by hidden power. He thus shows what Paul refuses to the teachers of the Church, and applies to Christ alone (I Cor. 3.7). Yet we must note that the Apostles were not so empty and deprived of the light of understanding as not to grasp a few elementary points; but as they had only tasted the surface, it is reckoned to be the beginning of their true understanding when the veil is taken away, and they see Christ in the Law and the Prophets.

Luke 24.46. *He said unto them, Thus it is written.* In this context we have the refutation of that false idea, that outward teaching would be superfluous unless our understanding were supplemented naturally by some faculty we possess. What point, they say, would there be in the Lord's talking to deaf ears? We see, however, that when the Spirit of Christ fulfils His role of Teacher within, then the effort of the minister who speaks aloud is a real thing. Christ gives a truly fruitful discourse on Scripture once He has gifted them with the understanding of the Spirit. Granted that the outward voice may vanish, as though dead, in the presence of the reprobate, yet they are none-the-less inexcusable. As far as touches on Christ's words—they are taken from the principle that what is written must be fulfilled, for God gave no testimony through His prophets but what He would certainly fulfil. The same words warn us of what we must principally learn from the Law and the Prophets: as Christ is the end and the soul of the Law (*finis et anima legis*), whatever we learn without Him or apart from Him, is vain and unsatisfying. Whoever then desires to make the most proficiency in Scripture, should always keep his eye on this object (*ad hunc scopum*). Christ puts His death and resurrection in first place, then the fruit that comes to us from them. Where do repentance and remission of sins come from unless our old man is crucified with Christ (Rom. 6.6) so that we might rise again by His grace into newness of life; and because our sins are covered by the sacrifice of His death, our filth washed off by his blood, and our righteousness won by His resurrection? So He teaches, that it is in His death and resurrection that the cause and ground of our salvation are to be sought, since there flow from them our reconciliation with God and regeneration into new and spiritual life. So it is explicitly stated that there can be no remission of sins, nor repentance, except as is preached in His Name. There is no hope of righteousness being imputed to us, nor denial of self and newness of life, except in so far as He Himself has been made our justification and sanctification. And as we have dealt with this heart of the Gospel fully elsewhere it is quite enough for readers to seek there what they do not happen to remember, than to burden them with repetition.

Luke 24.47. *Unto all nations, beginning from, etc.* At last Christ brings into the open what He had concealed before, that the grace of redemption, brought by Himself, is clearly for all nations, without distinction.

Though the calling of the Gentiles had been foretold by the prophets more than once, it had not been revealed in such a way that the Jews could easily admit them to join in the hope of salvation. So up to His resurrection Christ was only believed to be the Redeemer of one chosen people. Then, for the first time, the wall was torn down, so that those who before were outsiders, and dispersed, might be herded into the fold of the Lord. Yet meanwhile, that the Covenant of God might not seem without effect, Christ placed the Jews in first rank when He taught that a beginning should be made at Jerusalem. As God had peculiarly adopted the race of Abraham, it had to have preference over the rest of the world. This is the right of primogeniture that Jeremiah 31.9 applies to them. Paul everywhere kept to this order also (Eph. 2.17), saying that Christ announced peace to those who were near, and then to those who were strangers and afar off.

Luke 24.48. *Ye are witnesses.* He does not yet give them warrant to publish the Gospel, but only tells them the object of His appointing them, that they may be ready in time. Partly He relieves their sorrow, with this comfort, partly He guides their slackness, with this incentive. Seeing that they were aware of their recent failure, they were bound to be cast down in spirit. Christ gives them honour beyond their hope and belief when He lays on them the mission of publishing eternal salvation to the whole world. By this means He restores them to wholeness and utterly dispels the memory of their crime by the greatness of His new grace. At the same time He urges them (as I have said) to avoid slowness and delay over the faith of which they are appointed heralds.

Luke 24.49. *And behold I send forth.* In order that the Apostles may not be frightened of their weakness, He summons them to a hope of new and extraordinary grace, as if to say, 'Even if you know you are not equal to such a responsibility, there is no reason for you to despond, for I shall supply you with the power that I know you lack, from heaven.' To assure them the more in this confidence, He reminds them that the Holy Spirit was promised by the Father. To equip them for their task with eagerness, God already encouraged them with His promise, anticipating their diffidence. Now Christ, putting Himself in the place of the Father, undertakes to perform it, thereby claiming again for Himself divine authority. This is part of the glory that God swears, with an oath, that He will give to no other—to endow weak men with heavenly power. So if it belongs to Christ, it follows that He is God, who spoke through the mouth of the Prophet (Isa. 42.8). God promised particular grace to the Apostles, and Christ conferred it on them, but this is to be taken in general, that no mortal man of himself is fit for preaching the Gospel, except in so far as God invests men with His Spirit and comes to the aid of their nakedness and emptiness. Certainly

Paul is not declaring of Apostles only (II Cor. 1.16), 'Who shall be found sufficient for these things?'—but he states that none among mortals is equal to such a great task. Hence it must be that those whom God calls as ministers of the Gospel are imbued with the heavenly Spirit, and therefore it is promised always to all teachers of the Church, without exception. *But tarry ye.* In case they should rashly rush out and teach before time Christ enjoins them to peace and quiet, until He sends them out at His good pleasure and employs their efforts at the right moment. This is a useful test of their obedience, that endowed with understanding of Scripture, and inspired by the grace of the Spirit, they remain silent and dumb, because they are forbidden by the Lord to speak. We know how eagerly men go out into the open when they reckon they will gain praise and admiration for it. Perhaps Christ wanted to punish their lethargy by this delay, as they had not set out immediately for Galilee, on the same day as He commanded. Whatever it may be, we are taught by their example, not to attempt anything but at God's call. So though men may have some facility in public speaking, let them keep quiet as individuals, until God takes them by the hand and leads them to the public view. The command to stay at Jerusalem should be understood as applying after they had returned from Galilee. For (as we shall shortly hear from Matthew), although He gave them a sight of Himself at Jerusalem, He did not change His original instruction about Galilee. The sense of the words is that, after giving them commands at an appointed place, He wanted them to keep quiet for a time until He should endow them with new power.

But the eleven disciples went into Galilee, unto the mountain where Jesus had appointed them. And when they saw him, they worshipped him: but some doubted. And Jesus came to them and spake unto them, saying, All authority hath been given unto me in heaven and on earth. Go ye therefore, and make disciples of all the nations, baptizing them into the name of the Father and of the Son and of the Holy Ghost: teaching them to observe all things whatsoever I commanded you: and lo, I am with you alway, even unto the end of the world. (Matt. 28.16-20)

And he said unto them, Go ye into all the world, and preach the gospel to the whole creation. He that believeth and is baptized shall be saved; but he that disbelieveth shall be condemned. And these signs shall follow them that believe: in my name shall they cast out devils; they shall speak with new tongues; they shall take up serpents, and if they drink any deadly thing, it shall in no wise hurt them; they shall lay hands on the sick, and they shall recover. (Mark 16.15-18)

Matt. 28.16. *But the eleven disciples.* Matthew passes over what we have related from the other three, and only tells how the eleven disciples were appointed to their office. They had no intention (as we have often seen) to pursue every single part of the narrative, for the Holy Spirit who directed their pen was content to bring in the whole by their joint testimony, as we see. So Matthew chose what affected us most. When Christ appeared to His disciples, He then created them Apostles, to carry a mission of eternal life to all the regions of the earth. Though no mention was made elsewhere of a mountain, we gather that the place in Galilee was known through Mary. Yet it is remarkable that some, after Christ had been twice seen, still hesitated. If any like to apply this to the first appearance, it would be quite reasonable, as the Evangelists are sometimes used to mixing different events. But again, there is nothing strange if traces of apprehension led some into renewed indecision. We know that as often as Christ appeared, they were struck with fear and shock until they pulled themselves together and became used to His presence. In my opinion, the sense is that some hesitated at first until Christ approached them nearer and more intimately. When they knew Him in truth and certainty, then they wroshipped Him, as the brightness of His heavenly glory was revealed. Perhaps it was the same reason that suddenly drove them to hesitate, and later brought them to worship since He had now put away the form of a servant, and displayed nothing but what was heavenly.

Matt. 28.18. *And Jesus came to them and spake.* There is no doubt that His approach to them took away all doubts. Before relating that the office of teaching was laid upon them, Matthew says that Christ spoke first of His power, and rightly so. No ordinary authority would be enough for this. He had to hold supreme and truly divine power of command, to declare that eternal life was promised in His name, that the whole globe was held under His sway, and that a doctrine was published which would subdue all high-seeking, and bring the whole human race into humility. By this preface, Christ not only urged the Apostles to have a brave confidence in their powers to fulfil their task, but also established the faith of His Gospel unto all ages. The Apostles would never be persuaded to undertake such a task of difficulty unless they knew that their Champion sat in heaven, and that supreme power was given to Him. Without such a defence, it would have been impossible to achieve anything. When they hear that He, to whom they engage their efforts, has rule over heaven and earth, this is enough

—and more than enough—aid for them, to overcome every obstacle. As regards the hearers, if the appearance of those who announce the Gospel be contemptible and their faith is weakened or hindered, let them learn to lift up their eyes to the Author Himself, by whose power the majesty of the Gospel must be reckoned. It will turn out that they will not dare reckon contemptible the One who speaks through His ministers. He particularly makes Himself Lord and King of heaven and earth, because when He draws men into obedience by the preaching of the Gospel He is establishing the throne of His Kingdom upon earth, and when He regenerates His people to new life and calls them to the hope of salvation, He is opening the heavens, to raise them to blessed immortality with the angels—men who before, not merely crept upon the face of the earth, but were sunk into the abyss of death. Let us recall, that what Christ always had by right, at the Father's side, was also allowed Him in our flesh; that is (to speak clearly) in His Person as Mediator. He does not boast of the eternal power He enjoyed before the foundation of the world, but the power He now took, when appointed Judge of the world. We must note, His Authority was not openly displayed until He rose from the dead. Only then did He advance aloft, wearing the insignia of supreme King. This is the point of Paul's words (Phil. 2.9), 'He emptied himself: for that reason God exalted him, and gave him the name that is above every name', etc. Although in another place His sitting at the Father's right hand follows His ascension to heaven, as later in order, yet the resurrection and the ascension into heaven are inter-related events, and Christ rightly discourses now, with such impressive words, upon His powers.

Matt. 28.19. *Go ye therefore.* Mark, after telling that Christ appeared to the eleven disciples, soon goes on to the command to preach the Gospel, but does not make it a continuous episode, for we gather from Matthew's context that this was not done, until they had gone out into Galilee. Briefly, they were to lead all nations into the obedience of faith by publishing the Gospel everywhere and that they should seal and certify their teaching by the mark of the Gospel. In Matthew they are told at first simply to teach, but in Mark the type of teaching is specified, namely, preaching the Gospel. A little later, in Matthew himself, the condition is added that they should teach the observance of all that the Lord commanded. So we learn that the Apostolate is not an empty title of honour, but a responsible office; and that there is nothing more absurd nor more intolerable than that fake men should usurp the honour to themselves, live at ease as kings, and do away with their responsibility to teach.

The Roman Pope and his band proudly boast of their succession, as though they held a common role with Peter and his colleagues (*quasi communem cum Petro et eius collegis personam sustineant*), but they have no more concern for doctrine than the Luperci, or priests of Bacchus and Venus. How have they the face, I should like to ask, to put themselves in the place of those men who (they are told) were created heralds of the Gospel? Although they are not ashamed to show their impudence yet to all readers of sound judgment their futile hierarchy is absolutely toppled by this one, sufficient word; no-one can be a successor of the Apostles unless he uses his labours for Christ in preaching the Gospel. Whoever does not fulfil the role of teacher cannot rightly use the name of Apostle: this is the priesthood of the New Testament, to slay men by the spiritual sword of the Word, as a sacrifice to God. It follows that all sacrificers are degenerate, and lying, who are not engaged in the task of teaching.

Make disciples of all the nations. Here Christ removes the distinction and equates Gentiles with Jews, and admits both alike into the company of the Covenant. This is the point of the word *go* (*exeundi*): the boundaries of Judaea were prescribed to the prophets under the Law, but now the wall is pulled down and the Lord orders the ministers of the Gospel to go far out to scatter the teaching of salvation throughout all the regions of the earth. Though (as we have just remarked) the dignity of primogeniture stayed with the Jews at the first inception, yet the inheritance of life was shared with the Gentiles. Thus was that prophecy of Isaiah fulfilled (49.6) among others like it, that Christ was made a light to the gentiles, that He might be the salvation of God to the ends of the earth. Mark means the same by *every creature*: after peace had been announced to those of the household, the same messenger came to those far off, and even to the strangers. And it is obvious how necessary it was that the Apostles should be clearly told of the calling of the Gentiles, from the fact that even after receiving the commandment, it was with the greatest reluctance that they approached them, for fear they would pollute their doctrine (Acts 10.28).

Baptizing them. Christ orders that those who have subscribed to the Gospel, and professed themselves disciples are to be baptized, partly that Baptism may be for them a token of their eternal life in God's sight, partly an outward sign of faith before men. We know that God testifies to the grace of His adoption by this sign, for He ingrafts us in the body of His Son, to reckon us among His flock. Thus our spiritual washing, in which He reconciles us to Himself, and our new righteousness are there represented. But as God affirms His grace to us with this sealing, so those who offer themselves for baptism in turn ratify their faith, as if by appending their signature. And as the Apostles are explicitly given this role, along with preaching the Gospel, it follows that no others are rightfully ministers of baptism than those who minister the doctrine at the same time. As for the freedom to baptize being allowed to individual men, far less women, it is so contradictory to Christ's institution, as to be nothing other than idle blasphemy. Besides, as the first place is given to teaching, there is set a proper distinction between this mystery and the counterfeit titles of the Gentiles, by which they initiate themselves into their religion, for until God makes the earthly element come to life by His Word, the sacrament has no effect for us. Superstition competes ridiculously with all God's works, and foolish men devise various sacraments at their will, but as they have no basis in the Word—like a soul to them—they are empty and deceitful shades. Let us be sure, that it is by the power of teaching that signs put on their new nature, just as the outward washing of the flesh begins to be a spiritual pledge of regeneration when the teaching of the Gospel goes before. This is the true consecration, in place of which the Papacy has forced its magical exorcisms upon us.

So it is said in Mark, *He that believeth and is baptized*. These words not only exclude from the hope of salvation hypocrites who, empty of faith, are puffed out with the outward sign alone, but also He couples Baptism with a holy bond to teaching, that the one may be no more than an addition to the other. As Christ orders them to teach before baptizing, and only wishes believers to be received for baptism, baptism appears not to be rightly administered, unless faith has preceded it. On this pretext, the Anabaptists have raised a great tumult against Infant Baptism. Yet the solution is not difficult, if one considers the reason for the instruction. Christ wishes a mission of eternal salvation to be carried to all Gentiles: He confirms it by setting the seal of baptism thereon. The faith of the Word is rightly placed before baptism, since the Gentiles were utterly strange to God and had nothing in common with the chosen people. Otherwise, it would have been a lying gesture, offering remission of sins and the gift of the Spirit to unbelievers, who were not yet members of Christ. We know that they are gathered in to the people of God by faith, who before were astray. Now, it is asked on what condition God takes in as sons, those who before were strangers. Certainly we cannot deny that once He has embraced them into His favour He treats their sons and grandsons in the same way. He revealed Himself in common as Father, to Gentiles and Jews, at the coming of Christ: the promise then that formerly was given to the Jews, must now flourish today among the Gentiles also, 'I will be your God, and the God of your seed after you' (Gen. 17.7). Those who by faith have come into the Church of God are, we see, to be counted with His own stock, among the members of Christ, and likewise called to the inheritance of salvation. Nor is Baptism in this way separated from faith or doctrine, for though infant children do not yet perceive, for their age, the grace of God by faith, God includes them when He encourages their parents. So I deny that baptism is unwisely conferred on infants; the Lord calls them to it, as He promises that He will be their God.

Into the name of the Father. This passage teaches that the full and clear knowledge of God, which had only been darkly foreshadowed under the Law and the Prophets, had at last emerged under the Kingdom of Christ. The ancients would never have dared call God their Father unless they had taken their confidence from Christ, their Head. The eternal Wisdom of God was not altogether unknown to them, the Fountain of light and life. It was one of their acknowledged principles that God exerts His power by the Holy Spirit. But from the start of the Gospel God was far more clearly revealed under three Persons, then the Father showed Himself in the Son, His living and express Image, and Christ Himself, by the brilliant light of His Spirit, shone out upon the world and held out Himself and the Spirit to the minds of men. There is good reason here for the explicit mention of Father, Son, and Spirit, for the force of Baptism cannot otherwise be appreciated unless it begin from the free mercy of the Father who reconciles us to Himself through the only-begotten Son. Then Christ Himself advances into the midst, with the sacrifice of His death, and at last there comes the Holy Spirit also, through whom He cleanses and regenerates us all, and finally makes us partakers of all His benefits. So we see that God is not truly known, unless our faith distinctly conceives three Persons in one Essence; and the efficacy and fruit of Baptism flow from thence: God the Father adopts us in His Son, and through the Spirit reforms us into righteousness, once we are cleansed from the stains of our flesh.

Mark 16.16. *He that believeth.* This promise was added to draw in the whole human race to faith. As by contrast a severe warning of ruin follows, to frighten the unbelievers. And it is no wonder that salvation is promised to the faithful, for in believing in the only-begotten Son of God they are not only counted among the sons of God but, receiving free righteousness and the Spirit of regeneration, possess the sum of eternal life. Baptism is linked with the faith of the Gospel, that we may know that therein is engraved the mark of our salvation; for if it had not served to testify to the grace of God, Christ would not rightly have said that *those who believed and are baptised shall be saved.* Yet we must at the same time hold that it is not so necessarily required that all who have not received it must perish, for it is not so linked to faith as to be the half-cause of salvation, but as a testimony. I agree, the necessity is imposed on men in case they neglect the sign of God's grace, but although God uses such aids for their infirmity, I deny that His grace is bound by it. Hence we do not say it is necessary for its own sake, but only in respect of our obedience. In the second clause, where Christ condemns those who will not believe, He is meaning the rebels who in rejecting the salvation offered to them bring a heavier penalty on themselves. Not only are they involved in the common downfall of the human race, but they bear the blame of their own ingratitude.

Mark 16.17. *And these signs shall follow them that believe.* As the Lord had confirmed the faith of His Gospel by miracles as long as He was about in the world, so He extends the same power for the future, in case the disciples should think it was tied to His bodily presence. It was of great importance for the divine power of Christ to prosper among the faithful, that it might be a sure fact that He had risen from the dead, and that thus His teaching might survive and His Name become immortal. His equipping the faithful with this gift is not to be applied to each single one, for we know that His gifts were distributed variously, so that the power of miracles was confined to certain people. But as what was given to a few was common to the whole Church, and the miracles that one performed had the effect of strengthening all, Christ is right to name the faithful indiscriminately. The sense is, that the faithful would be ministers of the same power that had first been admired in Christ, so that in His absence the ratification of the Gospel might be the more certain, as he promises in John (14.12) that He will do the same things and greater. It was enough for a testimony to Christ's Glory and Godhead that a few of the believers should be honoured with this ability. Though Christ does not say exactly whether He wished this to be an occasional gift, or one to abide in His Church for ever, yet it is more likely that miracles were only promised for the time, to add light to the new and as yet unknown Gospel. It may be that through the fault of its ingratitude, the world has lost this privilege, yet I would say, that the real purpose for which miracles were appointed was to give enough assurance for the Gospel teaching at its outset. We certainly see that their use ceased not long after, or at least, instances of them were so rare that we may gather they were not equally common to all ages. It was the result of absurd greed and self-seeking among those who followed on, that they made up empty fabrications in order that they should not altogether lack miracles. This threw the door wide open to Satan's lies, not only with delusions taking the place of faith, but with simple men being pulled off the right road by the pretext of signs. It was only natural that men, over-anxious and dissatisfied with the proper proofs, should seek new miracles all the time and be fooled by such impostures. This is the reason why Christ foretold (Matt. 24.24) that the kingdom of Antichrist would be full of lying signs, and Paul testifies the same (II Thess. 2.9). For miracles rightly to strengthen our

254

faith, our minds should hold to that balance which I have spoken of. It follows that those who object that our doctrine is without miracles make a foul slander. As if it were not the same doctrine as Christ long ago sealed, enough and more. I can be quite brief over this point, as I have fully dealt with it in many places.

Matt. 28.20. *Teaching them to observe.* These words show (as I have said elsewhere) that Christ, in sending Apostles, does not resign all His role to them, as if He ceased to be the Master of His Church. He sends out the Apostles with this provision, that they do not obtrude their own opinions, but purely and faithfully pass down, from hand to hand (as they say), what He Himself commanded. Would that the privilege that the Pope claims for himself were subject to this rule: we would readily suffer him to be the successor of Peter or of Paul if only he did not lord it over souls as a tyrant. Seeing that he has made havoc of Christ's authority and tainted the Church with his rotten foolery, it is clear enough how far he has lapsed from the Apostolic office. Let us get the gist of it: these words show that the teachers set over the Church are not to put forward whatever they may think, but must themselves depend solely on the mouth of one Teacher, so as to win disciples for Him and not for themselves. *And lo, I am with you.* As Christ gave the Apostles a commission which, relying on human powers alone, they could not face, He fortifies them with the confidence of His heavenly protection. Before promising that He would be with them, He had said that He was King of heaven and earth, who governed all things by His hand and order. So we must read the pronoun *I* with emphasis, as if He had said, 'If the Apostles wished to perform their task with energy, they must not look to their own resources, but rely on the power enjoined upon Him under whose banners they campaign.' The nature of the presence that the Lord promises His people must be understood spiritually. To help us, there is no need for Him to come down from heaven, since the grace of His Spirit may help us, as by a hand stretched out from heaven. He who in respect to the body is separated from us, by an immense stretch of distance, not only works by His Spirit throughout the entire world, but also dwells in us truly. We must note besides, that this is said not only to the Apostles, for the Lord promises His aid not to one age alone, but to the end of the world. It is precisely as if He said, whenever the ministers of the Gospel are weak, and labour under the lack of everything, He would be their Guardian, so that they may come out victorious over all the world's conflicts. Thus today clear experience teaches that Christ works in a hidden way, marvellously, and the Gospel prevails over numerous obstacles. All the more intolerable is the sin of the papal clergy, who make this a pretext for their sacrilegious tyranny. They claim that the Church cannot err, being ruled by Christ, as if Christ, like a common soldier, hired Himself as mercenary to different leaders, and did not keep His authority firmly to Himself and declared that He would defend His doctrine, so that His ministers might confidently expect to be victorious over the whole world.

So then the Lord Jesus, after he had spoken unto them, was received up into heaven, and sat down at the right hand of God. And they went forth, and preached everywhere, the Lord working with them, and confirming the word by the signs that followed. Amen. (Mark 16.19-20)

And he led them out till they were over against Bethany: and he lifted up his hands, and blessed them. And it came to pass, while he blessed them, he parted from them, and was carried up into heaven. And they worshipped him, and returned to Jerusalem with great joy: and were continually in the temple blessing God. (Luke 24.50-53)

Mark 16.19. *So then the Lord.* As Matthew had extolled the reign of Christ over all the world he did not give an account of the ascension into heaven. Mark makes no mention of the place and manner of it, but both of these are detailed by Luke. He says that the disciples were *led out until they were over against Bethany*, in order that the Lord might ascend to His heavenly throne, from the Mount of Olives, from which He had set out to undergo the shame of the cross. As He did not wish to be seen in His resurrection state by all indiscriminately, so He did not allow men in general to witness His ascension into heaven: He wished this mystery of faith to be known more by the preaching of the Gospel than by the eyes. It follows in Luke, that Christ *lifted up his hands and blessed* the Apostles. This showed that the duty of blessing which under the Law was entrusted to the priests, was truly and properly His own. The blessings men give each other are no more than kind prayers. God's way is different, for He not only favours us with promises, but provides whatever is desirable for us by a simple act of His will. As He is the Author of all blessing, He wished His grace to be close to us, and from the beginning had priests give blessing in His name, as mediators. So Melchizedek blessed Abraham, and in Numbers 6.23 a perpetual law is handed down on this matter. This is also the intention of Psalm 118.26, reading, 'We bless you from the house of the Lord.' Finally the Apostle (Heb. 7.7) has taught us that it is a mark of promotion to bless others. The lesser, he says, is blessed by the greater. When Christ, the true Melchizedek and eternal Priest, was brought to light there had to be fulfilled in Him what was foreshadowed in the figures of the Law.

As Paul teaches (Eph. 1.3) we in Him are blessed by God the Father, that we may be rich in all heavenly goods. Therefore He blessed the Apostles once for all in a public and solemn way, in order that the faithful may go straight to Himself if they wish a share in the grace of God. In *lifting up his hands* we have the description of the old ceremony which we know the priests had used in ancient times.

Luke 24.52. *And they worshipped him and returned.* By the word *worship* Luke means first, that the Apostles lost their hesitation, for Christ's Majesty shone forth everywhere in such a way that there could now be no more doubt of His resurrection. Then, for the same cause, they began to worship Him with greater reverence than they were used to enjoy in His presence on earth. This is worship not of Christ merely as Teacher, or as Prophet, not even as Messiah, as though He were only half-known, but as the King of glory, and revealed as Judge of the world. As it was Luke's intention to develop his story further he only says briefly what the Apostles did during those ten days. Briefly, for the fervour of their joy, they broke out into the praises of God and were constantly at the temple, not that they passed night and day there, but that they went up to all the assemblies, and at the set and regular hours were there to offer thanksgivings to God. Their joy is contrasted with their fear which previously kept them shut in, hidden, at home.

Mark 16.19. *Sat down at the right hand of God.* I have expounded in other places the meaning of this expression: that Christ was taken up on high, that He should stand above the angels and all creatures, that the Father might rule the world through His Hand, that finally before Him every knee should bow. It is as if He were called God's Deputy, to act in His Person. It is not right to think here in terms of a particular place, since *right hand* is used metaphorically to mean second in power to God. Mark added this deliberately to tell us that Christ was not received into heaven to enjoy a blessed state of rest far from us, but to stand guard over the world for the salvation of all the godly.

Mark 16.20. *And they went forth and preached.* Mark here briefly touches on what Luke continues, in the narrative of his second book: how the voice of a feeble and low-born band of men resounded to the furthest ends of the earth. The less credible the thing was, the more surely the light of the miracle of heaven's power was seen. All would have thought Christ either utterly annihilated by the death of the cross, or so reduced that He would never again be mentioned, except in disgrace and hatred. The Apostles whom He had chosen as His witnesses had shamefully deserted Him and slunk off into the darkness: such was their ignorance, their inexperience, and in the end such the contempt in which they were held that they might scarcely ever dare raise their voice in public. Could anyone hope from uneducated and worthless men—deserters, in fact—that by the sound of their voice they should draw so many scattered nations to the rule of the Crucified? There is great weight in these words that they went forth and preached everywhere, recently after trembling in silence in their own prison-house. Such an unlooked-for conversion could not, by human means, take place in a moment, and so Mark adds, *the Lord working with them*, meaning that this was really divine work. Yet this form of speaking does not mean a sharing of their work and effort with the grace of God, as if they produced anything of themselves. He simply means they were aided by God because, according to the flesh, they would have gone out to no effect, whereas they achieved a perfect work. I grant that the ministers of the Word are called God's fellow-workers (I Cor. 3.9) inasmuch as He uses their ministry, but we must hold that they have no power but what He supplies. They do no good planting and watering, unless the secret effect of the Spirit produces increase. *And confirming the word*. Here in my opinion Mark gives an instance of what he had recently stated in general: the Lord worked with them by various means to prevent the preaching of the Gospel being vain, but here was an outstanding proof of His assistance, confirming it with miracles. This passage teaches what use we ought to make of miracles, if we are not to turn them into perverse corruptions: they must serve the Gospel. It follows that God's holy order is reversed if they are torn from God's Word, to which they belong, and are dragged in to decorate godless doctrines or to trick out misguided services.

THE EPISTLE OF JAMES

INTRODUCTION

THE THEME OF THE EPISTLE OF JAMES

We know from the testimony of Jerome and Eusebius that this epistle was originally only accepted by many churches after much controversy. Indeed, to this day, there are several who do not rate it worthy of authority. Yet I am glad to include it, without dispute, for I can find no fair and adequate cause for rejecting it. The apparent distortion (in chapter two) of the doctrine of free justification is a matter we may readily clear up when we come to it. If James seems rather more reluctant to preach the grace of Christ than an apostle should be, we must remember not to expect everyone to go over the same ground. See how the writings of Solomon differ widely from the style of David. The former was concerned with the training of the outward man, and with handing down rules of social behaviour, while the latter is noted for his profound attention to the spiritual worship of God, peace of mind, God's loving-kindness, and the free promise of salvation. Such diversity does not make us praise one and condemn the other. And what a difference there is between the evangelists in their portrayal of Christ's character. One may say that the first three, compared with John, have only fragments of the full glory and power: yet we love their work quite as much. I am fully content to accept this epistle, when I find it contains nothing unworthy of an apostle of Christ. Indeed, it is a rich source of varied instruction, of abundant benefit in all aspects of the Christian life. We may find striking passages on endurance, on calling upon God, on the practice of religion, on restraining our speech, on peace-making, on holding back greedy instincts, on disregard for this present life—these, and such like, which we shall deal with duly in their proper places.

Concerning the authorship, I find rather more reason for hesitation. Certainly this is not the son of Zebedee, whom Herod put to death shortly after the Lord's resurrection. Ancient opinion is almost unanimous that this was one of the disciples, surnamed Oblias, a blood-relation of Christ, who presided over the Jerusalem Church. He is reckoned to be the same man as Paul names (Gal. 2.9) along with Peter and John as 'pillars of the church'. But for a disciple to be counted amongst the three pillars, elevated above the other ten apostles, does not seem likely to me, and I rather incline to the conjecture that Paul is speaking of the son of Alphaeus; although I cannot say that there was not another, president of the Jerusalem Church, who was in fact taken from the band of disciples. It is not for me to say firmly which of these two was the author of this epistle. The very high position which Oblias held in the eyes of the Jews might be deduced from the fact of his cruel murder, the outcome of a plot instigated by the high priest: Josephus does not hesitate to assign the destruction of the city to that killing in some degree.

CHAPTER ONE

JAMES, a servant of God and of the Lord Jesus Christ, to the twelve tribes which are of the Dispersion, greeting.

Count it all joy, my brethren, when ye fall into manifold temptations; knowing that the proof of your faith worketh patience. And let patience have its perfect work, that ye may be perfect and entire, lacking in nothing. (1-4)

1.1. *To the twelve tribes.* When the ten tribes were led away, they were exiled by the Assyrians in various regions. As later empires rose and fell over the years, no doubt they wandered yet further afield, this way and that. Jews were dispersed over virtually the entire world. Thus all the number whom he could not address face to face, for the distances that lay between them, he calls up by written word. He does not treat of Christ's grace, or of having faith in Him, because he appears to be writing to those who have already received proper instruction from others, and who need, not doctrine, but effective lines of encouragement.

1.2. *All joy.* His first exhortation is to accept trials with a joyful mind, as being the testing of their faith. The Jews at that time were the first to need some comfort for the distress which all but engulfed them. The name of their race was so disparaged then that they were hated and despised by every people they encountered. The condition of Christians was worse still, for their own kin were their most bitter enemies; though, of course, the reassurance is not so closely tied to one period that believers may not always avail themselves of it; our life on earth is one long campaign. To be quite clear what *temptations* are, we can certainly understand them as those adversities which are a test of our obedience to God. He tells the faithful to rejoice when these beset them, not limiting them to the experience of one trial alone, but of many; not of one kind alone, but of all kinds and degrees. Though the fleshly plagues work death upon the flesh, they never fail to flourish: in the same way, these trials must keep coming. Moreover, we are afflicted with a variety of diseases, and so it is natural that we should treat them with a variety of cures. There are different troubles which the Lord brings on us, for it is not the same medicine which heals self-seeking, greed, jealousy, gluttony, over-fondness for this world, and the uncounted passions which throng around us. The effect of telling them to *count it all joy* is to have the whole sum put on the credit side, accounted only as a source of congratulation. There is, then, nothing in our distress which can spoil our rejoicing. He is teaching us both to bear adversity quietly and calmly, and to know why believing men are to be happy under affliction. We know that the natural trend of our feelings is to be grieved and saddened by any kind of temptation. Nor can any of us entirely escape the instinct to break down and cry, when trouble comes: but this does not prevent God's children from rising above fleshly pains, under the guidance of the Spirit. By this means, they may continue to rejoice, even in the midst of sorrow.

1.3. *Knowing that the proof.* We now see why he spoke of *temptations* as directed against us, for they serve to probe into our faith. This gives an explanation in support of the last paragraph. It might have been objected: how can it ever be that a bitter experience should be judged sweet? He demonstrates from the effect how we are to rejoice in our troubles; they produce a harvest of great worth, which is patience. If God is providing for our salvation, then He is giving us occasion to be glad. Peter uses the same argument, around the beginning of his first epistle, that 'the proof of your faith, being more precious than gold . . . unto praise' etc. (I Pet. 1.7). The point is that we take disease, famine, exile, prison, disgrace and death as objects of abhorrence, since we rate them as evils: but when we understand that by God's goodness they are changed into aids for salvation, then it becomes ungrateful to complain, and not willingly to offer ourselves to His paternal care.

Paul (Rom. 5.3) speaks of *glory* where James has *joy*. 'Let us also glory in our tribulations: knowing that tribulation worketh patience.' In his next phrase, he seems to contradict James' words, by putting probation in third place, as the effect of patience, while James puts it in first place, as the cause. This however is readily resolved: Paul uses the word in the active sense, James in the passive. James says that to be proved results in patience, for if God did not test us, but left us undisturbed, we would not have patience, which consists precisely in facing evil with a brave heart. Paul's sense is that our actual experience of overcoming evil leads us to grasp the value of God's help in the crisis. The reality then comes right home to us. It follows that we are encouraged to have more hope for the future, and our acquaintance with the truth of God wins more faith from us. Paul says that hope springs from such probation (that is, experience of divine grace), not as though hope started from that stage, but as it grows and gathers strength. The lesson of both is that trials produce patience. Now it is not natural for men's minds to find affliction bringing patience along with it. Paul and James are addressing themselves to the providence of God, not to human nature; the faithful may learn patience in the school of suffering, but the godless are driven by it ever deeper into madness; as the example of Pharaoh shows.

1.4. *Let patience have its perfect work.* We often feel an urge to do bravely, but the mood soon passes; so we must have perseverance. Real patience, he says, is such as will endure to the end. *Work* has the sense of effect here, victory not in one event only, but life-long persistence. One might relate this perfection to the sincerity of one's state of mind, meaning that men should yield themselves to God with full assent, not under a mask: but the addition of the word *work* makes me prefer an interpretation based on constant effort. As we said, many begin with a show of grand heroics, and very soon weary. For this reason he tells us to hold on to the end, as we wish to be perfect and entire. The significance of these two attributes is immediately given in his words 'lacking in nothing, not wearing out'. Those whose impatience gets the better of them will crack, and inevitably break up, until they go all to pieces.

But if any of you lacketh wisdom, let him ask God, who giveth to all liberally and upbraideth not; and it shall be given him. But let him ask in faith, nothing doubting: for he that doubteth is like the surge of the sea driven by the wind and tossed. For let not that man think that he shall receive anything of the Lord; a double-minded man, unstable in all his ways. (5-8)

1.5. *But if any of you lacketh.* Our reason, and indeed all our senses, find it strange that we should think ourselves blessed in time of woe, and so we are told to ask the Lord to bring us this wisdom. I refer the word *wisdom* exactly to the context, in the sense that if the doctrine is found to be beyond the reach of your intelligence, we must beg the Lord to give us the light of His Spirit. The only thought that could sufficiently relieve the pain of affliction is to find salvation for ourselves in the distress of the body: if we do not find comfort of this order, we are bound to succumb to despair. So we see that the Lord does not make demands on us beyond our powers, but is in fact all ready to send resources, once we ask for them. As soon as He tells us our task, we should learn to ask from Him the means to fulfil it. This passage, then, uses *wisdom* in the sense of yielding oneself to God in the face of all disaster, in the due consideration that He orders all things to fall out for our good: but the idea can be applied in general to the whole range of right understanding. Why does he say *if any* as though not all were lacking wisdom? The answer is that by nature all do fall short, but some are endowed with a spirit of prudence which others lack. Since all have not reached the point of finding joy in adversity, in fact only a few have such a gift, James takes the opportunity to say to those who are not yet convinced that the Lord brings salvation to us by the cross, so that they may pray to have this wisdom granted to them. However, all must take notice, and all make the same prayer. You may be some way ahead, but still lie far short of the goal. The only difference is praying for a start, and praying for an increase. When he says, *ask of God*, he means that it is He alone who can heal our sickness and supply our wants.

Who giveth to all liberally. By all, he means all who ask: those who look for no relief for their emptiness deserve to languish in it. But how impressive is this prayer of all the world, in which He invites all men to join, without exception. No man should cut himself off from such a benefit. With it goes the promise, which is directly linked to it. As sure as the command prescribes to every man his duty, so the promise declares that they will not be disappointed in its fulfilment, according to Christ's word (Matt. 7.7; Luke 11.9), 'Knock, and it shall be opened unto you'. The word *liberally* indicates promptness in giving. Thus Paul (Rom. 12.8) demands liberality of ministers. Again (II Cor. 8 and 9) discussing alms-giving, he repeats the same word a few times. So it means that God is so well-inclined and so ready to give that He will refuse none, none will be snubbed off—unlike miserly and grudging men who scowl and shuffle over every meagre payment, and even hold back part of what they were to give, or have a long debate with themselves whether to give or not.

And upbraideth not. This is added in case a man should fear that he is approaching God too often. Among men, the most open-handed remember their previous donations, even if a man approaches them for aid repeatedly, and make excuse for another time; so that we grow ashamed to bother our fellow man, however generous, with too much asking. But with God, says James, there is no comparison. He is prepared to heap new benefits on top of the old, with neither limit nor calculation.

1.6. *But let him ask in faith.* Prayer has its due order and method, and this is his first lesson. We are not able to pray, unless the Word leads our way: likewise, before we pray, we must believe. Our praying is a testimony that we look hopefully to God for the grace He has promised. A man who has no faith in the promises is praying in pretence. This brings us to learn what true faith is. Directly James has told us to ask with faith, he adds the explanation *nothing doubting*. Faith which relies on the promises of God assures us that we shall receive

264

what we ask for: consequently, it goes with a confidence and a certainty of the love God has for us. The word διακρίνεσθαι literally means to examine both sides of a question, like an arbitration. He would have us so convinced of God's once-and-for-all promise that we shall not raise any doubts as to our prayers being heeded.

For he that doubteth. He finds a neat comparison to say how God punishes those whose lack of faith makes them hesitate over His promises. They torture themselves inwardly with their own worries, for the soul never reaches calm waters until it rests on the truth of God. In the end he concludes that such men are unworthy of getting anything from God. This is a striking passage to rebut that sinful teaching, which has oracular appeal throughout the papacy, that we are to pray in diffidence, with no sure thoughts of succeeding. No indeed, it is to be our firm principle that the Lord only heeds our prayers when we bring to them the confidence that they will be heeded. Inevitably the weakness of our flesh exposes us to the assault of various temptations, which are like traps, to spoil our confidence; you will find no-one who is unaffected by the depressions and alarms of the flesh. But ultimately temptations of this sort must be overcome by faith, just as a tree puts down firm roots, and though it is shaken by the blast of the storm is not torn down, and in fact, it holds its ground all the more.

1.8. *A double-minded man.* This can be read as a separate sentence, expressing a general comment on hypocrisy, but I think it is more like a conclusion to the foregoing teaching. This provides a tacit antithesis between the single-mindedness of God, referred to already, and the split mind of man. As God gives us His bounty with an open hand, we in return should open wide our hearts to receive it. The incredulous, who tie themselves in knots, are called *unstable*, since they never settle on any one thing consistently. Sometimes they are bursting with fleshly assurance, sometimes they plunge into deep despair.

But let the brother of low degree glory in his high estate: and the rich, in that he is made low: because as the flower of the grass he shall pass away. For the sun ariseth with the scorching wind, and withereth the grass; and the flower thereof falleth, and the grace of the fashion of it perisheth: so also shall the rich man fade away in his goings. (9-11)

1.9. *The brother of low degree.* As Paul (I Cor. 7.22) encourages slaves to bear their lot with composure, and bids them take comfort in being God's freedmen, released by His grace from the thrall of Satan, warning the high-born, at the same time, to recollect that they are slaves of God, so in like terms, our author directs the poor to glory in their adoption as sons of God, while the rich discover the world's vanity and fall back to their place in the ranks. The former he would have content with their humble and depressed condition, while the latter are to have their pride checked. Since we have the supreme and incomparable honour of joining the assembly of the angels, yes, the company of Christ, any man who reckons God's goodness at its true price will treat all else with total indifference. Neither poverty nor contempt, nakedness nor hunger nor thirst, will shift his mind from the strength of this assurance: Since the master gave me the principal thing, I should manage without the lesser things. Should not the poor brother glory in his high estate, finding gratitude to God for the full and sufficient recompense of sheer adoption, and avoiding over much distress in straitened circumstances of life?

1.10. *And the rich, in that he is made low.* This is a case of the particular for the general. The caution applies to all who rise above their neighbours in rank or birth or other outward things. He tells them to glory in their lowliness, their smallness, to restrain those lofty notions that swell out of prosperity. He says *low*, because the revelation of the Kingdom of God should bring us to think little of the world, and to teach us that all things which earlier were greatly admired are really of no account, or only of the slightest. Christ Himself, Teacher of the poor, has a message which rejects entirely the pride of the flesh. In case the wealthy get enmeshed in the empty delights of the world, let them become used to glorying in the loss of their carnal splendours.

As the flower of the grass. I would not go so far as denying a certain allusion by James to the words of Isaiah (40.6), but I would not accept that he is citing a testimony from the prophet, who speaks not only of the benefits of fortune and the fading image of the world, but of the whole man, soul as much as body. James is concerned with the display of money and possessions. In a word, glorification over riches is folly and absurdity, since they are gone in a flash. Philosophy teaches the same, but the moral goes unheard, until men's ears are opened by God to heed the eternal reality of the Kingdom of heaven. This is why he speaks of *brother*, meaning that this doctrine can only begin from our entry into the ranks of the family of God. The standard reading is ἐν ταῖς πορείαις (in his ways), but I agree with Erasmus that we should read πορίαις without the diphthong, 'in his resources', or 'along with his resources', as I prefer later on.

Blessed is the man that endureth temptation: for when he hath been approved, he shall receive the crown of life, which the Lord promised

*to them that love him. Let no man say when he is tempted, I am tempted
of God: for God cannot be tempted with evil, and he himself tempteth
no man: but each man is tempted, when he is drawn away by his own
lust, and enticed. Then the lust, when it hath conceived, beareth sin:
and the sin, when it is fullgrown, bringeth forth death.* (12-15)

1.12. *Blessed is the man etc.* After bringing words of comfort to relieve
the sorrows of those who are hard dealt with in this world, and also
bringing down the haughty manners of the great, he comes to this
conclusion that men who have the courage to endure pain and various
trials, and to emerge from them victorious, are blessed. I know
temptation might be taken in another sense, referring to the darts of
desire, which prick the inward heart, but I consider that his praise is
for fortitude in the face of adversity, making the paradox that the
blessed are not those commonly so called (who get everything to suit
them) but those who are not crushed by their troubles.

For when he hath been approved. He gives a reason for that opinion:
the struggle leads to a reward. If it is the highest blessing to win a
crown in the Kingdom of God, it follows that the tests the Lord puts
us through are in the interests of our happiness. The argument is from
the end, or the effect. We see that the faithful are vexed with this
misfortune in order that their religion and obedience may be manifest,
and that in the end they may be ready to receive the crown of life. It
is quite a false deduction to say that we merit the crown by our
struggles. God has appointed it for us in His freedom, and only has to
train us to come up to it. And in adding that it is *promised* to them
that 'love God', his words do not imply that men's affections are the
cause, for in fact God has priority in His love towards us, but that
ultimately only those elect of God, who love Him, are approved. We
may take note that those who love God will be victorious over all
temptation, and if in temptation our heart fail us it will only be because
love of the world has prevailed upon us.

1.13. *Let no man say when he is tempted.* Here, without doubt, he is
discussing the other sort of temptation. We know very well that all
outward trials, of which we have been speaking so far, come to us by
God's will. In this sense God tempted Abraham (Gen. 22), and daily
tempts us: that is, He tests us to see what we are like, by putting something in our path which will reveal our inner self. But it is quite one
thing to draw the secrets of the heart into the open, and another to
harass the inner man with foul desires. Now he is dealing with inward
temptations, which are, simply, excessive lusts driving us to sin. Quite
rightly, he states that God is not the source of these, for they flow from
the evil of our flesh. This is a very necessary admonition, for it is the

commonest thing for men to pass the blame for their own misdeeds on to another—and what greater release than to turn it all over on to God! This somersault device has passed down from Adam to ourselves, and we copy it vigorously. For this reason James calls us to admit our own guilt, and not to put God in our place, as though He drove us to sin.

But does not the whole teaching of Scripture cry out against this version, when it says that men are blinded by God, driven to a state of ruin, exposed to degrading and illicit desires? I would answer that perhaps James had such arguments in mind when he was persuaded to state that we are not tempted by God, seeing how the wicked are always arming themselves with texts of Scripture to improve their case. There are two points to be noted. When Scripture assigns blinding or hardening of hearts to God (Exod. 9.12), it does not name Him as the first Mover, nor does it make Him the Author of the evil and so liable for the blame. James insists just on these two points. Does Scripture say that God gave men up to their vile passions (Rom. 1.26), or was it that God depraved and corrupted their hearts? No, their hearts were made subject to vile lusts, for they were already corrupt and vicious. And is it the case that, when God makes a man blind or hard, He is the instigator or accomplice of sin? No indeed, this is His vengeance upon sin, and the fair retribution He takes upon the evil-doers, who have spurned the direction of His Spirit. Consequently, neither is the origin of sin to be found in God, nor is its blame to be imputed to Him, as though He sought pleasure in wrong. We conclude that it is a vain manoeuvre for man to attempt to throw the blame of his errors upon God, for whatever the evil, it comes from no other source than from the perverse affections of man himself. This is certainly how we stand; we are under no other influence: for first and last, every man goes the way of his own wicked thoughts.

That God tempts no man, is confirmed by the fact that He *cannot be tempted with evil.* The reason why the devil chases us into sin is precisely that he is himself all aflame with a mad passion for it. God has no taste for evil, and so He is not the Author of our evil deeds.

1.14. *When he is drawn away by his own lust.* Since the urge and pressure to do wrong come from within, it is useless for the sinner to seek to hide behind an excuse of outward provocation; but we are to note these two effects of lust—it has charms to entice us, and it diverts our attention. And either of these will convict us.

1.15. *When it hath conceived.* First and foremost he speaks of *lust,* not as one particular motivation, but rather as the source of them all. We learn from this that a foul progeny is conceived, which finally comes out as sinful action. Perhaps it does not appear quite accurate, indeed rather opposed to scriptural usage, to restrict the word *sin* to outward acts, as if lust were not sin in itself, and every wicked desire that lurks secretly concealed in the heart was not equally 'sin'. The term, however, has a variety of uses, and there is nothing strange in taking it, in this instance, as in many other passages, for actual sins committed. Papists show their ignorance in seizing on this text, in a wish to prove from it that vicious, yes, filthy, criminal and unspeakable desires are not sins, so long as one does not fall in with them. James does not argue over the moment of sin's inception—granted that it is sin, and is so accounted before God—but treats of its coming to maturity. Step by step he makes the cause of eternal death to be the consummation of sin, sin itself to spring from our forbidden desires, and the desires to be rooted in lust. It follows that men gather the harvest of eternal ruin, sown by their own hands. By 'sin committed in the full sense', I do not mean the perpetration of some act in particular, but the full career of sin: though death is the price for every single offence, one speaks of the wages of a godless and wicked life. Thus we refute their foolish notion of taking from these words the sense that there is no mortal sin, until it breaks out into (what they call) an external act. This is not James's point, either: he is concentrating on the fact that the root of our destruction lies within ourselves.

Be not deceived, my beloved brethren. Every good gift and every perfect boon is from above, coming down from the Father of lights, with whom can be no variation, neither shadow that is cast by turning. Of his own will he brought us forth by the word of truth, that we should be a kind of firstfruits of his creatures. (16-18)

1.16. *Be not deceived.* The argument proceeds from opposites. As God is the Author of all good, it is absurd to count Him the Author of evil. It is, in plain terms, His property and nature to do good; from Him all good comes down to us, and to perform anything evil is outside His nature. Yet occasionally a man, who has generally distinguished himself throughout his life, may lapse in some respect. This is the doubt which is countered by the denial that God is changeable as men are. As in all things and at all times He is consistent with Himself, we may deduce from this constancy that the course of His well-doing in uninterrupted. This is quite a different line of thought from Plato's, when he holds that no disasters fall on men from God, because He is good. Men's crimes are properly punished by God, and in this regard we should not class the penalties, which He justly inflicts, as evils. Plato is out of his depth: James gives God His right and duty to punish, but allows no blame to fall on Him. We should learn from this passage, that we should be so impressed with the countless benefits of God, which daily we see fall from His hand, that we should turn all our minds to His glory, and any idea that occurs to us, or is suggested by others, which is not in accord with His praise, we should reject with all our hearts.

God is called *Father of lights* in the sense of all excellence and the well-framed universe. The next phrase continues the metaphor—*shadow that is cast by turning*: we must not measure the splendour of God by the way we see the rays of the sun.

1.18. *Of his own will etc.* Here he gives an important example of the divine goodness he has propounded: God has given us new birth, unto everlasting life. As each and every believer has recognized this inestimable benefit in himself, the universally proven experience of God's goodness should put all opposition out of court. In saying that God *brought us forth* of His own intention and volition, he means that He was not influenced by any external force—thinking of the contrast men make between God's will and counsel, and human merits. But to say that nothing led God to this course would be an understatement. In fact, he is saying that God brought us forth because of His own good-pleasure, that He was an influence upon Himself. Consequently, that it is God's nature to show benevolence. The passage also shows how our election, before the foundation of the world, was an act of freedom; and so we are brought to the light of the knowledge of truth by the sheer grace of God, and our vocation matches our election. Scripture teaches us (Eph. 1.4-5) that we were freely adopted by God before we were born. James goes some degree further, showing that we hold the right of adoption because God also freely calls us. We are further taught, that it is peculiarly God's task to give us spiritual birth. That this should occasionally appear to be ascribed to the ministers of the Gospel means only that God works through them. It is exactly in the uniqueness of God's work that men serve as His agents.

Bringing forth has the sense that we are made new men, to throw off our old nature, when we are effectually called by God. He also says how God regenerates us, which is, by the Word of truth, to teach us that we have no other access to the Kingdom of God.

That we should be a kind of first-fruits. 'A kind of'—τινά or *quaedam* —indicates comparison, as if to say 'in some fashion' we are made first-fruits. This is not to be restricted to any small number of the faithful, but is shared by all equally. Just as man excels all creatures, so the Lord draws His people out of the remaining herd, and sanctifies a separate offering to Himself. It is no cheap distinction which God awards His sons. To be 'set apart as first-fruits' is a worthy expression for men in whom the image of God is re-fashioned.

Ye know this, my beloved brethren. But let every man be swift to hear, slow to speak, slow to wrath: for the wrath of man worketh not the righteousness of God. Wherefore putting away all filthiness and over-flowing of wickedness, receive with meekness the implanted word, which is able to save your souls. (19-21)

1.19. *Let every man be swift to hear.* If this were a generality, its place in the argument would take some finding. It is placed, however, straight onto the last sentence about the Word of truth, without breaking the sense, and I am sure he is matching this exhortation exactly to his course of teaching. He propounds the goodness of God, then explains how we are to be in the proper frame of mind to receive this priceless benefit which He lays upon us: a most useful lesson. Spiritual birth is not the work of a mere moment. Since some traces of the old humanity still remain, we must ever be re-fashioned, until the flesh is done away. Our violent behaviour, our arrogance, or apathy, greatly obstruct God from finishing His work in us. When James wishes us to be quick in hearing, he means to commend a promptness of this sort: God offers Himself so freely to you, so you should be quick to learn, and not let your slowness get in His way. But we think ourselves so very wise, and cannot put up with the sober tones of God's instruction: we must hurry on, and so cut His lecture short. Hush, the apostle says to us, no-one will ever be a good student of God, if he will not listen to Him in silence. Now this is not the silence of the Pythagorean school, forbidding us to make inquiry whenever we need to know something of value for our understanding: it is only a check on our impatience, to stop us (as we usually do) from interrupting God out of turn. As long as His sacred lips are open towards us, our minds and ears are to be open towards Him, and we are not to seize the conversation for ourselves.

Slow to wrath. I think anger is condemned in like terms because its passion disturbs and blocks the attention which God asks to be given to Himself. We can only hear God with our minds composed. And, he adds, as long as wrath has the upper hand, there is no place for the righteousness of God. Until the rage of contention disappears, we shall never give to God the silence and restraint just referred to.

1.21. *Wherefore putting away.* How then are we to receive the Word of life? First, it cannot properly be gained unless it be implanted, and put down roots in us. The expression *receive ... the implanted word* must be taken in something of this sense: Receive it, as a seed right sown. We think of seed falling often on to dry places, not finding its way to watered and welcoming soil, or of runners that fall to the ground, or hang over dead wood, and wither. He insists there must be a lively implanting, an effective union with our hearts. At the same time, he stresses the manner of this reception—*with meekness*. The word is intended to cover the moderation and docility of minds apt for instruction, such as Isaiah describes (57.15): On whom will my Spirit rest, if not on the lowly and quiet? The reason for so few making progress in the school of God is that scarce one man in a hundred contains his impetuous moods, and controls himself decently in God's presence. The great majority approach Him with high and indignant looks. If we wish to live in the nurture of God, we must take care to order our instincts in humility, and let ourselves be led as lambs by their shepherd. Yet man is never tamed, peaceable, or quiet in mind, until his base passions are purged out of him, and so we are bidden to put away all filthiness and wickedness. As James borrows his illustration from gardening, we may say the practice to follow is to start by getting rid of the weeds. In terms of his general address, we may infer that these faults are inborn in our nature, inherent in us all. Yes, though he is speaking to the believing, he makes plain that in this life we are never entirely clear of these, but constantly find new outbreaks. Hence the call for energetic efforts to root them out. Since the Word of God is a holy thing, we should make a proper start by shaking off the dirt with which we are soiled, to make ourselves fit to receive it. The word 'wickedness'—κακίας—includes hypocrisy and contumacy, and the whole range of corrupt desires. Not content with naming the human soul as the abode of wickedness, he speaks of it as the home of vast evils, such as overflow and heap up mountains high. It is quite true, if a man search himself to the core, that he will find a huge maelstrom of vice.

Which is able to save. What a splendid affirmation of the heavenly message, that by it we find sure salvation. This is added that we may learn to search out this 'treasure beyond reckoning' (as we may say), set our hearts on it, worship it. Here is a stinging reproof to our idle thinking, to find the Word, to which we usually pay such careless heed, to be the means of our salvation; not that the power to save us is ascribed to the Word in the sense of salvation being included in the outward hearing of the utterance, or of God's saving task being put into other hands. James speaks of the Word which penetrates, by faith, to the heart of a man, and means only that God, as Author of salvation, accomplishes this by the agency of His own Gospel.

272

But be ye doers of the word, and not hearers only, deluding your own selves. For if any one is a hearer of the word, and not a doer, he is like unto a man beholding his natural face in a mirror: for he beholdeth himself, and goeth away, and straightway forgetteth what manner of man he was. But he that looketh into the perfect law, the law of liberty, and so continueth, being not a hearer that forgetteth, but a doer that worketh, this man shall be blessed in his doing. If any man thinketh himself to be religious, while he bridleth not his tongue but deceiveth his heart, this man's religion is vain. Pure religion and undefiled before our God and Father is this, to visit the fatherless and widows in their affliction, and to keep himself unspotted from the world. (22-27)

1.22. *But be ye doers.* The interpretation of 'doer' is not as at Rom. 2.13—the man who satisfies the Law of God, and fulfils it in every particular—but rather the man who embraces God's Word from the heart, and testifies by his life that he is a sincere believer, according to Christ's saying (Luke 11.28), 'Blessed are they that hear the word of God, and keep it.' He demonstrates by tangible effects what this indwelling he refers to really is. And of course we must notice that faith is included by James in our general performance, indeed it is put first, as being the chief response which God demands of us. We conclude, that we must try to get the Word of God to take root in us, so as to bring on its fruit.

1.23. *He is like unto a man.* Certainly the teaching of heaven is a looking-glass in which God allows us to gaze upon Himself—but in such style that we are transfigured into His likeness (compare Paul, at II Cor. 3.18). Here he is dealing with the mere outward glance of the eyes, not the intense and powerful contemplation which pierces to the very heart. It is an elegant simile, telling in a few words how unprofitable is the message which we simply hear, and do not fasten upon with the inner feelings of the soul, because, all at once, it has faded.

25. *Into the perfect law.* He has spoken of vain speculation, and comes on now to the perception which searches the depths, and transforms us into the likeness of God. Being concerned with Jews, he takes the word *Law,* so familiar to them, as suggesting the whole doctrine of God. But his reasons for speaking of *the perfect law, the law of liberty,* have eluded exegetes, who have failed to observe the contrast he makes, with reference to other passages of Scripture. As long as the Law is preached by man's outward utterance, and not written in the heart with the finger and Spirit of God, it is a dead letter, it is like a lifeless corpse. The Law may reasonably be held to be impaired, until it finds a place in the heart. The same argument applies to its lack of freedom. Divorced from Christ, it bears children unto

bondage (Gal. 4.24), and it can only affect us with profound apprehension and fear (Rom. 8.15). But the Spirit of regeneration, printing its message on our inmost being, confers in like manner the grace of adoption. It is as though James had said, Do not make a slavish thing of the Law's teaching, but rather a vehicle of liberty; don't be tied to the apron-strings, but reach out with it to perfection; you must receive it with whole-hearted affection, if you aim to find a godly and holy life. Further we may see from the witness of Jeremiah (31.33), and many others, that the re-fashioning which the Law of God will give us is a blessing of the new covenant. From this it follows that it could not be found, until the coming of Christ. He alone is the accomplishment and perfection of the Law. Hence James' addition of *liberty*, inseparably attached, for Christ's Spirit never gives us new birth without equally giving testimony and pledge to our adoption, so as to set our hearts free from fear and alarm.

And so continueth. That is, remains fixed in his knowledge of God. And when he adds, *this man shall be blessed in his doing*, he means that the blessing lies in the action itself, not in the empty sound.

1.26. *Thinketh himself to be religious.* Addressing himself to those who claim to be doers of the Law, he reprehends a fault which (as a rule) lies heavily on the hypocritical, namely, the sharp and censorious tongue. His previous comment on restraint in speech was to another purpose: we were told to keep silence before God, to be better composed for learning. The point now is, that the faithful should not use their tongues for miscalling others, and this is certainly a fault to underline in any discourse on the observance of the Law. When people shed their grosser sins, they are extremely vulnerable to contract this complaint. A man will steer clear of adultery, of stealing, of drunkenness, in fact he will be a shining light of outward religious observance—and yet will revel in destroying the character of others; under the pretext of zeal, naturally, but it is a lust for vilification. This explains his desire to distinguish the honest worshippers of God from the hypocrites, and the bloated pharisaical pride that feeds indulgently on a general diet of smear and censure. He says, If any man think himself,[1] meaning that in other respects he has the appearance of religiosity, but his zest for slander convicts him of insincerity in the service of God. Describing his religion as vain indicates that his other good features are spoiled by the taint of his foul tongue, and also implies that his professed interest in religion is bogus.

But deceiveth his heart. I do not favour the interpretation of Erasmus, 'He allows it to go astray'. This is the source of the invective to which the hypocrites are addicted, and we are to see how, blinded with ex-

[1] *seemeth to be*, RV mg.

cessive self-love, they persuade themselves to be far better than they are. This disease of character-killing stems from the way we sling it over our backs (to take up Aesop's fable) and never see it in ourselves. James does well to treat the symptoms—the appetite for passing censure—by adding the comment that the cause lies in the extreme self-indulgence of hypocrites. They would be more inclined to pardon if they recognized in turn their need for the forgiveness of others. Self-congratulation makes them falsely weak towards their own faults, and over-haughty in passing judgment on others.

1.27. *Pure religion.* He passes over those matters that are of greatest importance in religion, as he is not giving a general definition of it, and warns us that there cannot be religion where certain things fail. Suppose a man said outright that he was temperate, but yet was addicted to wine and drinking parties, and another said in retort that temperance meant keeping away from wine and banqueting: the latter is not giving a complete account of what temperance is, but is simply taking up one point relevant to the case in hand. These ματαιόθρησκοι —'men of vain religion'—who are in question here, are notorious for their display and their idleness. James's message is that we are to assess religion on a different basis from ceremony and parade, for there are definite activities in which God's servants should be engaged.

To visit in cases of need, means to stretch out a hand for the relief of those who are oppressed. Indeed there are a great many others whom the Lord commands us to help, but, by synecdoche, he refers to the widows and the orphans. There can be no doubt that by this single instance he is commending the general range of charity. In other words, if a man wants to be thought religious, he must show it by his self-denial, and by his compassion and well-doing towards his neighbours. He says, *before our God,* to indicate that men see differently, being impressed by outward forms, and that we are to find out what God prefers. *God and Father*—take this as, 'God who is the Father'.

CHAPTER TWO

My brethren, hold not the faith of our Lord Jesus Christ, the Lord of glory, with respect of persons. For if there come into your synagogue a man with a gold ring, in fine clothing, and there come in also a poor man in vile clothing; and ye have regard to him that weareth the fine clothing, and say, Sit thou here in a good place; and ye say to the poor man, Stand thou there, or sit under my footstool; are ye not divided in your own mind, and become judges with evil thoughts? (1-4)

At first sight, this admonition seems difficult and inconsistent. Among the duties of human society, it is not a negligible matter to pay respect to those who are of high rank in the world. And if acceptance of persons is to be faulted, then slaves must be freed from all subjection, for liberty and slavery are counted as 'persons' by Paul (Eph. 6.8-9; Col. 3.25). The same opinion will hold for magistracies. These questions will readily be settled, as long as we do not separate what James keeps together. He is not making a one-sided condemnation of the respect they pay to the rich, but of the fact that they do this to bring insult on the poor. This will be more obvious from what follows, when he brings everything under the obligation of love. We must keep in mind that the acceptance of persons censured is such as exalts the rich and hurts the poor. This is actually revealed by the context. It is, of course, the selfish and vain kind of honour which falls on the rich man, to the contempt of the poor. No doubt self and vanity hold sway when only the external features of this world are taken into account. We must remember the rule (Ps. 15.4), that those reckoned as heirs of the Kingdom of heaven are such as despise the reprobate, but give honour to the godfearing. Thus the contrary stands condemned, if respect for wealth counts so completely that a man heaps honour upon the evil, and is rude to the poor—as has been stated. If you take by itself the sentence, 'It is sinful to offer one's seat to a rich man', the idea is absurd. But if you put in conjunction with that, 'It is sinful to show honour only to the rich, and to look down on the hard-up, indeed to bring them to shame', this will be proper and true teaching.

2.1. *Hold not the faith ... with respect of persons.* He means that respect of persons is so inconsistent with faith in Christ that they cannot be put together: which is well said. By faith we are united into one body, in which Christ is supreme. When the spot-lights turn on to the grandees of this world, and Christ is put in the dark, then plainly our faith has lost its vitality. I have taken τῆς δόξης to mean 'in your estimation', following Erasmus, though one cannot find fault with the ancient interpretation which reads 'in glory'. The Greek word can take either sense, and glory can appropriately be referred to Christ without damaging the context of the passage. For such is Christ's splendour that all worldly glories are soon shrouded by His, once His radiance falls upon our eyes. Consequently, if we look at nothing else than the world's glory, we are detracting from Christ's. Yet the other sense also fits very well. While our estimation of wealth or honours dominates our attention, the truth, which should have pride of place, is being suppressed.

To *sit in a good place*—*sedere honeste*—implies a seat of honour.

2.4. *Are ye not divided?* This can be read as an affirmation, or as a question, but the sense is virtually the same. He emphasizes their guilt by the fact that they gratify themselves, they revel in this degrading behaviour. If you read this as a question, the sense will be: Does not your own conscience convict you, and make you need no other judge? If you prefer the affirmation, the effect will be to say: Here is a further evidence against you—you do not realise you are sinning, nor recognize that your thoughts are as degraded as they are.

Hearken, my beloved brethren; did not God choose them that are poor as to the world to be rich in faith, and heirs of the kingdom which he promised to them that love him? But ye have dishonoured the poor man. Do not the rich oppress you, and themselves drag you before the judgement seats? Do not they blaspheme the honourable name by the which ye are called? (5-7)

2.5. *Hearken, my beloved brethren.* He proceeds to show, by a double argument, how ridiculous it is for them to curry favour with the rich by slighting the poor. First, it is unworthy to bring down men whom God has raised up, or to treat with shame those He has honoured. God ennobles the poor, and it perverts God's ruling to reject them. The second is drawn from general experience. By and large, the wealthy harass plain, decent people, and it is quite absurd to give this rough treatment such a reward as to hold them more esteemed than the poor who actually help us, not hurt us. We shall be able to examine how far he takes each part.

Did not God choose them that are poor? Not only the poor, but He determined to start with them, in order to rebut the arrogance of the rich. This is Paul's observation (I Cor. 1.26), 'Not many noble, not many mighty of this world, but such things as were poor did God choose, to put the strong to shame'. It comes to this that God shed His grace on the rich and poor alike, but chose to prefer the latter to the former, that the great ones might learn not to live on self-appreciation, and that the humble and obscure might ascribe all that they were to the mercy of God: thus both would be trained to have a proper and sober-minded attitude. He calls them *rich in faith*, not because they had a great surplus of faith, but as men whom God had made rich, with the various gifts of His Spirit, which we receive by faith. The Lord offers Himself liberally to us all, and it is exactly according to the measure of every man's faith that each comes into possession of His gifts. Hence if we are destitute and without resource, that points to a defect in our faith. If only we open our arms to Him in faith, God is ever ready to fill us. He speaks of the Kingdom He *promised* to them, not meaning that the promise depends upon their love, but warning them that we are called by God to hope for eternal life on this condition and to this end, that we who are called should love Him. It is the end, not the beginning, that is noted.

2.6. *Do not the rich.* He appears to be stirring thoughts of revenge in them, by adducing the unfair domination of the moneyed classes, suggesting that those who have suffered their ill treatment should pay back like for like. Yet are we told at all times to do good to our enemies, who are against us? No, this is not James' plan. He only intends to explain that there is no reason or judgment for men zealously to pay respect to their own executioners, and at the same time to hurt men who are on their side, or at least have never done them any injury. It all shows more evidently a degree of vanity, where, without any incentive of favours shown, men admire the wealthy simply for being wealthy; yes, even when (to their own loss) they feel their injustice and cruelty, they still fawn and flatter in their court. Granted, there are some rich folk of equity and moderation, men who keep clear of any foul play, but there are not many to be found like this. The general trend of life, what we may call the everyday experience, is exactly as James says. Men discover their own strength by doing mischief; so the more a man can do, the worse he will be, and the more roughly he will treat his neighbours. Let the rich learn to take greater heed to themselves, and avoid the contagion which is so rife within their ranks.

2.7. *The honourable name.* I have no doubt that he means the name of God and of Christ which was called[1] over the faithful, not in prayer (as Scripture mentions at various places) but in the form of a profession;

[1] RV mg.

for example, the name of a father is said to be called over his offspring (Gen. 48.16), and that of a husband over a wife (Isa. 4.1). In other words, 'The good name in which you glory, or by which you wish to be known, as a mark of honour.' Now if these people, in their pride, defame the glory of God, surely they are unfit to have honour paid them by Christians?

Howbeit if ye fulfil the royal law, according to the scripture, Thou shalt love thy neighbour as thyself, ye do well: but if ye have respect of persons, ye commit sin, being convicted by the law as transgressors. For whosoever shall keep the whole law, and yet stumble in one point, he is become guilty of all. For he that said, Do not commit adultery, said also, Do not kill. Now if thou dost not commit adultery, but killest, thou art become a transgressor of the law. (8-11)

The point is now enlarged upon. He makes quite plain the reason for the reproof he has just given: they were busy pleasing the rich, but not for love's sake, rather for the futile purpose of trying to win their favour. He makes a prolepsis in debate, and seizes on the plea of the opposite party. For they might have pled that they were not to blame, if they should subject themselves, humbly, even to the undeserving. True enough, James agrees, but he reveals the falsity of the pretext, in the fact that they pay homage to persons, not to neighbours. You see, in the first part, he recognizes as right and laudable all the duties of love which we perform for our neighbours. But in the second, he denies that acceptance of particular persons should be rated on this level, for it is entirely divorced from the direction of the Law. His answer hinges upon the words *neighbour* and *persons*, as if he said, If you are cloaking your actions with a pretended charity, it will soon be stripped off. God bids us love our neighbours, not certain selected persons. Now the word *neighbour* is understood across the human race. Anyone who sets himself to serve a few of his choosing, and leave the rest, is not observing God's Law, but obeying the base interest of his own spirit. God expressly commends to us both the alien and the enemy, and all who in any sense might seem contemptible to us. Acceptance of persons is utterly opposed to this teaching. Hence James is right to say that this (προσωπολημψίαν) conflicts with charity.

2.8. *Ye fulfil the royal law.* At the beginning of the section, I take *law* simply as equivalent to rule or command, and *fulfilling* it as honest-hearted obedience, with 'no nonsense', as they say. This is as opposed to the one-sided obedience of certain people. It is called the *royal law* (in my opinion) in the sense of a state highway, level, straight, and open—with an implied contrast to the twisting and confusing side routes. And further (again, in my opinion) there is an allusion made to the slavish obsequiousness they produce for the wealthy, when they could give unaffected service to their neighbour, and enjoy the status of free men, indeed the privilege of kings. But in the second sentence, where he says they are *convicted by the law*, when they make acceptance of persons, he intends Law in the primary sense. While we are under God's command to welcome all fellow mortals, any man who turns the majority away and makes room for a few, and besides, gives high priority to the least deserving in face of better folk, is in breach of the divine bond, perverting the order of creation: thus he is well named a transgressor of the Law.

2.10. *For whosoever shall keep the whole law.* The effect of this is that God will not be given obedience with exceptions attached. He will not be taken piecemeal, permitting us to omit sections from His Law as it may strike our fancy. Some people, at first sight, find this a stern doctrine, as though it adhered to the paradox that the Stoics teach, that all sin is the same to the sinner, and asserted that there should be the same punishment for the single offence as for the whole life of wickedness and crime. But the context makes crystal clear that nothing of the sort was in the apostle's mind. We must always pay heed to his motive in each particular case. Here he is saying that we fail to love our neighbours when we give special favour to one section, and neglect the rest. Thus he proves that we fail in obedience towards God, since there is no equity in our efforts to do our duties, in terms of our response to the commandment of God. But God's rule is of one piece and one consistency: therefore we ought to make our behaviour consistent, and not let any commit the error of separating what God has put together. Keep a fair balance, then, if you wish to give proper obedience to God. For example, if a judge punishes ten thefts, and leaves one unpunished, he reveals, by his action, the distorted slant of his mind, suggesting that he hates the man, and not the crime. What he condemns in one man, he absolves in another. Have we grasped James' argument now? If we make an exception to God's Law, when something is inconvenient for us, even if in other matters we show ourselves obedient, we are convicted overall of violating the entire Law on that one count. This conclusion is drawn for the circumstances of the present discussion, but it depends on a general principle, that God has prescribed for us a rule of life which we are not allowed to chop about. It is not over one section of the Law that we are told, 'This is the way, walk ye in it', for the Law promises its reward only to complete obedience. And so it is foolish of the scholastics to imagine there is merit in some so-called 'partial' justice and morality. This passage, and many others, show quite clearly that there is none such, apart from the entire observance of the Law.

2.11. *For he that said.* This adds weight to the previous sentence, that we should take more note of the lawgiver than of the individual precepts. God's righteousness is contained in the Law as a single body. Whoever sins against one heading of the Law undermines, for his part, the righteousness of God. Further God wishes to test our obedience both in one portion, and in particular instances. The transgressor of the Law is he who offends in any ordinance, according to what is written (Deut. 27.26): 'Cursed be he that doth not accomplish all these.'[2] For James, then, we see that transgression of the Law is equivalent to guilt on all counts.

> *So speak ye, and so do, as men that are to be judged by a law of liberty. For judgement is without mercy to him that hath shewed no mercy: mercy glorieth against judgement.* (12-13)

2.12. *So speak ye.* Here is one interpretation: men are called back to face the court of law for being too easy on themselves. They acquit themselves by their own judgment simply because they do not approach the judgment of the divine Law. This will serve to warn them that all acts and words must be accounted for in that court, as God will judge the world by His Law. Considering, however, that such a summons might strike unbearable alarm on the hearer, it is said that the severity is limited, or relieved, by his addition, *a law of liberty.* Remember what Paul writes (Gal. 3.10), that, 'As many as are under the Law are liable to its curse'. In itself the judgment of the Law is a sentence of eternal death, and for this very reason the word *liberty* shows how we are delivered from the rigour of the Law. Now this sense is not altogether unapt; but if you think a little more deeply of the immediate development, you will see that James is making a different point: in other words, Unless you wish to undergo the rigour of the Law, you must be less severe on your neighbours. The law of liberty, then, is equivalent to God's clemency, which frees us from the curse of the Law. So we must take this, and what follows, in the one context of being tolerant towards weakness. This line of argument flows very well: since none of us would stand in God's presence if we were not absolved and made free from the rigorous application of the Law, our actions should follow a like course, and not exclude God's generosity by over-severity; in the end, we all need the same.

[2] RV: that confirmeth not the words of this law to do them.

2.13. *For judgment.* This is the application of the last sentence to his subject in hand, and confirms the second interpretation, which I gave. He shows that as we only stand by God's mercy, so we are to display it towards those whom the Lord Himself commends to us. Now this is a remarkable incentive to humanity and kind actions, the promise that God will be merciful to us, if we are the same to our brothers. It is not that the mercy—whatever it is—which we show men merits the mercy of God, but that God wills those whom He has adopted (to whom He would be a loving and kind Father), to show forth His image on earth, in the sense of the saying of Christ (Luke 6.36), 'Be ye merciful, even as your Father in heaven', etc. On the other hand, note that there could be no sterner or more awesome denunciation of God's judgment. Men are wretched and lost beyond words, if they do not take shelter in forgiveness.

Mercy glorieth. Or we may say, it is only the mercy of God which can deliver us from the fear of judgment. *Glory,* in the sense of being victorious or superior. The sentence of doom lies on all the earth, if mercy does not bring relief. It is a difficult and forced exposition to suggest that the person is indicated by the name of the quality. In any case, it is not man who glories over God's judgment, but rather God's mercy which heads the triumph, occupies the Kingdom single-handed, when the terror of judgment gives way. I do not, of course, deny that our confidence and boast begin from this moment, when the faithful see that the wrath of God yields, as it were, to His mercy, and that the latter has raised the siege brought by the former.

What doth it profit, my brethren, if a man say he hath faith, but have not works? Can that faith save him? If a brother or sister be naked, and in lack of daily food, and one of you say unto them, Go in peace, be ye warmed and filled; and yet ye give them not the things needful to the body; what doth it profit? Even so faith, if it have not works, is dead in itself. (14-17)

2.14. *What doth it profit.* He further encourages works of mercy. He has given warning that God will be a grim and fearsome Judge, if we do not behave warmly and generously towards our neighbours. But since the hypocrites would reply that faith is enough for us, being the basis of our salvation, he turns to counter this futile assertion. The point is, that faith without love gives no profit, indeed it is sheer loss. The question arises whether faith can be separated from love. There is a perverse exposition of this passage which has produced the tedious distinction of the sophists between faith *informis et formata*—'unformed and formed'. This was not in James' understanding. He is speaking of false profession, and his words make this certain. He does not start, 'If a man has faith', but 'If a man says he has faith . . .' Plainly he implies that there are hypocrites who make an empty boast of the word, when they have no real claim on it. For him to call this 'faith' is indeed a concession, in terms of rhetoric. When we are getting down to facts, it does no harm, indeed sometimes helps the case, to allow your adversary the word he wants, since, when the facts are proven, the word also immediately drops from his hands. James was content to refute the false pretext which the hypocrites assumed, and had no wish to argue over the term. Just remember, he is not speaking out of his own understanding of the word when he calls it 'faith', but is disputing with those who pretend insincerely to faith, but are entirely without it.

Can that faith. This has the same effect as saying, that with an indifferent and formal understanding of God we shall by no means attain to salvation. This is universally agreed. Our salvation comes from faith, which ties us to God, and the only pathway is our insertion into the Body of Christ, to live by His Spirit, and also to be ruled by Him. That dead representation of faith shows us none of this, and so it is no wonder if James refuses it effectiveness for salvation.

2.15. *If a brother.* He takes an example from the matter in hand. As we said, he is encouraging works of mercy. Should any man contradict this and boast of being content to have faith without works, James compares such flaccid faith to telling a starving man to 'have a good meal', while failing to supply the man with the food he has to get. Now, as it mocks a poor man to send him off with words, and not bring him any help, so men mock God, when they arrange their lives to avoid works, or any single action, of sincere charity.

2.17. *Is dead in itself.* He calls faith lifeless if it is empty of good works. Thus we deduce that it is not in fact faith at all, for being dead it can hardly keep the name. The phrase has been forced by the sophists to imply that faith 'in itself' may exist to some degree: but such flimsy speculation will not stand up for a moment, when it is abundantly clear that the apostle was reasoning in terms of an impossibility; compare Paul (Gal. 1.8), calling an angel 'anathema' should one try to subvert the gospel.

Yea, a man will say, Thou hast faith, and I have works: shew me thy faith apart from thy works, and I by my works will shew thee my faith.

Thou believest that God is one; thou doest well: the devils also believe,
and shudder. (18-19)

2.18. *Yea, a man will say, etc.* Erasmus represents this as a dialogue
between one side supporting faith without works, and another works
without faith, concluded by the apostle taking the middle course to
refute them both, but I think this is rather strained. He thinks that it
is absurd to put into James' mouth the words, *Thou hast faith*, when he
admits that there is no faith without works. But this is quite mistaken
—he fails to recognise the irony of the words. So I take ἀλλά ... τις
(RV 'But someone will say') as introducing a rebuttal of the vain boast
of those who imagine they have faith, but whose lives reveal their
faithlessness. James says that it will not be difficult for all godly and
decent folk to shatter the hypocrites' pride, on which they bloat
themselves.

Shew me. Although the most general reading in the Greek texts is
'from thy works', the old Latin is more apt, 'without', etc., and it is
the reading of a few Greek mss. I have not hesitated to choose it. In
commanding them to show faith without works, he is arguing from
the impossible, in order to prove there is none such. The device is
ironic. Should anyone prefer to follow the other text, it will come
back to the same: Show me faith from your works, for it is not
inactive, and must be shown in works. Which means: Unless you
show fruits for your faith, I shall say that you have none. It may be
asked whether outward probity of life can be a sure evidence of faith.
James says, *I by my works will shew thee.* The answer is, that men of
no faith do at times distinguish themselves with commendable works,
and in fact lead an excellent life, with no hint of ill-doing: so works,
outwardly splendid, may be unrelated to faith. James is not arguing
that every fine appearance leads straight to a man of faith. He only
wants to say that preaching faith without the testimony of good works
is useless, for fruits always come from the living root of the good tree.

2.19. *Thou believest that God.* This remark alone is enough to prove
that our whole discussion is not on the subject of faith, but on a certain
uninformed opinion of God, which no more brings God and man
together than looking at the sun lifts us up into the sky. It is certain
that we approach God by faith. So it is quite ludicrous for anyone to
say that devils have faith. At this juncture, James is preferring them
to the hypocrites. The devil *trembles*, he says, at the mention of God,
for when he recognizes his Judge he is struck with terror. So any who
despise the God they recognize are in even worse degree. *Thou doest*
well is a kind of compliment, as if to say: this is really an achievement,
to sink lower than devils.

But wilt thou know, O vain man, that faith apart from works is barren? Was not Abraham our father justified by works, in that he offered up Isaac his son upon the altar? Thou seest that faith wrought with his works, and by works was faith made perfect; and the scripture was fulfilled which saith, And Abraham believed God, and it was reckoned unto him for righteousness; and he was called the friend of God. Ye see that by works a man is justified, and not only by faith. And in like manner was not also Rahab the harlot justified by works, in that she received the messengers, and sent them out another way? For as the body apart from the spirit is dead, even so faith apart from works is dead. (20-26)

2.20. *But wilt thou know.* We must keep this question in its context. He is not taking up the matter of the cause of our justification, but only the worth and the place we should allow to a profession of faith without works. Thus it is quite mistaken to try to use this testimony as a proof that man is justified by works, since James intended nothing of the kind. The proofs he alleges are to be related to this statement, that faith without works is nothing, or at least, is a dead thing. It is not possible to understand what is being said, or to make any discerning judgment on the terms, unless one keeps an eye on the intention of the author.

2.21. *Was not Abraham.* The sophists leap on the word 'justification', and sing out in triumphant chorus that part of justification depends on works. A sober exegesis must be sought from the circumstances of the present passage. We have said that James is not here dealing with the source or the manner of man's attainment of righteousness (as is evident to all), but is stressing the single point, that good works are invariably tied to faith: so when he states that Abraham was justified by works his words are in confirmation of the justification. So when the sophists set James against Paul, they are deceived by the double meaning of the term 'justification'. When Paul says we are justified by faith, he means precisely that we have won a verdict of righteousness in the sight of God. James has quite another intention, that the man who professes himself to be faithful should demonstrate the truth of his fidelity by works. James did not mean to teach us where the confidence of our salvation should rest—which is the very point on which Paul does insist. So let us avoid the false reasoning which has trapped the sophists, by taking note of the double meaning: to Paul, the word denotes our free imputation of righteousness before the judgment seat of God, to James, the demonstration of righteousness from its effects, in the sight of men; which we may deduce from the preceding words, *Shew me thy faith, etc.* In this latter sense, we may admit without controversy that man is justified by works, just as you might say a man is enriched by the purchase of a large and costly estate, since his wealth, which beforehand he kept out of sight in a strong-box, has become well known.

When he says that *faith wrought with his works*, and was made perfect by them, he gives us further proof that there is no debate here over the cause of our salvation, but as to whether works necessarily go along with faith. In this sense, it is said to have co-operated with works, being not inactive. It is said to have been made perfect by works, not because it drew its perfection from them, but because they were evidence of its true quality. Sophists squeeze their miserable distinction of 'formed and unformed' faith from this argument, but they need no protracted refutation. Abraham's faith was formed, indeed it was burnished, before ever he was called to sacrifice his son. Nor was that action his dying gesture, so to speak, for there were many later occasions on which Abraham showed the increase of his faith. This was not the perfecting of his faith, nor was it taking form for the first time. James only means that his integrity was made certain in that action where he revealed the remarkable fruition of his loyalty.

2.23. *And the scripture was fulfilled.* Those who would prove that on James' testimony it was by the imputation of his works that Abraham was justified, would have to agree that he is distorting Scripture. Turn as they will, they can never make an effect come before its cause. A passage is cited from the books of Moses (Gen. 15.6). The imputation of righteousness which Moses there records preceded by more than thirty years the action by which they say Abraham was justified. Surely, when fifteen years before the birth of Isaac, faith was imputed to Abraham for righteousness, this could scarcely be the effect of his sacrifice. I have them here in a perfect tangle, pretending that righteousness was imputed to Abraham in the sight of God, because he sacrificed his son Isaac, for he was not yet born when the Holy Spirit was announcing that Abraham was justified. So we are bound to conclude that the reference is to the future. How does James speak of its accomplishment? Well, he wants to show what kind of faith this was, that justified Abraham, not inactive, not fading, but capable of making him obedient to God, as we may read at Heb. 11.8. The conclusion given immediately, which follows on this, is precisely in this sense. A man is not justified by faith alone—that is, only by a bare and empty awareness of God. He is justified by works—that is, his righteousness is known and approved by its fruits.

2.25. *And in like manner was not also Rahab.* This seems a strange procedure, to link such dissimilar characters. Why not select some one from the great number of the noble Patriarchs, to cite along with

Abraham? Why prefer a harlot to them all? He deliberately brought two such different people together, in order to exhibit more plainly that at no time was any person, of whatever condition or race or class, reckoned among the justified and believing if they did not show works. He has named a Patriarch of undoubted pre-eminence: now, in the person of a harlot, he includes all who, though they were strangers to the Church, are being brought in. So let any who will be rated just, though his station be of the lowest degree, reveal his character in good works. James follows his practice and declares that Rahab was justified by works: from which the sophists deduce that we achieve righteousness by the merits of our works. For our part, we deny that there is any question here of attaining righteousness. We agree that good works are required of righteousness, but we do not allow them the power of conferring it, since at God's tribunal they must draw back.

CHAPTER THREE

Be not many teachers, my brethren, knowing that we shall receive heavier judgement. For in many things we all stumble. If any stumbleth not in a word, the same is a perfect man, able to bridle the whole body also. Now if we put the horses bridles into their mouths, that they may obey us, we turn about their whole body also. Behold, the ships also, though they are so great, and are driven by rough winds, are yet turned about by a very small rudder, whither the impulse of the steersman willeth. So the tongue also is a little member, and boasteth great things. (1-5a)

3.1. *Many teachers.* The common, and virtually undisputed, interpretation of this passage, is that it is a deterrent against great enthusiasm for the teaching vocation, for the reason that one runs the hazard, indeed the risk, of serious judgment under God, in case of failure in the office. This assumes that he said, *Be not many*, because of course there must be a certain number. However, I take *teachers* to refer not to the men who perform public duties in the Church, but to those who usurp to themselves the right to pass censure on others. These are the critics, who like to be regarded as teachers of morality. The word is as common in Greek as in Latin in the sense of 'teachers' who turn a fault-finding look of superiority upon others. Forbidding the 'many', comes from the large number that behaved in this style. We may say it is an innate condition of the human make-up, to make one's reputation by scoring off other folk. The ill effect of this behaviour is two-fold—the few have the skill and influence, the many rush in and make confusion out of learning. Only a few feel any real interest, while the rest are prompted more by hypocrisy and ambition than any regard for their brethren's salvation.

Note that James is not discouraging those fraternal admonitions, which the Spirit so much and so often presses upon us, but is condemning an excessive passion, which springs from self-seeking and pride, whereby one man inveighs against his fellow, speaks against him, sneers at him, snaps and rummages about to find something to use to his harm. It is usually the case that persistent critics of this sort make wild claims for themselves in hunting down the faults of others. Such is the immoderate and arrogant behaviour from which James bids us turn back. And he gives a reason: those who are so stern with others will face a more heavy judgment themselves. They give themselves a hard standard when they force everyone's words and deeds to the utmost rigour; they do not find pardon, who cannot bear to pardon another. This is a thought to keep well in mind, that men provoke God's severity on themselves when they are too strict on their brothers.

3.2. *For in many things we all stumble.* This may be taken as concessive, as if to say, Come now, you find a point of blame in your brothers, but no man is free of faults, indeed every man has more than one. Do you think you are so perfect, when your tongue is nasty and offensive? But in my opinion, James uses this argument to urge a gentler attitude upon us: quite simply, that we are ourselves beset with a great number of weaknesses. It is unjust to deny others the pardon we need ourselves. Compare Paul, where he says that those who have lapsed are to be corrected with clemency, and in a spirit of leniency, adding directly (Gal. 6.1), 'Looking to thyself, lest thou also be tempted'. Nothing does more to temper extreme severity than recognizing our own weakness.

If any stumbleth not in word. After saying there is no-one who does not sin in various respects, he shows how the disease of censorious speech is repulsive above all other. He calls that man *perfect* who does not offend by his tongue, meaning that restraint in speech is an exceptional virtue, one of the finest. And this makes their behaviour so perverse—they fuss and probe into every little error, yet on their own account plunge in up to the necks. It is a neat point to bring home against the hypocrisy of the over-critical, that in self-examination they fail to notice the outstanding and most significant vice, which is malicious speech. Those who castigate others display a great zeal for perfect sanctity, but if they wish to be perfect they should start with the tongue. But, as they are quite incapable of restraining their tongues, and rather use their snarling, rasping words on others as an exhibition of false religiosity, then evidently they deserve more blame than any, for neglecting the primary virtue. To put the contrast like this, reveals to us what the apostle is thinking.

3.3. *Now if we put the horses bridles.* He employs these two similes to underline the great significance of the tongue for true perfection, the mastery (as he has just said) which it should exercise over our entire life. First he compares the tongue to a bridle, and then to a ship's rudder. If the wild spirit of a horse can be brought round to the will of the rider by the use of a bridle, no less is the achievement of the tongue in controlling a man. We must look the same way at the steering of a ship, which can overcome both its bulk and the force of the winds. Thus the tongue, which is a little member, has great influence on moderating a man's life.

Boasteth great things. The Greek word μεγαλαυχεῖν means to boast or parade oneself, but in this passage James is not hitting at ostentation so much as saying that the tongue may claim great effectiveness. This last sentence brings the foregoing comparisons into line with his present instruction. Empty boasting is not relevant to the control of horses or of ships. So he means, the great force which the tongue enjoys.

The impulse of the steersman (RV). 'Inclination' is my rendering, rather than Erasmus' 'impulse', which he takes from the Greek ὁρμή meaning 'appetite'. I agree the word is used in that language for passions which do not yield to reason, but James is simply dealing with the helmsman's power to choose.

> *Behold, how much wood is kindled by how small a fire! And the tongue is a fire: the world of iniquity among our members is the tongue, which defileth the whole body, and setteth on fire the wheel of nature, and is set on fire by hell.* (5b-6)

Now he shows the difficulties that come from intemperate speech, to teach us that the tongue has a considerable effect either way. If it is moderate and well-ordered, it serves as a bridle on our whole pattern of life, but if it is rude and dissolute, it can be the one match to set all ablaze. *How small a fire*, he says, to indicate that smallness does not keep the tongue from spreading its damaging forces far and wide. The addition, *the world of iniquity*, effectively implies a 'sea' or an 'abyss'. It is a well-framed expression to compare the immensity of the world with the smallness of the tongue. A tiny part of our anatomy has all the evil of the world within its touch.

3.6. *The tongue, is among our members* (RV mg). This clarifies what he intended by the term *world*—the tongue's contagion affects every part of life. Or rather, it explains his metaphor of 'fire'—it corrupts the whole body. He comes straight back to 'fire', in saying: *setteth on fire the wheel of nature* (or *birth* RV mg). Here the course of human life is compared to a wheel. Γένεσιν, as before, is used for 'nature'. The sense is, that while in the course of seasons and of years other vices are corrected, the tongue's vice is spattered and rife in every period of life. Unless you care to take this *setting on fire* as that fierce impulse, which we call 'burning' from the rage of its onset. Horace uses a comparable expression of 'wheels': they 'burn' in the race on account of the speed of the chariot's career. The sense then would be, that the tongue is like wild horses, whose frenzy tears a man headlong, like a chariot.

When he says, *is set on fire by hell*, it comes to saying that the tongue's fury is just like the flame of infernal fire. Exactly as the secular poets describe the pains of the wicked, burning from the torches of the furies, so it is true that Satan kindles on earth a fire of all kinds of evil, fanned by temptations: James' point, though, is that the fire Satan sends is most easily sparked off by the tongue, to give a quick blaze. In short, it is a likely instrument for catching, encouraging, and increasing the fires of hell.

For every kind of beasts and birds, of creeping things and things in the sea, is tamed, and hath been tamed by mankind: but the tongue can no man tame; it is a restless evil, it is full of deadly poison. Therewith bless we the Lord and Father; and therewith curse we men, which are made after the likeness of God: out of the same mouth cometh forth blessing and cursing. My brethren, these things ought not so to be. Doth the fountain send forth from the same opening sweet water and bitter? can a fig tree, my brethren, yield olives, or a vine figs? neither can salt water yield sweet. (7-12)

3.7. *For every kind of beasts.* This strengthens what has just been written. He demonstrates the amazing effectiveness of Satan's rule over the tongue, from the fact that it responds to no method of control; and he brings this out by various comparisons. There is no animal, he says, so fierce or savage that it cannot be tamed by human effort. Fish, who live in a kind of different world; birds, who are so agile and scattering; even snakes, the enemies of mankind, are sometimes made tame. So when the tongue admits of no restraint, it must surely possess some secret, hidden source of hell-fire. His reference to wild beasts, snakes, and other creatures, is not to be understood of them all: it is enough that human skill has managed to subdue even some of the most ferocious beasts—as snakes can sometimes be charmed. So he uses both tenses, present and past: the former indicates the power and ability we possess, the latter the lessons of custom and experience. His conclusion is well justified, that the tongue is full of deadly venom. Although in the first instance all this should be related to the context of the present passage—that it is quite absurd for men to set up as teachers over others, when they suffer from the worst of vices—yet we should appreciate the general message, that if we wish to keep our lives in good order, we must give the greatest attention to controlling our tongue, for it is the most lethal member we possess.

3.9. *Therewith bless we.* Here is an illuminating example of the poison's deadly power: it is able to alter its shape with fantastic caprice. It pretends to bless God, and in the same moment curses Him in His image, by speaking evil of men. If God is blessed in all His works, this should be true in men above all, on whom His image and His glory cast a particular radiance. So it is unbearable hypocrisy for a man to direct the same speech to the praises of God and the cursing of man. We simply cannot call upon God, our words of praise must die upon our lips, when malicious speech takes over. It is sinful profanation of the Name of God for the tongue, that slanders the brethren, to speak of Him in the guise of adoration. To give Him the worship we owe, we must first of all put right this vicious ill-speech against our neighbours. But hold on to the actual point he is making, that our solemn judges are shown up by the virulence of their own judgments, when they sing the sweet praises of God and spew out on their brethren all the malediction they can imagine. If it is objected, that the image of God in human nature was removed by the sin of Adam, we must admit that it was sadly deformed, yet in such a way that certain lineaments of it still appear. Righteousness, equity, the freedom to seek after good, these things have gone; but many gifts are left to us, by which we are superior to beasts. The man who has a true respect and reverence towards God will beware of being insulting towards people.

3.11. *Doth the fountain.* These similes are adduced to show that a cursing tongue is something prodigious, alien to the rest of nature, subversive of the order everywhere appointed by God. God has so distinguished things that are opposites, that inanimate objects should persuade us to avoid confusions and ambiguities, of the sort that a double-dealing tongue reveals.

Who is wise and understanding among you? let him shew by his good life his works in meekness of wisdom. But if ye have bitter jealousy and faction in your heart, glory not and lie not against the truth. This wisdom is not a wisdom that cometh down from above, but is earthly, sensual, devilish. For where jealousy and faction are, there is confusion and every vile deed. But the wisdom that is from above is first pure, then peaceable, gentle, easy to be intreated, full of mercy and good fruits, without variance, without hypocrisy. And the fruit of righteousness is sown in peace for them that make peace. (13-18)

3.13. *Who is wise.* As we may admit that a passion for malicious speech is the offspring of pride, pride itself is largely engendered by a false assurance of wisdom, which accounts for his mention of it here. It is the rule for hypocrites to vaunt and project themselves by their denunciation of all around. Similarly, in the old days, many a philosopher won his reputation by cynical railery directed at all classes. The self-satisfaction that inflates and blinds such foul mouths is rejected by James, who says that t⌐e notion of wisdom conceived by such selfishness had nothing of the divine about it. No, he urges, it is diabolic.

This is the sense: these haughty censors, so generous to themselves, so unsparing on others, think they have outstanding wisdom, but are greatly deceived. The Lord has trained His people quite another way, which is to be gentle and courteous to one another. The only men who have wisdom in God's sight are such as bring to this gentleness an honest manner of life. The harsh and unyielding, for all the other great virtues they may have, have no real measure of wisdom.

3.14. *But if ye have bitter jealousy.* He details the fruits that grow from overmuch severity, as opposed to meekness. It cannot be helped but excessive strictness will produce unworthy jealousies, which will at once break out into quarrelling. He is stretching language to speak of 'faction' in the heart, but this makes little or no difference to the sense. He intended to point to the source of these evils, which is a base passion of the heart. He calls it *bitter jealousy,* for it has no domination until our hearts are so affected with its poison that they turn everything sour. If we wish to make an honest boast that we are the sons of God, we are told to behave quietly and moderately with our brothers, or else he will say we lie, when we boast the name of Christ. It is quite relevant to include *faction* with jealousy, since disputes and rows always swell out of malice and envy.

3.15. *This wisdom is not.* Hypocrisy does not withdraw its claims readily, and so he returns to attack, with some energy, their arrogant attitude; he says it is not true wisdom (on which they pride themselves) to be so doom-ridden in belabouring the faults of others. Now he allows them the word *wisdom,* but qualifies it as earthly, animal, demonic, in contrast to the true definition, which is heavenly, spiritual, divine—giving each epithet its direct opposite. James takes it for granted that wisdom comes to us from no other source than the heaven-sent illumination of God through the Spirit. Thus, however far man may stretch his intellect, all his insight will be vain, indeed, will fall into Satan's trap at last, and come to mental ruin. *The senses* ('*anima*') are here contrasted with the Spirit, as in I Cor. 2.14, where Paul says, 'The natural man receiveth not the things of God.' No greater collapse could bring down the pride of man, than to find himself convicted of drawing all his wisdom from his own nature, without anything of the Spirit of God, and of letting his own nature go over to the devil's court. This comes to mean that men who follow their own feelings will quickly slip into Satan's wiles.

3.16. *For where jealousy.* He is arguing from opposites: the jealousy that drives on the hypocrites has an effect quite the reverse of wisdom. Wisdom requires a well balanced composure, while jealousy starts disturbance in the mind, makes it uneasy in itself, and has a disordered temper towards others. Some translate ἀκαταστασίαν as 'changeableness', and it sometimes has this meaning; but as it can also be 'civil strife' and 'uproar', the sense of 'confusion' seemed best for the present passage. James appears to imply something more serious than fickle behaviour, inasmuch as the ill-minded detractor handles everything in a chaotic and mistaken fashion, as though he were beside himself.

3.17. *But the wisdom that is from above.* He proceeds to list the effects of heavenly wisdom, which are the opposite of those above. It is, first of all, *pure*, that is, qualified as excluding hypocrisy and selfishness. Secondly, he calls it *peaceable*, meaning, unconnected with strife. Thirdly, *gentle* or reasonable, to teach us that it is far from that undue severity which shows a brother no tolerance. Then, it is *easy to be entreated*, approachable, indicating an abhorrence of pride or spite. Lastly, he says it is *full of mercy*, while the hypocrites are inhuman, forbidding. By *good fruits* he suggests all the good offices that well-intentioned men owe to their brethren, as much as to say, in one word, full of well-doing. Consequently it is downright dishonest to glory in dark austerity. Although he had gone far enough to condemn hypocrisy, by speaking of the *pure* and sincere, he ends by repeating the point still more plainly. We are warned that there is no reason for our being so very woeful, except that we are too indulgent towards ourselves, and are conniving at our own sins. It might appear odd that he wishes it also to be 'without discernment'[1] (ἀδιάκριτος). For the Spirit of God does not abolish every distinction between good and evil, or make us so unconcerned that we lose all judgment, and admire vice as virtue. I answer, that James intended the word to cover that over-anxious and scrupulous probing, of the kind we often observe amongst hypocrites, as they search over-particularly into a brother's words or deeds, and take every item in the worse sense.

3.18. *And the fruit of righteousness.* One can take this in two senses, either that a harvest is sown for the peacemakers, which they may later reap, or that they themselves, while they put up quietly with a good deal of trouble in their lives, do not fail to sow the seed of righteousness. He is anticipating an objection. Those whose lust for censoriousness drives them to speak ill, always have the pretext: What, are we to foster evil by our permissiveness? To which James replies, Those who have true wisdom from God are to be so calm, restrained, peaceable and merciful that they will neither conceal nor favour vice, but will

[1] RV *'variance'* or RV mg 'doubtfulness' or 'partiality'.

endeavour to correct it; but with peace, that is, in a way of moderation, such as will preserve unity unimpaired. This is our evidence that there is no intention here, as far as he has discussed it, of doing away with unruffled words of admonition, as long as those would-be practitioners of healing for sin do not become executioners. This *for them that make peace* ('*facientibus pacem*') is what grammarians call a 'seventh case'. We should read the passage thus: Men who work for peace are also concerned with the sowing of righteousness, and are not idle or ineffective in promoting and encouraging good works: but they temper their zeal with the seasoning of peace, while hypocrites throw all into uproar with their blind and frantic attacks.

CHAPTER FOUR

Whence come wars and whence come fightings among you? come they not hence, even of your pleasures that war in your members? Ye lust, and have not: ye kill, and covet, and cannot obtain: ye fight and war; ye have not, because ye ask not. Ye ask, and receive not, because ye ask amiss, that ye may spend it in your pleasures. (1-3)

4.1. *Whence come wars, etc.* Having discussed peace, and noted that vice is to be purged in such a manner that peace is sustained, he takes the opportunity to speak of the quarrels that tear them apart in themselves, and explains that they come more from inordinate desires than from any interest in the right. If each could hold himself in check, men would not incite one another. Conflicts boil up, because our passions range with impunity. Ovbiously, there would be more peace amongst ourselves if we all kept clear of doing mischief. But the vices that rule in us are like raiding forces, setting on the battle. By *members*, he means all parts of us. *Pleasures* are taken as all illicit and lustful desires, such as can only be satisfied by damaging the other side.

4.2. *Ye lust, and have not.* He seems to mean that man's spirit is inexhaustible, once it indulges in wicked desires. And indeed it is so. When a man allows his appetites free rein, he will never come to an end to his lust. Even if he were given the earth, he would long to have new worlds made for him. As a result men make themselves torments beyond the cruelty of any torturer. A true word of Horace: 'Sicilian tyrants could not find a torture worse than envy.' While some texts read φονεύετε (*ye kill*) I have no doubt that we are to read φθονεῖτε (*ye are envious*), as I have rendered it. The word 'kill' has no relevance to the context.

Ye fight. He is not thinking of the wars and battles waged among men with bare weapons, but contested arguments of any kind where one party tries to come out on top of the other. The fact that they make no headway in their contests, constitutes, he declares, the penalty they pay for their unworthy actions. God does well to frustrate them, as they do not acknowledge Him as the Author of good. They struggle by means outside the law, more ready to ask favour from Satan than blessing from God. No wonder if they fall back in their efforts, for victory is only to be found by those who wait upon the blessing of God alone.

4.3. *Ye ask, and receive not.* He takes it further: Even though they ask, they deserve a refusal, for they seek to make God the Agent of their own desires. They have no sense of restraint (such as He has taught) even in their prayers: but with reckless disregard they storm in to ask for things which one would be ashamed to share mention of with another man. This is the affrontery which Pliny mocks at some point, and rightly too, for men to make such shocking abuse of the ears of God. All the more intolerable in the case of Christians, who have been given by their heavenly Master, a rule of prayer. Certainly we can have no reverence for God, no fear, no appreciation indeed, if we dare to ask things from Him which even our own conscience would deny us. In short, James intends that we should control our appetites. And the means of control is by subjecting them to God. Our reasonable desires are to be put to God Himself. By this course, we shall avoid mean contentions, deceptions and all kinds of violence amongst ourselves.

Ye adulteresses, know ye not that the friendship of the world is enmity with God? Whosoever therefore would be a friend of the world maketh himself an enemy of God. Or think ye that the scripture speaketh in vain? Doth the spirit which he made to dwell in us long unto envying? But he giveth more grace. Wherefore the scripture saith, God resisteth the proud, but giveth grace to the humble. (4-6)

4.4. *Ye* [adulterers and] *adulteresses.* I attach this sentence to the preceding. He calls adulterers, as I think, in a metaphorical sense, those who are corrupted by the vanities of this world and are estranged from God, as he might call them 'degraded', or some other epithet. We know how frequently Scripture refers to the sacred tie of marriage that God has contracted with us. He would have us as chaste virgins (cf. II Cor. 11.2), and it is this chastity which is violated and spoiled by all the impure affections of the world. Reason enough for James to compare love of the world to adultery. If his words are taken without this application, the context is not being adequately understood. He continues with an attack on the human passions which bind men to the world and draw them away from God—as follows.

A friend of the world. What he calls friendship of the world is the state of men who become addicts and slaves of the corrupt side of life. The nature and extent of the world's disagreement with God is such that every step a man takes towards the world is one step further away from God. Hence the repeated command of Scripture to renounce the world, if we would serve God.

4.5. *Or think ye.* The next sentence appears to be almost a direct citation from Scripture, and many commentators distort it for this reason: there is no such passage to be found in Scripture, no close testimony at least. But there is nothing to prevent reference to what we have just discussed, namely, the friendship of the world being inimical to God. We have said that this is a lesson often found in Scripture. He omits any pronoun, which might have made his train of thought more distinct, but we need not be surprised, as he is always very concise. We shall note this again.

Doth the spirit. Some think this is said of the human spirit, or soul. Thus they read the verse affirmatively, in this sense, man's spirit, being malevolent, being also envious, is ever soiling its affections with jealousy. But the better interpretation refers it to the Spirit of God. It is He who is given to us, that He may dwell in us. So I take this of the Holy Spirit, and take the verse as an interrogative. He wants to prove from their enviousness that they are not ruled by the Spirit of God, for His instruction of the faithful is of another order, as he stresses in the next few words where he adds, *But he giveth more grace.* Again, he is arguing from opposites. Jealousy is a symptom of ill-will, but the Spirit of God displays a generous nature, by the gifts which He lavishes. Nothing could be more repugnant to His nature than envy. In short, James says that the Spirit of God cannot rule where mean lusts flourish and tease us into quarrels with each other, for it is the character of the Spirit to invest men more and more with renewed benefits. I shall not waste time on refuting other interpretations. Some read this as saying that the Spirit yearns to overcome envy, but this is too difficult and forced. Some take *giveth more* [divine] *grace* of the Spirit working to tame envyings, to keep them in check. But the sense I have expounded is more authentic, showing that His beneficence actually reclaims us from spites and jealousies. The continuative particle δέ has the force of an adversative ἀλλά or ἀλλά γε, and so I have rendered it with *quin* [nay, but].

Be subject therefore unto God; but resist the devil, and he will flee from you. Draw nigh to God, and he will draw nigh to you. Cleanse your hands, ye sinners; and purify your hearts, ye doubleminded. Be afflicted, and mourn, and weep: let your laughter be turned to mourning, and your joy to heaviness. Humble yourselves in the sight of the Lord, and he shall exalt you. (7-10)

4.7. *Be subject therefore.* It is the submissiveness of the humble heart which he commends. This is not a general encouragement to obey

298

God, but a demand for self-abasement in terms of the Spirit of the Lord resting on the humble and peaceable (cf. Isa. 57.15). The connecting particle shows an inference is to be drawn. Having stated that the Spirit of God is generous in the increase of liberality, he infers that we should lay our enviousness aside, and be subject to God. Many texts contain an intervening sentence: Wherefore it *saith, God resisteth the proud, but giveth grace to the humble.* As other manuscripts do not have it, Erasmus suspects that it was a marginal note of some student, which later crept into the text. This may well be, though it would not be out of accord with the trend of his argument. We can easily clear up a difficulty some have found, suggesting that a citation is made as from Scripture, which can only be traced to Peter. I would conjecture that this was something of a proverbial expression, then common among the Jews. And its content is just what we find in Ps. 18.28 [v. 27, RV]: 'For thou wilt save the humble people, O Lord, but the haughty eyes thou wilt bring down.' There are many other passages.

Resist the devil. Now he discloses the direction in which we have to join battle, in the manner of Paul (Eph. 6.12), where he says that we do not struggle against flesh and blood, but must be keen to wage the warfare of the Spirit. Therefore in teaching us to be restrained towards men and submissive towards God, he points to Satan as our enemy, against whom we should fight. He adds a word of promise—that Satan will flee—which daily experience seems to contradict. Surely the more bravely we resist, the sharper we feel his pressure. Satan can be very tricky, if he is not driven back with a vigorous effort, for when men maintain their resistance, he really uncovers his power. And fighting never wearies him, for he can be beaten in one engagement, and at once take up another. My answer must be, that *flee* is taken as 'go to ruin'. Certainly for all that he brings attack after attack, he must go away, if he is not allowed in.

4.8. *Draw nigh to God.* He tells us again, that God's help will not fail us as long as we give Him opportunity. To *draw nigh to God,* in order to feel that He is near us, is a commandment that implies we were drawing away from Him, and so losing His grace. With God upholding our cause, there is no reason for us to be afraid that we may succumb. Of course, should someone infer from this passage that the initiative lies with us, and God's grace follows after, this is miles from the intention of the apostle. For though this is our duty, it does not directly follow that it is within our power. When the Spirit of God nerves us for our task, there is no derogation of His own person or prowess in fulfilling in us the very thing He commands. Briefly, James's sole object at this point is to show that unless we keep ourselves away from Him, God never fails to help us in the manner, for instance, in which someone leads starving men back to the table, or thirsty men to the spring. The only difference is, that our feet must be directed and supported by the Lord Himself, for our steps falter. The sophistry which asserts that God's grace is secondary to, and as it were a 'hanger-on' of, our preparation, on the grounds that James speaks of God's approach in second place, is quite ridiculous. We know that it is nothing new for Him to give greater gifts of grace beyond the first, thus making us ever more richly endowed, though we have received much already.

Cleanse your hands. Here the appeal is to all those estranged from God. It is not that he designates two classes of mankind, but the same people are *sinners* and *double-minded.* They are sinners in a particular sense, men of wicked and downright corrupt living, as we read (John 9.31), 'God heareth not sinners', or in the sense which Luke intends (7.37) of the 'woman . . . a sinner', and Luke again (with the other Evangelists) says, 'He eateth and drinketh with . . . sinners' (Mark 2.16). Thus not all are called, without distinction, to a show of penitence, as noted here, but from those whose hearts are depraved and corrupt, whose lives are base and appalling, or at least criminal, from such he demands purity of heart and a cleansing of their works. We can gather from this what is the true means and nature of repentance: it does not only correct the outward life, but starts from the purging of the soul, just as the opposite is true, that the fruits of inward repentance must reveal themselves in wholeness of action.

4.9. *Be afflicted, and mourn.* Christ calls 'mourning' down upon the heads of those who laugh (Luke 6.25), as a word of woe. Now James, a little later, to the same effect, cries sorrow upon the rich. Only here he treats of that saving sorrow which leads us to repentance. He calls to men who are fuddled in their minds, and have no sense of the judgment of God: which is why they indulge themselves in vice. To dispel this fatal torpor from them, he tells them to learn a lament, have their consciences touched with a note of grief, and stop—at the approach of ruin—their self-adulation and applause. *Laughter* must be taken as the pleasure-seeking, which the godless arrange for themselves; doped with the seduction of wickedness, they forget the judgment of God.

4.10. *Humble yourselves.* These thoughts lead to the conclusion, that the grace of God will be revealed to raise us up, when He sees that we have laid down our lofty aspirations. We are jealous and envious, because we long to be high and mighty. We could not be more mistaken. It is God's own pleasure to raise up the lowly, especially those who willingly resign themselves. The man who sets his heart on a sure high place should be so cast down by a sense of his own incapacity, that he will only think humbly of himself. There is a good saying of

Augustine: 'As a tree must drive its roots deep down, in order to grow up tall, the man who does not have his soul rooted in humility will find height to be his downfall.'

Speak not one against another, brethren. He that speaketh against a brother, or judgeth his brother, speaketh against the law, and judgeth the law: but if thou judgest the law, thou art not a doer of the law, but a judge. One only is the lawgiver and judge, even he who is able to save and to destroy: but who art thou that judgest thy neighbour? (11-12)

4 11. *Speak not one against another.* We can observe how insistently James reproves the passion for censoriousness. The hypocrite is ever proud, and by nature we are all hypocrites, eager to push ourselves forward at the shame and expense of others. It is a further disease, inborn in the human constitution, for every man to wish the rest to live at his own direction. In this place, just such a headstrong attitude falls under James' reproach: we dare to impose a law of life upon our brethren. Detraction—*speaking against*—covers all sorts of slander and smearing remarks, all that flows from spiteful, slanted views. The evil of defamation spreads wide. But, as I say, there is one particular aspect which he underlines here, namely our judgments superciliously handed out on the deeds and words of others, as if our grim expression was to be their law; we blandly condemn anything that displeases our eyes. The argument that follows makes clear that it is this self-assurance which he is criticizing.

He that speaketh against a brother. This means that the Law loses to the extent that we usurp its function against our brethren. To speak against the Law is contrasted with the reverence we owe it. Paul covers much the same argument in Rom. 14, albeit provoked by another subject. Some people were firmly attached to their scruples over the choice of foods which they held to be illicit, and they condemned the actions of others. He tells them, in this matter, that the Lord is one, and that all of us stand or fall by His decree, that we all must appear before His judgment seat. He concludes that the man who judges his brethren from his own feelings is taking on himself a function which belongs to God. Now James is reprehending those who condemn their brethren with the object of winning a reputation for themselves; whereby they set their own spleen into the position of the divine Law. This is really using the same reasons as Paul, to convict us of headstrong action in seizing to ourselves the domination of our brethren's lives, when the Law of God puts us all without exception on one level.

Judgment, let us be well taught, is only to be taken from the Law of God.

Thou art not a doer of the law, but a judge. The passage comes out like this: If you claim authority as censor, superior to the Law of God, then you remove yourself from the government of the Law. Thus the man who is bold enough to pass judgment on his brother, is shaking off God's yoke, for he does not submit himself to the common rule of life. Thus the argument runs from opposites, since the observance of the Law is very different from this state of arrogance, where men accord the force and authority of Law to their own foolish opinions. Consequently, we really observe the Law when we are entirely and solely dependent on its teaching, and take no other course of deciding between right and wrong; as indeed all man's deeds and words should be measured. If one objects, that the saints will judge the world (I Cor. 6.2), we may readily reply that they did not come to an honour of this order by their own right, but in as far as they are members of Christ. That they do now give judgment according to the Law, does not mean that they are to be rated judges over it, for they obediently subscribe to God, their own Judge and the Judge of all. And if we think of God, He should not be reckoned as a 'doer' of the Law, since His righteousness is superior to it. The Law flows from the eternal and vast righteousness of God as a stream flows from its source.

4.12. *One only is the lawgiver.* By attaching the power of life and death to the function of the legislator, he means that men who claim for themselves the right of laying down the law are snatching at the whole majesty of God. These are the people who force their will on others as a law. Remember please, that we are not here treating of external polity, the field where there is a place for the edicts and laws of the magistrates, but of the spiritual government of the soul, in which only the Word of God should have supremacy. God is one, rightly holding in His sway the consciences subject to Him, as He alone has in His hand the salvation or ruin of the soul. So we can have no doubt what we are to feel about those human precepts, which fling a snare of necessity upon our consciences. Some people would have us speak more softly, if we call the pope Antichrist, when he exercises a tyranny upon souls, making himself a legislator on a par with God. In fact, this passage takes us much further in logic: members of Antichrist they must be, who willingly accept these snares, and renounce Christ to the degree that they associate with him a man, not merely mortal, but one who sets himself up as his foe. I call it prevaricatory obedience—the devil's goods— to accept any other than God as Legislator for the government of souls.

Who art thou. Some think this is directed against those who criticise others for their own faults, that they should start the scrutiny with themselves, and finding they are no better than others cease to be so strict. I think he is putting men's condition, simply, before their eyes, to make them realise how far they are from that position to which they aspire; in the words of Paul (Rom. 14.4), 'Who art thou that judgest the servant of another?'

Go to now, ye that say, To-day or tomorrow we will go into this city, and spend a year there, and trade, and get gain: whereas ye know not what shall be on the morrow. What is your life? For ye are a vapour, that appeareth for a little while, and then vanisheth away. For that ye ought to say, If the Lord will, we shall both live, and do this or that. But now ye glory in your vauntings: all such glorying is evil. To him therefore that knoweth to do good, and doeth it not, to him it is sin. (13-17)

4.13. *Go to now, etc.* Here he condemns another form of pride. Many who should wait upon the providence of God, announce their future plans with assurance, arrange their policies for the long term, as though they had in their grasp a full course of years, and all the while they have no certainty even for the moment. Solomon takes an elegant and amused view of this obtuse self-assertion when he says (Prov. 16.1), 'The preparations of the heart belong to man: but the answer of the tongue is from the Lord.' It is really senseless for us to presume to carry through a purpose, which we cannot even determine with our tongues. James is not criticizing the manner of speaking, though, but rather the dumbness of the mind, that men grow so used to forgetting their own weakness. There may well be times when godly folk, with a modest opinion of themselves, recognizing their steps to be led by the will of God, may say unconditionally that they will do this or that. Let us, however, say it is right and useful, when we make any promise for future time, to make a habit of these expressions: 'God willing', or, 'God permitting'. Naturally I do not want to make a fetish of this, as though the omission should be an offence. For we frequently read in Scripture how the holy servants of God spoke of future events without qualification, although all the time they were sure in their minds that they could do nothing without God's assent. So as regards this habit of speech, 'If God will', 'If God grant it', I see it as a careful practice for all men of religion. James means to arouse those who take no respect for the providence of God from their unconcern, who take charge of the whole course of a year when they have no power over one single minute: they promise

303

themselves a profit far off, and scarcely possess the ground beneath their feet.

4.14. *What is your life?* He might have used a variety of arguments to put the brake on this crazy race of projects. Every day we see how God frustrates these proud men, who lordly promise they can do anything. But this single proof is enough for him: Who has promised you life for the morrow? If you die, will you achieve your very assured purpose? When the brevity of life comes to our minds, over-boldness is soon restrained, and our plans are kept from running too far ahead. The only reason why profane men are so careless with themselves is that they forget they are men at all. The simile of *a vapour* neatly describes how counsel is all too fleeting and only exists under the shadow of life.

4.15. *If the Lord will.*[1] There is a two part condition set out: If we survive long enough, and, if the Lord allows; for there are many things that might intervene to upset what we had decided on. The outcome of future days is hidden from us. *Will* indicates, not what is expressed in the Law, but His counsel, by which He governs all things.

4.16. *But now ye glory.* We may gather from these words that James finds fault with something more serious than stray words. *Ye glory,* he says, in your vauntings, meaning surely that in robbing God of His dominion, they are entirely pleased with themselves. Not that they openly put themselves above God, even those most puffed up with self-confidence; but their infatuation with the vanity of their own opinions makes them reduce respect for God to a minimum. And as warnings of this sort are usually treated with contempt by profaners— indeed we can hear their immediate reply, They know all too well, what is alleged, and need no warning: so he turns their awareness back upon themselves (they boast of it!), and declares that their sin is the more heinous for being the sin not of ignorance, but of contempt.

[1] Calvin reads: 'and if we shall live, etc.'

CHAPTER FIVE

Go to now, ye rich, weep and howl for your miseries that are coming upon you. Your riches are corrupted, and your garments are moth-eaten. Your gold and your silver are rusted; and their rust shall be for a testimony against you, and shall eat your flesh as fire. Ye have laid up your treasure in the last days. Behold, the hire of the labourers who mowed your fields, which is of you kept back by fraud, crieth out: and the cries of them that reaped have entered into the ears of the Lord of Sabaoth. Ye have lived delicately on the earth, and taken your pleasure; ye have nourished your hearts in a day of slaughter. Ye have condemned, ye have killed the righteous one; he doth not resist you. (1-6)

5.1. *Go to now.* In my opinion it would be mistaken to think that James here is urging repentance upon the rich. Rather, I think this is a straightforward declaration of the judgment of God, to strike them with terror and to remove all hope of pardon; all he says is in a vein of despair. He does not approach them with words which invite a change of heart; no, he is really looking to the men of faith, that they may attend to the sad ruin of the wealthy, and not be envious of their prosperity. Further, that they may know God will avenge the hurts they now suffer, and so learn to bear them with an untroubled and peaceable mind. It is not just any rich man he denounces, but such as devour all in their paths, like gaping throats, and harass others with tyrannical rage: this will appear from the context.

Weep and howl. Sorrow has a part in repentance too, but it is mixed with consolation, and does not go to the extremes of anguish. James means that the severity of the curse of heaven will be so appalling and awesome to the rich, that they will be driven to shrieks of distress, as he might say in a word—Woe unto you! Actually, his form of speaking is more by way of the prophetic, confronting the ungodly there and then with the penalties which await them, by presenting them already in vivid terms. Even while they flatter themselves, assure themselves that the fortune on which they base their supposed joys will go on for ever, he gives utterance to the fearful torment that hangs over them.

5.2. *Your riches.* We may take this two ways, either as a mockery of their foolish confidence, since the wealth on which they found their happiness is altogether transitory, and turns to nothing at one whisper of God's voice, or as a reproof of their inexhaustible avarice, since the only result of all their piling up goods is to see it perish with benefit to no-one. The latter sense fits better. True enough, the rich are out of their minds to glory in such fading things as clothing, gold, silver, and the like, for this only comes to putting their glory into the hands of rust and moth. And we all know the saying, 'Ill gains sink fast', for God's curse wears them all down. Nor is it right or proper for the wicked or their heirs to enjoy wealth that they have taken with violence, as from the hands of God. However, James here is listing the vices by which the rich draw ruin (as we noted) upon themselves, and in my opinion the context demands that we take this as his stricture on the vast acquisitiveness of the rich, for clutching at anything they can pull in, from any side, and for putting it to rot uselessly in their hoards. With the result, that what God created for human use they turn to ruin, and so they may be seen as enemies of human kind.

Now we must note, that the vices condemned here do not apply to each and every one. Some employ their wealth in a life of luxury, some lay a great deal out on display and ostentation, some cheat the social virtues and live like misers in squalor. So note that various faults are blamed on various sorts, but there is a general condemnation passed on all who either accumulate unjust riches for themselves or make a wrongful abuse of riches. James' present discussion applies not only to those who hang on to riches with the extreme parsimony of Plautus' *Euclio*, but to those whose manner of life is fine and expansive —yet they would rather see their store of possessions wasted before their eyes than let it out for necessary employment. Some have such a spite in their characters that it hurts them to share daylight or fresh air with other folk.

5.3. *For a testimony against you.* This confirms the exegesis I have outlined above. God did not appoint gold to go to waste, or clothes to be eaten by moths, but intended them to sustain human life. So to see them consume away without use testifies to the inhumanity of the possessor. The corruption of gold and silver will serve to inflame the fire of God's wrath, to burn them up in its heat. *Ye have laid up your treasure.* Even this phrase can be taken two ways—either that the rich, as if they would live for ever, are never content, but always struggle to lay things up sufficient to last to the end of time, or, that they are piling up God's wrath and curse unto the last day. I am more taken with the second interpretation.

5.4. *Behold, the hire.* He proceeds to attack the cruelty, which is the inseparable companion of avarice. One sort in particular he inveighs against, and it may well be rated more odious than the rest. For if the humane and fair man has regard for the life of his beast (Prov. 12.10), what unnatural savagery we see when man has no pity for man, whose sweated labour he exacts for his own profit. In the Law, the Lord strictly forbids us to sleep on the wages of our hired servant (Deut. 24.15). Further, James does not name workers in general, but to be complete, farmers and harvesters. What is more unworthy than bringing starvation and famine on those whose toil supplies us with our bread? Yet the fearsome deed is no rarity. There are many of such tyrannous cast of mind that they believe the human race exists for them alone. *Crieth out*, he says of their *hire*, for anything that does not belong be it kept back by fraud or by violence, demands retribution with a true, resounding call. Note what he adds, that the *cries* of the destitute reach the ears of God, telling us that injuries will not go unavenged. So let those who are under unjust oppression endure it with patience, for God shall be their champion. Let those who have it in their hands to do hurt avoid it, or they will call God down upon themselves, the Guardian and Patron of the poor. For this reason he calls God the Lord of *Sabaoth*, to indicate His power and might, and make His judgment more to be dreaded.

5.5. *Ye have lived delicately.* Now he reaches another vice, namely soft living, luxuriousness. Those who have means above the average rarely put a check on themselves, but waste their abundance on excessive splendour. I have remarked that there are some wealthy men who starve, for all their means. There is reason behind the poet's representation of Tantalus, sitting hungry at the well-plenished table. There have ever been Tantaluses in the world, but as I say James is not referring to each and every individual. We know well enough that it is a common vice which prevails upon the rich to spend overmuch and over-foolishly upon the delights of their own voracity. Though the Lord permit them to live generously at His supply, yet one must ever beware of being lavish, and keep respect for plain living. Not for nothing does the Lord by His prophets throw sharp words at those who sleep on ivory couches, who pour on precious unguents, who entrance their palates with sweetness to the notes of the zither, to all intents like fat cattle in rich pastures. All this is said to make us keep a perspective in all our creature comforts; self-indulgence wins no favour with God.

Nourished your hearts means indulgence beyond the satisfaction of nature, to match the rate of our cravings. He gives a comparison: 'as' [RV omits] *in a day of slaughter*: it was the practice on days of ritual sacrifice to feast more freely than daily use. So he says, the rich spend all their lives as one long celebration, plunged in an unending run of revelry.

5.6. *Ye have condemned.* One more type of inhuman behaviour follows—the power oppression by the rich of the weak, their campaign of ruin. It is by metaphor that he says the righteous are slain and condemned by them. They do not strangle with their own hands, they do not sit on the bench of judgment, but in directing the strength of their authority to cause hurt, by corrupting justice and arranging various schemes to destroy the innocent, truly they are agents of death and doom. When he adds that *the righteous one . . . doth not resist,* he means that the audacity of the rich increases, since those they crush are without any means of resistance. Yet at the same time he gives warning that the vengeance of God will be all the more ready and swift, as on man's side the poor are unprotected. I grant that the reason for the just making no resistance is that he ought to bear injuries with patience: at the same time, I think the reference is to his essential weakness, which is, that he does not resist because he has no force, and has no human assistance.

Be patient therefore, brethren, until the coming of the Lord. Behold, the husbandman waiteth for the precious fruit of the earth, being patient over it, until it receive the early and latter rain. Be ye also patient; stablish your hearts: for the coming of the Lord is at hand. Murmur not, brethren, one against another, that ye be not judged: behold, the judge standeth before the doors. (7-9)

5 7. *Be patient therefore.* The inference shows definitely that all that has been said to this point against the rich pertains to the comforting of those who, for the present time, appear to be exposed to their violence. After reviewing the reasons for the disasters which threaten the rich, amongst which he records their proud and heartless domination of the poor, he at once goes on to say that we who are unjustly harassed have real grounds for patience, as God will be our Judge. Such is his intention when he says, *until the coming of the Lord*: the confusion which we see in the world today will not go on for ever, for the Lord, by His coming, will bring all back to order, and for that we must gather our spirits to have good hope. There is substance in his promise to us of a universal restoration. Though the day of the Lord is frequently named in Scripture as one of judgment, and of grace revealed, succour to His own, and chastisement for the ungodly, I should prefer to take this passage of the final deliverance.

Behold, the husbandman. Paul touches on the same simile at II Tim. 2.6, where he says that the farming man must labour, before he gathers the crop.[1] James puts it more fully. He describes the long patience of

[1] cf. RV ad loc.

308

the farmer; how he entrusts the seed to the soil, then waits with mind detached, or at least patient, until the time of harvest comes; he does not grudge the fact that the earth does not immediately produce the mature fruit. We are to realize that we should not be unduly anxious if this should be our time of labour and of sowing, and not yet the appearance of the day of the Lord—our harvest-time.

The precious fruit. I take the epithet to suggest its nourishment, its power to sustain life. James means that as the farmer allows his life, which is so precious to him, to lie hidden in the bosom of the earth, and patiently contains his desire for harvesting the crop, we would surely be too hurried and demanding if we did not wait for the day of our redemption, with calm minds. There is no need to go through every detail of the rest of the comparison.

The early . . . rain. Two seasons are noted by these terms, the former which comes a little after sowing, and the latter while the crops mature. This was the language of the prophets, when they wished to describe the right seasons for rain, as Moses promised (Deut. 28.12; cf. Joel 2.23 and Hos. 6.3). He records them both, to express more ably how the farmers are not worn out with the tedium of such a long period that they cannot bear the delay.

5.8. *Stablish your hearts.* In case any object, that the time of deliverance is put off too long, he anticipates their thoughts by saying that the Lord is at hand, or (to say the same thing), His coming is near. Meanwhile he tells them to cure softness of heart, which may make us weak and unable to persevere in hope. The time appears long, of course, because we are feeble and frail. Hence we must gather strength, and be firm, and from what better source, than from the hope, the virtual sight, of the close coming of the Lord!

5.9. *Murmur not.* Since there are complainers all about us, claiming to be worse treated than others, some expound this passage as James' instruction to every man to be content with his lot, not to envy others, and not to be upset if other people have an easier life. My interpretation is on different lines. He has discussed the wretched end of those who tyrannize and molest decent and peaceable men: now he urges the faithful to treat each other on a level, and to be tolerant in condoning offences. The continuation of the argument shows that this is the true sense. Do not be querulous, he says, *one against another, that ye be not judged*, all of you. Perhaps we may murmur, if some misfortune gives us pain, but he means murmuring in accusation, which some take to God with claims one against the other. He makes a declaration that the only outcome of this will be for all to be condemned, for there is no-one who does not offend his brother, and give grounds for complaint. So if they all grumble, they will accuse each other in turn.

No-one is blameless enough, not to have hurt somebody, and God will be the common Judge of them all. The inevitable consequence will be that each will bring on himself the judgment he asked for the other; all will be heard, all will come to grief. Better for no-one to ask vengeance upon others, unless he wish to involve himself in the same. And to stop such protests being launched without thought, he reminds them that the Judge is standing at the door. We have a great propensity to take God's Name in vain, and call on Him to judge the most trifling offences. No bridle is more suited to holding back our headstrong temper than the thought that our imprecation does not go off into thin air, for close at hand there is the judgment of God.

Take, brethren, for an example of suffering and of patience, the prophets who spake in the name of the Lord. Behold, we call them blessed which endured: ye have heard of the patience of Job, and have seen the end of the Lord, how that the Lord is full of pity, and merciful. (10-11)

5.10. *Take . . . for an example.* The comfort he applies is not on the level of the proverbial 'Beggar help beggar'. As companions in distress he names those whose company one might well wish to join, and with whom it would be no beggary to share conditions. By necessity we should be cast into profound sorrow if some disaster struck us, such as never before was known by the sons of God: but here is our extraordinary comfort, in knowing that we suffer nothing different from them, yes, recognising that we are being formed to undergo precisely the same yoke as they bear. When Job heard his friends say (Job. 5.1), 'Turn to the holy ones, and see if you will find any, who may be like yourself?'—this was the voice of Satan, willing to throw him into desperation. By contrast, when the Spirit, through the utterance of James, wishes to fill us with staunch hope, He shows us all the Saints who go before, who (as it were) stretch out their hand to us, and by their example invite us to undergo, and surmount, the same afflictions. The life of man is subject to pain and conflict quite indiscriminately, but James does make an example of the generality of men (for there is no advantage in perishing with the crowd), but picks upon the prophets, whose fellowship is blessed. A feeling of wretchedness is peculiarly able to cause our breakdown and collapse. So it is a real consolation to know that what the world takes to be misfortune is for us a means of salvation. To the understanding of the flesh, this is strange: but the faithful may be sure that when they are tried by the Lord with various pains, they are blessed.

To press home his point, James tells us to consider, in the person of the prophets, what was the end of their afflictions. In our troubles, we are taken up with sorrow and grief and all kinds of extreme emotions, and cannot form a judgment. We are like men tossed on the storm under a lowering sky, amidst the sweeping gales—we can see nothing. So we must turn our eyes elsewhere, and find the clearer skies, the calm air. When we read of the sufferings of the Saints, none of us would call them wretched, but indeed blessed. James is right to put this example before our eyes, that we may learn to consider it in any time of trial when we lose patience or hope. He draws out the principle that the prophets are reckoned blessed in their afflictions because they endured them with constancy. It follows that we should make the same conclusion when we are in affliction.

He speaks of *the prophets who spake in the name of the Lord,* by which he means that these were under God's favour and approval. Hence if it had been better for them to have been excused their distresses, doubtless God would have kept them free of them. But He did not: it follows that affliction is salutary for the faithful. In this sense he wants them taken as an example of suffering, but not to the exclusion of patience, which is the true testimony of our obedience: the two are conjoined in his appeal.

5.11. *The patience of Job.* He has spoken of the prophets in general, and now chooses one outstanding example from them all. No-one, as far as our narratives reveal, was ever overcome with such hard and various torments, and yet he came out of that profound abyss with head high. Should any man imitate his patience, no doubt he will likewise feel the hand of God come at last to his relief. Observe the end to which these accounts are written. God did not allow His servant Job to be vanquished for he endured his pains with patience: so the patience of no man will be wasted. But one asks, why does the apostle so greatly commend the patience of Job, who in fact under the shock of the blind catastrophe showed considerable signs of impatience. The answer is, that even though on occasion he lapses through weakness of the flesh, and actually wrestles with himself, yet he always comes back to entrusting himself wholly to God, and offering Himself to His restraining and controlling arm. So though his patience lack a little here and there, it well deserves praise.

The end of the Lord. The point of the word is that affliction is always to be assessed by its conclusion. At the outset, God seems to be far away, and at this time Satan takes the liberty of working upon this sense of alarm, and the flesh suggests within us that we are deserted and betrayed by God: so we must stretch our understanding further, as in the short view there is not enough light. And a further reason for saying, *the end of the Lord*: it is for Him to turn adversity to happy effect. If we do our duty of obeying and enduring, He will not fail on His part. Only let hope direct us on our course, and at the end God will reveal Himself in turn even more merciful, for all that in time of trouble He seemed stern and severe.

But above all things, my brethren, swear not, neither by the heaven, nor by the earth, nor by any other oath: but let your yea be yea, and your nay, nay; that ye fall not under judgement. Is any among you suffering? Let him pray. Is any cheerful? let him sing praise. (12-13)

5.12. *But above all things*, etc. It has been a common vice in almost all ages to swear without reason or consideration: our thoughts are evil, and we do not reckon how atrocious a crime it is to dishonour the Name of God. But as the Lord meanwhile enjoins us in solemn terms to have reverence for His Name, men devise various subterfuges by which they may swear with impunity. They pretend that there is no harm as long as they do not openly bring in God's Name—this is an old device. When the Jews, therefore, swore by heaven and earth, they thought it was no abuse of the Name of God, for they did not speak it. Yet all the time men think they are being ingenious, and putting up a smoke-screen in front of God, they are only deluding themselves with frivolous excuses. Christ inveighed against this sort of folly, as we see at Matt. 5.34, and now James endorses his Master's rule, by telling us to avoid indirect turns of phrase of this sort, for in fact a man does abuse the Name of God by swearing vainly, and for no consequence, however he may dress up his words. In short, it is no more permissible to swear by heaven and earth, than by the Name of God outright. Christ gives the reason: God's glory is set on all things, and His light is everywhere. So there is no other sense or purpose in men taking the words *heaven* or *earth* for their oaths, than if they named God Himself: to speak like this, effectively names the Creator in His created things.

He says, *above all things*, for it is no light offence to profane the Name of God. When the Anabaptists make pretext of this passage to condemn all oath-taking, they display some lack of vision. James is not discussing the taking of oaths in the widest sense, any more than is Christ, in the place I referred to: both in fact refute the misguided plea, which had been invented to cheat the Law, by men endeavouring to enjoy a freedom to swear without actually naming God. A freedom (I say) quite opposed to the prohibition of the Law. Now the words quoted make this absolutely clear: *neither by the heaven, nor by the earth.* If we were dealing with a more fundamental issue, would there be any point in noting these expressions? I am quite sure, that in the words of both Christ and James, a reproof is given to the current childish notion of those who thought they could swear without trouble, as long as they went round in a circle. To grasp James' message, we must give first place to what the Law lays down: 'Thou shalt not take the Name of thy God in vain.' This makes certain that there is some legitimate use of God's Name. They are, however, attempting to abuse it by a circle of words, and this the Law condemns.

But let your yea be yea. The treatment he prescribes to correct the condition noted above is most effective—to practise in all one's utterance a habit of telling the truth and sticking to it. This custom of false swearing stems entirely from our giving no credence to plain speech, amongst all the vanities of life. If our speech showed a proper respect for honesty, there would be no need for all these unnecessary oaths. Thus men's lack of trust, their inconsistency, is the source from which springs the corrupt use of swearing, and to remove the latter vice James says we must deal also with the former. The means of cure must start with the cause of the disease. Some texts read, 'Let your speech be, Yea, Yea: Nay, Nay.' The true reading is the one I have given, which is actually more accepted. It means, as I have explained, that we should be truthful and steady in all that we say. In the same sense Paul testifies in II Cor. 1.17-18, that he had not been brought to task for changing 'Yea' to 'Nay' in his preaching, but had kept to the same lines on which he began.

That ye fall not under judgment. There is a variant reading, due to affinity of sounds—ἀπόκρισιν and ὑπόκρισιν.[1] If we read, 'into judgment', or, 'into condemnation', the sense will be clear, that the Name of God will not be taken in vain with impunity. However there is appropriateness in reading, 'into hypocrisy', for (as we have just said), when plain dealing flourishes in our midst, futile oaths have lost their whole support. If we are trusty and sure in all our words, then pretence is done away, the very incentive to wild oaths.

5.13. *Is any among you suffering.* He indicates that there is no time at which God does not call us to Himself. Sufferings should stimulate us to pray, prosperity should provide material for the praise of God. Men are so depraved, that they cannot enjoy themselves until they forget about God, and when they are in trouble they go into depressions, and sink into utter despair. Here is a balance we must preserve,

[1] The former, if read, could read 'to give answer', but κρίσιν itself is 'judgment' of RV; the latter is 'hypocrisy'.

313

that the enjoyment which usually inclines us to be forgetful of God should stir us to declare His goodness, and the sorrows should give us a mind for prayer. The word *sing praise* (*psallendi*) is contrasted against the profane or abandoned revelling of those who celebrate good fortune which does not lead them, as it should, to God.

Is any among you sick? let him call for the elders of the church; and let them pray over him, anointing him with oil in the name of the Lord: and the prayer of faith shall save him that is sick, and the Lord shall raise him up; and if he have committed sins, it shall be forgiven him. (14-15)

5.14. *Is any among you sick.* At that time, the gift of healing still flourished, and he teaches that they, in sickness, should have recourse to this remedy. Now we are sure that not all were healed, but that the Lord gave this grace as often and as far as He recognised it to be expedient. Nor is it likely that anointing of oil was given indiscriminately, but only where there was a positive hope of success. Along with the healing power, the ministers were given a discernment, in case they should profane the symbol by abuse. James' sole purpose was to commend this charism of God, which the faithful could at that time enjoy, and prevent its benefit being lost by contempt or neglect. And for this reason, he wants the elders [*presbyteros*] summoned. The use of unction must be restricted to the effective working of the Holy Spirit. Papists make a great song and dance over this passage, when they want to peddle their 'extreme unction'. The difference between their corrupt version of the old institution (as noted by James) is something I shall avoid discussing at the present. This is a subject readers may find treated in the *Institutio*. I would only say that the passage is mistakenly and foolishly distorted, to give any sense of 'extreme unction', or to have it called a Sacrament, which should for ever be allowed to continue as a use of the Church. I quite admit that its use was seen as sacramental by Christ's disciples (and rebut the opinion that it was regarded as a medicament); but as the true effect of the sign did not last beyond this period, I would say that the symbol itself was only temporary. This is really quite evident: there is nothing more absurd than to call something a Sacrament which is empty, and does not truly offer us the matter signified. That the gift of healing was temporary, all are bound to confess, for events themselves confirm it: so its sign should not be perpetual either. Consequently, they are not true imitators of the apostles, but apes, when they place 'Unction' among the sacraments today, and do not bring us back the effect, which God withdrew from the world fourteen hundred years ago. Thus I have no argument over unction ever having been a sacrament, but over this question: Was it given to us in such fashion that it would still be in use amongst us to this day? To which I answer, No, as it is certain that the matter signified has long since departed.

The elders of the church. I would include all in general who had a place of government in the Church. Not only Pastors are called *presbyteri*, but the men chosen from the people to act as 'censors' for the oversight of discipline. Each separate Church had its own quasi-senate, chosen from reliable men, of proven integrity. Since it was the practice to choose those endowed with more outstanding gifts, he accordingly tells them to summon the elders, being those in whom the power and grace of the Holy Spirit were most exerted.

Let them pray over him. The object of the rite of praying over a man was, as it were, to set him in the presence of God, for when circumstances are brought home to us, we find a greater warmth in our prayers. Compare Elijah (II Kings 4.34), and Paul (Acts 20.10), and Christ Himself (John 11.41-42), all using this action to arouse the ardour of prayer, and commend the grace of God. We must note how he attaches a promise to the prayer, for it must not be made without faith. Hesitant requests are neither the proper mode of approach to God, nor deserve to be successful—as we read in the first chapter. The man who wishes to be heard must assure himself that he is not praying in vain. Similarly, James draws attention to the particular thing given, and added simply as an external rite. We are thus to understand that without faith there is no proper application even of the oil. Now since we find papists so completely devoid of any assurance in their use of unction, that we may take it as evident that the gift is not in them, obviously their practices are bogus.

5.15. *And if he hath committed sins, etc.* This is added, not simply as an expansion of the point, as if to say that God will give the invalid something greater than health of body, but inasmuch as diseases are most often inflicted upon us for our sins, he speaks of their being forgiven, meaning that the cause of the evil will thereby be removed. Can we not see how David, afflicted with illness, sought relief by wholehearted prayer for his sins to be pardoned? Was it not his only motive, to recognise the effect of his guilt in the pains he suffered, and to find no other remedy than for God to desist from imputing his offences to him? The prophets are full of this teaching, that men are delivered from their ills when they are cleared of the guilt of their misdeeds. Eventually we come to admit that the treatment most fit for our sickness, and other misfortune, is to take thought for the favour of God, and pardon won for sin, and to be diligent in self-examination.

Confess therefore your sins one to another, and pray one for another, that ye may be healed. The supplication of a righteous man availeth much in its working. Elijah was a man of like passions with us, and he prayed fervently that it might not rain; and it rained not on the earth for three years and six months. And he prayed again; and the heaven gave rain, and the earth brought forth her fruit. (16-18)

5.16. *Confess . . . one to another.* In several texts the particle 'therefore' is included, and it is quite appropriate; even though it is not expressed, one has to understand it so. He had said that sins are remitted to the sick, over whom the elders have made prayer. He proceeds to show what benefit there is in uncovering our sins to our brethren, since surely by their prayers we may obtain pardon. I know this passage is often interpreted of offences being reconciled, as those who wish to return to favour must first acknowledge their fault and make confession. The upshot is that ill-feeling grows roots, becomes firm set, if not irreconcileable, while each party stubbornly defends his own case. Many believe that James is presenting them here with a way to fraternal reconciliation, by mutual admission of sins: however, he had a different object, as we have stated. He puts mutual prayer together with mutual confession, and he means that the advantage of confession is to find assistance from the prayers of our brethren in the sight of God. Such as appreciate our real needs are prompted to intercede on our behalf, while those who have no knowledge of our troubles are less forward in bringing help. I am amazed at the folly of the papists—or is it wickedness?—who attempt to extract their whispering confessional from this proof. You could readily make James' words imply that only priests ought to make confession. The mutual, or 'turn-about' confession (to speak rather insensibly), here required is certainly imposed in terms of those men confessing their sins who are in return fitted to hear the confession of others. Now, priests say that they alone have this office, and that confession is appointed solely for them. Really, their fatuous ideas are not worth the time spent on their refutation, and we should be content with the true and authentic exposition which I have produced. The words are quite unambiguous: confession is only taught us to the end that those who know our troubles may have more care to lend us their aid.

Availeth much. In case anyone should think that there is no benefit gained by others praying for us, he sets out the usefulness and the effect of prayer. He explicitly calls it the *supplication of a righteous man,* for God does not listen to the wicked, and the only approach to God is through a good conscience. Not that our prayers depend on our own worthiness, but because we must have a heart purged by faith, in order

316

to present ourselves before God's sight. James therefore testifies that there is benefit, and no lack of effect, in the righteous and faithful men praying for us.

What then is the sense of the last words, *in its working*? It appears to be superfluous: if prayer is greatly to our advantage, doubtless it works effectively. The old interpretation rendered it as 'assiduous', but this forces the sense. James uses the Greek participle ἐνεργουμένη, which has exactly the force of *operans*—*in its working*. One might resolve the question of prayer thus: It is of great benefit, because it is effective—an argument deriving from the principle that God does not wish the prayers of the faithful to be frustrated or idle. The inference would be quite proper, that they have great force. However, I prefer to restrict this to the present context: our prayers may well be said to be working, when we are faced with some emergency and are moved to a serious attitude of prayer. Day by day, we pray for the whole Church, that God may remit her sins, but our prayers are really engaged when we struggle to win help for those who are in the toils. Such an effectiveness cannot be in our brothers' prayers unless they know of our plight. So it is not a general reference back to the cause, but something that should be matched closely with the logic of the previous sentence.

5.17. *Elijah was a man.* There are countless instances in Scripture of the matter he wishes to prove, but he selects one that outshines the rest. It was a notable event for God to put heaven, in some sense, under the control of Elijah's prayers, to be obedient to his requests. By his prayers, Elijah kept heaven shut for two years and a half. Then he opened it, and made it suddenly pour with a great rain, from which we may see the miraculous power of prayer. The narrative is familiar, indeed famous, and is to be found at I Kings 17 and 18. Although it is not there stated explicitly that Elijah prayed, we may easily gather that the drought and the rain were granted in answer to his prayers. Now we must observe the application of the case. James does not say that we must ask a drought from the Lord, because Elijah achieved one. (Our unthinking zeal might make us imitate the prophet in rash and mad requests.) We must keep to the rule of prayer, that it be by faith. This is the example he presses upon us, that if Elijah gained a hearing, we too shall gain one for prayers, duly offered. There is one rule of prayer, one promise, and consequently there will be one effect.

If it be objected that we are a long way from the standing of Elijah, he sets him on our level by saying, he was a mortal *man of like passions with us*. We lose some benefit of the saints' examples when we imagine them to be demigods or heroes, who enjoyed a special relationship with God. We gain no increase in confidence from the fact that they win their petitions. James would have this gentile or pagan super-

317

stition knocked clean away, and tells us to consider the saints in the infirmity of their flesh, and learn to attribute all they have won from God not to their merits, but to the efficacy of their prayer. This reveals the childish whimsy of the papists, who bid us have recourse to the inheritance of the saints, since their voices were heard by the Lord. Their argument is: Because, while he lived in the world, he obtained what he requested, he will now be, after death, the best patron for us. The Holy Spirit knows nothing of this sophistry. The opposite is James' reasoning: because their prayers had such force, we ought to follow their example today in a like fashion, and this we shall do and not be disappointed.

My brethren, if any among you do err from the truth, and one convert him; let him know, that he which converteth a sinner from the error of his way shall save a soul from death, and shall cover a multitude of sins. (19-20)

5.20. *Let him know.* I wonder whether the original was not γινώσκετε —'know ye' [RV mg]? In either case the sense will be the same. James commends to us the correcting of the brethren from its effect, in order that we should pursue it with more enthusiasm. There is nothing more noble, or more to be desired, than to wrest a soul from eternal death, and this is what a man does when he recalls his erring brother to the way. We must not neglect such splendid work. To give food to the hungry and drink to the thirsty—we know how Christ values these: but the salvation of the soul is far more precious to Him than the life of the body. So we must beware, or souls redeemed by Christ may perish by our carelessness, for their salvation to some degree was put into our hands by God. We do not confer salvation upon them, but God uses our ministry to deliver and preserve what otherwise seemed near destruction. Some texts read 'his soul', without changing the sense in any way. I prefer the alternative reading for its greater energy.

Shall cover a multitude of sins. This is an allusion to a saying of Solomon's, rather than a direct citation. He says (Prov. 10.12), that 'love covereth all transgressions, while hate stirreth up strife'. Those who have hatred, burn up with a mutual passion for defamation, while those who have love, freely condone many matters amongst themselves: so with men, love buries sins. James' message has a deeper significance, that they are also removed from the sight of God, as one might say, Solomon declared that it was the fruit of charity to cover

318

transgression, but the finest and most salutary means of concealment is that which leads to their complete removal from the presence of God. And this is what happens when the sinner, by our word of warning, is brought back onto the road: to this end we should turn our chief and unremitting energies.

THE EPISTLE OF JUDE

INTRODUCTION

THE THEME

This epistle also has been the subject of controversy among former critics, of differing opinions, but it is useful to read it, and it does not contain anything divergent from the pure apostolic doctrine. All the best authorities have long since accepted its worth, and I am happy to include it with the rest. Its brevity asks for no lengthy word of preface, and its essence is very close to II Pet. 2. Under the cloak of Christianity, there had been subtle inroads made by ungodly deceivers, with a supreme desire to tempt the unthinking and the insecure into a profane contempt for God. Jude's principal point is to show that the faithful should not be swayed by devices of this sort, which have always been tried against the Church, and he adds words of encouragement, that they should keep themselves awake and prevent such trouble-makers. To make the enemy more hateful and detestable, he calls down upon them in stern language the near vengeance of God, to fit the merits of their wickedness. And if we think what Satan has engineered against this generation, in the time of the rebirth of the Gospel, with what craftiness he labours to subvert faith, and the fear of God, then the warnings which were profitable in the time of Jude are all the more needed in our own. All this will be better understood from the reading of the Epistle.

JUDAS, a servant of Jesus Christ, and brother of James, to them that are called, beloved in God the Father, and kept for Jesus Christ: Mercy unto you and peace and love be multiplied. (1-2)

1. *Judas, a servant of Jesus Christ, etc.* Calling himself a servant of Christ, he is not considering the general sense, in which this title belongs to all faithful people, but rather his apostleship. Men, upon whom Christ has laid some public office, are to be taken as His servants in a particular sense. And we are aware of the implications of this title, which is customarily worn by the apostles. No-one will boldly claim the right and authority to teach, unless he has been called, and so the apostles take it as a witness to their calling that they do not practice on their own choice. Of course it would not be enough in itself to be appointed to office, if they did not apply themselves to it faithfully. Both are included, when a man states that he is God's servant—God is the source of the work he is given to do, and he must perform with good faith what is entrusted to him. I say this, because there are many who use the title to deceive, and falsely profess to be something that is very far from them, but we must always see if the substance corresponds to the profession.

Brother of James. He sets down a name better known and recognized among the Churches. The faithfulness and authority of doctrine do not depend on any mortal, but it is a great help to faith when we are sure of the integrity of the man who assumes the role of teacher. Besides, presenting James' authority is not like that of any ordinary individual, but as of a man regarded in all the Churches as one of Christ's leading apostles. This was the son of Alphaeus, as I have noted elsewhere. To my mind, this passage tells against the view of Eusebius and others who say that it was some disciple, James surnamed Oblias, who (compare Luke at Acts 15.13 and 21.18) had a superior position to the apostles in the Church of that time. Quite certainly, Jude names his brother here for the high reputation he had amongst the apostles. Likely this is he whom Luke describes, as receiving the highest dignity amongst the rest.

To them that are called . . . in God. Thus he designates all the faithful, as the Lord has separated them to Himself: the calling, being merely the effect of outward election, is sometimes found to stand for it. At this point, it makes little difference which way we take it. Without doubt, he is commending the grace of God, by which He has condescended to attach them to His flock. He indicates that men never take the initiative over God, or ever approach Him, until He starts to draw them. He also calls them sanctified [RV, *beloved*] *in God the Father*, which we may translate as 'through God the Father'. I have kept the form of his expression, to allow the reader to judge for himself. One could read in this sense: They find in God the sanctification, for what in themselves was profane. The means of sanctification, is by His Spirit giving us regeneration. The alternative reading ἠγαπημένοις, that is, 'beloved' in God the Father, is followed by the Vulgate, and is rather more difficult. I take it to be a corruption [i.e. of ἡγιασμένοις], and certainly it is only found in a small number of manuscripts.

He goes on to add, *kept for Jesus Christ*. We are always open to Satan's fatal stroke. At any moment he might snatch us a hundred times over into his ready clutches, were we not safe in the protection of Christ. Indeed the Father gave Him as our Guardian for this cause, that none of those whom He had taken under His trust and influence should be lost. So Jude declares, there is a threefold blessing of God upon all men of religion: He calls them to share in the Gospel, He re-creates them by His Spirit unto newness of life, and, by Christ's arm, He defends them, lest they are cut off from salvation.

2. *Mercy unto you*. The word 'mercy' has virtually the same effect as 'grace' in the greetings of Paul. If you want to make a more precise distinction, grace is strictly an effect of mercy, for the one reason for God embracing us in His love is the regard He has for our sorry state. *Love*—you may understand as God's love towards men, or of men's to each other. In the former sense, he wishes it to increase in them, and day by day may the assurance of divine love to be established in their hearts. The latter sense is quite agreeable, that God may kindle and encourage their affection one for another.

Beloved, while I was giving all diligence to write unto you of our common salvation, I was constrained to write unto you exhorting you to contend earnestly for the faith which was once for all delivered unto the saints. For there are certain men crept in privily, even they who were of old set forth unto this condemnation, ungodly men, turning the grace of our God into lasciviousness, and denying our only Master and Lord, Jesus Christ. (3-4)

3. *While I was giving all diligence*. I have translated σπουδὴν ποιούμενος as 'applying energy'; the strict rendering would be 'making diligence'. Many interpreters take the sentence in the sense that a great burst of

323

energy drove Jude to write—in the way that we say, of those who are burning with a real enthusiasm for their subject, that they cannot stop themselves. Some kind of compulsion, according to them, seized upon Jude, till he could not contain his urge to put pen to paper. But I rather think there are two distinct things here: that he was already well-inclined, and diligently engaged upon his letter, when he felt the further pressure of necessity. That is, he was glad and indeed anxious to write to them, but he was also compelled by events to take it in hand, since (as the context goes on to show) they were attacked by forces of evil, and had to get instructions for battle. In the first place, Jude testifies to the great interest he had for their salvation, leading to his free inclination to write them, yes, his enthusiasm. Secondly, to raise their attention, he says that force of events demanded his action. Necessity makes a sharp spur. If they had not been advised in advance of the urgency of his appeal, they might have been careless and taken no action about it. To say, in his preface, that he is writing to meet their actual needs, is like sounding a trumpet to rouse their dull minds.

Of our common salvation. Some texts have the insertion 'your'— wrongly, in my judgment, since he is treating of salvation as shared between him and them. It adds a good deal of weight to the message one is putting across when a man speaks out of his own understanding and experience. Our words will be quite ineffective if we discuss salvation with others, and have no taste for it in ourselves. Jude declares himself to be (what I may call) a practising instructor, when he joins himself to the number of the godly in one fellowship of the same salvation.

Exhorting you, etc. is the literal reading, but as the argument indicates the purpose of his proposal, we should read thus: 'To have you exhorted', etc. My translation, 'to aid the faith by your endeavours',[1] is intended to give the effect of striving to hold on to the faith, and bravely standing up to the hostile assaults of Satan. He warns them to stand by their faith; and so they must meet a number of trials, and hold out for a long campaign. Faith he describes as *once for all delivered*, so that they may realise the terms on which they are won, and never fail or falter.

4. *Crept in privily.* Though Satan always wages war on the godly, and goads them without ceasing, Jude is now alerting those to whom he writes of an immediate crisis. Now, he tells them, Satan has a special scheme of attack and provocation: they must therefore take up their weapons and fight back. We gather how the good and faithful pastor must take prudent note of what the present circumstances of the Church require, in order to suit his advice to the occasion. The word

[1] RV, *contend earnestly for.*

324

παρεισεδύσαν which he uses means an indirect and furtive insinuation, by which Satan's agents deceive the unwary. It is by night, when the farmers sleep, that Satan sows his tares, to waste the pure seed of the Lord. We are also told that the evil is within their ranks. This is another device of Satan's, to suborn mischief from those who are of the flock, that they may sneak in more readily.

They who were of old set forth. He speaks of the *condemnation* or 'doom' or 'reprobate condition' which lies at the end of those who subvert the teaching of the truth. It is an action no man can pursue, except to his own ruination. The metaphor derives from the fact that God's eternal purpose, wherein the faithful are ordained to salvation, is called a Book. When the faithful hear that these men are set on the path of eternal death, they should beware of being caught up in the same destruction, though (at the same time) James is wanting to anticipate the danger that they will be disturbed or shaken by the suddenness of the affair. If these men were long since 'written down', it follows certainly that, what the Church experiences, comes from the sure counsel of God.

The grace of our God, etc. He explains more exactly what is the nature of this plague. He says, they have perverted the grace of the Lord, prostituted themselves and others to a foul and blasphemous career of sin. The revelation of the grace of God was to a far different intent, namely, that we should deny ungodliness and earthly desires, and live soberly, righteously and religiously in this world. Let us realise how pestilential above all other is this breed of men, who seize upon the grace of Christ as a pretext for licentiousness. As we teach that our salvation comes to us through the freely given mercy of God, the papists bring this false charge upon us. But is there any point in refuting their impudence in words, when at every turn we insist on penitence, the fear of God, and newness of life?, while they are corrupting the whole world with their wicked example, and indeed, by their unholy doctrine, are abolishing the real sanctity of life and the pure worship of God? However, I tend to think that Jude is speaking of such as are comparable to the 'free thinkers' of our day; as we shall see better from the context.

God . . . the only Master [RV mg]. Some old texts read, 'Christ, who is the only God and Master'. Certainly, in II Pet. 2.1, there is reference only to Christ, and He is called Master [RV, 'Lord'] there. *Denying . . . Christ*, he says, of those who have been redeemed by His blood, and now enslave themselves again to the devil, frustrating (as best they may) that incomparable boon. That Christ may keep us within His fold, let us remember that He died for us and rose again, to be the Lord of our living and our dying.

325

Now I desire to put you in remembrance, though ye know all things once for all, how that the Lord, having saved a people out of the land of Egypt, afterward destroyed them that believed not. And angels which kept not their own principality, but left their proper habitation, he hath kept in everlasting bonds under darkness unto the judgement of the great day. Even as Sodom and Gomorrah, and the cities about them, having in like manner with these given themselves over to fornication, and gone after strange flesh, are set forth as an example, suffering the punishment of eternal fire. (5-7)

5. *To put you in remembrance.* It may be tactful modesty of approach, avoiding an impression of telling them, like a beginner's class, things they never knew; or it may be (and I think this is better) to add force to his words, that he states that his appeal has nothing strange or unheard-of about it, and so what he is about to say should be given more trust and weight. He says, I am only recalling to you what you have already once learnt. Just as he refers to the knowledge they have for themselves, to make them more alert and careful, so, in case they should think the effort he is expending on them is unnecessary, he says that they are in need of words of caution. It is the way of God's Word not only to teach us what we never knew before, but also to give us an impulse to ponder seriously on the lessons we have covered, and not to allow our knowledge to sink into dull indolence. To sum up: once we have been called by God, we must not idly glory in His grace, but rather walk circumspectly in His paths, for if a man mocks God in this fashion, his contempt of grace will come to cost him dear. He proves this by three instances. The first records the vengeance that God took on the unbelievers whom God had redeemed by His mighty work, and gathered into the ranks of His people. Paul makes almost the same comparison at I Cor. 10. In short, those on whom God had lavished the highest blessings, lifted to an equal rank of honour, as we today enjoy from Him, were afterwards punished severely. Vainly will men boast of the grace of God, who do not respond to His calling. *A people* is a title of honour, indicating the holy and chosen Race. In other words, it did them no good, to receive the singular privilege of admission to the covenant. *That believed not* describes the source of all the wrong. From this source flow all the sins that Moses records against them—they did not suffer the Word of God to be their rule. When we put on the yoke of faith, then in all parts of our lives we maintain a sure obedience towards God.

6. *And angels, etc.* The argument is from greater to lesser. The state of the angels was higher than ours, yet the example of the vengeance God brought upon their disloyalty is terrifying. Our treason,

therefore, will not be forgiven, if we turn back on the grace to which He has called us. Certainly the penalty that was inflicted on the inhabitants of the skies, on the great and exalted ministers of God, should never leave our thoughts, for fear that, when we may be led to spurn the grace of God, we fall headlong into the abyss.

Principality. Ἀρχή in this passage may well be taken either as 'beginning' or 'dominion'. Jude means that they paid the penalty for despising the goodness of God and lapsing from their original vocation. The exposition follows directly, when he says, *left their proper habitation.* For, exactly as we are used to seeing with deserters in wartime, they abandon the post to which they were stationed. We must note the dreadful picture of the penalty which the apostle draws. Not only had they been free Spirits, but also heavenly dominations: now they are held in the grip of perpetual bondage. Not only had they enjoyed the glorious light of God, but His splendour was reflected in them, that they might diffuse themselves, like rays of the sun, to every corner of the earth. Now, however, they are plunged into darkness. We must not try to imagine the place where the devils are imprisoned. The apostle intended simply to show how wretched was their state, since they lost their honour, by their own apostasy. Wherever they may travel, they draw their chains after them, and remain involved in their own shades. And meanwhile their final torment is put off to the last day.

7. Even as Sodom and Gomorrah. This example is more general, giving testimony that God punishes without discrimination, without excepting any race of mankind, every sort of wickedness. Jude himself goes on to record that the fire in which the five towns were consumed is a type of the everlasting flame. So at that time God set forth a striking demonstration, to impress His fear upon men, even to the end of time. And so it is mentioned very frequently in Scripture. As often as the prophets desire to mark some memorable or fearful judgment of God, and paint it in terms of that fire and brimstone, they make allusion to the overthrow of Sodom and Gomorrah. Good reason, then, for Jude to bring forward the same image to deter all ages.

When he says, *and the cities about them, having in like manner with these given themselves over to fornication,* I take it he is not referring to the Israelites, or to the angels, but to the contact with Sodom and Gomorrah. It does not matter that the pronoun 'with these'—τούτοις —is masculine, for he is thinking of the inhabitants rather than the localities.

Gone after strange flesh is to be understood to mean that they were seized with unnatural lusts. We know that the Sodomites were not

327

satisfied with the ordinary way of fornication, but were stained with a more loathsome and filthy practice, contrary to nature. Note that he consigned them to eternal fire; we gather from this that the awesome spectacle, which Moses describes (Gen. 19.24), was only the surface view of a grimmer torment.

Yet in like manner these also in their dreamings defile the flesh, and set at nought dominion, and rail at dignities. But Michael the archangel, when contending with the devil he disputed about the body of Moses, durst not bring against him a railing judgement, but said, The Lord rebuke thee. But these rail at whatsoever things they know not: and what they understand naturally, like the creatures without reason, in these things are they destroyed. (8–10)

8. *Yet in like manner.* The likeness is not to be pressed exactly, as if to compare those he is dealing with to the Sodomites in all respects, or to the apostate angels, or to the unbelieving people. But he makes it plain that these are vessels of wrath appointed to destruction, who cannot escape from the hand of God, which will work an equal proof upon themselves. His purpose is to frighten the faithful, to whom he writes, that they may not be involved in the company of these men. From this point he goes on to describe the impostors in plainer terms. First, he says that they pollute their own flesh, as in a dream. His words are directed at their foolish impudence, and imply that they launch out into the depths of depravity, from which even the most dissolute would shrink, unless sleep removed his shame and so his awareness. The expression, then, is metaphorical, meaning that they are so dull that they give themselves over to all kinds of shaming behaviour without a blush. We should observe his contrast between *defile the flesh* (that is, dishonouring what has lesser excellence) and 'setting at nought', as beneath contempt, that which has highest rank in the human race. This second part shows that they were trouble-makers, set on anarchy, undermining the fear of the laws, to be free for their sins. The two almost always go together—those who turn their steps to evil-doing try at the same time to have all order overthrown. Allowing then that this was their aim, to throw off the yoke and run wild, we can see from Jude's words that they made a habit of speaking insolently and rudely about the magistrates. It is just the same today, that fanatics rage against the authority of the magistrates holding them down, and all the time are declaiming against every sort of government. They say, the use of the sword is a blasphemy, contrary to our religion, and

328

ultimately they would exclude all kings and magistrates from the Church of God.

Dignities ['Glories']. So he names the ranks who are given a pre-eminence, who are promoted with honour.

9. *But Michael the archangel.* Peter touches on this argument rather briefly, and in general terms, telling how the angels for all their lofty position above mankind still do not dare to make an insulting judgment upon us. There are some who reckon this episode is taken from an apocryphal book, and as a result, give the epistle less weight. But seeing that the Jews kept a great number of the traditions of their fathers, I see nothing strange in saying that Jude related something which had been passed from hand to hand over many centuries. I know very well that a lot of nonsense is handed down in this manner (as the papists of today put under this heading all the ignorant notions of the monks), but this does not prevent the Jews holding certain narratives, which were not put down in writing. It is beyond dispute that Moses was given burial by the Lord, which is to say, that his tomb was concealed by the unfailing purposes of God. The reason for the hidden tomb is clear to all, namely, that the Jews should not take his remains as material for superstitious practice. Need we be surprised if Satan attempted to bring the body of the prophet into the open, once God had put it out of view? And the angels resisted him, for their assistance is ever ready on God's behalf. This is a stone which we may observe Satan moves in almost every generation—to make the bodies of the servants of God become the idols of deluded men. For these reasons, we should not allow the epistle to become suspect amongst us through this testimony, even though it does not appear in Scripture.

As for representing Michael alone in controversy with Satan, this is nothing new. We know that hosts of angels are always ready at God's command, but He uses this one and that, at His choice, to do His work, according as it may please Him. What Michael is related by Jude to have said, is also found in Zechariah (3.2), 'The Lord rebuke thee', or, 'shut thy mouth, Satan'. It is what they call a comparison of greater and lesser. Michael would not dare ill-name Satan (for all that he was reprobate and damned) in any degree, beyond handing him over to the rebuke of God, but these powers, in their turn, to which God awards such singular honour, are incessantly attacked by these people with extreme insults.

10. *Whatsoever things they know not.* He means that their intelligence is so thick, one may say bovine, that they simply do not appreciate what is deserving of respect; yet they reach such a pitch of boldness that they do not shrink from condemning things beyond their grasp. The other fault they labour under is to lose all shame, when they plod, cow-like,

into fields where they can stuff their bodies to capacity, while in this case they cram themselves full, just like swine rolling in their own muck. The adverb *naturally* is contrasted with the use of reason and judgment. In dumb animals, only the instinct of nature reigns: reason should hold sway with men, and restrain their appetites.

> *Woe unto them! for they went in the way of Cain, and ran riotously in the error of Balaam for hire, and perished in the gainsaying of Korah. These are they who are hidden rocks in your love-feasts when they feast with you, shepherds that without fear feed themselves; clouds without water, carried along by winds; autumn trees without fruit, twice dead, plucked up by the roots; wild waves of the sea, foaming out of their own shame; wandering stars, for whom the blackness of darkness hath been reserved for ever.* (11-13)

11. *Woe unto them!* We may be surprised that he inveighs so vigorously against them, when he has just said that the angel was not allowed to pass a wounding judgment, even upon Satan himself. But he did not mean to set that as a general rule, but only used the case of Michael as a ready comment on the intolerable temper of those who revile, with affrontery and insult, that which God has honoured. Michael might well have thundered out a final anathema upon Satan, and we may observe how violently at times the prophets lay into the ungodly. Yet Michael held back from extreme rigour (justified though it was). Thus is it not the height of frenzy to lose all control against beings that are superior in glory? But anyhow, when he turns to deal with these people, he is not so much calling evil down upon them, as warning them of the ruin which awaits them, and his purpose is to prevent them dragging some unwary soul into the same destruction. He says, they are imitators of *Cain*, who lost God's favour, perverted His worship by the sin and wickedness of his heart, and rejected his right as firstborn. He says, like *Balaam* they have been deceived by bribery, for to gain filthy lucre they adulterate the teaching of religion. Actually the metaphor used expresses something further —he says they *ran riotously*, for their dissipation flooded out like gushing water. Thirdly, he says they imitate the *gainsaying of Korah*, by reason of the upset they cause to the well governed state of the Church.

12. *Hidden rocks* [RV mg 'spots'] *in your love-feasts.* Those who read 'among your works of charity' (*caritates*) do not sufficiently (in my view) elucidate the true sense. By ἀγάπας he means the feasts which the faithful held amongst themselves, to witness to their brotherly

concord. He says that these feasts are treated with disrespect by offensive men, who afterwards treat themselves to an orgy. On these occasions, there used to be complete frugality and restraint. It went beyond all propriety to allow these gluttons in, when afterwards they would go off to another place and stuff their bellies till they burst. Several texts [as RV] read 'feasting with you' [as against 'among themselves'], and if this reading is preferred, the sense will be that they bring not only degradation, but also a burden and nuisance upon the Church, daring to cram their own bellies out of its common funds. Peter's point is slightly different (II Pet. 2.13), when he describes them as revelling in their errors, and feasting with the company of the faithful, as if to say that the Church there is not thinking what it is doing, to foster such harmful snakes, and doubly stupid to pay the cost of their extravagant indulgence. Would that there were more judgment among good men I could name today, who try to be too kind towards the bad element, and so bring great harm on the whole Church.

Clouds without water. The two similes found in Peter are combined to give the one effect: both condemn empty ostentation, since the clouds are the kind that promise much but are dry within, empty things, like the clouds driven before the gales, which make one hope for rain, but quickly turn to nothing. Peter adds the comparison of the dry and waterless spring. Jude heaps up his metaphors to the same effect—the trees *withered*, as we see them in *autumn* when their vigour fades, and *without fruit; plucked up by the roots*, and *twice dead*, as if to say, that there is no sap in them, for all that they show are leaves.

13. *Wild waves of the sea.* The object of this addition may best be inferred from Peter's words: they are swollen with pride, they puff out great rounded phrases in a high-flown style, or rather, they belch them out. All the time they contribute nothing of the spirit, but actually reduce men to the apathetic stupor of senseless beasts. As we remarked above, these are the kind of 'free thinkers' of our own day, as they call themselves, these madmen. Their speeches are sheer rolls of thunder: they scorn common speech, and produce for themselves I know not what foreign-sounding jargon, but once they have lifted their disciples to the heights of heaven, they immediately subside into the follies of beasts. By their way of it, there is no difference between right and wrong; by their way of it, life is of the spirit, wherein each must put fear aside and enjoy his own mood, and we become gods, as God absorbs the spirits released from their bodies. Let us heed the simplicity of Scripture with more attention and respect, in case our over-ingenious philosophizing leads us, not to heaven, but rather to the bewildering labyrinths of the depths beneath. *Wandering stars*, he calls them, for they throw a tricky sort of light upon our eyes.

And to these also Enoch, the seventh from Adam, prophesied, saying, Behold, the Lord came with ten thousands of his holy ones, to execute judgement upon all, and to convict all the ungodly of all their works of ungodliness which they have ungodly wrought, and of all the hard things which ungodly sinners have spoken against him. These are murmurers, complainers, walking after their lusts (and their mouth speaketh great swelling words), shewing respect of persons for the sake of advantage. (14-16)

14. *And to these . . . prophesied.* I think this is an ἄγραφον ('unwritten') oracle, rather than one cited from an apocryphal work. It may be that an earlier generation passed on this saying to their descendants as worth remembering. If one should ask, why, seeing there are frequent references in Scripture to like effect, he did not quote a written testimony from one of the prophets, the answer is straightforward, that he wished to go back to the furthest antiquity for evidence of what the Spirit said about these people: which is the effect of these words.

The seventh from Adam, as he is explicitly named, is a commendation of the antiquity of the oracle, going back as it does to that world before the flood. As for my comment that the prophecy became familiar to the Jews by oral tradition, if there is another opinion I do not dispute it; nor indeed do I dispute over the epistle, whether it is Jude's or some other man's. When there is uncertainty, I am content to adopt the likely answer.

Behold, the Lord came. Past tense, expressing the future, as is the manner of the prophets. It says, He will come *with ten thousands of his holy ones,* and by these words includes both men of faith, and the angels. Both will adorn the tribunal of Christ, when He comes down to earth to give judgment. He says 'thousands' (as Daniel also (7.10) speaks of myriads of angels) lest the multitude of the wicked, like a stormy sea, should overwhelm the children of God, while they may rest their thoughts on the time when God will choose to gather in His own, some already dwelling in heaven beyond our sight, some concealed in the great pile of chaff around us. As for the fate that hangs over the reprobate, it should keep the elect in a condition of apprehension and concern. He speaks of both deeds and words, for these traffickers of corruption did their harm not only by wicked living, but to a great extent by impure and improper speech. He says they are *hard* words, for the downright audacity displayed in their high-riding insolence.

16. *These are murmurers.* Those who indulge in degrading passions are at the same time awkward and gloomy people, never willing to be satisfied. As a result, they always grumble and complain, however kindly decent folk go out of their way to please them. He tackles

them for their pompous tongue, their style of self-adulation, and also (by contrast) their mean minds, cringing like slaves to make money. Such inconsistency is commonly seen in rogues of this sort. Where there is no-one to resist their rudeness, or no consideration stands in their way, their arrogance is insufferable, they are so imperious in their claims for themselves. But those whom they fear, or from whom they hope to get some advantage, they will lick their boots for them! *Persons* he takes as outward magnificence or power.

But ye, beloved, remember the words which have been spoken before by the apostles of our Lord Jesus Christ; how that they said to you, In the last time there shall be mockers, walking after their own ungodly lusts. These are they who make separations, sensual, having not the Spirit. (17-19)

17. *But ye.* To that most ancient prophecy, he now adjoins the admonitions of the apostles, whose memory was still fresh. It does not greatly matter whether you read the verb μνήσθητε as indicative or imperative (i.e. 'remember' or 'ye remember'), the sense remains the same, that they should not be cast down when they have the protection which he cites.

In the *last time*—his meaning is that period in which the renewed body of the Church will hold its order securely, until the end of this world. He starts from the first coming of Christ. *Mockers*, as he calls them, using the scriptural term, are men drunk with a wicked and profane scorn for God, who burst out with a savage contempt for spiritual things, until there is no restraint of religion to hold them to their profession any longer, no more fear of judgment lingering in their hearts, and no hope of life eternal. They are like the Epicurean scorners of God which swarm upon us on all sides today, who have quite thrown their sense of religion overboard and sneer angrily at the whole teaching of our faith as 'fairy tales'.

19. *Who make separations.* Several Greek texts make the participle absolute, others add ἑαυτούς ('separate themselves'), but there is virtually the same sense. He means that they make a disruption from the Church, since they cannot endure the yoke of discipline, being so addicted to the flesh that they find the spiritual life abhorrent. The soul[1] is here set against the Spirit, that is, the renewal effected by grace; hence, the senses in their depraved condition, such as in men not yet born again. In our degenerate nature, which we derive from Adam,

[1] RV, translating 'sensual' ψυχικοί

there is only the base and earthly material, no part of us aspiring to God, until we are renewed by His Spirit.

But ye, beloved, building up yourselves on your most holy faith, praying in the holy Spirit, keep yourselves in the love of God, looking for the mercy of our Lord Jesus Christ unto eternal life. And on some have mercy, who are in doubt; and some save, snatching them out of the fire; and on some have mercy with fear; hating even the garment spotted by the flesh.

Now unto him that is able to guard you from stumbling, and to set you before the presence of his glory without blemish in exceeding joy, to the only God our Saviour, through Jesus Christ our Lord, be glory, majesty, dominion and power, before all time, and now, and for ever-more. Amen. (20-25)

But ye, etc. He shows the means by which they may be able to throw down all the contrivances of Satan; if to their faith they add love, and be like men that stand watch for the coming of Christ. He is, however, always ready to pack in his metaphors, and here also there are forms of expression which require brief comment.

In the first place, he speaks of *building up yourselves on . . . faith,* meaning that they must keep an underlayer of faith, but that the first principles are not sufficient unless they proceed to finish the work, with constant efforts, after they have laid their foundation upon true faith. He calls their faith *most holy,* that they may rest upon it in confidence, and rely on its firmness, and never be shaken. But as man's whole perfection holds together by faith, it seems odd that he tells them to put on any further building, as if faith only made part of a man. This question is settled by the apostle, when he goes on directly to say that men are built on faith, with the addition of charity—unless perhaps some prefer to say, that men are built up on faith, in the sense that they make progress in it. Certainly, the effect of daily advances in faith is to cause it to rise up, to the true proportions of the building. Thus the apostle's message would be that we are to increase in faith, be persistent in prayer and hold to our calling by charity.

Praying in the Holy Spirit. This order of perseverance depends on our being equipped with the mighty power of God. Whenever we need constancy in our faith, we must have recourse to prayer. And as our prayers are often perfunctory, he adds, 'in the Spirit', as if to say, such is the laziness, such the coldness of our make-up, that none can succeed in praying as he ought without the prompting of the Spirit of God. We are so inclined to lose heart, and be diffident, that none

334

dares to call God 'Father', unless the same Spirit puts the word into us. From the Spirit, we receive the gift of real concern, ardour, forcefulness, eagerness, confidence that we shall receive—all these, and finally those groanings which cannot be uttered, as Paul writes (Rom. 8.26). Jude does well indeed to say that no-one can pray as he ought to pray, unless the Spirit direct him.

21. *Keep yourselves in the love.* He makes love the guardian or overseer of our lives, so to speak, not opposing it to the grace of God, but as we find the true course of our calling in the pursuit of love. Since many things tempt us to give up, suggesting the thought that it is hard for us to stay blameless before God to the end, nonetheless it is on the last day that he sets the sights of the faithful. Only as we wait upon that day may we be able to endure, and never let our hearts despair; or else, at any minute, we shall be bound to collapse. And note, that he does not wish our hopes to be set on eternal life except through the mercy of Christ. For He is to be our Judge, and on these terms: that the free blessing of redemption, which He Himself has gained, is to serve Him as His rule of procedure.

22. *And on some have mercy.* He gives a further word of exhortation, telling the faithful how to behave in the matter of correcting their brethren and restoring them to the Lord. He says, they are to be treated in various ways, that is to say, each according to his own character, for the meek and biddable sort are to be shown clemency. But the rest show a harder front, and they are to be brought round by terror. This is the sifting out process [*diiudicatio*] which he refers to. I do not know why Erasmus preferred to take the participle διακρινόμενοι in the passive mood [RV, 'being in doubt'], which makes for ambiguity, while the active mood suits the context far better. This is the point: if we wish to be concerned for the salvation of the heretics, we must consider the nature of each individual, so that the mild and tractable can be quietly called back to the road, as deserving mercy, and such as are contumacious be given a harsher correction. Sharp treatment is never very agreeable, so it is excused for necessity's sake; without it they would not accept rescue, as they do not choose to follow good advice. And he uses a neat metaphor: where there is danger of burning, we do not hesitate to take violent hold on a man we want to bring out unhurt; it would not be enough to beckon with a finger, or politely hold out one's hand, for we must care for their salvation with the thought that, unless they are roughly handled, they will not come to God. The old interpretation is quite different, but the reading is found in many Greek texts. 'Put to the test those who have been set apart in judgment' is the literal sense of the old rendering. But my version above suits the sense better, and in my opinion is the

335

true, authentic version. The word *save* is applied to men by transference, for they are not the authors of salvation, but its ministers.

23. *Hating.* This passage might appear obscure in some respects, but will present no difficulty once the metaphor is well understood. He would have the faithful not only to beware of any contact with vice, but, for fear that some contagion may fall on them, he advises them also to avoid any association or approach. For example, if it were a matter of unchaste living, every provocation to lust must be put out of the way. This will be made more evident if we expand the passage to read, that we are to hate not only the flesh, but the very garment that is infected by contact with it. The effect of the particle καί (even) is to increase the emphasis. So far is he from allowing evil to be shown favourable treatment, that he actually orders all the preliminary and accessory (as they say) factors to be cut away.

24. *Now unto him that is able to guard.* He closes his epistle with the praise of God, showing thereby that our words of exhortation, our energies, can do nothing unless the effect derives from the mighty power of God. There is some evidence for 'guard them', and if we take that reading the sense will be, 'It is your part to attempt their salvation, but God's alone to provide it.' But I prefer the other reading, which picks up the foregoing sentence. After encouraging the faithful to save what is perishing, he makes them understand that all efforts will be vain apart from the working of God, and testifies that neither can they be saved themselves except by His virtue. I grant that in this latter part the verb is different, that is to say, φυλάξαι (literally, 'to guard'), but this would look back to an earlier verse (21) where he said, 'Keep yourselves' or 'Keep watch on yourselves'.

INDEX TO THE HARMONY

INDEX OF SCRIPTURE REFERENCES

INDEX OF NAMES

GENERAL INDEX

Abel, Cain, 65, 330
Abraham's faith, 286
  guests, 244
Adam, children of, 117,333
ἀδιάκριτος, 294, cf. 335
Adoption, 17, 24, 38, 65, 115, 221, 266, 270
ἀγαπάς, 330
ἄγραφον, 332
ἀκαταστασίαν, 294
Allegory, 38f., 109, 137
Anabaptists, 252, 312
ἀνακεφαλαίωσις, 94
analogia vel similitudo, 136
Anarchy, 328
anima, 293, cf. 333
ἀνθρωποπάθειαν, 69
Antiochus, 85, 141
Apocrypha, 31
Apostles, 50, 61f., 80, 82f., 106, 141, 214, 221, 231, 239ff., 244, 249ff., 255, 322
Ἀρχή, 327
Arians, 99

Baptism, 102, 109, 134, 251f.
Bishop's, jurisdiction, 145
Brotherly love, 36ff., 51, 57, 116, 279

Caiaphas, 164, 197
Calling, 20, 47, 322
Ceremonies, rites, 4, 17, 40, 123, 223
Children, 7
CHRIST
  Ascension, 238, 250, 256
  Divinity, 41f., 99, 127
  Eternal Wisdom, 69
  Head of Church, 51, 92, 129
  'Ignorance', 98f.
  Innocence, 179, 184
  King, 3, 7, 113, 199
  Kingdom of, 44, 74f., 91f., 94f., 108ff., 250, 308
  Lord of Living, 32, 325
  Majesty, 3, 43, 71, 94, 111, 206, 257
  Mediator, 71, 99, cf. 164, 208, 211, 236
  Messiah, 6, 7, 11, 76, 145, 166f., 235

CHRIST (contd.)
  Miracles, 6, 8, 199, 254, 258
  Preserver, 203
  'Pretence', 236f.
  Priest, 3, 211, 256
  Prophet, 3, 233
  Redeemer, 41, 67, 71, 96, 139, 145, 167, 180, 185, 233ff.
  Sacrifice, 119
  Self-emptying, 153, 163, 198, 206, 235, 250
  Son of God, 11, 18, 116, 165, 174, 213
  Sorrows, 147, 168, 189, 207
  Sun, 106
  Teacher, 3, 25, 181, 245f., 225, 266
  Victim, 120, 125, 180, 235
  Will of God, 150f.
  Wounds, 242
Christian, name of, 279
Christs, false, 77
Civil order, 27, 159, 180, 276, 328
coercitio, 185
complementum, 93
Confession, 316
Consecration, 134
conversio (in sacrament), 134
'Corban', 175
Covenant, 30, 32, 35, 87ff., 139, 188, 247
Cursing, blessing, 8, 114, 189, 256, 291

Daniel, 85
David, 18f., 41f., 194f., 198, 259, 315
debitas poenas, 99
Depravity, 333
Doubt, 9, 265
δόξης, 277

Elect, 65, 88, 114, 225
Elijah, 317
ἐνεργουμένη, 317
ἐνθουσιασμούς, 245
Epicureans, 29, 333
Essenes, 46
εὐχαριστήσας, 133
'Extreme Unction', 314

343

quievit Divinitas, 99, 147

rationibus ostensam, 235
Reconciliation, 130, 138, 182, 199, 221, 236, 246
regnum auspicatus, 113
Reprobate, 52, 64, 79, 89, 96, 101, 117f., 131, 207, 225, 229, 325
Resurrection, 29ff., 99, 137, 211f., 221ff., 232
Righteousness, 13, 37, 115, 246

Sacrament, 133ff., 237, 314
sacramentalis unio, 135
Sadducees, 29, 46
Saints, petitions to, 318
salutis caput, 225
salutis firmitas, 90
Samaritans, 38
Sanctification, 323
Satan, 27, 28, 41, 55, 77, 82, 90, 118, 125, 140, 157, 161, 172, 175, 198, 200, 208, 291, 299, 321, 323, 329
Scripture, 18, 30, 31, 63, 75, 87, 129, 160, 166, 235, 244ff., 268
Sects, 30
sedere honeste, 277
Self-denial, 72, 102, 246, 297
Sin, 'outward act', 269
Sodom, 100, 327
Solomon, 131, 259, 318
Sorbonne, 37
SPIRIT, 9, 21, 42, 66, 69, 81, 86, 120, 122, 125, 134, 153, 162, 170, 208,

231, 244, 247, 249, 255, 268, 274, 278, 298, 314f., 334
Discernment, 25f.
Seal, 31, 239
σπουδήν, 323
Stephen, 174, 210, 233
Stoics, 280
Sweated labour, 307
Symbols, 6, 56, 123, 218, 223

τέλος ἔχει, 145
Temple, 2f., 55, 66, 70, 74f., 86, 165, 198
Titus, 88
Traditions, 329
Transubstantiation, 135

umbratilis cultus, 211
'Under the Cross', 77, 81, 93, 109, 158, 179, 184, 190
Unity and Doctrine, 70, 77, 92, 103, 228, 276

'Vessel', 6
Vestments, 49
voluntatem duplicem, 69

Witness, 7
Word, 9, 13, 21, 23, 47, 64, 67f., 98, 106, 121, 251, 264, 270ff., 326
Works, 35, 111, 115, 284

Zechariah, 65f., 141f., 177